Campaigns of Knowledge

In the series *Asian American History and Culture*, edited by Cathy Schlund-Vials, Shelley Sang-Hee Lee, and Rick Bonus. Founding editor, Sucheng Chan; editors emeriti, David Palumbo-Liu, Michael Omi, K. Scott Wong, and Linda Trinh Võ.

Also in this series:

Crystal Mun-hye Baik, *Reencounters: On the Korean War and Diasporic Memory Critique*
Michael Omi, Dana Y. Nakano, and Jeffrey Yamashita, eds., *Japanese American Millennials: Rethinking Generation, Community, and Diversity*
Masumi Izumi, *The Rise and Fall of America's Concentration Camp Law: Civil Liberties Debates from the Internment to McCarthyism and the Radical 1960s*
Shirley Jennifer Lim, *Anna May Wong: Performing the Modern*
Edward Tang, *From Confinement to Containment: Japanese/American Arts during the Early Cold War*
Patricia P. Chu, *Where I Have Never Been: Migration, Melancholia, and Memory in Asian American Narratives of Return*
Cynthia Wu, *Sticky Rice: A Politics of Intraracial Desire*
Marguerite Nguyen, *America's Vietnam: The Longue Durée of U.S. Literature and Empire*
Vanita Reddy, *Fashioning Diaspora: Beauty, Femininity, and South Asian American Culture*
Audrey Wu Clark, *The Asian American Avant-Garde: Universalist Aspirations in Modernist Literature and Art*
Eric Tang, *Unsettled: Cambodian Refugees in the New York City Hyperghetto*
Jeffrey Santa Ana, *Racial Feelings: Asian America in a Capitalist Culture of Emotion*
Jiemin Bao, *Creating a Buddhist Community: A Thai Temple in Silicon Valley*
Elda E. Tsou, *Unquiet Tropes: Form, Race, and Asian American Literature*
Tarry Hum, *Making a Global Immigrant Neighborhood: Brooklyn's Sunset Park*
Ruth Mayer, *Serial Fu Manchu: The Chinese Supervillain and the Spread of Yellow Peril Ideology*
Karen Kuo, *East Is West and West Is East: Gender, Culture, and Interwar Encounters between Asia and America*
Kieu-Linh Caroline Valverde, *Transnationalizing Viet Nam: Community, Culture, and Politics in the Diaspora*
Lan P. Duong, *Treacherous Subjects: Gender, Culture, and Trans-Vietnamese Feminism*
Kristi Brian, *Reframing Transracial Adoption: Adopted Koreans, White Parents, and the Politics of Kinship*
Belinda Kong, *Tiananmen Fictions outside the Square: The Chinese Literary Diaspora and the Politics of Global Culture*
Bindi V. Shah, *Laotian Daughters: Working toward Community, Belonging, and Environmental Justice*
Cherstin M. Lyon, *Prisons and Patriots: Japanese American Wartime Citizenship, Civil Disobedience, and Historical Memory*

A list of additional titles in this series appears at the back of this book.

Campaigns of Knowledge

∽

U.S. Pedagogies of Colonialism and Occupation in the Philippines and Japan

∽

MALINI JOHAR SCHUELLER

TEMPLE UNIVERSITY PRESS
Philadelphia • Rome • Tokyo

TEMPLE UNIVERSITY PRESS
Philadelphia, Pennsylvania 19122
tupress.temple.edu

Copyright © 2019 by Temple University—Of The Commonwealth System
of Higher Education
All rights reserved
Published 2019

Chapter 2:
Copyright © 2014 Johns Hopkins University Press. Parts of chapter two first appeared in JOURNAL OF ASIAN AMERICAN STUDIES, Volume 17, Issue 2, June, 2014, pages 161–198.
Chapter 4:
Parts of Chapter 4 first appeared in Malini Johar Schueller, "Negotiations of Benevolent (Colonial) Tutelage in Carlos Bulosan," *Interventions* 18.3 (2015): 442–449, https://doi.org/10.1080/1369801X.2015.1026371.
Parts of Chapter 4 first appeared in Malini Johar Schueller, "Unthinking Consumption and Arrested Melancholia in Bienvenido Santos' 'The Excursionists,'" Eds. Anastasia Aulanowitz and Manisha Basu, *The Aesthetics and Politics of Global Hunger*, 2017, Palgrave Macmillan reproduced with permission of Palgrave Macmillan.

Library of Congress Cataloging-in-Publication Data

Names: Schueller, Malini Johar, 1957– author.
Title: Campaigns of knowledge : U.S. pedagogies of colonialism and occupation in the Philippines and Japan / Malini Johar Schueller.
Description: Philadelphia : Temple University Press, [2019] | Series: Asian American history and culture | Includes bibliographical references and index. | Summary: "This book examines colonial education as a technology of U.S. power in the Philippines and Japan, tracking discourses on U.S. tutelage in policy, textbooks, short stories, novels, films, and essays by writers in the Philippines, Japan, and the diaspora."—Provided by publisher.
Identifiers: LCCN 2019009200 (print) | LCCN 2019980583 (ebook) | ISBN 9781439918555 (cloth : alk. paper) | ISBN 9781439918562 (paperback : alk. paper) | ISBN 9781439918579 (ebook)
Subjects: LCSH: Educational change—Japan—History—20th century. | Educational change—Philippines—History—20th century. | Education—Philippines—American influences—History—20th century. | Education—Japan—American influences—History—20th century. | Philippines—History—1898-1946. | Japan—History—Allied occupation, 1945–1952.
Classification: LCC LA1291.82 .S38 2019 (print) | LCC LA1291.82 (ebook) | DDC 370.95—dc23
LC record available at https://lccn.loc.gov/2019009200
LC ebook record available at https://lccn.loc.gov/2019980583

9 8 7 6 5 4 3 2 1

For John, Divik, Maya, Neena, and Kavita

Contents

List of Figures ix

Acknowledgments xi

Abbreviations xiii

Introduction: Colonialism, Occupation, and the Burden of Tutelage 1

1 "Among a Tropical People": Little Brown Brothers, Individual Liberty, and Self-Government 33

2 Americanism and Filipino Nationalism in English Readers in the Philippines, 1905–1932 61

3 Unhomeliness and Educational Anxieties in the Neocolonial Philippines: Tiempo and Cordero-Fernando 89

4 Articulations of Decolonial Thinking and Collective Subjectivity in Bulosan, Santos, and Linmark 109

5 Mapping the Japanese Tutelary Subject in the Classroom and Brides Schools 155

6 Mourning, Nationalism, and Historical Memory in Kojima,
   Shinoda, Albery, Houston, and Otsuka   201

7 Occupation Tutelage and the Pragmatics of Individual Memory   229

   Epilogue: The War on Terror and Education for Democracy   249

   Notes   259

   Works Cited   269

   Index   287

List of Figures

FIGURE I.1.	"The White Man's Burden"	9
FIGURE I.2.	"The First Lesson"	10
FIGURE 2.1.	Making sugar	66
FIGURE 2.2.	Farmer and carabao	67
FIGURE 2.3.	Filipina child reading	68
FIGURE 2.4.	American girl reading	68
FIGURE 2.5.	At the market	69
FIGURE 2.6.	Teaching subtraction with flags	70
FIGURE 2.7.	"This is a Flag"	71
FIGURE 2.8.	Flag in the distance	81
FIGURE 2.9.	Saluting the flag of the Philippines	82
FIGURE 5.1.	"Another Puzzler for World Scholars"	163

Acknowledgments

It is a pleasure to have this opportunity to publicly thank the numerous people who have made this book possible. Foremost, I thank Cathy Schlund-Vials for her indefatigable support of my project and for her insightful comments. From the very first time Cathy heard me present part of this book at an Association for Asian American Studies (AAAS) conference, she expressed confidence in the project and urged me to send the manuscript to Temple University Press (many thanks to Joan Vidal, whose scrupulous copyediting greatly improved the quality of the book). Subsequently, she attended several of my talks, provided useful feedback, and diligently helped me trim the book to its current size. Over the course of almost ten years, I have benefited from conversations with and critiques by several scholars who have enriched my arguments. Tim Marr has been an incredible resource regarding the Philippines, and my regular meetings with him have been wonderfully productive. I am also grateful to Leslie Bow, Julian Go, Kenneth Kidd, Lee Quinby, and Anastasia Ulanowicz, who generously read and commented on different portions of the manuscript and helped me refine my ideas.

In fall 2015 I had the opportunity to teach at the University of the Philippines, Diliman. My interactions with students and faculty and my teaching experience there shaped this book in fundamental ways. I am indebted to Lily Rose Tope for undertaking the bureaucratic paperwork to make the visiting professorship possible and for her kind hospitality. Neil Garcia pointed me to many useful sources, as did Judy Ick, who also allowed me to take over her course.

Over the years I have taught several courses in which I have had the opportunity to discuss ideas that were germane to this project. This book has benefited from stimulating discussions with students in my "Postcolonial Theory," "Cultures of U.S. Imperialism," and "Empire and Asian American Studies" courses. Thanks also go to my colleagues Apollo Amoko, Pamela Gilbert, and Leah Rosenberg for their participation in invigorating reading groups.

Chapters of this book were presented at invited talks at Ateneo de Manila University; the University of Alabama, Huntsville; and Kyungpook National University and at American Studies Association and AAAS conferences. I am grateful to the hosts of and audiences at these meetings for the stimulating discussions that took place.

I began working on this book at a difficult period in my life, following the death of my mother, Mrs. Usha Johar, my anchor and support. I am immensely grateful to the friends and family who comforted me and kept me going. In addition to my nuclear family, I wish to thank Kavita Nayar, Manju Vadhera, Fiona Barnes, Marsha Bryant, Jayshree Mahajan, Deepa Ranka, Cora Suri, and Amy Vollmer.

It has been delightful to see Divik, Maya, and Neena grow into thoughtful and caring adults. Frequent visits from Neena, the good fortune of having Maya live at home, and weekly talks with Divik add joy to my life. I am proud of all of them and thrive in their love and affection. As ever, my greatest debt is to my soul mate, John, who has steadfastly and selflessly supported me. He was never too busy to help me with computer problems or manuscript issues or to drive me to the library at night so I didn't have to contend with campus parking. This book would not have been possible without him.

Abbreviations

Affairs: *Affairs in the Philippine Islands: Hearings before the Committee on the Philippines of the United States Senate*
Annuals (chronologically)
  Eighth Annual: *Eighth Annual Report of the Director of Education*
  Ninth Annual: *Ninth Annual Report of the Director of Education*
  Tenth Annual: *Tenth Annual Report of the Director of Education for the Philippine Islands*
  Thirteenth Annual: *Thirteenth Annual Report of the Director of Education*
  Fifteenth Annual: *Fifteenth Annual Report of the Director of Education*
  Sixteenth Annual: *Sixteenth Annual Report of the Director of Education*
  Twenty-First Annual: *Twenty-First Annual Report of the Director of Education*
  Twenty-Second Annual: *Twenty-Second Annual Report of the Director of Education*
  Twenty-Fourth Annual: *Twenty-Fourth Annual Report of the Director of Education*
  Twenty-Eighth Annual: *Twenty-Eighth Annual Report of the Director of Education*
ARWD Philippine Commission: *Annual Reports of the War Department for the Fiscal Year Ended June 30, 1903: Vol. VII Report of the Philippine Commission*
CK: *Camp Kokura Brides School*

FE: *Far East Asia American Red Cross Brides School*
Guide: *Guide to New Education in Japan*
PR: *The Philippine Readers*
Primer: *Primer of Democracy*
Report: *Report of the United States Education Mission to Japan*
Survey: *A Survey of the Educational System of the Philippine Islands by the Board of Educational Survey; Created under Acts 3162 and 3196 of the Philippine Legislature*

CAMPAIGNS OF KNOWLEDGE

Introduction

Colonialism, Occupation, and the Burden of Tutelage

> One of the most remarkable chapters in the history of education has been written since the opening of the twentieth century in the Philippine Islands.... With the coming of Americans a system of education embodying the ideals of universality, practicality and democracy, was brought into the Islands.... Under the very guns of the American troops schools were established; wherever the American flag went, a school was found.
>
> —*A Survey of the Educational System of the Philippine Islands*

> General MacArthur, firm in his conviction that a sound educational program was basic to the development of a new and democratic Japan, directed the Japanese Government to establish immediately a normally operating school system and to encourage the inculcation of concepts—and establishment of practices in harmony with representative government, international peace, the dignity of the individual.
>
> —LIEUTENANT-COLONEL D. R. NUGENT, *Chief, Civil Information and Education Section*

In the Hollywood film *Teahouse of the August Moon* (1956), set in postwar Okinawa (arguably Japan's first colony), the earnest but doltish Colonel Wainwright Purdy, a parody of the colonial official convinced of his civilizational superiority, sends Captain Fisby on a mission to the village of Tobiki to build a schoolhouse. Early in the film, the Okinawan Sakini, Fisby's interpreter and the mouthpiece of satire, speaks directly to the audience, informing them in his broken English, "Okinawans most eager to be educated by conquerors." Fisby arrives in Tobiki ready to build the schoolhouse, immediately establishes a Ladies League for Democratic Action, and sets in motion elections for mayor. The film satirizes the U.S. occupation of Okinawa and the occupation goals of education, democracy, and capitalism. The people of Tobiki want a teahouse instead of a schoolhouse, democracy gets carried too far when women want to exercise their rights and complain to Washington, and the handicrafts the villagers produce at the behest of Fisby find no market. Illustrating the imperial objectives of occupation, orders from Washington are to construct a pentagon-shaped schoolhouse. As Fisby explains to the villagers nonplussed by the word "pentagon," "It's like a building in Washington, folks, and everybody is going to learn about democracy." When Fisby proclaims the benefits of U.S. rule, a thin elderly villager presents him with a gift and artlessly connects the occupation with the U.S. colonization of the Philippines. To Fisby's surprise, the villager speaks in English and explains, "In my youth I work in Manila. How is McKinley?"

Of course, what the film satirizes is bad occupation and colonial paternalism, but it also suggests that Americans should, in fact, be good occupiers who, with the aid of some Yankee ingenuity, can help the natives realize their own dreams. Indeed, by contrasting good and bad paternalism, the film reinforces the value of good American occupation. It also invites viewers not to take the natives seriously by having Marlon Brando play the role of Sakini. Fisby blends in so easily with Okinawans that he is not really colonial. He goes native, wearing his bathrobe all day instead of a kimono; enjoys the company of his geisha, Lotus Blossom; savors the local custom of drinking tea while watching the sunset in silence; and lets the villagers get their teahouse. The mock ending of the film, when Purdy fires Fisby (only to finally rescind because Tobiki is going to be showcased as an exemplary occupation site), provides the occasion to articulate a sentimental imperialism. Gently refusing entreaties of marriage from a tearful Lotus Blossom, Fisby prepares to leave and declares complete identification with Okinawans: "I think I felt an awful lot like you people felt, always being conquered. You know, now, I'm not sure who's been conquered and who's the conqueror. I've learned in Tobiki the wisdom of gracious acceptance." So with a sleight of hand, the film declares that the occupation of Okinawa is not really an occupation and effaces the power dynamic between occupiers and natives.

But while the film glosses over the Battle of Okinawa—the most brutal in the Pacific War, in which a quarter of the local population was decimated, where abysmal poverty prevailed during an occupation far harsher and more martial than that of the mainland, and where the U.S. Army paid no compensation for its appropriations of land—the first few minutes of *Teahouse of the August Moon* comically set out the themes that are central to this book: the importance of schooling and the creation of suitable pedagogical subjects to the project of U.S. imperialism; the paternalist, colonial conception of teaching natives; the ability of natives to challenge, question, and reroute the tutelary enterprise; the ultimate defeat of the educational project; and, interestingly, the continuity of U.S. colonial-educational projects in the Philippines and Japan. Thus, when Fisby attempts to represent the government's Americanization mission benevolently, he is upended by the villager, who reminds Fisby of the U.S. colonization of the Philippines by William McKinley. The film is diegetically noncommittal about English being mandatory in the Philippines, but the language's very use by the villager reminds viewers extradiegetically about the imposition of English on the archipelago through schooling. The film, set in 1946, the year of the Philippines' independence from the United States, and made in 1956 while Okinawa was still occupied, momentarily alerts viewers to the continuity of U.S. colonialism (the United States occupied Okinawa until 1972) and its tutelary projects. Yet it is the villagers who also reverse colonial tutelage and "teach" Fisby, who assents to the building of a teahouse instead of a schoolhouse.[1]

Campaigns of Knowledge argues that beginning in 1898, the creation of a suitable pedagogical subject through schooling emerged as a central technology of U.S. power overseas, one that was therefore deployed in the materially different circumstances of the colonization of the Philippines and the occupation of Japan. Although separated by half a century, in vastly different sociopolitical landscapes, and with disparate agendas, the creation of a new school system in the Philippines and educational reforms in Japan, both with stated goals of democratization, speak to a singular vision of America as savior following a pattern of a politics of violence followed by a pedagogy of recovery in which schooling was central. More than a means for disciplining individual bodies in space (although it was undoubtedly that, as well), schooling was conceived as a process of subjectification, of creating particular modes of thought, behavior, aspirations, and desires that would render them docile subjects, amenable to American-style colonialism in the Philippines and occupation in Japan. Although *Campaigns of Knowledge* focuses on the Philippines and Japan, subjectification through schooling as a strategy for controlling racialized Others was worked out first in the United States through reservation schools started by Richard Pratt and in Hampton and Tuskegee. Overseas, this biopolitical technology has been exercised in diverse ways to buttress and consolidate U.S. imperialism wherever it was deemed feasible: in Hawai'i Puerto Rico, Haiti, Cuba, the Dominican Republic, South Korea, and, arguably, now in Afghanistan and Iraq.[2] Indeed, military personnel are well versed in theories of hegemony and continue to look at schooling in the Philippines as an exemplary instance of counterinsurgency that should be followed today (see Ruscetta).

Behind the construction of this racialized pedagogical subject and the articulation of the project of benevolent tutelage, however, were doubts and hesitancies of administrators, and Filipinos and Japanese were not willing and supine subjects. As John Willinsky points out, despite colonial schools instilling ideas about the European nation-state, "the young often sought to repay this instruction with articulate, defiant, and sometimes violent expressions of a home-grown nationalism" (92–93). *Campaigns of Knowledge* uses a contrapuntal method, examining educational documents of the colonial and occupation archive and putting them in conversation with native cultural texts that register these subjectifications. These educational documents reveal at once the scripting of tractable pedagogical subjects amenable to U.S. rule or military power through enculturation, based on a presumed racial difference; the constant renewals, assertions, and defenses of this subjectification as educators attempt to justify the tutelary project and reconcile their lived experiences of students (who question or refuse this subjection and do not mimic the colonial/neocolonial order in expected fashion) with the colonial mission; and the contradictory desire of educators to create Americanized subjects and yet to maintain the separation of "almost but not quite" (Bhabha, *The Location of Culture*, 91). Well-known Filipinos and Filipino Americans and Japanese and Japanese Americans, including Nobuko Albery, Carlos Bulosan, Gilda Cordero-Fernando, Jeanne Wakatsuki Houston, Kojima Nobuo, R. Zamora Linmark, Julie Otsuka, Bienvenido Santos, Masahiro Shinoda, and Edith Tiempo, have offered a wide array of fictional, cinematic, and autobiographical responses to the tutelary project and its legacies. Thus, representations of the classroom and the encounter with the American text, learning, teaching, being taught, and the desire for colonial knowledge reveal a complex interplay of assent and coercion, collaboration and defiance, and hegemony and resistance, as well as ambivalence between resentment and guilt.

Yet none of these cultural texts simply accepts the discourses of racialization and imperialism that undergird the U.S. colonial/occupation rhetoric of tutelage. The colonized, as Frederick Cooper (16) and many others have argued, have always deflected and reinterpreted colonial strictures. Thus, while Filipino and Filipino American, Japanese, and Japanese American literary and cultural works may testify to the continued resonance of—and, indeed, attraction to—forms of colonial knowledge, they also complicate and challenge the project of subjectification in different ways: using civilizational logic to dismantle the paternalism of tutelage, strategically acceding to a colonized pedagogical subjecthood to advance their interests, drawing on the resources of the folk and community to proffer different epistemologies, offering forms of decolonial thinking, invoking intersectional memories to challenge the discourse of singularity in the educational project, seeing colonial tutelage ambivalently or as melancholia, and rewriting history affectively.

By reading educational documents as both policy statements and ideas in the making, using a contrapuntal methodology of viewing the colonial archive alongside native cultural texts and comparing colonial Philippines and occupation Japan, *Campaigns of Knowledge* puts forward a series of interrelated arguments. First, as mentioned earlier, the subjectification of natives as suitable pedagogical subjects was essential to the Philippines' colonization and Japan's occupation. Second, this subjectification relied on a racial (often gendered) difference that constantly had to be reiterated and modified, revealing the hegemonic yet malleable nature of colonial racial ideologies. Circumstances, cultures, educators, and legislators on the ground affected both the goals and the technologies of governance in the Philippines and Japan. Third, while both Filipinos and Japanese were objects of colonial tutelage, they were racialized in strikingly different ways. Filipinos, often seen through the lens of domestic racial categories, had to be culturally uplifted, while the Japanese, seen as foreign, had an excess of culture. Fourth, pedagogical inscription is contested by formulating different forms of collective subjectivities and through forms such as collaborative dissent, which often contest hegemony by laying claim to aspects of it. Finally, the tension between the ideal subjects scripted by colonial pedagogy in official documents and the resistance to and uneven materialization of this pedagogy, as seen in cultural texts that register its operations, suggests a failure of inscription; the mission of schooling, that is, was destined to remain incomplete.[3]

My study of the pedagogical subject of U.S. educational policies in the archives of colonialism and occupation in the Philippines and Japan, as well as in Filipino and Filipino American, Japanese, and Japanese American texts, is a history of ideas that tracks the inception, as well as the subjective afterlife, of a specific form of imperial governance. It is situated at the nexus of U.S. empire studies and Asian American studies, as well as within the specific fields of occupation studies (*senryo kenkyu*); the burgeoning field of postcolonial Filipino studies; and the nascent field of postcolonial education studies, which, despite the publication of Gauri Viswanathan's *Masks of Conquest* in 1989 has not seen much growth.[4] *Campaigns of Knowledge* performs the important task of integrating these fields and putting them in conversation with one another in the interdisciplinary manner of postcolonial studies while contributing to them through a cultural studies lens.

By attempting to change language and education by requiring the use of English and disallowing the use of Spanish and vernaculars in public schools in the Philippines, and by promulgating the use of *romaji* in public schools in Japan, in addition to inculcating the "American" values, American forces were pursuing a complete colonization of the linguistic symbols of nation and culture, the signifiers of ideas, communal and familial identity, self and the Other.[5] It was, as Bernard Cohn aptly argued in relation to British colonialism in India, not just the occupation of physical space but the occupation of "epistemological space" (4). However, unlike the British in India, who even after the Mutiny of 1857 did not attempt to enforce a singular language (although English was undoubtedly the language that allowed entry into the administrative structure) and left cultural institutions relatively intact even as they embraced the civilizing mission, the Americans followed to an extent the putatively more egalitarian French model of assimilation, which assumed, at least in theory, that all could become French. As discussed in Chapters 1 and 5, American colonialism and occupation were at once egalitarian in the French sense in that they assumed that natives could learn to be citizens of a liberal, capitalist democracy; hierarchical in that these natives were Othered through racialization and gendering; and hegemonic in attempting to create subjects who would desire a mythologized America—a wealthy, egalitarian, unified nation unfractured by race or class, based on the virtues of a masculinist, possessive individualism, industry, and freedom. Thus, from the very beginning of the colonization of the Philippines, American officials proclaimed their intention to oversee the country's independence premised on the idea that Filipinos, like Americans, could learn democracy. But they continued to insist on delayed independence because Filipinos needed guidance, and they often racialized Filipinos as lazy, lacking (muscular) vigor, and dishonest. Similarly, the Japanese were seen as inherently conformist, compulsive, ritualistic, feudal, and subservient (see Minear, 41–42)—qualities that allowed them to be recruited for ultranationalism—but also capable of overcoming these cultural characteristics and building a society of individualism and capitalist democracy.

What also distinguished the program of American schooling in the Philippines from those of colonial powers such as Britain, France, and Spain was the speed, thoroughness, and intensity with which schools were established in the colony. After all, less than a month after Admiral George Dewey's destruction of the Spanish fleet in Manila Bay in May 1898, American soldiers opened the first school on the island of Corregidor. By 1900, a Department of Public Instruction had been established under the direction of the U.S. Army, and by the end of the year, Fred Atkinson, a high school principal from Massachusetts, was established as the general superintendent of public instruction. Atkinson immediately centralized all public schools under the Board of Education and stipulated English as the medium of instruction as soon as possible. A year later, the *USA Transport Thomas* brought five hundred American teachers to the Philippines, followed by six hundred more in a few months; these teachers came to be known as the Thomasites. All of this happened while the United States engaged in a bloody war with Filipinos who had proclaimed independence in 1898 with a constitution modeled on that of the United States. The Philippine-American War, which has been relegated to national amnesia and introduced infamous techniques such as the water torture, claimed anywhere from 250,000 to a million Filipino lives and continued for several years after the U.S. invasion. Trying to subdue an intransigent rebellion, General Arthur MacArthur, then the military governor, asked for school funding specifically as an "adjunct to military operations, calculated to pacify the people and procure and expedite the restoration of tranquility" (Forbes, 423).

Seeing education as a hegemonic counterinsurgency mechanism and themselves as liberators of the populace from the Spanish, Americans immediately secularized Spanish Jesuit education. Unlike the Spanish, who conducted schools in both Spanish and the vernacular, Americans quickly mandated English-only instruction, striving to create an Americanized populace through a standardized curriculum.[6] While the Spanish prioritized higher education until 1863, when they established a nationalized primary school system, Americans stressed primary education, thus creating the conditions for both increased mass literacy and English proficiency. Accordingly, by 1939 a quarter of the population could speak English (Rafael, "Anticipating Nationhood"). As detailed in Chapter 1, within a decade texts conducive to colonialism, such as Daniel Defoe's *Robinson Crusoe* and Henry Wadsworth Longfellow's *Evangeline* and *The Song of Hiawatha*, alongside hagiographies of American presidents, were introduced in elementary schools. Many of the elite, however, continued their education in parochial schools and remained fluent in Spanish in addition to learning English (Rafael, "Anticipating Nationhood," 72).

The establishment of an Americanized school system in Japan shortly after the beginning of the occupation in August 1945 followed a similar speed and urgency. Schooling, as D. R. Nugent stated, was integral to the mission of radically changing Japanese society and aligning it with new geopolitics. Although the presence in Japan was putatively an Allied occupation, General MacArthur, who held the sovereign title Supreme Commander for the Allied Powers (SCAP), ensured that the occupation bore the stamp of U.S. power and catered to U.S. interests. As discussed in Chapters 5 and 6, iconic photographs of MacArthur stepping off the airplane, pipe in mouth, to accept the surrender and the famous photograph of him towering over Hirohito dramatized the more powerful masculinity of the United States over the diminutive masculinity of Japan. Little wonder that even historians who are highly critical of Japanese imperialism, such as Renato Constantino, refer to MacArthur as the new *shogun* (*The Second Invasion*, 9).

With MacArthur we witness a remarkable continuity between colonialism in the Philippines and Japanese occupation. Douglas MacArthur, whose father had been the military governor-general of the occupied Philippines in

1900, had himself served in the Philippines in the 1920s; he was appointed field marshal of the Philippines in 1935 and liberated the country from the Japanese. MacArthur thus had intimate knowledge of the Philippines before he came to Japan as SCAP and waxed eloquently about the educational work in the Philippines as "one of the most romantic chapters in Philippine history" (*Reminiscences*, 24). Writing about his governance of Japan, the "world's greatest laboratory for an experiment in the liberation of a people from totalitarian military rule," MacArthur worried about the problems of prolonged occupation; he recalls trying to learn from "the lessons my own father had taught me, lessons learned out of his experiences as military governor of the Philippines" (*Reminiscences*, 282). Arguably, his experience in the Philippines was instrumental in SCAP's focus on educational reform. The *Report of the United States Education Mission to Japan*, completed in March 1946, became the veritable guide for educational reform during occupation. As discussed in Chapter 5, the reforms recommended the adoption of *romaji*, based on the Romanized alphabet, rather than on *kanji* (logographic Chinese characters used in Japanese along with *kana*); a grade system that followed the American school system; the removal of Shinto shrines from schools; a veritable interdiction of traditional Japanese sports, which were perceived as martial; and, as in the Philippines, progressivist instructional methods geared toward child-centered learning.

This book argues that despite the urgency of both missions as a means of biopolitical reproduction of colonized and occupied subjects, U.S. educational policies in the colonial Philippines and occupied Japan were contrasting projects of Orientalist racial management. Two cartoons—one from the early colonial period in the Philippines, and the other from the period of Japanese occupation—succinctly illustrate the contrast. In February 1899, several months after soldiers began running rudimentary schools in the Philippines as a means of quelling the insurgency, the *Journal of Detroit* documented this schooling in a political cartoon that demonstrated the colonial racial difference at the heart of this benevolent project. Titled "The White Man's Burden" (echoing the sentiment of virtuous colonization manifest in Rudyard Kipling's contemporaneous poem), the cartoon depicts a tall, muscular, white American soldier, armed with a rifle, forcibly carrying an unwilling Filipino (see Figure I.1). The soldier tirelessly climbs uphill in long strides across a battlefield strewn with corpses, to which he pays no heed, to a schoolhouse displaying an American flag, thus marking schooling as a colonial project. He tramples on a bloody past and looks ahead to a benign future. The soldier and the Filipino are contrasted in relation to the school: the Filipino has his back toward it, unmindful of the benefits of colonial education, while the soldier determinedly faces up to his task to tutor the native. The Filipino is an unruly

FIGURE I.1. "The White Man's Burden."
(*Literary Digest* 27, no. 7 [February 18, 1899].)

savage, represented through stock signifiers of Indianness, wearing only feathers and crude adornments but also caricatured as African American through his thick lips; he stares at the viewer, eyes wide open, hair standing up, as if in shock. He does not know where he is going to be taken at the end of conflict, but it is clear that this savage will be "uplifted" and civilized.[7] Such representations, as Servando Halili points out, were potent in demonstrating Filipino savagery and backwardness (59–80).

The second cartoon, published in 1945 in the *Pittsburg Post-Gazette*, also dramatizes forcible schooling (see Figure I.2). Four children sit in a Tokyo classroom with their backs to the viewer. The classroom has been taken over by the Americans, as the U.S. flag displayed on the teacher's desk makes clear. An American officer, presumably MacArthur (his cap has three stars), strides into the classroom, displaying muscle, vigor, and a determined agenda. The movement of his body is akin to that of the American soldier in the first cartoon; however, instead of carrying the white man's burden, he is here to disabuse Japanese children (who are civilized enough to be in the classroom) of any ill-founded ideas about Japanese power or pride. The teacher is caught in a running posture, barely entering the classroom in time to teach the children, suggesting the Americans' need for vigilance. The children appear shocked at the first lesson being emphatically presented to them: Japan lost the war. The classroom is a metonym for the nation: clearly what these

FIGURE I.2. "The First Lesson."
(*Pittsburgh Post-Gazette*, September 8, 1945. Created by Cy Hungerford.)

children need is reeducation. The Japanese are also racialized but as ugly Asians: their faces turned to the blackboard reveal the horrendously oversize buckteeth familiar in demeaning representations of East Asians.

Thus, although both Filipinos and Japanese were seen as racial Others, the racializations were different, as were the natures of the racial projects to be carried out in the two sites.[8] Once Filipinos had been effectively tribalized through anthropologists and lay journalists and denationalized,[9] they were seen as savages or little brown brothers to be uplifted and deemed fit for industrial education, as were Indians and African Americans. And while some distinguished between educated Malays and "primitive" Negritos, many perceived a savage element in all classes and deemed Emilio Aguinaldo (the president of the First Philippine Republic, who resisted U.S. rule until his capture in 1901) barbaric (Miller, 54–55, 65). In broad terms, while Filipinos lacked culture, the Japanese had an excess of culture. Bound by Shintoism, emperor worship, obsessive rituals, and fanaticism, the Japanese at the time of occupation were viewed as victims of an arcane hyper-Orientalized, if also technologically modernized, culture and had to be appropriately decultured and reeducated (Dower, *War without Mercy,* 18–20, 124–125).[10] "Reeducation," as discussed in Chapter 5, was an official term repeatedly used by the military and education officials in policy documents. Unlike in the Philippines, in Japan industrial education and vocational training were never objects of concern for the educators who oversaw reform. In sum, while Filipinos were racialized like racial Others within the nation, Japanese were racialized as threats without. And while the Reverse Course of occupation lifted the more punitive measures, since Japan began to be seen as an ally, specific ideas about deculturation and reeducation remained. Little wonder, then, that in the mid-1980s Japanese economic power was often represented through tropes of militarist invasion (Makin, 8–16). However, as discussed in Chapters 1 and 5, both Filipinos and Japanese were seen as imitative rather than creative, irrational rather than rational, and, ultimately, behind the West in the teleology of civilization. Both Filipino and Japanese subjects were asked to distinctly imagine the nation. Theirs were to be modern nations, rejecting effete pasts and built instead on principles of liberal capitalist democracy that upheld freedom and social equality, but on an individual rather than a structural level, and premised on the unstated fairness of market relations. Educators in the Philippines emphasized the urgency of inculcating in students the importance of materialism while those in Japan affirmed learning practices suited to a Taylorist efficiency.

Just as important, Filipinos and Japanese were encouraged to value a possessive individualism over commitments to tribe or community. The pedagogical subject Americans strove to engender was the modern subject of Anglo-American culture, a "unitary-expressive and rights-bearing bourgeois subject," as Dipesh Chakrabarty puts it (143). Such a subject was, as Frantz Fanon recognized, conducive to colonialism, which had "hammered into the native's mind the idea of a society of individuals where each person shuts himself up in his own subjectivity" (*The Wretched of the Earth*, 47). A collective subjectivity, or nonindividualist practices that were often the basis for resistance to colonialism and occupation, such as the Filipino concept of *bayanhihan* and cooperative endeavors invoked by the revolutionary leader Apolinario Mabini in the 1896 revolution, were not encouraged (Delmendo, 14). In Japan, kinship norms of respect for elders were deemed inimical to learning and creativity. In addition to resistance, what educators effectively attempted to control was what Anibal Quijano saw as essential to colonialism: a repression of indigenous "modes of knowing" and producing knowledge (169). Colonial logic dictated that for Filipinos what was advocated was individual self-reliance (Defoe's *Robinson Crusoe* and Ralph Waldo Emerson's "Self-Reliance" were exemplary teaching tools here) but not political enfranchisement; the Japanese were offered individual freedom from militarism but not the freedom of protest for leftist teachers and students deemed subversive or freedom from U.S. hegemony. Japanese and Filipinos were both enjoined to be model citizens of their own nations paradoxically by being grateful to the United States as a guarantor of their nations' freedom and celebrating U.S. culture and its icons as symbols of equality.

John Willinsky sees a pattern in schooling for the colonized in which "it was made to stand against family and community, against a culture that seemed to fly in the face of the ostensible rationality and enlightenment of the colonial power. Schooling, in this sense, was meant to wean the child away from the learning and life associated with what was regarded as an expired era, an eclipsed form of life" (95). Willinksy's argument about controlling forms of culture that challenge colonialism's purported rationality and enlightenment get complicated, however, in the case of Japan, itself an erstwhile colonial power. In the wake of the Russo-Japanese War, many intellectuals in the United States had dubbed Japan the "Britain of the East." George Kennan, for instance, had seen the Japanese as having access to discourses of modernity (Lye, 23, 33). Japanese schooling under occupation, unlike that of the Filipinos, was thus devised for a defeated nation, yet one that had been a major military threat and rival imperial power and therefore had been admired in some ways by educators. Japan's was not so much a culture of the past (despite characterizations of its rituals as feudal), as famously theorized by Johannes Fabian, as a nonviable form of the present. For example, *bushido* (codes of conduct for Japanese men and soldiers, variously emphasizing loyalty, self-sacrifice, and pure Confucian values), which had been admired by many in the West, was seen during and after the war as a dangerous hangover from an earlier period. In sum, Japan's imperial culture had to be changed rather than uplifted; Filipinos had to be civilized, while the Japanese had to be de-civilized. Filipinos had to be educated while the Japanese had to be reeducated. Yet both were Asians and correspondingly racialized and gendered as inferior in relation to whites. Germany, which was also subject to postwar reeducation, for instance, was not seen as tuitionary and, as is made evident in Chapter 5, wrought feelings of timidity in U.S. educators handed the task of changing German education, while Italians were seen as inherently good, malleable people on whom fascism had been imposed (Buchanan, 219–220; Dower, *War without Mercy*, 33). By contrast, Japanese and Filipinos were racialized by educators through the discourses of Orientalism and tropicalism, respectively, and sometimes through distinctly different forms of Orientalism.

In describing the project of schooling and the subjectification therein as a form of power, I am drawing on Michel Foucault's idea of governmentality, which—following the lead of postcolonial studies scholars—I would argue began in the colonies alongside or after brutal suppression. Based on life-inducing mechanisms, governmentality addressed the problems of "how to govern oneself, how to be governed, how to govern others, by whom the people will accept being governed" ("Governmentality," 87). Foucault further goes on to explain governmentality as an "ensemble formed by the institutions, procedures, analyses, and reflections, the calculations and tactics that allow the exercise of this very specific albeit complex forms of power, which has as its target population, as its principal form of knowledge political economy, and as its essential technical means apparatuses of security" ("Governmentality," 102–103). A particular form of biopower exercised at the level of population, governmentality transforms earlier forms of power based on the sovereign's will and represented by laws, as well as forms of disciplinary power, to work instead through mechanisms that provide populations with the structures they require to live, to feel secure about their lives, and to reproduce their social conditions. Foucault clarifies that governmentality does not simply replace a society of sovereignty or a disciplinary society based on punishment. Rather, the three form a triangle of "sovereignty-discipline-government" ("Governmentality," 102). Although Foucault conceives of this triad and its functioning only in Western liberal democracies, and his formulation has justly been taken to task for being Eurocentric (see Stoler), I find the formulation useful with the modifications of the colonial and imperial contexts.

Here I take seriously Partha Chatterjee's powerful critique of Foucault's idea of governmentality, the universality of the "modern regime of power" that works by making social regulations part of self-disciplining and makes power more productive and humane. Chatterjee posits instead the centrality of the "rule of colonial difference" and argues that colonial power was "a modern regime of power destined never to fulfill its normalizing mission because the premise of its power was the preservation of the alienness of the ruling group" (15, 18). He demonstrates that just as modes of biopower were being put into place by the colonial state in India, the more prominent racial difference became (19). Gyan Prakash similarly argues that "colonial governmentality could not be the tropicalization of its Western form but rather its fundamental dislocation." The colonial state, estranged from "ideals of law and liberty" could not develop civil society and mobilize "capillary forms of power," which depend on the positioning of the state's knowledge and regulations "as disciplines of self-knowledge and self-regulation" (Prakash, 31).

Chatterjee and Prakash rightly point to the ubiquity of the rule of colonial difference, which challenges the normalizing function of governmentality. Both in the colonial Philippines and occupation Japan colonial (racial) difference was presumed and operative in different modes of power. Yet because colonialism in the Philippines after the Philippine-American War always included the rhetoric of self-government, and because the occupation of Japan was presented as a step toward a democratic future, forms of governmentality could function to a limited extent and in certain contexts.[11] Filipinos were promised independence if they were capable of self-government, the route to which was being the ideal pedagogical subject envisioned by educators. The United States operated through a colonial governmentality, inducing colonial conduct but carried out through what David Scott has called the "desiring subject." Scott uses the example of the jury system in Sri Lanka, which established a technology of regulation that "reach[ed] down to the very 'motives' of the native and not only constrain[ed] or induce[d] him to alter them but also to encourage[d] him to appreciate the alteration" (111, 113). Analogously, the pedagogical subject of U.S. empire was clearly a construct of colonial difference/racism, a subject who would believe the mythos of American freedom (despite Jim Crow and colonialism) and see it as coterminous with individualism, a desiring subject of governmentality.[12] Manuel Quezon's oft-quoted comment, "Damn the Americans, why don't they tyrannize us more?" comes to mind (Thomson, Stanley, and Perry, 120). The limited rights and forms of local self-government offered Filipinos at different moments were not a change from colonial rule to democracy but, rather, a change in tactics of colonial rule that masked its workings even more. In Japan, forms of democracy inspired by progressivism and a rights-centered ideology were enacted through authoritarian rule in a manner that John Dower refers to as "schizophrenic." Dower also argues that although the populace's weariness after decades of war may have made it more amenable to embracing occupation, there was no singular Japanese response to occupation (*Embracing Defeat*, 24–27).

The workings of the sovereignty-discipline-governmentality triad were starkly evident in the colonial Philippines and occupation Japan, where overt punitive machineries of colonial violence and disciplining of individuals coexisted with salubrious technologies of governmentality of which pedagogical biopolitics were central. As discussed later, arrangements of the classroom, forms of physical activity, the apportionment of the school year, and the management of space were all central to the project of subjectification in the Philippines and Japan. In the Philippines, a remarkable conjunction of sovereign thanatopolitics and salutary governmentality through schooling emerged as key to U.S. colonial rule and occupation. The centralization of all public schools in the Philippines in 1901 and the standardization of courses of study for primary schools under David Barrows in 1903, the secularizing of schools in Japan, and the mandatory textbooks on democracy introduced under occupation all speak to a structure through which governmentality was enabled. The fact that by 1914 Dean Worcester could confidently claim that "baseball is emptying the cockpits, and thus aiding the cause of good order and morality" (928) was in no small measure the result of introducing baseball in schools in the Philippines.

Comparative Imaginations and Specters

I invoke the titles of two magisterial studies—George M. Frederickson's *The Comparative Imagination* and Benedict Anderson's *The Spectre of Comparisons*—to explain my focus on the Philippines and Japan and the dialectical pairing of official documents with fictional, cinematic, and autobiographical representations. For Frederickson, historical comparison, more than a method or procedure, is an "antidote to parochialism," which actually "makes the experience of individual nations more meaningful" (7). Paradoxically, a key to comparison is establishing a common international context, which for Frederickson was the global struggle against imperialism and racism (9). For Anderson, comparisons are specters that haunt our perceptions. Anderson uses the experience of José Rizal's protagonist, Ibarra, in *Noli Me Tángere* when he returns from a colonial education and sees Manila's botanical gardens through their sister gardens in Europe as if through an "inverted telescope." He cannot simply experience them but sees them simultaneously near and afar through comparison (*The Spectre of Comparisons*, 2). Comparisons estrange the familiar and enrich our understandings of the discrete.

This comparative study uses two very distinct sites, with disparate histories and relationships to the United States, to demonstrate the structural similarities and political goals of colonial and occupation schooling and, yet, the particular contingencies and difference of both sites. Colonial rule in the Philippines was justified on the grounds of freeing Filipinos from tyrannical Spanish rule and preparing them for self-government; the Allied occupation of Japan was consequent on a military victory over an imperial power that had brought misery to its population (a fact emphasized by occupation forces to the virtual neglect of the suffering inflicted on other Asian populations) and was justified as a period of demilitarization and democratization by decree. U.S. colonialism in the Philippines continued for close to half a century, while the military occupation of mainland Japan lasted six years. Unlike the period of the occupation of Japan, the Philippines became a colony during the high tide of U.S. colonialism, which included taking over Puerto Rico, Hawai'i, Guam, and Samoa. Filipinos and Japanese have also experienced different restrictions on immigration to the United States. Allowed entry into the United States as nationals consequent on the colonization of the Philippines, Filipinos found their entry severely curtailed through the Tydings-McDuffie Act of 1934, which pronounced them aliens and limited their immigration to fifty per year. The Japanese, by contrast, experienced both legal racial exception and racism. The Gentlemen's Agreement of 1907, signed into law by Theodore Roosevelt, who had placed the Japanese in the same rank as the Englishmen and Irish (M. Hunt, 79), allowed entry to parents, children, and spouses of Japanese immigrants (while barring the entry of laborers) and had the effect of increasing migration. The "Japanese exclusion clause" in the Immigration Act of 1924, however, effectively singled out the Japanese as "aliens ineligible for citizenship" because the 1917 and 1921 acts had already excluded all other Asians (Koshiro, 229).

Given these contrasts, one might reasonably ask why I have chosen to compare the Philippines and Japan rather than, perhaps, the Philippines and Puerto Rico or the Philippines and Hawai'i. I have no argument against the comparison of these concurrent colonizations; indeed, the few comparative studies of these colonizations have been extremely rich.[13] However, the juxtaposition of the Philippines and Japan is useful for several reasons. First, the comparison of the production of colonized subjects through schooling in a formal colony and then during occupation reveals the continuity of this tactic of U.S. imperialism in areas of military occupation, arguably a major strategy of neocolonial and neoliberal control until the present. Second, the radically different sociopolitical landscapes of the Philippines and Japan are testaments to the ubiquity of U.S. tutelage as an arm of empire. Third, the temporal contiguity of colonialism in the Philippines, which ended with the beginning of occupation in Japan and includes some of the same historical actors, allows a fascinating glimpse into how technologies of pedagogical biopolitics changed from formal colonialism to a military occupation that itself changed during the Reverse Course. Although imperial violence and recovery through education was a pattern of U.S. colonialism and occupation in Cuba, Puerto Rico, Haiti, the Dominican Republic, South Korea, and, arguably, Afghanistan and Iraq, the Philippines and Japan offer the most radically different sociopolitical landscapes. In no other country than the Philippines was U.S. sovereignty and governmentality pitted against a nation that had just fought a colonial power and declared its independence. The Philippine proclamation of independence in June 1898, its ratification by the Malolos Congress later that year, and the Malolos Constitution of 1899, which proclaimed popular sovereignty, were all ignored by the United States, which proclaimed the Philippines as its territory ceded from Spain. The first American schools were accordingly opened against the backdrop of revolutionary nationalism and intense Filipino-American hostilities.

In contrast, Japanese schooling was devised for a defeated nation, yet one that had been a major military threat and rival imperial power and had been admired in some ways by educators. In the aftermath of the Russo-Japanese

War, the Japanese were seen as both a threat and a nation belonging to modernity. The popular novelist Jack London, for instance, accepted the appellation of the Japanese as the British of the Orient but was clear that the Japanese were still Asiatic and thus inferior to whites. The Japanese were seen as better than other Asians, but their conduct in World War II had convinced Americans that Japanese imperialism had fostered a dangerous militarism that necessitated cultural overhaul. By the same token, concerned Americans attributed the anti-American feelings of Filipinos (after a short period of gratitude following the defeat of the Japanese) to Japanese rule, which had created antipathy toward the white race and diminished respect for the white man (Koshiro, 18).

However, despite these major differences, educators and colonial officials often compared the two peoples, their cultures, and the strategic value of the two sites for the United States. For instance, in the Senate hearings on affairs in the Philippines held shortly after the Philippine-American War, senators and colonial administrators spent appreciable time considering Filipinos and Japanese. Senator Albert Beveridge testified to "an inherent difference in physical and nerve vigor between the Japanese and Filipino" while deliberating industrial capacity in the Philippines (*Affairs*, 711). David Prescott Barrows, superintendent of education in the Philippines, drew contrasts between industrial growth in Japan and the Philippines, arguing that while population density drove the Japanese to hard work and industrial growth, nothing of a similar nature could occur in the Philippines for centuries (*Affairs*, 710). Others wondered about the introduction of English in the Philippines. Senator Fred DuBois quizzed Barrows about the effects of English education, using as a comparison the introduction of English in Japan in high schools. Both DuBois and Barrows concurred that the addition of English had not been a threat to the Japanese national character (*Affairs*, 700). Two years later, in his annual report, Barrows demonstrated clearly the significance of Japan in considering education in the Philippines. He wrote, "We look to the Japanese for illustration of very much that is helpful in solving Philippine problems. There the most notable educational achievement of modern times has been effected."[14]

Japan as a rising power and as a nation that, after the Meiji Restoration, was selectively following Western modernity fascinated leaders and colonial educators, particularly because American teachers had been hired to advise the Japanese Ministry of Education in the 1870s. Indeed, William S. Clark, selected the first president of Sapporo Agricultural College in Hokkaido in 1876, was also asked whether a group of Americans wanted to establish a colony in Hokkaido (Maki, 165). Some lessons, it seemed, could certainly be learned. Conversely, educators and administrators of occupied Japan often reflected on their experiences in the Philippines. Commenting on the *Report of the United States Education Mission to Japan*, the major educational document of occupation, William Bagley, an established educator, wrote that if the report was followed, the occupation would hold "a place in history that [would] rival, if not surpass, the record of American idealism now written so large in the annals of the Philippines and of China" (389). MacArthur, the virtual sovereign of occupation Japan, conceived of the Japanese in a tutelary manner, similar to ideas educators had about the Philippines. Despite their "antiquity measured by time," he argued, the Japanese "were in a very tuitionary condition."[15]

While both Filipinos and Japanese as a race may have been conceptualized as tuitionary, some of the methods envisioned for teaching them were not different from the methods being implemented in schools in the United States. Educators in the United States propounded child-centered, progressivist models of learning, particularly after the publication of John Dewey's *Democracy and Education* in 1916, and the same methods were proposed in the Philippines and occupation Japan. But while this similarity suggests that educators may have viewed American (white) children and Filipinos and Japanese as equally adept, they did so in a contradictory manner. As Thomas D. Fallace maintains, many progressivists, including Dewey, rejected theories of biological determinism but believed in the theory of recapitulation, which argued that individual development "retraced the development of the human race" and that people of color represented earlier stages of human development (2–3). Nonwhites could improve but were ontologically inferior to whites. Consequently, progressive educators rationalized differentiated curricula based on the perceived predispositions of racial groups, even if they argued for similar methodologies of teaching. Such rationales, Fallace argues, governed the education of American Indians, African Americans, and the students of color in colonized territories such as Puerto Rico, the Philippines, and Hawai'i (13). Japanese deculturation could also be written into recapitulation.

By comparing the U.S. colonial Philippines and occupation Japan, this book also reveals the ubiquity and persistence of racial difference in the creation of Asian pedagogical subjects. At the same time, however, it continuously explores and foregrounds the fact that colonial racism, even when directed toward Asian subjects, proceeds from discourses that are multiple, fragmented, nuanced, and ever shifting both spatially and temporally. Discourses of race, empire, and tutelage are not fixed but malleable concepts of analysis, but that does not make them any less hegemonic in a particular time and space: witness the different racial justifications offered for language reform in the Philippines (discussed in Chapter 1) and in Japan (discussed in Chapter

5), as well as the racialized discourses at play in the creation of Brides Schools in postwar Japan (discussed in Chapter 5). While the documents of governmentality reveal the technologies of attempting to create docile raced bodies amenable to U.S. colonialism and, later, strategic militarized outposts in the Pacific Rim, Filipino and Japanese writers and filmmakers invite us to see these technologies from an inverted telescope, as it were. Nabuko Albery, Carlos Bulosan, Gilda Cordero-Fernando, Kojima Nobuo, R. Zamora Linmark, Camilo Osias, Bienvenido Santos, Masahiro Shinoda, and Edith Tiempo variously critique, resist, and strategically accommodate to, but almost always question, the ubiquity of U.S. pedagogical biopolitics. Their works not only reveal the paradoxes of desire and resentment, appropriation and critique, but also delineate the particularities of racial formations and practices and point to the plural and contingent process of colonial racial subjectification as it intersects with discourses of class, gender, and community.

Japanese Occupation of the Philippines

My focus on the Philippines and Japan should not be taken to mean an equation of the geopolitics of the two nations or a forgetting of the Japanese occupation of the Philippines, which itself is a different area of study. As established in Chapter 5, some of the technologies for creating suitable Japanese subjects under occupation and those for creating tractable Filipinos under U.S. colonialism eerily resembled those used by the Japanese in the Philippines. During their occupation of the Philippines from 1942 to 1945, the Japanese took seriously the task of spreading the use of Nihongo, as the Japanese language was called. Military Order 2 of 1942 called for the "diffusion" of Nihongo, which was taught at all levels of education and became a graduation requirement at the University of the Philippines.[16] However, in keeping with wanting Filipinos to take pride in their culture, and in contrast to U.S. policy in the Philippines, Tagalog and Nihongo were declared as the two official languages under Military Ordinance 13. Spanish was banned and English continued piecemeal, despite intentions to prohibit its use, because it was the only common language between the Japanese and Filipinos (Steinberg, 51). Filipino educators strove to circumvent the rules about Nihongo as much as possible, with Camilo Osias (whose readers are discussed in Chapter 2) managing to change the curriculum so that the requirement for teaching a national language, renamed "Filipino language," was instituted from the first grade and Nihongo was not introduced until the fifth grade (D. Martin, 142–143).

Hoping to capitalize on anticolonial sentiment, the Japanese attempted to erase what they saw as the degenerate materialism, individualism, and epicureanism of Anglo-American cultural influences and promote instead an Asian moralism and culture—indeed, a pre-Spanish indigenous culture—as long as it aligned with Japanese interests. In a much publicized speech, the Japanese military commander-in-chief declared that Americanism had created a spiritual degeneration among Filipinos that would lead them to "the very brink of racial extinction."[17] At a meeting of a training camp for schoolteachers in Manila in August 1942, the Director General of the Japanese military stated in a speech that "the guiding spirit of education shall be such as will eradicate undesirable Anglo-Americanism, such as the government of the masses, self-centered lack of restraint and the craving for things material and easy living."[18] Japanese educators likewise promulgated a pedagogy of discarding Western influence. As Professor Masanori Oshima put it, "With respect to Western civilization, [the policy] is one of discriminate rejection; with respect to Eastern civilization, it is one of discriminate acquisition" (quoted in Gosiengfiao, 230). Thus, the Textbook Examining Committee compiled new textbooks and, in a foreshadowing of SCAP's methods, issued orders to eliminate "improper and unsuitable parts," such as references to the Gettysburg Address, "The Star-Spangled Banner," and Thanksgiving Day (Gosiengfiao, 231, 234).

To curry favor with nationalists, Japanese educators created a commission of Japanese and Filipino scholars to study aspects of Philippine culture and make recommendations for education. However, Japanese officials expressed frustration with not being able to find an authentic pre-Spanish culture and having to improvise with existing folklore and legends (Gosiengfiao, 240). Like the Americans, the Japanese promoted the celebration of Rizal as a hero both in schools and in the society at large but also insistently publicized Japanese aspects of Rizal's life, including his death, which was seen as samurai-like, and the fact that his great-great-grandfather was Japanese (D. Martin, 157–158). At the same time the dissemination of Japanese culture in schools was effected by the introduction of stock signifiers of nation: singing "Kimigayo," the Japanese national anthem; celebrating holidays such as Emperor Hirohito's birthday; and using Japanese *radio taisō* for physical exercises in schools rather than free play. A major and substantial difference between American colonial tutelage and that of the Japanese, however, was that there was no discussion of, or desire to continue, the child-centered, Deweyan models of learning that had preoccupied American educators in the Philippines since the 1910s. The focus was on what students learned rather than on how they learned.

Japanese exhortations to Filipinos to exorcise the demon of American (and Spanish) colonialism and their attempts to foster indigenous pride were, in fact, not different from sentiments expressed by Filipino educators in the commonwealth period. For instance, in a speech at Centro Escolar University in 1939, Benito Soliven lamented that Filipinos, "fascinated by the allure of foreign ideologies . . . [had] embraced them with eagerness and enthusiasm, neglecting that which is legitimately and typically his own." He beseeched, "Let there be a reflowering of the Filipino soul in its pristine beauty" (19, 24). However, Japanese occupation came at a time when English had been adopted in all public schools, U.S. and Filipino troops were fighting together, and the commonwealth status of the country had outwardly ensured Filipino leadership in public and political spheres. As a result, the occupation was seen as a foreign invasion even as Japanese cultural propagandists played an anticolonial tune and granted the Philippines its putative independence under Jose P. Laurel, arguably a puppet president. No less significant was the public resentment against prescribed forms of behavior, including bowing before Japanese sentries and forms of shaming, such as slapping in public, sometimes even for failing to bow correctly (Dower, *War without Mercy,* 7; Rafael, "Anticipating Nationhood," 78). Such norms of behavior contrasted sharply with those of Americans in the Philippines, even though structural inequalities persisted. Thus, although the Japanese propagated a Greater East Asia Co-Prosperity Sphere, they also made clear that the center of this sphere was a superior Japanese culture and race, and in this sense they bought into Western paradigms of racial hierarchy. As Yukiko Koshiro has suggested, the United States and Japan often cultivated a common racial ideology, acclaiming the other's suitability for world leadership (3).

Colonizing and Decolonizing the Mind

In his book declaring his farewell to English, Ngugi wa Thiong'o famously wrote, "Berlin of 1884 was effected through the sword and the bullet. But the night of the sword and the bullet was followed by the morning of the chalk and the blackboard. The physical violence of the battlefield was followed by the psychological violence of the classroom" (9). By equating the violence of battle with that of the classroom, Ngugi presented a searing indictment of the project of colonial education. For Ngugi, colonial education created a cultural deracination that could be resisted only by forging alliances with the peasantry and writing in the native language. Although Ngugi's uncompromising stance on language has been critiqued by many writers—most notably, Chinua Achebe, who considered an Africanized English an African language he intended to use—resisting the cultural legacies of colonial education has been central to the thinking of postcolonial writers. Echoing the title of Carter Woodson's *The Miseducation of the Negro,* Renato Constantino presented a scathing critique of American education in the Philippines, holding it responsible for hampering creativity, inhibiting nationalism, and creating an Americanized populace divorced from its culture. In "The Miseducation of the Filipino," Constantino famously wrote, "The education of the Filipino under American sovereignty was an instrument of colonial policy. The Filipino had to be educated as a good colonial. Young minds had to be shaped to conform to American ideas" (5).

Notwithstanding the coerciveness of colonial education and the missionary zeal of the United States' conception of itself as teacher, having received the mantle of empire from Europe, the legacy of this education has been fraught with contradictions. As discussed in the Epilogue, U.S. educational practices in the Philippines and Japan have been seen as both oppressive and liberative; some of the reforms initiated there have endured, while others have been discarded. This is not surprising, given the paradoxical nature of the educational apparatus. School, as Louis Althusser famously argued, is an ideological state apparatus that drums the ruling ideology into children for several hours a day and finally ejects them into production to take the roles set for them in class society ("Ideology," 155–156). But as Paulo Freire has argued, education can also foster *conscientizaçao* (critical consciousness) that liberates (35). Although established through sovereign power, colonial and occupation schools were not simply exercises of a one-way project of biopolitical racial management producing docile pedagogical subjects. Filipino students of the school system such as Camilo Osias, who had studied at an American-run high school, emerged as educators who worked within the system and used U.S. tutelary, civilizational logic to challenge U.S. authority. Here Foucault's idea of power as something circulating and "exercised from innumerable points, in the interplay of nonegalitarian and mobile relations," is useful (*The History of Sexuality*, 94). Colonial education could work to maintain the status quo, but for the student it could be a means of accessing power within the status quo; it could function to colonize the native mind with ideas of its inferiority and the inherent superiority of Anglo-American culture, but it could also be seized by the native to subvert and resist these very ideas, as James C. Scott has brilliantly theorized in *Weapons of the Weak*. And no matter what the intent, tutelage could have unintended consequences. Filipino and Filipino American, Japanese, and Japanese American writers have registered American tutelage by variously embracing, acquiescing to, questioning, opposing, and resisting its imperatives through affective responses to the contradictions it engendered. I am concerned specifically with works that depict colonial/occupation education and its afterlives. Thus, although many Filipino works, such as Jessica Hagedorn's *Dogeaters*, Peter Bacho's *Entrys*, and Han Ong's *The Disinherited*, depict the ongoing cultural repercussions of U.S. colonial rule, I do not include them here. Instead, I focus on works that explicitly foreground American schooling or its aftermath. For similar reasons, this work does not deal with the occupation fiction of writers such as Kenzaburō Ōe, Shōtaro Yasuoka, and Fumiko Hayashi. Rather than being comprehensive, the purpose is to delineate the multiple ways in which writers have wrestled with colonial and occupation schooling and its legacies.

Campaigns of Knowledge tracks these different discourses on U.S. tutelage in textbooks, short stories, novels, films, and essays by writers in the Philippines and Japan and in the diaspora in the United States. The intention here is not to collapse differences between Asia and Asian America but to suggest that an engagement with the technologies of colonial and occupation instruction in the Philippines and Japan necessarily connects America and Asia, Asian American and Asian, and renders fluid the boundaries between them. In addition to individual migration and travel, state programs created conditions of fluidity. For instance, under the *pensionado* program started in 1903 in the Philippines, students were recruited to study at U.S. universities and return to the Philippines as potential leaders.[19] These recipients of American tutelage, some of whom became educators in the Philippines, contributed to cultural interchange. Arguably, *pensionados* challenged the boundaries between Asia and America and some, such as Bienvenido Santos, between Asian and Asian American.

Sociopolitical continuities in technologies of surveillance and tutelage also question boundaries between Asian and Asian American. Thus, precisely because they were suspected of transnational loyalties to an imperial and rapacious Japan rather than to the United States, Japanese Americans were interned in camps, where they could be taught loyalty and where children were "appropriately" schooled. In turn, observations of internees' behavior and character by anthropologists, sociologists, and intelligence officers, who treated them as objects of study, were used to plan the occupation of Japan (Hayashi, 204–206). Indeed, the Manzanar, Topaz, and Tule Lake internment camps remained open for a short while after the beginning of occupation. And *nisei* interpreters and soldiers were part of the occupation forces. Little wonder, then, that Japanese American texts about internment, such as Julie Otsuka's novel *When the Emperor Was Divine* and Jeanne Wakatsuki Houston and James D. Houston's *Farewell to Manzanar*, subtly or overtly reference the Allied occupation of Japan or that Filipino writers almost seamlessly connect scenes of instruction in the United States with those of colonial instruction in the Philippines. Asian and Asian American texts registering the legacy of the U.S. project of tutelage thus reveal a complex cultural history of imperial and colonial relations that this book explores.

My use of the term "tutelage" refers to a mode of governance of U.S. colonialism and occupation in which populations were conceived of as needing instruction, encompassing but not limited to specific projects of schooling, methods of teaching, and educational reform, although teaching methods and reform remain the particular objects of study. The book builds on the work of scholars such as Julian Go, Paul Kramer, and (more recently) Meg Wesling, who have seen tutelage as a central metaphor for the U.S. colonial state in the Philippines and a way of thinking about Filipinos.[20] Thus, writings about the strategies and goals of teaching or the methods of preparing teachers are simultaneously reflections on the kinds of tutelary relationships envisioned among Americans, Filipinos, and Japanese. They also reveal the racialized ways in which Filipinos and Japanese were perceived and the different ways in which they could be imagined as the ideal (Americanized) subjects of colonialism and occupation, what I refer to as "pedagogical subjects." I reserve the term "instruction" to refer most often to the distinct ways in which different activities, thought processes, subjects, and behaviors were being taught; sometimes, however, I have found it useful to address the tropological significance of scenes of instruction represented in the various texts engaged in this study. Finally, "schooling" describes both the mundane sense of the regime of education as well as the diverse material apparatuses that it deployed in the colonial and occupational contexts.

The Filipino and Filipino American and Japanese and Japanese American texts examined in this study are in the English language, English translations, or subtitled works. In the case of the Philippines, I have used English-language texts because the very use of English by Filipinos evinces complex forms of hybridity, affiliation, and dissociation with U.S. colonial and racial formations that are central to this study. Bulosan's education in English in a public school during colonial rule, for instance, is important in his comical, yet critical, renditions of schooling in his short stories. The use of English in the premier public university of the Philippines, the University of the Philippines in Diliman (as in other universities and schools)—an institution with highly nationalist and anticolonial leanings that nurtured a number of Filipino writers in English—demonstrates the contradictions emergent from English education. My use of English-language texts brings to light particular forms of affiliation that would be different from those of texts written in the vernacular and that therefore are not part of this study. However, because English was never instituted as a language in schools in Japan, even though it was promulgated through daily language programs on the radio such as "Come, Come English," some of the texts used for this part of the study are translations of Japanese texts or, in the case of some interviews, are aided by translators. However, because it was the language of occupation, all the official documents examined in this book are in English.

Chapter Overview

Chapter 1 focuses on the outlines of the Filipino pedagogical subject as it emerges in the statements of educators, beginning with the establishment of schools run by soldiers in 1898 until the harshly critical Board of Education survey done by Paul Monroe in 1925. The annual reports of the directors of education are fascinating archival documents of colonial management that include statements, summations, hesitancies, and reflections on teachers' trials and tribulations. Despite the policy changes among the major educators—Fred Atkinson, David Barrows, and Frank White—significant commonalities also emerge in these documents. The chapter analyzes the representations of Filipino "racial character" and the formulation of the ideal Filipino subject in the annual reports and in U.S. Senate hearings on the Philippines, as well as in H. C. Theobold's *The Filipino Teacher's Manual*, a text used for several years by the Board of Education to train teachers and that performs the task of pedagogical biopolitics by instructing teachers on hygiene, diet, class discipline, and layout. Filipinos are characterized in four basic ways: as lazy, contented, and demasculinized through the discourses of a tropicalized Orientalism; as imitative and unoriginal through a traditional racialized Orientalism; as rendered subservient by Spanish aristocratic rule; and as illogically defiant. The ideal, tractable pedagogical subject is contradictory: one democratized and Americanized through the teaching of the English language (a language racialized as resilient and powerful) and American history, yet a proud Filipino; one taught individualism and self-reliance through the practices of progressive education, yet content with colonial rule because Filipino and American interests could be seen as congruent; and one integrated mechanically as labor through the manufacture of goods in schools.

Chapter 2 focuses on children's primers and readers in the Philippines as sites of subject making and contestation. I argue that these texts are invaluable ideological documents of colonial rule. By comparing the construction of the Filipino in English primers and readers written by American teachers in the Philippines in the first two decades of colonial rule to the later, immensely popular Osias Readers written by the well-known Filipino nationalist and educator Camilo Osias, which continued to be taught and reprinted until the 1950s, I demonstrate how the earlier American readers attempted to indigenize the content of readers popular in the United States but were clearly invested in Americanizing Filipinos. Is it possible to articulate an anticolonial nationalism while working within the structures set out by colonizers? The second part of the chapter attempts to answer this question by looking at the Osias readers. Using James Scott's ideas on how subaltern groups work within hegemony to contest its workings, I propose that Osias's readers demonstrate nationalism as a form of what I call "collaborative dissent," thus suggesting interesting possibilities of contesting American colonialism through its own exceptionalist rhetoric. Osias's nationalism incorporates American culture within a Filipino schema even as it buys into some of the colonial racial hierarchies of Filipinos.

Chapter 3 turns to Filipino fiction to trace the different ways in which the specter of colonial education haunts the short stories of Edith Tiempo and Gilda Cordero-Fernando, who have written in the Philippines to a Filipino audience. Both are recognized as major writers in the Philippines, and their representations of the impact of American education in the postcolonial nation form an important component of the engagement of Filipinos with the aftermath of the project of colonial schooling. Tiempo and Cordero-Fernando register the legacy of colonial tutelage through their Filipino teachers of English who, to use Homi Bhabha's term, are "unhomely" and steeped in Anglo-American culture. Cordero-Fernando's faith in the (colonial) educational project is evident in her characterization of Miss Noel, who, particularly in the short story "A Harvest of Humble Folk," resembles the glowing portraits of erstwhile Thomasites heroically bringing knowledge to an ignorant populace, representations that continue to circulate in the Philippines even today. Yet the story also dramatizes the disconnect between the teacher and the barrio dwellers through the figure of the mysterious (and ultimately evil) Lazaro, who raises the class consciousness of the people. Tiempo's educators, by contrast, are anxious, lonely, middle-aged characters who dramatize the ambivalent position of the postcolonial pedagogue through their nonheteronormative sexuality and yet have doubts and uncertainties about accepting native self-definitions, such as *bakla*, that challenge Western ideas of gender and sexuality. These bumbling educators are unable to assert power or order in the school. Both writers register the legacy of the tutelary project ambivalently—Tiempo through her tormented and feckless educators estranged from local forms of gender and sexual expression, and Cordero-Fernando by eulogizing educators while simultaneously pointing to the bankruptcy of neocolonial knowledge in dealing with the needs of the poor. Tiempo's and Cordero-Fernando's stories explore the failure of the new nation's Americanized schooling through conflicts of class, gender, and sexuality and express a postcolonial disillusionment with the workings of the educational system that deserves separate analysis.

Chapter 4 addresses the reworkings of the pedagogical subject by three Filipino American writers: Carlos Bulosan, Bienvenido Santos, and R. Zamora Linmark. All three have had a wide reception in both the Philippines and the United States, and Bulosan, in particular, has been canonized within

Asian American literature. Writing almost three generations apart, Bulosan and Linmark explore the possibilities of what Walter Mignolo has called "decolonial" thinking, epistemologies that offer an alternative to the discourses of colonial tutelage. In his magical real, folkloric short stories in *The Laughter of My Father* (1942) and in his fictionalized autobiography *America Is in the Heart* (1943), Bulosan posits the world of community as a space of gendered and classed subaltern resistance to colonial order and knowledge; at the same time, Bulosan problematically celebrates the lone artist in search of knowledge, even if the knowledge is anticolonial. In *Leche* (2011), Linmark both poses and questions the possibilities of what I call "unlearning" in a hyperexperiential world connected through circuits of popular culture, consumption, and mobile labor, a world in which globalization and neocolonialism coexist. He articulates possibilities for a collective subjecthood through an intersection of personal and collective histories and through a queer subjecthood while also registering the anticolonial limits of a queerness that is classed. Santos, whose writing career began with Bulosan's but spanned several decades, dystopically registers in his novel *The Volcano* (1965) and in his short story "The Excursionists" (1960) the incorporation of colonial knowledge as melancholia that results in an estrangement from fellow natives—nationalists in *The Volcano* and tribals in "The Excursionists." In *The Volcano*, the melancholic pedagogical subject is also excluded from a heterosexual compact with white America. Bulosan's communal world, Santos's melancholic incorporation, and Linmark's exploration of unlearning, although distinct visions of subjecthood, are all attempts to grapple with the hegemony of colonial tutelage that continues its conflicted legacy and demands ethical response.

Chapter 5 turns to the construction of the Japanese pedagogical subject in educational policy documents and textbooks, as well as in popular manuals, all produced during the occupation. This pedagogical subject was different from the Filipino one because he or she had to be reeducated—taught, for instance, the practicality of *romaji* over the arcane *kanji*. In light of Japanese fascism, a specific kind of Orientalism was marshaled to explain Japanese deviance. It was argued that Japanese cultural practices—ritualism, mystical nationalism—and behavior such as conformity with community were more feudal than modern, despite the nation's rise to industrial power, and lent themselves to totalitarianism rather than democracy. Policy documents related to educational reform reflect the deployment of this kind of Orientalism, which limits civic modernity to the West. The chapter examines key occupation documents: *Report of the United States Education Mission to Japan* and the best-selling and widely read *Primer of Democracy*, required high school history volumes published under the direction of SCAP. In these documents, the Japanese were at once Orientalized as conformist, obsequious, and uninventive and feared as possibly threatening and imperial, yet they could be seen as potential subjects of a capitalist democracy. The chapter then shifts to the self-Orientalization by Japanese officials in the widely disseminated *Guide to New Education in Japan* and briefly examines the critical registering of the contradictions of democratic reforms in the memoir of educational officer, Jacob Van Staaveren. Finally, it examines the construction of a different kind of pedagogical subject emerging from Brides School texts produced by the American Red Cross—the Japanese wife as metonym for a new Japan, ready to unquestioningly occupy her class position in a racially stratified United States and thereby function as racial capital for the nation.

Chapter 6 examines how Japanese and Japanese Americans have registered these tutelary imperatives in their fiction, film, and personal reminiscences, reflecting the volatile and vertiginous landscape of postwar devastation and hope, imperial occupation, and wariness about Japanese militarist nationalism coupled with a forgetting of the country's own imperial violence, humble acceptance of defeat, and belief in cultural resilience. Examining Kojima Nobuo's "The American School" (1955), a short story about education under occupation; Masahiro Shinoda's film *MacArthur's Children* (1984), which views occupation through the prism of schoolchildren; and, briefly, Nobuko Albery's novel *Balloon Top* (1978), which looks at occupation from the perspective of the 1960s, I argue that these texts upset the unblemished narrative of loving, democratic tutelage by questioning its assumptions about Japanese character while simultaneously distancing themselves from Japanese imperial nationalism. All the works seize cultural representation to open up the contradictions of racial difference under the trope of tutelage and interrogate the (gendered) filiality inherent in it. More importantly, they articulate possibilities of subjecthood outside that of U.S. imperial governmentality. Nobuo posits a unique conjuncture of emasculation and resistance in the Bartleby-like figure of the schoolteacher Isa, suggesting a complex idea of power in defeat and a questioning of a tough (American) masculinity as power; Shinoda postulates a pacifist, feminized nationalism, mourning, and historical memory as alternatives to a rugged, masculinist, capitalist individualism and Americanization; and Albery articulates an alter-education to Japanese incorporation into a Pax Americana. Finally, I examine how Japanese American writers Jeanne Wakatsuki Houston and James D. Houston, in *Farewell to Manzanar*, and Julie Otsuka, in *When the Emperor Was Divine*, use intersectional historical memory to challenge the singular narrative of democratic occupation by linking the tutelage of internment camps to occupation.

In Chapter 7, I turn to the different route of ethnographic research. I was reminded by Shinoda's film that MacArthur's children, the objects of education reform, still survive and carry with them their histories, stories, and memories. Convinced that their oral narratives would be an invaluable cultural register, I sought out Japanese who had been schooled under occupation and were willing to share their memories. The chapter examines these oral histories in light of theories of collective memory studies begun by Maurice Halbwachs and continued by scholars such as Michael Schudson and Barbie Zelizer, who argue that memory is collective and social rather than individual. My conversations with this group of Japanese suggested that while their memories often meshed with the rhetoric of the occupation in critiquing Japanese wartime nationalism, militarism, and censorship, they simultaneously expressed cynicism about the "education for democracy" promulgated by SCAP. These complex and messy accounts of reflection and memory questioned the occupation goal of molding Americanized subjects and demonstrated ambivalence toward the project of tutelage, which was seen as both liberating and tactical.

In the Epilogue I briefly sketch the continuities of subjectification through education in other sites of U.S. empire and address the implications of this subjectification in a neoliberal, globalized world. I argue that the introduction of educational reform in other sites of U.S. occupation and the construction of pedagogical subjects there were also intimately related to forms of racialization. For instance, while restructurings in Korea focused on redesigning academic training to a progressivist model to change transform Asiatic/"Oriental" minds, changes in Haiti involved attempting to dismantle the French system of education and promote vocational training for a primitive people. I also briefly address the aftermath of U.S. educational reforms in the postcolonial Philippines and in postwar Japan to show how Japan particularly illustrates the fact that despite Japanese economic and military alignments with the United States, the project of cultural colonization introduced through schooling has had limited success. However, in the twenty-first century, despite the self-consciousness about articulating tutelary missions and the need to express cross-cultural tolerance, military violence followed by recovery through education and pacification through schooling remain major strategies of neoliberal imperialism. Nongovernmental organizations such as the Initiative to Educate Afghan Women, ideas of education for democracy used in the opening of the American University of Iraq, and projects such as Beauty without Borders (which involved teaching female Afghan hairdressers Western beauty methods) collude with the neoliberal imperial project and help reformulate pedagogical subjects for U.S. occupation and empire today.

My inclusion of Filipino and Filipino American and Japanese and Japanese American texts in this study of colonial tutelage points not only to the importance of the legacy of American schooling to the cultural imaginary but also to the significance of empire to Asian American literary and cultural production. This does not mean that the imperative to claim America so memorably articulated by Frank Chin is outdated but, rather, that this claim has a different valence when articulated by populations that have been colonized or occupied by the United States and, further, that this claim needs to be supplemented by colonial histories (xii). Here Augusto Espiritu's call for an Asian American studies that is simultaneously national and transnational is apropos (xvii).[21] Recent works in Asian American studies, such as Eiichiro Azuma's *Between Two Empires* (2005), Victor Bascara's *Model Minority Imperialism* (2006), and Jodi Kim's *Ends of Empire* (2010), have emphasized the centrality of empire to Asian America. Through her discussion of coolie labor in *Intimacies of Four Continents* (2015), Lisa Lowe has superbly demonstrated the imperial and transnational valences of Asian and Asian American studies. By situating Asian American literary and cultural production within the ambit of U.S. colonial tutelage, *Campaigns of Knowledge* significantly broadens the trajectory of Asian American empire studies and contributes to the burgeoning field of transnational Asian American studies (see, e.g., Cruz; Grewal; E.-B. Lim; S. Lim et al). In broad terms, this book also contributes to the now established field of U.S. empire studies, with its cultural studies beginnings in works such as Richard Drinnon's *Facing West* (1980); its consolidation in the academy, with Amy Kaplan and Donald Pease's *The Cultures of United States Imperialism* (1993); and many works too numerous to mention here. The amnesia about the colonization of the Philippines and the Philippine-American War has also been addressed in major collections devoted to U.S. imperialism, such as Alfred McCoy and Francisco A. Scarano's *Colonial Crucible* (2009).

This book also builds on the rich and growing body of cultural studies scholarship within Filipino studies that focuses on U.S. rule over the archipelago, including works by Paul Kramer, Vicente Rafael, Julian Go, E. San Juan Jr., Glenn Anthony May, and others.[22] It also builds on the field of occupation studies (*senryo kenkyu*), which includes works by John Dower, Takemae Eiji, Michael Molasky, and others.[23] However, although locatedness and historical specificity are crucial to this study, this is not a work of empirical history. Rather, it is a history of ideas, a cultural history that draws from Filipino studies and occupation studies.[24] Within both fields, there have been a few studies dealing with education. Critics of Filipino studies have focused on points of ambivalence and contradiction, such as colonial schools as a mixture of "oppressive and liberating opportunities" for Filipino children and American teachers' perception of fissures between their experiences and their roles within empire (Alidio, 2, 21, 94); education as a means of addressing ethnoreligious conflict, a "key mechanism in the internal colonization of Muslim Filipinos" (Milligan, 10); the use of American literature as a source of value and a means of colonial pacification (Wesling 7, 31–34); the use of English instruction for naturalizing occupation (Hsu, 4); American colonial education as promoting Philippine patriotism while quelling anticolonial fervor (Francisco, 3); and the creation of a hybrid nationalism using American and local influences to manipulate colonial education for nationalist purposes (Coloma, "Empire and Education," 85–112).[25] Studies devoted specifically to SCAP's educational reforms are largely descriptive and empirical and have argued that reforms were democratic but executed in authoritarian fashion (Nishi); that the advocacy of *romaji* under occupation was not an instance of cultural imperialism but, rather, a necessary script reform often discussed by the Japanese themselves (Unger); and that manuals for teaching democracy were important (Trainor).[26]

All of these studies (with the exception of Roland Sintos Coloma's, which examines Osias's writings in relation to those of colonial administrators) focus on colonial and occupation texts, thus unwittingly privileging the power of colonial discourse alone. I argue, by contrast, that by dialectically pairing the educational archives of U.S. empire with the literary and cultural texts of Filipinos and Japanese both at home and in the United States, we can see how the educational project is variously rerouted, appropriated, reinterpreted, and resisted, thus challenging the ubiquity of imperial power and demonstrating how colonial and occupation tutelage remain incomplete.[27] Furthermore, none of the studies of U.S. educational projects in the Philippines and Japan has been comparative.[28] By comparing the tutelary subjectification of Filipinos and Japanese, *Campaigns of Knowledge* points to the differences between the transnational nexus we think of as "Asian America" and to continuities of a tactic of U.S. empire that arguably continues into the present.

1

"Among a Tropical People"

Little Brown Brothers, Individual Liberty, and Self-Government

In a now well-cited letter, William Howard Taft, governor-general of the Philippines, assured President William McKinley that "our little brown brothers" would need fifty to a hundred years of American guidance "to develop anything resembling Anglo-Saxon political principles and skills" (Miller, 134). Taft's turn-of-the-twentieth-century statement captures in a nutshell the attitudes toward Filipinos within U.S. colonial policy that would be fleshed out, albeit in different ways, over the next three decades. It indicates clear racial-cultural differences between Filipinos and white Americans, the former in a state of intellectual underdevelopment and needing the supervision of the latter. Two years later, Taft praised the Bureau of Education, responsible for public instruction in the Philippines, for "preparing the people of the Philippine Islands to be fit to understand and enjoy individual liberty and self-government."[1] In articulating the colonial tutelage of Filipinos as ruling them in order to teach them freedom, Taft created a fraternal rhetoric that would be echoed over the next three decades as a distinctly American vision in which colonizers envisioned that their little brown brothers deserved, and would be capable of, self-rule through American education. A few years later, Frank R. White, who as director of education promoted industrial training in schools, would marvel at his mission, writing, "Never before in history was a practical educational system built up among a tropical people" (*Tenth Annual*, 25). White saw the project of education as unprecedented and characterized the subjects of this tutelage as "tropical," a moniker that defined Filipinos in relation to their temperate climate, marking them as easygoing natives unburdened by material care. Similarly, Charles Burke Elliott, a member of the Philippine Commission and a believer in anthropological racial theories,[2] subtitled his monograph on the Philippines "A Study in Tropical Democracy."

This chapter examines the multiple and often contradictory ways that American officials imagined Filipinos in educational documents constitutive of the colonial state's racial projects. While many educators saw Filipinos through the discourses of what we can call "tropicalism" (used to define happy islanders and similar to what Paul Lyons has admirably described as pacificism, with the difference that tropicalism includes knowledge gathering)[3] or Orientalism (with its raced and gendered binaries of East and West), or through domestic racial discourses in which Filipinos would be declared similar to inferior races such as African Americans and Indians, a few saw Filipinos as the intellectual equals of Americans. Yet despite their differences, educators believed they were creating subjects who would emulate qualities of individualism, self-reliance, equality, industry, and respect for labor, and who envisioned themselves as subjects of American tutelage. Although a pedagogical subject constituted by discourses of self-reliance and equality, on the one hand, and benevolent tutelage, on the other, seems contradictory, the contrast is only apparent. Starting in the 1910s, for instance, Ralph Waldo Emerson's "Self-Reliance" and an excerpt from Booker T. Washington's *Up from Slavery* were taught in all high schools. But as Jennifer McMahon suggests, Washington's success could be attributed to an equality of opportunity (which Americans argued they had bestowed on Filipinos), while impressing on students the idea of the dignity of labor (which would keep Filipinos satisfied in menial jobs); moreover, the self-reliance, freedom, and equality encouraged were not sociopolitical but individual and could be perfectly congruent with colonialism (57, 63, 65). Little wonder that the export of these ideas has been central to pedagogical subjectification for both colonialism and occupation. Indeed, the doctrine of individualism served the colonial government well by undermining native communal and family ties that could and did foment anticolonial revolt.

This is not to suggest that all of the directors of education, superintendents of provinces, or teachers had identical ideas about how best to educate Filipinos or that there was complete consistency over time. Indeed, as many scholars have pointed out, policies concerning industrial education, for instance, changed from the first director of education, Fred Atkinson, to his successor, David P. Barrows, to Frank R. White (G. May, 89, 96; Coloma, "Empire and Education," 70; San Juan, *The Philippine Temptation*, 28–29). However, changes in policy did not necessarily reflect a radical revision of how Filipinos (other than those in Mindanao) were viewed. More often than not, Filipinos were seen as belonging to a backward culture with native languages incapable of artistic or intellectual expression; they were a people indolent, deficient in reason, and accustomed to feudalism and mechanical imitation because of a pernicious Spanish inegalitarianism. The Filipino was to be made a desiring subject, eager to be taught the values of democracy, individualism, and capitalism, all of which were exemplified in the United States. The texts I examine are major policy documents, particularly the *Annual Reports of the Director of Education* and the 1902 Senate hearings on the Philippines, as well as a teacher's manual. I focus mainly on the period between 1900, when schooling moved from the War Department to the Bureau of Education, to 1925, the year that the harshly critical findings of the *Survey of the Educational System of the Philippine Islands* (the Monroe Report) were published—that is, roughly the first generation when the American system of schooling was implemented. Such an examination, in turn, points to subject construction as an integral component of forming U.S. colonial policy in the Philippines.

Pacification and Resistance: Schooling under Military Rule, 1898–1900

Before examining the manner in which educators wished to mold their pupils, it is important to understand the strategic role of schools at the beginning of colonial occupation. As noted in the Introduction, American soldiers opened the first school in Corregidor just a month after the victory over the Spanish fleet in May 1898. By 1900, there were ten thousand pupils in the three provinces of Bataan, Bulacan, and Pampanga alone (*Annual Report of Major General Arthur MacArthur*, 94). The speed with which schools were established reflected the urgency of finding a mechanism to combat Filipino nationalism and the insurgency. After all, the Philippine Republic had been formed in 1899 with Emilio Aguinaldo as president, and revolutionary attacks continued after Aguinaldo's surrender in early 1901. As General Arthur MacArthur commented to the Philippine Commission, "I know nothing . . . that can contribute more in behalf of pacification than the immediate institution of a comprehensive system of education. . . . [T]he matter is so closely allied with the exercise of military force in these islands that in my annual report I treated the matter as a military subject and suggested a rapid expansion of educational facilities as an exclusively military measure."[4] General James F. Smith, as secretary of public instruction, concurred, arguing that schools "operated as a restraining influence" to prevent families from joining the insurgency, "with which many of them undoubtedly sympathized" (quoted in Forbes, 420).

Charles Burke Elliott, member of the U.S. Philippine Commission, was clear about the role of American teachers as symbolic markers of an occupying force, even as he enthused about the institution of mass education as something that "had never been attempted in the Orient" (224). Describing the recruitment of American teachers, Elliott wrote:

> Arrangements were promptly made for enlisting a small army of teachers in the United States. At first they came in companies, but soon in battalions. The transport *Thomas* was fitted up for their accommodation, and in July 1901 it sailed from San Francisco with six hundred teachers—a second army of occupation—surely the most remarkable cargo ever carried to an Oriental colony. (228–229)

According to Elliott, teachers were battle-ready to combat Filipinos through their pupils and benevolently cement the work of military occupation. Little wonder that decades later, Renato Constantino saw this passage as an admission of the teaching of English as a technology of colonial oppression ("The Miseducation of the Filipino," 2). This description of the "Thomasites" through military metaphors is also echoed in the memoirs of teachers such as Mary Helen Fee, who refers to the "pedagogical invasion of Manila" (34) in *A Woman's Impression of the Philippines*, suggesting a consciousness of teachers' roles in buttressing occupation through the creation of amenable colonized subjects.

Indeed, as W. W. Rodwell, the superintendent of Cagayan and Isabela provinces, noted at the superintendents' convention in 1903, "The military people say that the schools are the only thing that is doing any good" (*ARWD Philippine Commission*, 894). The massive school system and the teaching of English had the potential to act as a counterinsurgency mechanism in several ways: by demonstrating Americans' genuine interest in the welfare of the Filipinos, by stemming peasant unrest through the promise of economic betterment promised by schooling, by creating a new Americanized community through the teaching of English, and by luring community leaders into an alliance with colonialism via offers of minor positions of power within the system. Years later, the Monroe Report would succinctly link occupation and schooling, noting that schools were established under the aegis of the military and followed the flag (*Survey*, 11–12).

Most scholars have noted the function of schools as mechanisms of pacification, integrally linked with occupation. However, scholars have ignored the early reception of these schools, as well as the often coercive ways in which they were established. Despite laudatory accounts, Filipinos did not, in fact, greet American teachers with open arms. As Frank White, then assistant to the general superintendent of education, reported in 1903, the establishment of schools by military authorities amidst violent suppression of insurrections meant that they had to be accepted by natives. White based his statements on the reports of officers in different provinces. For instance, a first lieutenant in the Fourth Infantry from Cavite recounted that the sergeant in command at Rosario

> stated to me yesterday that some of the school children at Rosario had told the school-teacher there that they did not want to learn English, but did want to learn Spanish. Sergeant went to the *presidente* of the town and told him that such talk was treasonable; that the United States had come here to stay and the people were to learn English; that he did not want to hear of any more of such defiant and treasonable talk. He asked me to report the matter to regimental headquarters. (*ARWD Philippine Commission*, 705)

Further investigation into the affair revealed that some families had chosen to remove their children from the American school to a barrio school where Filipino teachers were teaching Spanish and Tagalog. The lieutenant concluded that the *presidente* was innocent because he had recommended "American school-teachers for the largest two barrios [and] the arrest of the Filipinos now teaching Spanish, and [had] published notices that if the children [did] not go to school their parents [would] be arrested and fined" (*ARWD Philippine Commission*, 706). Thus, at this early stage of the establishment of colonial schools, not only were punitive measures taken to ensure attendance and compliance with the institutionalization of English, but alliances were also made with the native elite to discipline those who resisted the system. The reason teachers were welcomed by communities, White concluded, was that "there were few Filipinos at that time who did not wish to assume a semblance of loyalty to the purposes of the government as expressed by its military representatives" (*ARWD Philippine Commission*, 705).

At the same time, there were provinces where distrust of the American regime, including its school system, manifested itself openly. According to White, in Camarines Province people at first expressed scorn for American schools (*ARWD Philippine Commission*, 710), while in Iloilo Province, Division G. N. Brink reported that during a cholera epidemic the local populace refused the help of American teachers, and in four cases American teachers were "openly charged with having poisoned wells" (*ARWD Philippine Commission*, 761). W. E. Lutz, division superintendent of Lacuna, reported "blind opposition" to schools at their inception (*ARWD Philippine Commission*, 765). Yet in all cases there was a marked change in attitude toward the teachers and the schools a year or two later. E. G. Tubneb, division superintendent of Bulacan, the last province to lay down its arms against Americans, noted that the populace exhibited confidence in the schools they had not had earlier (*ARWD Philippine Commission*, 748). A combination of cooptation of the local population and coercion, along with teachers doing the job of colonial diplomacy—representing Americans not as an occupying force but as emissaries of beneficence—had worked. As Taft put it, "In the policing of the islands, in the collection of taxes, the attitude of the government necessarily encounters opposition, but in the work of the educational department the government is simply a giver, a donor, an almoner. The opportunity, therefore, for the American school-teacher and the division superintendent to ingratiate themselves with the Filipino people exceeds that of any other class of servants" (*ARWD Philippine Commission*, 907). However, it is clear that even when Filipinos attended schools, they were not simply obedient disciples. In 1907, one finds David Barrows formulating rules about dealing with a recalcitrant school population striking to protest school policies and effect changes. An indignant Barrows found the attitude intolerable and the "encouragement in local feeling" unacceptable, and stipulated that striking students would not be readmitted (*Eighth Annual*, 26). As late as 1912, the annual report records strikes at several schools and notes that strikes were a means to express displeasure at the policies of the Bureau of Education and represented attempts to change these policies. As part of the recording and ordering task of the colonial project, the Bureau of Education was compelled to document these outbreaks but was also free to interpret them. Thus, the report alleges that strikes were simply the machinations of politicians and lacked the support of parents (*Thirteenth Annual*, 14–15).

Tropicalist Orientalism: Indolence and Imitativeness

Once schooling was moved from the military to civilian control with the appointment of Fred Atkinson as the general superintendent of public instruction in 1900 and the establishment of the Bureau of Public Instruction in 1901, specific policies and ideas about programs of study began to be outlined, and the project geared itself to educating rather than simply pacifying Filipinos (G. May, 79). Yet, as is clear from Barrows's injunctions about insubordination, tutelage and pacification could never be completely separated, and education remained a major vehicle of colonial rule. Euphemistically referring to U.S. colonial rule as "the peculiar conditions existing here," Atkinson recommended a "centralized control of the public-school system" in which district superintendents would inspect schools, regulate courses of study, decide on the hiring of teachers, and report to the general superintendent ("The

Present Educational Movement in the Philippine Islands," 1325). The Bureau of Education divided the country into school divisions, initiated a system of reports, bulletins, and journals, and required staff to deliver monthly and annual reports on attendance and school supplies. In time, as discussed later in the chapter, teachers were instructed to report on hygiene and diseases within their communities; the bureau began reporting on public health and became, as Roland Sintos Coloma puts it, a mechanism of colonial surveillance ("Empire and Education," 33). This highly centralized technology was also racialized according to colonial parameters. Despite the criticism of Spain's rule as excessively hierarchical, the posts of district superintendent continued to be held by Americans alone until 1915, when Camilo Osias, a former *pensionado*, attained the position. Atkinson created an advisory board that included Filipinos but made amply clear that the board lacked the power to implement recommendations. It was to be strictly advisory and consultative ("The Present Educational Movement in the Philippine Islands," 1338–1339).

At the heart of this extensive educational system was the belief that schools could unify the archipelago, uplift the Filipinos, and foster a culture amenable to the exigencies of American colonial rule. Ideas about the intellectual, social, and cultural capabilities of Filipinos were thus crucial in devising educational strategies. For many educators, teaching natives in the new colony meant thinking about means of managing a racially different, backward population. The schooling of Native Americans and African Americans provided possible blueprints. Thus, General Superintendent Atkinson, conscious of his duty to "Americanize" the archipelago through children ("Education in the Philippines," 832), visited the Carlisle Indian Industrial School, as well Hampton and Tuskegee, before leaving for the Philippines. Atkinson wrote to Booker T. Washington for advice and argued for agricultural schools on the basis of intellectual ability, that Filipinos be taught "those things for which they have a capacity, i.e., industrial and mechanical pursuits" ("Education in the Philippines," 1327). Articles in popular publications such as *National Geographic*, *Scribner's*, and *Judge* and cartoons in newspapers routinely represented Filipinos as Black or Indian (Halili, 59–80). Not surprisingly, when Estelle Reel developed the Uniform Course of Study for Indian Schools in 1901, three thousand copies were printed for Indian schools, but six thousand copies were soon printed for use in Puerto Rico and the Philippines (Lomawaima, 12). The Annual Lake Mohonk Conference on the Indian and Other Dependent Peoples, begun in 1883, was enlarged in 1904 to include the Philippines, Puerto Rico, and other dependencies. Here it is important to emphasize the centrality of racialization to educational policies. Notwithstanding the fact that the occupation of Japan a half-century later put into place new, neocolonial mechanisms such as permanent bases and that the American attitude to the Japanese was, as John Dower puts it, colonial (*Embracing Defeat*, 23, 72), the Japanese were not racialized as Black or Indian. Although they could not be seen as equal to whites, Japanese generally were not thought of as primitive or as barbarous as other Asians.[5] Thus, the question of deemphasizing academic education did not arise.

Filipino racialization was otherwise. Although the successive general superintendents in the first generation of American schooling—Atkinson, Barrows, and White—proposed somewhat different educational policies, they were united in thinking of Filipinos as a backward race (not inherently but rendered so by history) needing guidance. What varied was how they represented Filipinos and how they envisioned their prospects for improvement. Engraved in the American imaginary through writers such as Herman Melville, who immortalized Fayaway and the Typees as happy, indolent people blessed with a fertile climate (*Typee*, 144, 187), educators in the Philippines drew on this tropicalist discourse even as they sought to learn from educational strategies used for Native Americans and African Americans. Like journalists and scientists who attempted to typify Filipinos as devious, sullen, indolent, and immature, educators classified Filipinos into racial types (Becker, 748–749; Palmer, 77) Atkinson's summation about Filipinos in his 1902 report is worth quoting: "They are slow, take life leisurely, putter over their work, and lack responsibility. That, however, is not strange, considering the climate. . . . [T]he Filipino lives only for to-day, and it is not surprising. In a land where little clothing is required and where food grows without cultivation there is not much incentive for the average person to work" ("The Present Educational Movement in the Philippine Islands," 1434–1435).

Using the discourse of tropicalism by representing Filipinos as lackadaisical, contented, arguably demasculinized natives at a time when insurrections against Americans were still rampant allowed for a discounting of resistance as well as the independent thinking evidenced by criticisms of schools by locals. The challenge of tropicalism was to classify those who resisted categorization. Thus, the idea of Filipinos as lazy continued even when educators acknowledged their work potential. For instance, William B. Freer, who would become division superintendent, contrasted Filipino students who deprived themselves of sleep in their intense desire to learn with Native Americans who were "dull" with their books; still, Freer continued to characterize Filipinos as "indolent constitutionally" (275–276). Almost two decades later, the Woods-Forbes report, commissioned by President Warren Harding to determine Filipino readiness for independence, would similarly portray Filipinos as "light-hearted and inclined to be improvident as are all people who live in lands where nature does so much and people require so little" ("Report of the Philippine Commission," 682).

Other explanations of Filipinos' racial difference derived from the discourses of Orientalism, which, as Edward Said argues, represented "Orientals" variously as childlike, depraved, passive, treacherous, superficial, sensual, and accustomed to despotism (40, 102, 286) Filipinos were essentially different from Westerners and inferior to them in intelligence, rationality, and innovation—hence, a people needing uplift. For many educators, the Philippines was part of a citational Orient. Emblematically, in his statement in the 1903 annual report, Freer quoted a stanza from Rudyard Kipling's "The Ballad of East and West" as part of his argument about the incomprehensibility of "the inner spirit of the oriental" (*ARWD Philippine Commission*, 894). The Monroe Report of 1925, while severe in its criticism of the educational practices in the Philippines, positively stereotyped Filipinos as "traditionally polite, courteous, and generous," like other "oriental peoples," but cautioned against placing too much emphasis on these outer mannerisms. Yet even if they exhibited qualities that evidenced the attainment of culture and refinement, such qualities were seen as superficial and not proof of their caliber. It would be a lapse, the report warned, to mistake "outward manners of politeness for depth and strength of character" (*Survey*, 242).

If logic and rationality were the hallmarks of modernity, colonial administrators, including those heading the educational establishment, were loath to grant Filipinos these capacities, for to do so would be to admit both the legitimacy of earlier insurrections and demands for immediate independence that leaders such as Teodoro Sandiko had formally articulated as early as 1905. Orientalist discourse perfectly served the purpose of not admitting Filipino autonomy by marking Filipinos as devoid of reason and therefore incapable of articulating nationalism. Hence, while outlining a program of study for the Philippines, Atkinson intimated that although Filipinos could be taught, "in studies which require the use of reasoning powers [they] are slow, and much tact and patience are required on the part of the teacher" ("The Present Educational Movement in the Philippine Islands," 1353). But the official archive, as Antoinette Burton has so eloquently argued, need not be just panoptic, for to think of it as such is to fall prey to the "seduction of the total archive" (140). The colonial archive itself has fissures and cracks through which we can hear the voice of the Other, the native. For instance, David Barrows's Orientalizing of Filipinos as deficient in scientific thinking and reasoning in his 1904 annual report reveals his frustration with gaining the assent of his pupils: "Education in the Philippines is concerned with a people whose lack of exactness, especially in their mental processes, is a conspicuous racial fault. The Filipino has an instinctive and intense reluctance to admit ignorance. . . . He fails to appreciate the desirability of accuracy" (*Annual Report of the General Superintendent of Education*, 30–31). While Barrows racializes mental faculties (calling to mind Alfred Lyall's statement to Lord Cromer, "Accuracy is abhorrent to the Oriental mind" (Said, 38), he is also frustrated by his inability to convince Filipinos of their deficiencies and, arguably, about their need for American tutelage. Still, the Orientalist discourse deeming Filipinos weak in reason was so powerful that even educators convinced of the capabilities of the Filipinos felt the need to acknowledge the received wisdom about the natives. Thus, William A. Phillips, superintendent of Ok I'akagua Province, found Filipino students comparable to Americans and testified that the best Filipino students' "work in mathematics is superior to that of any American class I ever saw." Concurrently, he felt compelled to begin his comments by first acceding to the received colonial wisdom about Filipinos and presenting his own findings as tentative and possibly aberrant: "The Filipino is said to be deficient in reasoning power and that is true to a great extent. Yet the results obtained in sciences have been very good" (*ARWD Philippine Commission*, 825).

While the colonial discourses of Orientalism and tropicalism influenced the perception educational administrators had of Filipinos, these views were also affected by the need to distinguish American rule from that of Spain. Roberto Fernández Retamar has written eloquently about the creation of the "Black Legend," the idea of Spain as a monstrous empire created by newer colonial powers to justify their own rapaciousness (57–60). Thus, while educators saw the benign influence of Spain in Christianizing the archipelago, they criticized Spain for its pernicious creation of a highly stratified class culture mirroring its own and transmitted in the Philippines as the culture of *caciquismo*. The earliest education reports berate the Spanish for preventing the enlightenment of the masses and for friars' condemning freethinkers as troublemakers.[6] Spain's introduction of mass primary education in 1863 was often deemed inadequate because there were only two schools for each *pueblo*. Years later, Charles Burke Elliott would write that Spanish methods had "accentuated the worst feature of an aristocratic as distinguished from a democratic system of education" and lament that, almost twenty years later, Filipinos remained Spanish in their culture and that their "mental processes [were] those of Latins, not Anglo-Saxons" (Preface [n.p.], 220). The result of this inadequate system of education, according to Barrows, was to create a society sharply bifurcated into the rich, who owned haciendas and adopted charming Spanish manners, and the rest, who lived in poverty and ignorance and were dominated economically and intellectually by the *ilustrado* class

(*ARWD Philippine Commission*, 696–697). The mass of Filipinos had been conditioned to accept the dominance of the *ilustrado* and lacked free will.⁷

Other characteristics ascribed to Filipinos derived both from the perceived scourge of Spanish rule and the influence of progressive theories of education. The beginnings of U.S. colonial rule in the Philippines coincided with major developments in education, the most famous being the concepts introduced by John Dewey. His "My Pedagogical Creed," which outlined the idea of learning that takes place organically when the school is a form of community life rather than apart from it, was published in 1897 and aroused the interest of teachers and parents nationwide. Two years later, he delivered a series of lectures that further crystallized his ideas. Dewey argued that the industrial revolution had destroyed the home as a site of production in which family members had different tasks and children learned in the process of doing. What had replaced this process was the school, similar to a factory, with rows of geometrically placed desks and an emphasis on listening, which for Dewey marked "the dependency of one mind upon another." For Dewey, this listening meant the passive absorption of standard materials in the shortest time (*The School and Society*, 32). The solution was learning through activities, where the center of gravity would move from the teacher to the child with the result that children would "individualize themselves" and "become ... distinctive beings" (*The School and Society*, 33, 35). Educational administrators in the Philippines did not necessarily implement strategies of progressivist pedagogy because they clashed with colonial imperatives. Indeed, as Glenn Anthony May argues, many colonial educators were conservative (72). Yet when these administrators wrote about schools in the Philippines, they valorized aspects of progressivist learning and found the schools and students wanting in spontaneity, creativity, and innovation. Atkinson's early evaluation of Filipinos as mimics and rote learners who were incapable of original thought continued to be reiterated by later educators. Schooling for the average Filipino, Atkinson wrote,

> has not tended to broaden his intelligence, and has hardly developed independent thought and action. One could observe in the schools a tendency on the part of the pupils to give back like phonographs what they had heard or read and memorized without seeming to have thought for themselves. . . . When the Spaniards came here[,] . . . the Philippine Islanders could read and write their own languages. At the present time, after three hundred years, the mass of people have been taught so mechanically that they can hardly do more than this." ("The Present Educational Movement in the Philippine Islands," 1319)

If, as discussed in the Introduction, progressivist educators were not biological determinists but bought into the theory of recapitulation, which argued that human development retraced that of the races and that some races were behind in evolution, Atkins seemed to argue that Filipinos were indeed behind their Western counterparts but that the reason was cultural rather than racial. Spain had inhibited the development of Filipinos. Educators such as E. G. Turner, division superintendent of Bulacan, who found Filipinos lacking in originality, stated, "The Filipino people as a race are very imitative" (*ARWD Philippine Commission*, 888). But Americans continued to paint Filipinos as mimics even when lived experience belied their pronouncements. In impressionistic memoirs of teachers rather than statements of administrators making educational decisions, attestations of Filipinos' derivativeness plainly contradict teachers' impatience with Filipino spunk. Thus, Mary Helen Fee, reflecting on her years of teaching Filipinos, notes with annoyance in her memoir how, in contrast to American children, Filipinos refused to admit any wrongdoing, that "the attitude of dissent" was present in the quiet as well as the loquacious, and that this refusal to assent was based on a conviction of the teacher's ignorance (65). Yet a little later, in the same chapter on Filipino traits, Fee depicted Filipinos as good at memorization but poor at independent thinking, apt to be "discouraged quickly when they have to puzzle out things for themselves" (66). Such statements reflect not only the conflicting realities teachers might have noticed—students could refuse to admit wrongdoing and yet become discouraged by some tasks given them—but also the logic of colonial racial difference that demands that, at some level, the colonized remain essentially learners rather than creators of knowledge. This logic helps explain why, despite their different subjectification, the Japanese were also viewed as mechanical imitators.

Thus, Orientalist discourses about Filipinos' superficial manners and love of form (learned from the Spanish) intersected with tropicalist discourses about indolent, contented, happy natives to produce what we might think of as a tropicalist Orientalism. This was an Orientalism different from that of the British in India or Egypt, where part of the colonial mission was to restore the glory of past civilization from the degeneration of the present through a vigorous, masculinized Anglo-Saxonism (Said, 35). Filipinos were seen as possessing not a worthy past civilization or culture but, rather, a barbarism that had been partially redeemed through Spanish colonialism and needed further amelioration through contact with Anglo-American culture. If they were seen as "Oriental," it was of a different type. Thus, almost a decade after the opening of American schools, Barrows wrote:

Their indigenous culture, which frequently is spoken of by Filipinos as the standard toward which to return, was a wild barbarism left behind centuries ago.... From this jungle life they were rescued by contact with the civilization of the Hindu. Subsequently they came under the civilization of the Arab and the European, and through these various foreign influences the Malayan people have steadily developed in culture until in the Philippines their civilization approximates that of western Europe. (*Eighth Annual*, 35–36)

Although Barrows clearly disagreed with Filipino culturalists, he had a Lamarckian evolutionist view of Filipinos—though only of the Malayan elite—whom he thought could absorb the cultures with which they came into contact. This optimism about cultural absorption was not at odds with Barrows's conviction about the civilizing mission of Western colonialism (evident, for instance, in his praise for the Dutch colonization of the East Indies) but was, instead, one of its many benefits as Filipinos learned the route to colonial modernity (Barrows, "Memorandum on Public Instruction in Netherlands-India," 61).

English as Pacification and Civilization

If Filipinos could be redeemed through education, the teaching of English would play a major role. Strategically, the introduction of a vast number of English-only schools was seen as a way to create a population unified through an Anglo-American language and culture and hence potentially supportive of the American presence, which continues to the present. The 1902 U.S. Senate Hearings before the Committee on the Philippines reveal how language is racialized at once as a carrier of culture and values, a technology of colonial subjectification, and a mechanism of uplift. In his testimony, Governor-General Taft responded to questions about insurrections related to different linguistic groups in the following manner: "The insurrecto leaders in Samar, in Panay, and of course in Batangas, are all Tagalogs.... They carry with them the Tagalog language where they go, though they learn other dialects, and therefore you will find in many places persons who speak Tagalog" (*Affairs*, 49). Taft saw Tagalog as a linguistic unifier and a dangerous accessory to insurrection in a country where, despite U.S. attempts to catalog and divide people according to tribes, there was a "homogeneity in appearance, in habits, and in many avenues of thought" (*Affairs*, 50). Race, language, and culture are interwoven here. Tagalog is seen both as a language that enables unity and anticolonial community and a threatening racialization, with insurrectionary

Filipinos carrying and perpetuating Tagalog as an incendiary weapon. For Taft, the teaching of English was necessary to break down anticolonial resistance. Simultaneously, Taft justified the wholesale adoption of English in schools not simply on strategic but also on civilizational and racial grounds, stating: "One of our great hopes in elevating those people is to give them a common language and that language English, because through the English language certainly, by reading its literature, by becoming aware of the history of the English race, they will breathe in the spirit of Anglo-Saxon individualism" (*Affairs*, 50).[8]

In Taft's formulation of resistance leaders as "Tagalogs" we see the workings of what Paul Kramer has described as the two-pronged strategy of imperial racial formation in the Philippines, the first of which "Anglo-Saxonized" Americans, while the second "tribalized" Filipinos. Kramer writes, "Contemporary social evolutionary theory held that societies, in evolving from 'savagery' to 'civilization,' moved in political terms from 'tribal' fragmentation to 'national' unity." Successfully identify "tribes"—"marked by language, religion, political allegiance"—and "one had disproven a nation's existence." This strategy of discounting the Philippine Republic formed under Aguinaldo in 1898, presented in terms of sovereignty and "civilization," was worked out through the formation of Philippine commissions that, in their first report in 1900, reduced the Philippine Republic to the "Single Tribe" of Tagalogs (Kramer, 121–122).

For Barrows, who would later articulate a Jeffersonian yeomanry for Filipinos, English was a leveling, democratic force that could challenge *caciquismo* because knowledge of English would be "a possession as valuable to the humble peasant for his social protection as it is to the man of wealth for his social distinction" (*ARWD Philippine Commission*, 701). Because Barrows was such an influential figure in the early years when the school system was being established, it is important to understand the relationship between his advocacy of English and his often derogatory views of Filipinos, which were strongly affected by his conviction that the U.S. colonization of the Philippines was necessary and its practices moral. In the Senate hearings on the Philippines in 1902, Barrows was closely interrogated by skeptical anti-imperialists on the wisdom of foisting a foreign language on Filipinos and on Filipino attitudes toward Americans. Barrows made clear his remarks were limited to the Christianized population and to what he called the Malay race. Barrows fervently believed that U.S. colonial rule (although he never used the word "colonial" in relation to the United States) was established for the enlightenment of the population, unlike that of the British or Dutch in Malaysia (*Affairs*, 692). Thus, when questioned by senators about torture, he refused to entertain any possibilities of wartime atrocities, testifying that the water cure had never harmed any natives (*Affairs*, 723). Likewise, he downplayed Filipino demands for independence, maintaining that Filipinos were given liberties and freedoms under the United States (*Affairs*, 703). Filipinos, in his view, were capable of development, but only to a point. They could endure manual labor and would provide a workforce capable of tolerating the tropical heat but could never hope to be manufacturers and posed no threat to U.S. industry (*Affairs*, 710).

Barrows's firm views about the necessity of English were based on a similarly paternalistic solicitude for Filipinos. While his experiences with Indian education had convinced him about the undesirability of trying to obliterate native languages, he thought English was necessary for civilization and growth. Here the Senate hearings become particularly interesting. Avoiding Senator Albert Beveridge's question about the feasibility of fusing different native languages into a common one, Barrows draws on a geopolitical argument that without English there would be "the isolation of the Philippine Islands which has gone on for so long." Other senators refused to accept Barrows's civilizational hierarchy to pathologize non-Western languages. While interrogating Barrows, Senator Edward Carmack, who had denounced what he called the "rape" of the Philippines, argued that the problem of communication was the same for any country, that communication with the world was carried out by only the educated few. Barrows's responses reveal both his belief in the possibilities of Filipino advancement through education and his raced skepticism about emancipatory possibilities of native languages: "If we are seeking the enlightenment of the population . . . the population would have to have some language and literature upon which to rest that . . . if the Filipino is to be enlightened at all, he has to have some medium of exchange from tribe to tribe and from himself with the white race, and it is an exceedingly fortunate thing I think that his ambition at the present time is to acquire English" (*Affairs*, 695).

Pressed by the anti-imperialist Senator Joseph Rawlins, who pointed out that British civilization had grown and learned about other cultures by translating European languages into English, and that "the native language would grow as the English language had grown," by incorporating foreign words (*Affairs*, 698), Barrows emphatically dissociated any native Filipino language from a similar incorporative growth and capacity: "It would be impossible to take one of the Filipino dialects, like the Tagalog, for example, and develop it; that is, to carry it along, incorporating into it words and materials for which there is no Tagalog, and making it a language suitable for wide commercial use or for literature" (*Affairs*, 698). What Barrows argued about the capacities of Tagalog was similar to his views about Filipinos: as a people, they were not resilient enough to enter modernity, and their language reflected the weakness of the race. Writing about Filipino literature during U.S. colonial rule, Isabel Pefianco Martin suggests that this racialization of Filipino languages was perpetrated in classrooms—Pilipino was not allowed to be taught in schools until 1940—and in scholarly assessments of Filipino literature, in which excessive sentimentalism was seen as a reflection of the emotional nature of the people and the crispness and sharpness of English was seen as difficult for an Oriental people ("American Education and Philippine Literature," 120). Barrows's racialization of language resonated with his view that Filipinos needed American tutelage until they were fit for self-government. Although he believed Filipinos could progress, and had progressed, and was critical of American entrepreneurs who wanted to keep Filipinos submissive, he believed in what Kenton J. Clymer calls "humanitarian imperialism" because it was Americans who could effect the social transformation of Filipinos. Thus, U.S. rule over the Philippines was important for the sake of the Filipinos themselves (495–517). Barrows resigned in protest in 1909 partly because funds for the education of Filipinos were being cut.

Not surprisingly, when Barrows wrote his first report as director of education, he couched his unequivocal support of English by virtue of its rank in linguistic evolution. He wrote, "One has but to examine the literature which has appeared in the past fifty years in each of those tongues to see how unlikely of literary development is any one of them. The masterpiece of Tagalog literature is a satirical poem entitled 'Ang Salit ang Buhay ni Florante,' which was composed years ago by a Filipino 'filosofo' named Baltazar.... His result is not a success, and the poem, while of great interest, promises little for the future of a Tagalog literature. For common intercourse, as well as for education, the Filipino demands a foreign speech" (*ARWD Philippine Commission*, 700). Tagalog was both a reflection of Filipinos' underdevelopment and, given the limited nature of the language, the cause of this underdevelopment. Thus, in a novel process of race making, Barrows argued that Tagalog oppressed Filipinos, hampering their intellectual development. He then justified the use of English as the lingua franca of the world.

The teaching of English could not only ameliorate the race by introducing it to Western ideas but also continue the task of pacification past the cessation of military hostilities. Barrows could not conceive of Filipinos being other than desiring subjects of American rule. Thus, when asked by Senator Rawlins about the "political effect of a thorough understanding of English literature, or American literature, so to speak, upon [Filipino] aspirations to stand upon a plane of equality with American citizens," Barrows gave a utilitarian response, the contradictions of which were characteristic of colonial aspirations for Filipinos. Literary education would paradoxically create pedagogical subjects well versed in (it is implied) American democratic institutions and hence, paradoxically, contented to be under colonial rule. Barrows stated, "We hope that is will have a beneficial political effect; that is, the more they know of America and Americans and American institutions the more satisfied they will be under American rule" (*Affairs*, 702).[9] Even when pressed for further clarifications by the more skeptical Senator Rawlins and Senator Carmack, who felt that Filipinos would not be content with the mere knowledge of American institution unless accorded rights, Barrows continued to present evidence to the contrary. So tenacious was this policy that it would be a generation before primary school teachers were allowed to use local languages to supplement English.

Flags, Heroes, and the Americanization Project

Schools were seen as ideal sites for inculcating allegiance toward the colonial state even after they were handed over to civilian authorities, who remained in close contact with the constabulary (the major arm of surveillance). The layout of the classroom, the structure of the school day, and the curriculum could all reinforce this allegiance. In response to Atkinson's request for his opinion about the effect of American teachers on the populace, C. J. Bailey, senior inspector of the constabulary for Tarlac Province, noted the effect of American schooling in dissipating demands for independence. He wrote, "When native school children daily gather in groups on the streets and plaza and sing 'America' and 'The Star Spangled Banner,' in good English and with a vigor that would have made our pilgrim forefathers envious, they voice the beginning of the end [of demands for independence]" ("The Present Educational Movement in the Philippine Islands," 1390). Other accounts blatantly touted schooling as a means of inculcating Americanization. In an article significantly titled, "The Kindergarten as an Americanizing Influence," published in 1906 in the *Philippine Teacher*, a magazine started by the Bureau of Education but that soon became independent, the author, Austin Craig, recounted an episode in which a visitor to a provincial capital school asked of the pupils, "'Why do you come to school?' The answer was, 'To learn.' 'To learn what?' 'To learn American ways.' 'And why do you want to learn American ways?' 'Because they are the best ways'" (26–27). Such displays of deference to the United States, while initially instituted and encouraged as means for quelling opposition, became part of the school culture of the Philippines and a salient feature of the historical memory imaginatively recuperated by writers such as Carlos Bulosan, Edith Tiempo, and Bienvenido Santos.

However, tutelary colonialism did not always propagate Americanization in such a palpable manner. Instead, it cleverly attempted to make Americanization compatible with a Filipino identity. Allegiance to the United States did not have to be at odds with loyalty to selected icons and figures of Filipino history. William B. Freer, speaking at the superintendents' convention in Manila in March 1903, for instance, suggested that school decorations be a means of marking a congruence between Filipino nationalism and fealty to the United States: "The American flag should not be used sparingly. In our school we had [José] Rizal's portrait under the American flag, and it had a good effect, a number of teachers thereafter decorating their rooms in like manner" (*ARWD Philippine Commission*, 890). The memorialization of Rizal as a national hero by the United States was strategically designed to honor an iconic Filipino martyr who had been executed by the Spanish and who could be presented as an ally of Americans who had "liberated" the Philippines from Spain. Filipino and American nationalism could thus be seen as one.

If nationalism, as Anne McClintock has argued, is constituted through fetish spectacles such as flags, so is colonial nationalism (374). Thus, the liberal use of flags and marches of loyalty in schools and normal institutes continued to be a spectacular part of the technology of governance. The annual report of 1920, for instance, displayed a photograph with multiple American flags outside a building with the caption, "Pupils in training department of Philippine Normal School participating in a patriotic drill" (*Twenty-First Annual*, n.p.). Likewise, the annual report of 1922, in which Luther B. Bewley, the newly appointed director of education, noted that public schools from the beginning of U.S. occupation had "constituted propaganda centers for the spread of progressive ideas," contained a similar photograph. Students participated in a garden-day celebration flanked by multiple U.S. flags (*Twenty-Second Annual*, 20). The ideal pedagogical subject thus was one who would recognize that loyalty to the United States (and an acknowledgment of American exceptionalism concomitant with U.S. control) was indeed loyalty to the Philippines, a theme reiterated in school curricula and textbooks. As Prescott Jernegan suggested in his civics textbook *The Philippine Citizen* (1907), the Bill of Rights approved in 1902 gave Filipinos with a stroke of the pen "rights which they had been fighting in vain for hundreds of years to obtain from Spain" (182). Culturally, socially, and politically, Filipino interests could be presented as congruent with American interests. Thus, Jernegan's proposal for a Filipino history course for second-year high school students with the aim "to present the history of the Philippines from the Filipino point of view" involved a teleological progression from primitive Filipino civilization to Spanish influence and the new ideals introduced by American rule (*ARWD Philippine Commission*, 830).

Foremost among these new ideals were the rights and liberties denied under the autocracy of Spanish rule, which had suppressed differences. Educators felt that forms of local government established by Americans allowed

Filipinos to express their wishes. Division Superintendent H. H. Buck of Cavite Province wrote about the Filipino, "In the town council he may discuss questions which were formerly denied him; thus his mind is developed and fitted to take part in more important deliberations" (*ARWD Philippine Commission*, 881). Filipinos were to be prepared for self-government, and the prime vehicle for that goal was education. As Taft stated, the Bureau of Education was responsible for "educating and preparing the people of the Philippine Islands to be fit to understand and enjoy individual liberty" (*ARWD Philippine Commission*, 907). Yet individual liberty did not mean political liberty, and educators were convinced of the inability of Filipinos to govern themselves. More than a decade after the institution of American schools, Freer concluded his memoir by comparing Filipinos to caged birds: safe, well cared for, and with a cage large enough to roam, but unable to care for themselves outside the cage (334).

Filipinos as Fit for Industrial Education

But while Filipinos were viewed as a people to be trained in the exercise of democracy, original thinking, and, eventually, self-government, educators also saw them as best equipped to handle manual tasks. The teaching of practical skills, agriculture, and craftsmanship, along with training in different trades, were seen as essential pedagogical functions. As mentioned earlier, educators sought to learn from the models offered by Tuskegee, Hampton, and Carlisle, all of which stressed the value of manual training. Samuel Chapman Armstrong, the son of missionaries in Hawai'i and founder of the biracial Hampton, saw Indians and African Americans as "a thousand years behind us in moral and mental development"; they were "backward" races suited to industrial education.[10] Indians were simply "grown-up children" for whom book knowledge would be an absurdity (Armstrong, 407). Booker T. Washington, who had graduated from Hampton and founded Tuskegee, was consulted by Atkinson before Atkinson went to the Philippines.

Scholars of the Philippines have written extensively about the changes in educational policy in the first two decades of American schooling. Glenn Anthony May suggests that the inconsistent policies of different directors of education created a lack of continuity that diluted the educational efforts of Americans (77). Others have written about the total shift in emphasis from academic to industrial education, particularly after Frank White took over the post of director of education from David Barrows in 1909, and continuing through the tenures of Frank I. Crone, Walter W. Marquardt, and Luther Bewley (G. May, 92–93, 99–117; Coloma, "Empire and Education," 70; San Juan, *The Philippine Temptation*, 28). However, despite the increasing emphasis on the commercialization of industrial education, I suggest that most educators and, certainly, the directors of the Bureau of Education who standardized curriculum and made policy changes, subscribed to a greater or lesser degree to colonial racial difference when thinking about the capabilities of Filipinos, whom they thought were ill-suited to strenuous mental activity, even if they could be trained to improve. In a 1900–1901 report, David Gibbs, division superintendent for Pampanga, Bulacan, and Bataan, and who later wrote primers for Philippine schools, noted, "The public elementary and provincial schools must interest the coming generations in the soil and in manual occupations. The Filipino will never be a philosopher, nor deeply a scientist. He may develop linguistic and literary powers, but on the whole he must remain a man of the soil and of the saw" (in Atkinson, "The Present Educational Movement in the Philippine Islands," 1355). Atkinson concurred with Gibbs, arguing emphatically for the establishment of schools of agriculture so that "Filipinos may be taught those things for which they have a capacity, i.e., industrial and mechanical pursuits. . . . These instructors should follow the plan of work of Hampton and Tuskegee." Atkinson concluded his long report by warning against "overdoing the matter of higher education. . . . We should heed the lesson taught us in our reconstruction period when we started in to educate the negro. The education for the masses here must be an agricultural and industrial one, after the pattern of our Tuskegee Institute at home" ("The Present Educational Movement in the Philippine Islands," 1327, 1439).

With the directorship of Barrows came a shift in emphasis for a few years. Much has been written about his following a Jeffersonian tradition of wanting to create a literate, independent yeomanry. Indeed, in his 1903 report, Barrows wrote poetically about this figure:

> I believe we should . . . seek to develop here in the Philippines, not a proletariat, but everywhere the peasant proprietor. . . . If he has his small home and plot of ground, the possession of English, the ability to read, the understanding of figures . . . will, I hope, increase his contentment as it increases his independence. (*ARWD Philippine Commission*, 702)

This vision, which Thomas Jefferson premised on the assumption that the yeoman was white (slavery for Jefferson destroyed the industry that the yeoman embodied), was different from the ideal of the African American or Indian as skilled laborer. This ideal is probably the reason Barrows strongly defended teaching the three "R's" in primary school in his 1908 report. Answering critics who advocated more practical instruction, Barrows held firm that literacy was important in advancing societies from barbarism to civilization (*Eighth Annual*, 15). However, Barrows's propagation of literacy did not diminish his view of the importance of industrial education for Filipinos. In the same report in which he touted literacy in primary schools, he was clear that, unlike in the United States, industrial training could not be delayed until high school but had to be introduced in the intermediate grades to affect "the industrial efficiency" of the population (*Eighth Annual*, 17).

Barrows also saw the necessity of reforming Filipinos toward materialism. For that end the refinements of arts and culture were secondary. The function of American education, he argued, was to mitigate the "strongly materialist tendencies of American life," which were part of "environmental conditions and racial temperament" and had led to "high material advancement." Academics in the United States were "a guard against the stifling of the nonmaterial." The Filipino, on the other hand, would benefit from more materialist propensities. "The great need of Filipino national life," Barrows wrote in his 1904 report, "is precisely in the direction of effort to acquire material benefits. The graces of the culture studies may well await other lessons. The crying need now is for a stimulus which environment and racial history have for centuries denied, as stimulus to 'practical' activity" (*Annual Report of the General Superintendent of Education*, 30).

Other directors of education emphatically saw schooling as the opportunity to create Filipino subjects as labor for industrial capitalism. While the Bureau of Education had been gathering data about the industrial needs of the country even under the tenure of Barrows, the use of students as labor for the colonial market was cemented under the directorship of Frank White and continued thereafter. Educational administrators in the Philippines were not immune to the structures of colonialism in which they participated, even as individual educators were genuinely interested in improving the lives of Filipinos.[11] Frank Crone's annual report for 1915 clearly delineates the role of schools as part of the structure of a colonial, capitalist world system, with extraction of value from the periphery to the center (Wallerstein, 18–19, 65). With the disruption in commerce caused by World War I, buyers in the United States looked at the Philippines: "Representatives from big commercial concerns in the United States quickly made their way to the Philippines in search of embroidery, and incidentally became interested in lace and in the products of hand weaving. This brought to the Bureau of Education, through its interest in these industries, many requests and propositions of a commercial nature" (*Sixteenth Annual*, 39–40). In other words, students were not simply being taught skills to become tradesmen or future labor for industry but were already participating as labor. Crone further specified that for industrial instruction to follow commercial lines, children had to be taught one specialized skill beginning in elementary school and continuing through intermediate grades and that their products had to be standardized and uniform (*Affairs*, 38). In effect, they were to be seen as factory labor producing handicrafts such as embroidery, lace, woodwork, and bamboo-rattan furniture. In a few years, the production of these goods in schools was so established that directors documented earnings in their annual reports. In his report for the year 1920, Luther Bewley catalogued the earnings by schoolchildren, noting with satisfaction the 126 percent increase over the year from 1918 to 1919 (*Twenty-First Annual*, 34).

But whether or not students were viewed as labor for colonial markets, the particularly vaunted American subjectification of capitalism and possessive individualism were seen as important to inculcate in Filipinos. Again, in "The Kindergarten as an Americanizing Influence," Craig argues that the most important values taught are not academic but those leading to happiness made possible "by those ways which are characteristic of the America people." He further specifies that the kindergarten "calls attention to property rights and cultivates individual responsibility" (26–27). Such a Lockean emphasis on capitalism as essential to individual formation meant challenging the importance of communal and family ties in marking the pedagogical subject, a project that continued to be carried out in occupation Japan, as well. As Rafael Palma put it in his inaugural address as the president of the University of the Philippines, the "ideal of communal life in the family" was a pristine element of Filipino character, in contrast to the "individualist family organization" of Americans and their "utilitarian and materialist spirit" (quoted in Fonacier, 89). Thus, even the American educators most critical of U.S. pedagogical practices in the Philippines thought it was important to inculcate capitalist individualism. Although it was severely critical of schools, the landmark 1925 *Survey of the Educational System of the Philippine Islands*, carried out by distinguished educators and headed by Paul Monroe, a professor of education at Columbia University, was clear about the importance of disseminating capitalist values. Contrasting the family and community as loci of value in the Philippines with the valorizing of individualism in the "Western World," the report noted the lack of a "completely developed sense of property rights," something Filipinos needed to cultivate. It saw a major objective of American education as teaching Filipinos to move from their simple social organizations based on "community possessions and customs" to the complex and highly individualized social organization of the West. The absence of a fully developed sense of property rights was responsible, it was felt, for the "too common trait of dishonesty among the school pupils" (*Survey*, 96). Presumably Filipino students were dishonest because their family and community values interfered with the development of property rights and, therefore, character. A clearer statement about the normalization of the Lockean view of the propertied individual as central to the formulation of national character can hardly be found (Locke, 19).

Yet the writers of the Monroe Report were conflicted about the immediate translation of these values into the production and selling of goods as part of school curricula. Although the report commended industrial education for removing the antipathy to manual labor often noted in the Philippines and praised the quality of goods produced in schools, it criticized this education on two very different grounds: commercial and educational. The commercial critique noted the lack of demand for goods such as baskets and embroidered lace and the fact that students rarely used their skills after leaving school. The educational critique questioned the value of students' monotonously continuing the same tasks (basket making, for instance) after having acquired mastery and the gearing of education toward commercial ends (*Survey*, 59–62). Interestingly, when the report discusses industrial education under the rubric of "moral education," pedagogical and capitalist values intersect. Industrial education can indeed have moral value, the report asserts, if there are economic rewards, and it concludes, "Work done under compulsion and without developing the moral qualities and economic motives for which it was designed is not educative" (*Survey*, 97). There thus was no contradiction between capital and labor; rather, there were reciprocal relations and an idealized redemptive value that Filipino subjects needed to acquire.

H. C. Theobold's *The Filipino Teacher's Manual* (1907)

While the annual reports of the directors of education offer fascinating characterizations of Filipinos and the ideal student, teacher training manuals exemplify the execution of these precepts. Thus, they are compelling directives on attempting to create the perfect pedagogical subject for U.S. colonialism. Here I briefly discuss *The Filipino Teacher's Manual*, a text used by the Board of Education to train teachers, written by H. C. Theobold, principal of the provincial high school in Batangas. The manual is a comprehensive document that establishes the school at the center of the community with material instructions on school layout, beautification, and furniture; directives on overseeing the physical well-being of students, such as eyesight, posture, and exercise; and close guidance on curriculum, pedagogy, and moral training. It also aims to instill in the teachers an appreciation of benevolent American colonialism.

The manual compellingly illustrates the paramount significance of schooling in the project of U.S. colonial governmentality because the school is also a means of reforming the community's habits of eating, hygiene, child-rearing, play, and physical activity. Repeatedly, Theobold makes clear that the role of the teacher is not limited to the classroom because the teacher is simultaneously the vehicle of salubrious governmentality and surveillance. Teachers are instructed to visit the homes of their students to ensure that children are being adequately fed and housed. Concern for performance in the classroom thus extends to surveying, cataloging, and attempting to affect bodily and behavioral changes in the community. Thus, teachers are urged to find out what families are eating; inform them about the dangers of a Filipino a diet of fish and rice; and instruct them to eat a healthy, American-style diet of vegetables, meat, and bread (Theobold, 66). Warwick Anderson has brilliantly demonstrated how hygienic reform in the Philippines, carried out by medical and health officers, was central to the civilizing process and Americanization: the "medico-moral uplift" of Filipinos involved transforming an immature, contaminating, and feeble race into a strong and healthy one (1, 5). Teachers were to become an integral part of this apparatus of surveillance and were often chosen to serve on the Municipal Board of Health (Theobold, 64). As purveyors of hygiene, they are guided by Theobold to inspect the homes of their students to ensure adequate sanitation and cleanliness, examine parents for signs of disease, and introduce them to American norms of parenting. Lamenting the Filipino practice of inculcating adult behavior too young, Theobold urges teachers to promote play and physical activities in Filipino homes until a later age (68, 90) and to advise parents against the Filipino habit of introducing infants to a variety of foods too early. The teacher thus serves as a relay point for different forms of governmentality.

At the same time, the manual suggests forms of pedagogical biopolitics that can engender both Americanized and tractable children. Practices such as organizing "the noisy crowd of children" into effectively managed grades, ensuring that children have neat desks subject to daily inspection, and dividing the school day into short periods punctuated by a recess belong to a fairly standard repertoire of modernity and class discipline (Theobold, 13, 22). However, recommendations to decorate classroom walls with portraits of George Washington, Abraham Lincoln, Ferdinand Magellan, Christopher Columbus, and only one Filipino—José Rizal—speak to the power of the school as prime colonial apparatus (12). Furthermore, the very structure of the school year as mandated by the Bureau of Education clearly marked schooling as a process of Americanization. School holidays celebrated not only American social and political culture but also colonization. Included among the holidays were Independence Day on July 4; Thanksgiving; Washington's birthday; Rizal Day on December 30, the day of his execution by the Spanish; and Occupation Day on August 13 to mark the American occupation of Manila (*Philippine Education*, 8). The holidays normalized American colonialism in different ways. Filipino students participated in celebrating America's declaration of independence from colonial Britain and thus in a nationalism that was only partially theirs—Filipinos could be nationals but not citizens of the United States. With Thanksgiving they celebrated the unity of the nation and the myth of settler colonialism as a nonviolent encounter, and with Occupation Day they marked their own colonization as something to be celebrated. Thus, it is hardly surprising that when Theobold urges teachers to initiate more physical activity, he recommends "setting up" exercises used by the U.S. Army for use by young boys and popular American games such as baseball, tag, handball, basketball, and tug-of-war, all of which are explained in detail (89, 93).

Perhaps the most interesting chapter in the manual is the one on industrial training. The chapter begins with a pronouncement about the relative insignificance of the intelligentsia to the nation: "The wealth of the country is not produced by orators, politicians, lawyers, doctors, or artists" (197). Theobold quickly goes on to lay the blame for the poor economy of the Philippines on the indolence of its people, their aversion to manual labor, and their thoughtless tropicalism: "The smallness of production that we see in the Philippines has its causes. . . . Some of the people are indolent; that is, they do not like to perform much hard labor. If they have enough food for to-day, they do not think about tomorrow" (197). However, Theobold does not see this tropicalism as solely inherent. Relating pedagogy to the U.S. colonial project, Theobold speculates that the "indolence" of the Filipinos has resulted from the hopeless conditions of *caciquismo* under Spanish rule, where peasants were routinely cheated by corrupt officials, a condition that could be changed through the conditions of U.S. colonial rule, which promote equality and opportunity: "Such changes as have been made by the American government will gradually bring better times for all the people, but it will take years to change the habits that have been formed during generations of bad government. . . . Now under the present form of government the intention is that every man who is industrious shall have a chance to become prosperous" (198). Schools could initiate this process of industry: "By teaching trades and industries in the schools, we shall give dignity to every occupation that produces wealth for the nation, whether it be carpentry, iron-working, mat-weaving, wood-carving, hat-making, pottery-work or shoe-making. . . . With many lines of industrial training carried on seriously and persistently in the schools, a great army of young workers will soon be formed" (200–201).

Clearly, for Theobold schooling is integral to the colonial project. It is through the industrial training given to students, training designed to create handicrafts and other artifacts of a dependent economy, that an appropriate labor force for the colonized nation will be created. Furthermore, just as Booker T. Washington urged African Americans to pursue trades, this incipient labor force is urged to think of itself as having awakened to its appropriate task of dignified manual labor through the beneficence of U.S. colonialism, which has promised Filipinos individual freedom, though not social and political equality with Americans. In an ideological recruiting of pedagogical subjects for the colonial state, Theobold offers the mythos of America—the promise of freedom, equality, and economic opportunity—as one available to the colonized Filipino subject. Vividly illustrating the Althusserian rendition of schooling as a means of producing subjects ready to take their assigned position in the social order, Theobold offers a vision of student labor nourished on visions of upward mobility ready to enter the world of handicraft production. In the putative training manual, what the teachers are being trained in is not simply imparting industrial education but understanding the exceptional benefits of U.S colonial rule and arguably, later, a neocolonial and military presence.

The manual also makes clear that schooling should teach more than industrial skills and literacy. At a time that the idea of moral instruction in schools was being questioned in the United States, Theobold vehemently argued for the importance of teaching morals to students. Theobold writes, "The purpose of moral instruction is to influence the child's character. We want a child to become a person who always tries to do what is right" (98). Although Theobold's list of what doing right amounts to includes innocuous and, one might argue, universal virtues, such as honesty, kindness, and helpfulness, the practical lessons suggested to teachers are, not surprisingly, geared toward making schooling a means of promoting conciliation to the minutiae of colonial rule. As discussed in Chapter 3, American rule exacerbated entrenched systems of tenantry and did little to address poverty, an issue addressed in Gilda Cordero-Fernando's story "A Harvest of Humble Folk." Theobold uses the occasion of civics instruction to suggest lessons on pacification: "Some children have heard their fathers talk about how the government takes money that is called *taxes*. . . . Possibly, too, some of these boys may have taken the idea from their elders that this tax money is paid to rich men who become richer still upon it, and that it is only a wrong act to take it from the poor man" (225–226). Theobold suggests that teaching children the "benefits of a good government" will result in their agreement "that all people ought to be loyal to the government" (226). Arguably, such lessons would be a means of countering popular cynicism, distrust, and, most important, class consciousness. Thus, a decade into colonial rule, schooling was still seen as a means of creating subjects with fealty to the colonial state and a means of quelling peasant rebellion.

In tandem with instruction about benevolent colonial structures, the Americanization of students was viewed teleologically as a progression from a crude, shallow, authoritarian, misogynist Oriental culture to an advanced, humane, polished, modern (Westernized) one. Questioning the oft-noted polite manners of Filipinos, which many educators and travelers had ascribed to their racialization as "Oriental," Theobold characterizes these as simply superficial. Using the familiar tactic of deploying feminism in the service of colonialism, a stratagem famously characterized by Gayatri Spivak as "saving brown women" (92), Theobold not only critiques what he views as the backward practices of women bearing the brunt of physically taxing housework but also posits American norms of politeness and gentlemanly behavior as normative and enlightened. Instead of simply bowing and smiling, Theobold suggests, "boys should learn to step aside and allow the girls to pass out of a door before them" (103). Americanization and morality work in tandem. Thus, Theobold suggests inculcating morals and values by using iconic historical figures from the United States. Having read about Lincoln or Washington, Theobold suggests, "The question may be asked 'Are we hard workers and honest like Lincoln?' Or, 'Can we not be as truthful as Washington was?'" (106).

Thus, in the first generation of the introduction of the American school system, educators envisioned a contradictory pedagogical subject. Filipinos were schooled to aspire to democracy, liberty, and equality because, as the national myth went, these were the foundations of U.S. nationalism. But they were to desire democracy, liberty, and equality on a personal rather than a sociopolitical level. They were to firmly believe that as little brown brothers, these rights were best available to them through colonial rule that scarcely named itself as such. Educators vehemently believed they were not attempting to Americanize the natives but, rather, preparing them to be better Filipinos; yet the decisions at the national and local levels to prioritize English, promote myths of American exceptionalism, celebrate American culture, teach American habits, and not provide instruction in local languages were undoubtedly attempts at Americanization. A review of Freer's *The Philippine Experiences of an American Teacher* aptly captured these contradictions. The reviewer acknowledges that the policy in the Philippines has been "severely criticized, especially for the attempt to 'Americanize' the natives in language and institutions" but suggests that Freer's book puts such critiques to rest because it documents the Filipinos' desire to learn English and use it as a common language of communication. At the same time, the review notes with equanimity that "the instruction is all in English, but aims at immediately practical results. American songs are taught, American games are played, and all over the school American flags fly" (*The Dial*, 71).

Educators expressed a Deweyan skepticism of rote learning and advocated independent thinking but concurrently stressed the suitability and importance of industrial education for Filipinos over education in art, culture, or science. Filipinos were to be rescued from subservience to an aristocratic order bequeathed by Spain. Still, by no means were school strikes to be read as signs of sociopolitical discontent or disagreement with teachers and school policies (thus demonstrating autonomy and independent thinking, as well as the power of community ties) but simply as machinations of wily politicians who manipulated gullible individuals. The pedagogical subject envisioned by educators was thus the paradoxical one of U.S. colonial policy—granting personal freedom while denying political rights—and the vehicle for hegemonic colonial rule once insurrections had largely subsided. Arguably, this subjectification served to consolidate a later neocolonial U.S. military presence. Yet, as Chapter 2 shows, Filipinos such as Camilo Osias used these contradictions to their advantage, claiming aspects of the hegemony to argue for decolonization.

2

Americanism and Filipino Nationalism in English Readers in the Philippines, 1905–1932

> The stately march of history has evolved the axiomatic truth, that the power of a colonizing country invariably wanes, while the colonies wax in strength and influence. If the American Republic, "conceived in liberty and dedicated to the proposition that all men are created equal," violates this fundamental principle of national life, she must fall.
> —CAMILO OSIAS, *The Story of a Long Career of Varied Tasks*

As discussed previously, schools in the colony could function as apparatuses of pacification by teaching American political, social, and economic ideals, which implicitly promised to create (Christian) Filipino citizens fit for self-government. Because the burden of inculcating values capable of fostering capitalist democracy relied on English-language teaching, the series of English readers introduced in Philippine public schools represented prime pedagogical vehicles for making future citizens who were Filipino Malay, geographically in the Philippines, and under American tutelage.[1] Such readers correspondingly functioned as important cultural sites where metropolitan power and local realities met and often collided and where colonialism could be legitimated, but also where emergent forms of postcolonial nationalism could be articulated. At the same time, these readers worked as convergence points that drew together colonial technologies and market-based colonies. With the introduction of the American school system in 1901, reading was instituted as the major subject in the primary schools (grades 1–4), although grammar, composition, and reading also figured keenly in intermediate school (grades 5–7), where students could choose different programs. To be sure, standardization of curricula was central to colonial governance. By 1904, the general superintendent of education had issued uniform courses of instruction for the archipelago, except for the designated non-Christian tribes, and by 1908, a textbook advisory committee had been appointed to review texts and make recommendations for adoption for a five-year period (*Fifteenth Annual*, 33).

The potential for profit in this colonial market was enormous, and publishers in the United States competed furiously with one another to produce readers specifically designed for the Philippines. In his review of Philippine schoolbooks, most of them English readers, Frederick Starr commented:

> We were rather slow in realizing the opportunity the Islands offered. Now, however, we have grasped it. Today the leading textbook publishers vie with each other in the effort to have their books introduced into the Philippine field. Personal representatives are sent to Manila to push the claims of their texts. It is a growing field; there is a steady demand. And it will be a long time before local publishers will be at all equal to the occasion. (12)

The John C. Winston Company, the American Book Company, and Ginn and Company were among the most prolific in producing textbooks for the Philippines. Officials in the Bureau of Education were aware of the burden these expensive, U.S.-produced books put on Filipino families but thought it prudent not to compete with private companies, which, they argued, could produce better-quality illustrations than the local printing office (*Twenty-Eighth Annual*, 93). English readers were thus not only vehicles of tutelage but also, in themselves, highly productive vehicles for the colonial market. This chapter examines the overlaps and differences between forms of nationalism and the construction of the Filipino subject articulated in readers for the Philippines compiled by the American teachers Mary Helen Fee, David Gibbs, and Orlando Scheirer Reimold before 1915, and *The Philippine Readers* series of the 1920s, written by Camilo Osias, a Filipino nationalist and the first Filipino superintendent of schools. At stake in this chapter is the extent to which these early readers attempted to inculcate American political, social, and economic ideals in Filipino children; just as important is the degree to which *The Philippine Readers* contested colonial hegemony via a paradoxical critiquing and claiming dominant ideologies of citizenship and selfhood. I demonstrate how Osias, despite his position within the colonial hierarchy and the colonial apparatuses through which the genre functioned, strategically used the genre to open up a space for an anti-imperial, independence-now Filipino nationalism.

Correspondingly, my analysis of the readers demonstrates the ways in which this nationalism works by laying claim to a legible colonial hegemony. Neither the project of Americanization nor the project of Filipino nationalism is fully worked out in these readers; instead, the texts represent—via the teaching of English—battles over the legitimation of both colonialism and nationalism. I argue that Osias's readers demonstrate nationalism through what I call "collaborative dissent," a phrase that encapsulates the possibilities of contesting colonialism through hegemony itself. My idea of collaborative dissent is influenced by the pioneering work of James C. Scott, who contested both Marxist economic determinism and Gramscian ideological determinism and demonstrated how subordinate classes constantly challenge hegemony through everyday forms of resistance, or what he calls "hidden transcripts," which escape attention in a surface-level review of power situations, or "public transcripts."[2] Most germane to this chapter's overall argument is Scott's assertion that most struggles take place within hegemony, that hegemony itself provides the tools for its critique: "the very process of attempting to legitimate a social order by idealizing it always provides its subjects the means, the symbolic tools, the very ideas for a critique that operates entirely within the hegemony" (*Weapons of the Weak*, 338). By not privileging revolution, Scott accentuates calls for reform that function as the only plausible bases for revolutionary change (*Weapons of the Weak*, 317–318).

English Readers as Colonial Battleground

By the late nineteenth century, schools in the United States were institutionalized into spaces in which national culture was propagated via the codification and confirmation of racial, ethnic, and classed hierarchies. In her exhaustive survey of textbooks in nineteenth-century America, Ruth Miller Elson maintains how supporters of universal public schools repeatedly assured upper classes that "a judicious education of the poor" would not "lead them to forget their station and their duty" (313). Likewise, the ideal American in these textbooks is white, northern European, Protestant, and self-made. Primers and readers were major vehicles for inculcating this ideal. The two most important readers were the McGuffey and the Baldwin. The McGuffey Readers, started in 1836 by the ordained minister/professor William Holmes McGuffey, went through several editions and were immensely popular in schools until the end of the century. They taught virtue through biblical quotations, prayers, and explicit morals. The Baldwin Readers, launched in 1897, eschewed biblical materials and direct moralizing and professed to pay more attention to the literary qualities of the selections. Like the McGuffey Readers, however, they stressed the values of thrift, hard work, and conformity. Schools could uplift African Americans and pacify Native Americans, all the while teaching them through primers that would privilege white middle-class living. These readers were initially used in the Philippines, and 200,000 of Baldwin's primers and readers were en route to the islands by January 1901 (Wesling, 90).

Shortly thereafter, American teachers, conscious that schooling was the benevolent face of occupation, paid particular attention to the creation of elementary school primers geared to the needs of the colony.[3] Like the Baldwin and McGuffey readers, these readers emphasize U.S. exceptionalism via examples of industry as hagiographically fixed to "Founding Father" figures such as Benjamin Franklin and lessons in American democracy. Despite the jingoistic nature of such inclusions, these readers—when compared with extant experiences inside and outside the classroom—lay bare the complex work of colonial management. Readers smoothed over native intransigence. For instance, Fee, who taught for several years in the Philippines, noted impatiently that Filipino children were arrogant and that they refused to accept her authority or opinion about learning functional rather than literary English (64–66). By contrast, the readers presented Filipino children as obedient and eager to learn. Invested in domesticating both the Filipino landscape and Filipino people, the authors of such works more often than not were engaged with this diversity labor. The readers strive to domesticate the Filipino landscape and people while naturalizing colonial difference; taken together, participation in U.S. nationalism and American culture is rendered seemingly inherent. The readers demonstrate what Raymond Williams called the dynamic nature of hegemony, which exists not just passively as dominance but "has continually to be renewed, recreated, defended and modified" (112). Of the many readers and primers compiled by American teachers, I concentrate on those written by Fee, Gibbs, and Reimold, all published before Osias completed the manuscripts of *The Philippine Readers* series in 1917, and I briefly address the *Rizal Readers*, which were published after Osias completed work on his readers. Fee taught in the Philippines longer than most teachers and published a popular memoir, *A Woman's Impression of the Philippines* (1910), which went through a second edition. Gibbs and Reimold each served as division superintendents of schools in the Philippines. Both Fee's and Reimold's books were part of the *Philippine Education* series published by the World Book Company, and covered the first four grades. Fee's reader and Gibbs's series, although published before 1910, remained in use for more than twenty years and were used in the first three grades.

The most striking difference between the Baldwin Readers and the early readers used in the Philippines is how the former appeal to a bourgeois sense of culture, refinement, and class; by contrast, despite occasional representations of the upper class, the latter readers focus primarily on farming, weaving, and carpentry. Filipino children are represented as rustic and casual in a manner congruent with major educational policies. As discussed in Chapter 1, despite a few early debates about industrial versus academic education, by 1904 industrial education was seen as central. David Barrows, the second director of education, who began his tenure by envisioning an educated Jeffersonian yeoman, also emphasized industrial education. In a glowing introduction to Reimold's *Industrial Studies and Exercises*, Barrows characterizes Filipinos as possessing two qualities: nimbleness of hands and an artistic sense, which was relegated to making crafts for household industries (iii–iv). Decrying the influence of Spanish aristocratic culture, which denigrated manual labor, educators praised the dignity of labor in the United States and tactically used Booker T. Washington's *Up from Slavery* as a text (*Survey*, 342–343). Yet early readers in the United States, unlike those in the Philippines, rarely depicted manual labor.

Even a cursory glance at the illustrations in the texts brings to light differences between the Baldwin Readers and those used in the Philippines. The Baldwin Readers used illustrations to present to children a white, middle-class, leisured Victorian lifestyle as normative. Highly ornate pictures of women in hats and long dresses contemplating a country landscape, pictures of children sitting in rooms decorated with elaborate furniture, curtains, and artwork, and pictures of young blonde girls with perfectly curled hair attired in lace collars, stockings, and boots constitute a large quantity of the illustrations in the Baldwin and McGuffey readers. The illustrations in the readers for the Philippines, by contrast, depict laboring characters in the countryside. Gibbs's readers present women in the market, boys carrying water in buckets, and women washing clothes at the river. And, as befits a colony being integrated into the economic needs of the metropole, there are illustrations and questions about the harvesting of sugarcane and the making of sugar (Figure 2.1). Reimold's *Composition Leaflets on Philippine Activities*, also part of the *Philippine Education* series, most explicitly casts Filipinos in vocational roles through sections such as "The Carpenter," "The Blacksmith," "Weaving," "Sugar-Cane," and "Hemp." The same is true in his *First Primary Language Book*, which includes illustrations of ploughing with a carabao, thatching a house, and cutting rice (46, 60) (Figure 2.2).

Fee's reader similarly includes illustrations of Filipinos in the countryside, with most characters casually dressed and their feet bare—nature's children. The contrast between the cultivated child of the first-year Baldwin Reader and the natural child of Fee and her colleagues' *The First Year Book* (1907) is evident in the frontispiece of Fee's reader and on the cover of the Baldwin reader (see Figures 2.3 and 2.4). In Fee's book, a Filipino girl, clad in a simple dress, sits barefoot amidst a sea of strewn books; she uses her index finger to read. By contrast, in the Baldwin reader, an older girl with curled hair, lace shirt, and boots sits on a carpet, absorbed in a book while another book lies neatly beside her. The instructions to the teacher in the Baldwin reader privilege reading as a path to culture, refinement, and the development of an

3. When is it planted?
4. How is it planted?
5. On what kind of land does it grow best?
6. How tall does it grow?
7. What are the men in the second picture doing?
8. Why is the sugar cane crushed?
9. What is done with the crushed sugar cane?

10. Where is the juice put?
11. How is the juice made into sugar?
12. Into what is the sugar first put?
13. What color is new sugar?
14. Have you ever seen white sugar?
15. For what is sugar used?
16. How is molasses made?
17. For what is molasses used?

FIGURE 2.1. Making sugar.
(David Gibbs, *Lessons in English*
[New York: American Book Company, 1905], 181.)

aesthetic sense: "Thought has been given to the cultivation of a love for the pure, the beautiful and the good . . . towards the contemplation of things lovely and inspiring and away from objects that are, at their best, merely gross and commonplace" (3). The Preface to *The First Year Book*, however, emphasizes everyday situations in children's lives, lessons being based on "attractive children, clean and wholesome in mind and body" (3). Filipino students were fully aware of the politics of colonial representation and resisted being interpellated as less civilized and of a lower class than their American counterparts. In *A Woman's Impression of the Philippines*, Fee recollects that one of her former students, on seeing a copy of Fee's primer, was "enraged because

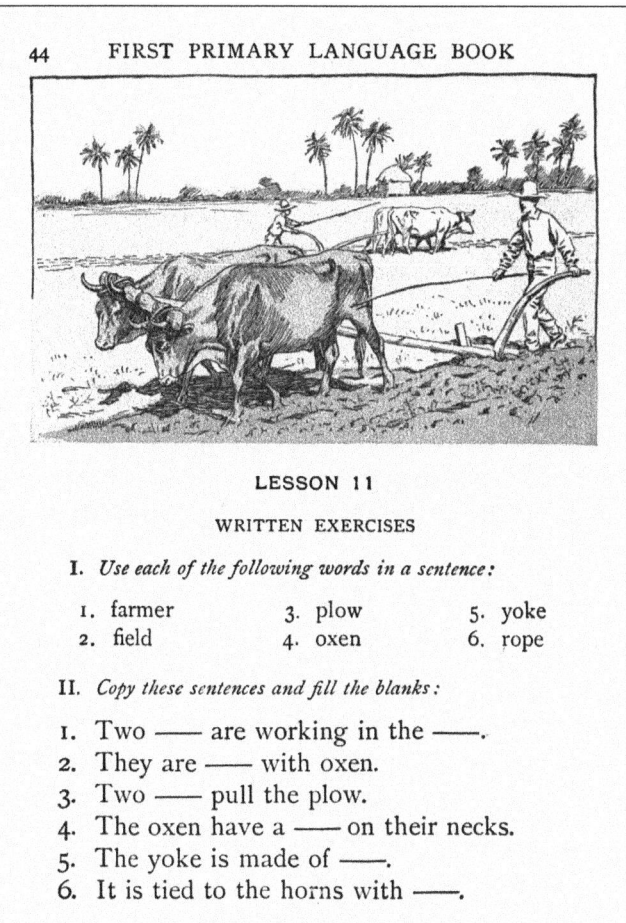

FIGURE 2.2. Farmer and carabao.
(Orlando Scheirer Reimold, *First Primary Language Book*
[New York: World Book Company, 1914], 44.)

the Filipino boys and girls in my book were sometimes barefooted, sometimes clad in *chinelas*, and wore native camisas instead of American suits and dresses.... The children in the American readers wore natty jackets and hats and high-heeled shoes, and winter wraps, even at play, and she wanted the Filipino children to look the same" (67). While the student sought representational parity, Fee strove to maintain colonial difference—almost the same but not quite—through markers of class.

The attempts of Fee and Gibbs to domesticate an unfamiliar landscape and people and suggest the naturalness of English as part of Filipino life are most evident in the deployment of illustrations. Yet the efforts to naturalize

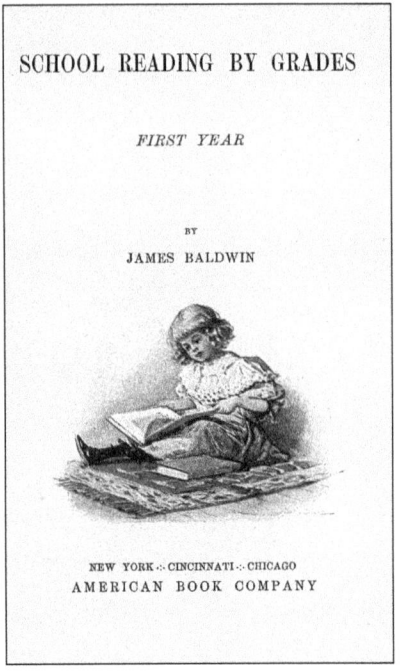

FIGURE 2.3. Filipina child reading. (Mary Helen Fee, *The First Year Book* [New York: World Book Company, 1907], n.p.)

FIGURE 2.4. American girl reading. (James Baldwin, *School Reading by Grades: First Year* [New York: American Book Company, 1897], n.p.)

the landscape and people often appear strained. Gibbs's *Lessons in English* (1905), a book intended as a two-part supplement to the second and third insular readers, advertises itself through its cover almost as if it were a tourist book inviting Filipinos to venture on a leisured trip through the archipelago. However, some of the picture studies depict unwilling subjects oddly caught in an anthropological refusal of the gaze even as they hold up items presumably for the market (see Figure 2.5). In these texts it is clear that the hegemonic order needs to be more viscerally reinforced through the parading of colonial insignia, particularly flags. This display of icons of the colonial order needs to be viewed in relation to both the nationalism in readers in the United States and nationalist flag politics in the Philippines. While Noah Webster's *The American Spelling Book*, which was originally published as part 1 of *A Grammatical Institute* (Webster 1783), explicitly taught students the merits of the American system of government, the number of pages overtly devoted to nationalism steadily declined in subsequent readers (Banton, 35, 50). The Baldwin and McGuffey readers promulgated a homogenous, white, middle-class nationalism, but patriotic history lessons and the use of flags were rare. By 1913, *The Beacon Reader* had just once patriotic selection: Edward Everett Hale's "Salute the Flag" (Banton, 50).

The English readers for the Philippines counter this trend of overt depo-

> I. Tell the names of the things that you see in this picture.
> II. Copy these names of boys and girls:—
>
> Juan   Maria   Pablo   Ina
> Anna   Louisa   Vincente   Marcos
>
> With what kind of letter does each name begin?
>
> III. Copy these names of things:—
>
> desk   door   chart   chair
> pencil   window   crayon   bell
> floor   clock   bench   flag
>
> With what kind of letter does each name begin?
>
> IV. Write the names of five boys or girls.

FIGURE 2.5. At the market.
(David Gibbs, *Lessons in English* [New York: American Book Company, 1905], 8.)

liticization, thus suggesting the need for affirmations of the colonial order in the face of continuing demonstrations of Filipino nationalism. Flag politics were important to this display of nationalism. In 1907, for instance, supporters of the Nacionalista Party paraded through the streets of Manila with the Katipunan flag, much to the outrage of an American observer, and worse, one marcher trampled the American flag in the dirt (Kramer, 330–331). Shortly thereafter, the governor-general issued an order for the confiscation of all goods bearing the Katipunan flag or its insignia, not only in Manila, but also everywhere else in the Philippines, and promoted overabundant displays of American flags all over Manila (Kramer, 332). As Paul Kramer suggests, "The U.S. flag became central to the marking of the outer boundary of U.S. sovereignty precisely because its triumph was disputed" (329).

FIGURE 2.6. Teaching subtraction with flags.
(Mary Helen Fee, *The First Year Book*
[New York: World Book Company, 1907], 32.)

The symbolic economy of the flag also finds its way into the readers written by Americans. While Fee, Gibbs, and Reimold organize many lessons around Filipino lives and include illustrations depicting only Filipino children, the U.S. flag circulates in all, and the school, as an icon of the colonial order, frequently appears with the flag. In *The First Year Book*, the innocuous teaching of basic arithmetic is done through flag politics, where children learn subtraction by seeing all but the American flag fall (see Figure 2.6); another illustration represents the normalization of the Philippines as a U.S. territory by depicting a cluster of happy Filipino children playing in front of the schoolyard, with a Filipino teacher watching over them and the American flag flying in the distance (Fee et al., 72). Perhaps the starkest iconography of the flag, reinforcing James Scott's argument that domination needs lavish display (*Domination and the Arts of Resistance*, 12), is evident in Gibbs's primer, where the U.S. flag is presented as the *Ur*-flag, defining what a flag

FIGURE 2.7. "This is a Flag."
(David Gibbs, *Revised Insular Primer*
[New York: American Book Company, 1906].)

means—that is, the American flag is both "a flag" and "the flag" (Figure 2.7). These readers demonstrate the imbrication of schooling and colonialism and teachers' needs to stave off insurrectionary ideas by demonstrating the authority of U.S. insignia while naturalizing them as part of children's everyday learning.

While it was important for early American educators to represent Filipino children learning about and milling around the U.S. flag, it was imperative to the racialized colonial order that these objects of uplift and eventual self-government be represented as Malay. Negritos, Igorots, and Moros—all people designated non-Christian, administered separately, and denied degrees of autonomy given to Christian Malays—are virtually absent from all readers. Their occasional presence, indicative of a pedagogical challenge, is emblematized by a grammar exercise in Gibbs's *Lessons in English* titled "The Moro Girl." The Moros were a particularly abrasive tutelary problem because they brought with them Islamic practices and actively resisted colonial (as well as Filipino neocolonial) rule long after insurrections had largely subsided in the rest of the archipelago. Often analogized to resistant Native Americans, they marked the limits of integration through tutelage and were represented as uncivilized, misbehaving children (Milligan, 47–48, 56).

Gibbs's grammar lesson is, in the end, a lesson about good and bad colonial subjects. The exercise, which accompanies a photograph of a traditionally attired Moro girl, represents the girl only through negation:

1. This is a picture of a Moro girl.
2. We do not know her name.

. . .

6. She does not go to my school.
7. She ___ not know how to read or write.
8. She ___ not live on the island of Luzon. (*Lessons in English*, 40)

As this exercise makes clear, Gibbs accesses binaried divisions between "good," pacified, American-educated Filipino schoolchildren and the intransigent Moro who, instead of being a thorn in the side of the colonial order, is simply not one of "Us"; she is untutored, illiterate, ignorant, and savage. Similar representations of Negritos as savages are evident in Gibbs's "Arwa, the Negrito Boy" and a picture study of a black boy (*Revised Insular Second Reader*, 116; *Revised Insular Primer*, 63). Such technologies of racial inscription circulated among different texts. Gibbs's photograph of the Moro girl, undoubtedly part of a repertoire of U.S. colonial photography, reappears in Henry S. Townsend's *Primary Geography* (1917), a textbook written for the Philippines in which Moros, along with Negritos, are described as uncivilized (16).

By 1909, Gibbs had established a repertoire of topics designed to inculcate an admiration for U.S. institutions and democracy while learning about Spanish colonialism and Filipino heroes. Writing exercises for children include answering questions about the biographies of George Washington, Benjamin Franklin, and Christopher Columbus; the story of John Smith and Pocahontas; the discovery of the Philippine Islands by Ferdinand Magellan; and a biography of José Rizal (Gibbs, *Elementary English Grammar and Composition*). In addition, the readers in the Philippines teach through the glorification of fictional colonial heroes. Both Reimold's *Second Primary Language Book* and Sidney Newsom and Levona Payne Newsom's *Third Reader* in the Philippine English Series, for instance, teach through cycles of Robinson Crusoe stories, which emphasize Crusoe's industry, inventiveness, and perseverance (Newsom and Newsom, 54–58; Reimold, *Second Primary Language Book*, 3). Reimold's reader also includes a lesson on Crusoe's saving Friday and Friday's abject gratitude as he places Crusoe's foot on his head and offers to be his servant.

Nationalism in Camilo Osias's *The Philippine Readers*

In 1917, Osias completed the manuscripts of books one through seven of *The Philippine Readers*, for grades 1–7, the first textbooks to be published by a Filipino author. Published in 1920, Osias's readers met with almost immediate success, with books five to seven distributed to be used as supplementary reading volumes (*Twenty-First Annual*, 55). By 1923, the Philippine Textbook Board had chosen books two to seven as the official primary textbooks in public schools for the next five years (*Twenty-First Annual*, 32–33), after which they continued to be taught and reprinted until the late 1950s. To appraise the ideological function of these readers, one must understand the peculiar trajectory of Osias's career: to wit, as he operated firmly within the rubrics of the American educational apparatus set up for colonial governance, Osias simultaneously supported nationalism and independence from American rule. Osias was well schooled in revolutionary pedagogy, having learned the principles of the Katipunan from his uncle; he subsequently translated these principles from Tagalog to Ilokano to advance the revolution, a cause he supported when the U.S. occupation forces entered the country (Coloma, "Empire and Education," 93). He continued his education, however, as did many poor and middle-class Filipinos, under the auspices of the U.S. troops and, later, the American school system. Chosen as a *pensionado*, Osias began his career as an educator, receiving a normal diploma from Western Illinois State Normal School and an education degree from Columbia University before returning to the Philippines to teach and become the first Filipino division superintendent of schools in in 1915. Back in the Philippines, Osias, as a member of the Nacionalista Party, which advocated immediate independence, participated active in politics and was part of the First Philippine Independence Mission to the United States in 1919. His career in politics began with his election as senator for the second senatorial district in 1926 and continued in the postindependence Philippines with his position as senator-at-large in 1947, president of the Senate in the 1950s, and president pro tempore of the Senate in the 1960s.

Roland Sintos Coloma refers to Osias's navigation between the forces of assimilation and separatism, creating a "third space of possibility," as a "disidentifying nationalism." He borrows the term "disidentification" from José Esteban Muñoz, who proposes it as different from identification or counter-identification. "To become a revolutionary educator," Coloma suggests, "Osias had to first learn, then distance himself from, and finally use the knowledge acquired" ("Disidentifying Nationalism," 21). Although Coloma's attempt to analyze Osias's thinking through a theory that eschews binaries is useful, it sets up a temporal schema that is at odds with Osias's own writings, and certainly with *The Philippine Readers*.[4] By contrast, I maintain that Osias never distanced himself from the key aspects of American tutelary hegemony: a belief in the exceptional nature of American freedom, the civilizing force of education, and differences in the intellectual capabilities of races. Like other nationalist leaders, such as Kwame Nkrumah of Ghana and Jomo Kenyatta of Kenya, Osias used his education in the metropole to further champion independence, yet he fulfilled a key purpose of the *pensionado* scheme: to become an ambassador for "American values." As he recalled in his autobiography, "I deepened my devotion to the cause of independence as a student in freedom-loving America with its Declaration of Independence and its galaxy of patriots who fought for freedom's cause. I made it my avocation to read about revolutionary movements and constitutional governments" (*The Story of a Long Career of Varied Tasks*, 180). These sentences exemplify Osias's collaborative dissent: he operated firmly within the hegemony of American exceptionalism that promoted the mythos of America as a site of freedom, despite Jim Crow at home and colonialism abroad, but this hegemony itself—via writings of revolutionary leaders—provided him with the tools of critique and supported his demand for immediate independence.

Unlike other *pensionado* elites, such as Victor Buencamino, who recognized the racism directed at both African Americans and Asian Americans in the United States, Osias, who needed American patronage, resolutely downplayed questions of racism (37, 71, 224). Warned against traveling in the South because of racial prejudice, Osias cautiously accepted the advice and reported only that he had had "no unpleasant experiences" during his three-year stay in the U.S. Midwest (*The Story of a Long Career of Varied Tasks*, 99). Interestingly, Osias begins his autobiography by announcing Booker T. Washington as his political and intellectual forebear, thus deliberately linking U.S. internal racism and colonialism, but what Osias identified with was Washington's rise to power from slavery (*The Story of a Long Career of Varied Tasks*, 13). Yet Osias was also impressed with Washington's ideas about Black uplift and cited them as formative for his own thinking about *barrio* schools (*Barrio Life and Barrio Education*, 16).[5] Little wonder that Osias's recollections about attending a colonial high school reflect an admiration for the class mobility, cleanliness, and hygiene that the teachers represented. Osias writes: "I liked to see them [teachers] come to school every day in clothes clean and well pressed. . . . I admired them and my ambition was to be a high school teacher" (*The Story of a Long Career of Varied Tasks*, 70). Simultaneously, Osias valued native languages and decried the effects of colonialism on education. Writing in 1940, a few years after the implementation of the Independence Act, Osias argued, "If the country is to be a mere colony or is to be made a permanent part of the American empire, it is obvious that the educational philosophy must be defined in terms of such a relationship or status" (*The Filipino Way of Life*, 29). The pluralized philosophy he proposed could be illustrated only through his native Ilocano (*The Filipino Way of Life*, 29).

For the young Osias, there was no contradiction between lavishing praise on American teachers who came as part of the colonial mission of lifting Filipinos out of ignorance and stridently demanding the complete independence of the Philippines. In an oratorical competition in 1908, Osias declared, "Believing that our salvation lay in popular education, America sent hundreds of her leading educators to our shores. Grand and praiseworthy have been the achievements of those who came to our relief" ("The Aspiration of the Filipinos," 164). But in the same speech, he challenged the premise of William McKinley's "unfit for self-government" logic by challenging assumptions about native ignorance: "Those who doubt our capacity for independence ... forget that capacity for self-government is not only an attainment but also an inherent quality of a people" ("The Aspiration of the Filipinos," 166). The altruism of teachers who came to the Philippines did not negate the importance of immediate decolonization.

Yet Osias's nationalism, like that of the United States he admired, was premised on racial hierarchies, even as he criticized the colonial use of the term "Non-Christian Tribes" as inimical to national unity (Osias, *The Story of a Long Career of Varied Tasks*, 51). Indeed, as postcolonial theorists such as Partha Chatterjee and Homi Bhabha have argued, the quest for a unified modern nationalism cannot help but be based on exclusions. This logic is perhaps all the more applicable to Osias, who often demanded nationalism through some of the same rhetoric as U.S. Eurocentric nationalism. Calling on the American public to support the independence of the Philippines, the young Osias appealed to the civilizing power of English and the rhetoric of uplift that had been used under the banner of benevolent assimilation: "Ten years ago, practically none could speak the English language. In less than a decade of intimate relationship with the American people, twenty percent of the inhabitants speak the new language. What an achievement. It is not with the savage Igorotte nor the heathen Negrito that you have to do, but with the enlightened and Christian Malay" ("The Aspiration of the Filipinos," 164). Drawing on the very racial typologies used by the colonial administration in its division of natives into Christian and non-Christian—divisions that neatly differentiated racial groups—Osias turns them to his own ends, arguing that the majority Malay population, which has received the benefits of the English language and has been enlightened, deserves independence. An older Osias continued to look at Negritos as primitives suited to schooling only in health and athletic activities and Mangyans as "simple creatures of nature" who needed instruction on "Soap, Soup, [and] Salvation" (Osias, *The Story of a Long Career of Varied Tasks*, 132, 136–137).

If the colonization of the Philippines was justified as a temporary measure to educate a citizenry for eventual self-government, Osias was simply arguing for immediate self-government. If colonial administrators routinely touted America as a beacon of freedom and democracy, Osias concurred with their assumptions. He critiqued the colonization of the Philippines not as a demonstration of the imperial nature of American nationalism or in keeping with the colonization of minorities within the nation, but, rather, as a transgression of American ideals. "The policy of colonization," Osias argued, "is contrary to the American instinct. It is a violation of the spirit of the Declaration of Independence" ("The Aspiration of the Filipinos," 165). Osias's nationalist rhetoric, that is, accepted the rhetoric of hegemonic American exceptionalism and used the language of exceptional American democracy to critique the nation for not following its own ideals.

When Osias became the first Filipino superintendent of schools in the Philippines in 1915, arguments for Filipinization were well under way, and the Jones Act of 1916 gave Filipinos a major share in their government. Osias's *The Philippine Readers*, the first compiled by a Filipino, contain biographies and historical accounts, among other genres, and do not question the intentions of American occupation, the virtues of the Founding Fathers, or Western narratives of discovery. As the readers progress, they increasingly include stories about the voyages of Magellan and Columbus, as well as biographies of George Washington, Thomas Jefferson, and Abraham Lincoln. Six of the seven readers end with biographies of or writings by Rizal. A cursory glance at the table of contents of these readers might not differentiate them from readers produced by earlier American educators. After all, a reformist rather than revolutionary Rizal had been promoted as a national hero by colonial administrators (Wesling, 94), and public schools were already commemorating the anniversary of Rizal's execution. However, the difference between the framing of Rizal in the Osias readers and in the *Rizal Readers*, which were commissioned by the United States, is stark. In the *Rizal Readers*, Rizal the educator is often used to normalize the colonial school through illustrations that depict him teaching rows of neatly dressed Filipino children and biographies comparing him to American heroes (W. Lewis et al., *Rizal Readers, Fifth Reader*, 253, *Rizal Readers, Seventh*

Reader, 1). Questions in the *Rizal Readers* about Rizal's exile in Dapitan refer to his love for his sister, while those in Osias's readers ask students to think about Rizal's courage in withstanding Spanish colonialism (W. Lewis et al., *Rizal Readers, Fifth Reader*, 255; Osias, *PR, Book Six*, 174). Similar differences can be seen in the representation of American heroes. While Gibbs's books on grammar and composition—*Elementary English Grammar and Composition* (1909) and *Advanced English Grammar and Composition* (1908)—include several selections on Washington, venerating him as industrious, a great general, the first president, and a leader of the Revolution, Osias includes Washington only in book seven and focuses on him as a soldier in the Revolutionary War. By concentrating on Washington as a soldier and placing him alongside Philippine nationalist heroes such as the revolutionary Andrés Bonifacio and Apolinario Mabini, who never accepted U.S. rule, Osias encourages students to think about nationalism in both nations and about Washington as a revolutionary hero to be emulated in present-day Philippines.

Osias's declaration of cultural independence is also evident in the prefatory materials to the readers, where he makes clear the difference of his materials from those of others through appeals to authenticity. While the readers that American educators such as Gibbs, Fee, and Reimold compiled also made bids to local culture by mentioning their sincere attempts to include materials from Filipino daily life, Osias claimed a cultural insiderism and intimacy with the students' experiences that was not possible for his American counterparts. Indeed, the prefatory materials speak as much to his American colleagues in the Philippines as to Filipino teachers. In the preface to the revised edition of book two, Osias writes, "Both the author and the illustrator, Mr. Fernando Amorsolo, being Filipinos, depict not only what they have heard and seen, but in many instances what they themselves have actually experienced" (*PR, Book Two*, iv). The ability to include what one has seen and heard by living in the Philippines does not match the experiential potential of "being Filipinos," a state available only to the native. Similarly, in the preface to book three, Osias validates his inclusion of Filipino folktales in the volume by claiming a special familiarity with them: "Several of the native folk tales and legends in this volume were told to the writer in childhood by his mother and are generally known in the Islands" (*PR, Book Three*, v).

This idea of cultural transmission, which assumes fixity and desire to reclaim lost origins, has been critiqued by numerous poststructuralists, including Stuart Hall, who writes: "This 'return to the beginning' is like the imaginary in Lacan—it can neither be fulfilled nor requited, and hence is the beginning of the symbolic of representation" (402). As Renato Rosaldo reminds us, imperialist nostalgia also seeks to freeze the native in a timeless precolonial past (107–122). Osias's statements about compiling folktales preserved from the past to transmit Filipino culture to students might well be seen to privilege pure Filipino origins, but it is important to read the statements in the context of increasing calls for independence and U.S. statements about the continued needs for tutelage. By 1921, Manuel Quezon had declared that the stable government stipulated in the Jones Act as a precondition for independence had already come to pass and demanded that "the time to fulfill that promise has arrived" (960). Yet, as Gertrude Emerson, reporting about the special mission to the Philippines, averred, "We are morally bound to the conception of a free Philippines. But in national epics thirty or forty or even fifty years' time is a brief period of tutelage" (959). Osias's readers were notable in the sheer number of folktales they included, surpassed by only the three volumes of Harriot Ely Fansler and Isidoro Panlasigui's *Philippine National Literature* series, which were used as supplementary texts for grades 2–4. As Damiana L. Eugenio writes, "Many of us first encountered Philippine folk tales such as 'Why the Sky [I]s High' and 'The Legend of the First Bananas' in this series" (177).

Of course, Osias knew well that what was being constructed as Filipino culture was the result of a collaboration between colonial and native scholars and educators. Given the establishment of the U.S. school system for almost a generation, a clear demarcation between native and colonial knowledge would have been difficult. In book one, for instance, Osias acknowledges the assistance of the U.S. anthropologist H. Otley Beyer and "other Oriental scholars" in collecting material (*PR, Book One*, 4). Beyer, who had a lifelong career as an anthropologist of the Philippines, including serving as head of the Department of Anthropology at the University of the Philippines for more than twenty years, had been appointed as an ethnologist for the Philippine Bureau of Science by the colonial administration, and his classifications of mountain peoples were widely cited by policy makers.[6] In the revised edition of Book Two, Osias acknowledged the American teachers Muzetta Williams, Hertha Cornish, and Bertha Shanks Chaney. Yet Osias wanted to impress on readers the fact that *The Philippine Readers* were different from earlier texts. The contents of *The Philippine Readers* were evaluated by a qualified cadre of Filipino educators from all regions of the Philippines (except Mindanao), and the list of more than thirty evaluators, with their regions identified, appears in almost all of the readers. Osias's claim of native access to cultural purity thus needs to be seen as strategic, necessary for articulating a unified nationalism.

In books five through seven, where he substituted the preface with the more direct "A Talk with the Pupil," written for more mature students, and used the occasion to include exhortations to good citizenship, Osias makes clear that this citizenship is a postcolonial, Filipino one. Within the bounds of an American educational structure, yet chafing at the limits of paternalist, progressivist practices of American educators, Osias inculcated a nationalism that incorporated American culture within a Filipino schema. Thus, in the address in book six, Osias implicitly suggests that Magellan and Lincoln, who exemplify diligence, in fact prefigure Rizal: "People who work hard succeed best, and the men who succeed, like Lincoln and Magellan, often do so only because they never cease trying.... At the close of the book you will study the hymn in which Rizal tells us of the dignity of labor" (*PR, Book Six*, iii). In the revised edition of book seven, the "Talk" becomes a strident call in which he urges students to use their readings to further national pride and become commendable citizens: "I know you admire men and women who were brave and unselfish and patriotic.... A knowledge of the lives and deeds of such men and women will make you stand a little straighter... and wish to be patriotic and useful yourself.... You will learn of great characters of all times and countries, and of our own heroes, Bonifacio, Mabini, and Rizal." The address ends by instructing students to take the selections in the volume as lessons that will enable them to become "good and useful Filipino citize[ns]" (*PR, Book Seven*, iii). The provocative question the address poses is that of citizenship. If the purpose of the hagiographic selections is to inculcate "patriotism," what is the *patria* that the students should imagine and have loyalty toward? If the *patria* is the Philippines, how can the students become useful Filipino citizens in 1932, long before the Philippines gained independence and three years before it became a commonwealth? The "Talk with the Pupil" here declares an independence that questions the slow process of Filipinization under the shadow of colonial rule. And yet, Osias is careful to reassure his readers that his brand of Filipino nationalism is not a revolutionary one. The national heroes celebrated in the volume are all "heroic in peace," men of peace rather than the sword.

For Osias, the political necessity of immediate independence was clear; at the same time, as the first Filipino superintendent of schools (a title he proudly displayed in all of *The Philippine Readers*), working within the most elaborate systems of colonial management while arguing for Filipino control of it, Osias was also part of a system that was slowly being Filipinized. *The Philippine Readers*, while continuing the task of teaching English, had also become vehicles of cultural expression. Unlike Gibbs, Fee, Reimold, Newsom, and many others who used American illustrators for their books, Osias chose Fernando Amorsolo, a painter well versed in Western classical and modern art and committed to representing idealized Filipino landscapes and peoples. By the time he started illustrating *The Philippine Readers* series, Amorsolo's famous painting *Rice Planting* (1922) had already started to appear on calendars and in tourist brochures. Clearly, Osias selected an illustrator whose works could be used to sell the Philippines as a tropical tourist destination and thus someone who could be seen simply as a tool of colonial management. Renato Constantino, for instance, would deride Amorsolo for his idealized pictures of rural Philippines ("The Miseducation of the Filipino," 9). But Amorsolo was also symbolic of the Filipino artist who could rival his American and European peers in reputation, his works having been exhibited in Belgium and New York. Osias's use of Amorsolo, who is credited prominently on the title page of all of the readers, speaks of Osias's abilities to use the tools of colonial management to demonstrate pride in Filipino art and culture.

We have seen how, in the early readers, insignia of colonial authority such as flags were featured in ostensibly innocuous pedagogical acts such as teaching simple arithmetic. Gibbs's and Fee's books continued to be used as primary official texts for the early grades when Osias's later volumes were contracted as supplementary reading in 1920, but by 1923, the *Rizal Readers* were adopted as primary texts for grade 1 and as supplementary texts for grades 2–7, while Gibbs's readers continued to be used as supplementary texts. The *Rizal Readers* had largely turned away from overtly political subject matter and displays of flags, but other than the obligatory section on Rizal, they had virtually no Filipino content. Osias, however, continued to use flags as pedagogical objects, but instead of being emblems of American hegemony, they represent the vexed state of Filipino nationalism—at once permitted and withheld by the colonial power. Osias used his readers to challenge the logic of delayed independence, what Peter Schmidt called Jim Crow colonialism in describing education for African Americans and the colonized post-Reconstruction.

The text of the very first of Osias's *Philippine Readers* begins with an illustration of an ordered and peaceful Filipino landscape (Figure 2.8). The palm tree, signifying the tropics, stands tall over the countryside, with its vistas of farmland and neat rows of nipa-thatched homes. In the distance are signs of religious order (the church) and secular order (the schoolhouse with a flag). The flag, too small to be discerned yet asking to be identified, stands at the edge of the landscape, visible yet ambiguous. Close to the end of the reader, however, Osias invites students to participate in Filipino nationalism: by depicting a schoolboy saluting the flag of the Philippines, he suggests that the indeterminate flag of the first page is that of the Philippines (Figure 2.9). In 1919, not long before the publication of *The Philippine Readers*, the 1907 act declaring the exhibition of the Philippines flag illegal had been repealed, and a year later the Philippine legislature had adopted the Philippines flag, originally designed by Emilio Aguinaldo, as the official flag. However, as

FIGURE 2.8. Flag in the distance.
(Camilo Osias, *The Philippine Readers: Book One*
[New York: Ginn and Company, 1927], 8.)

befitting a colony, U.S. and Filipino flags flew alongside each other until the Japanese invasion in 1941. Patriotic drills in schools, however, were often executed with an overabundance of U.S. flags, with the Philippines flag nowhere in sight.[7] Osias was undoubtedly aware of the seditious nature of this call for nationalism, preferring to bury it at the very end of the book and surrounding it with text that referred only to the flag's colors (red, white, and blue) and not to its gold sun or three golden stars (Figure 2.9). It would not be specious to speculate that the politics of book one challenged colonial policy, for it remained the only one of *The Philippine Readers* not to be adopted as an official textbook for the five-year period starting in 1923, when Osias's readers were first adopted.

But even in the other readers, in which the flag of the Philippines never flies alone, Osias uses these patriotic emblems to question colonial authority

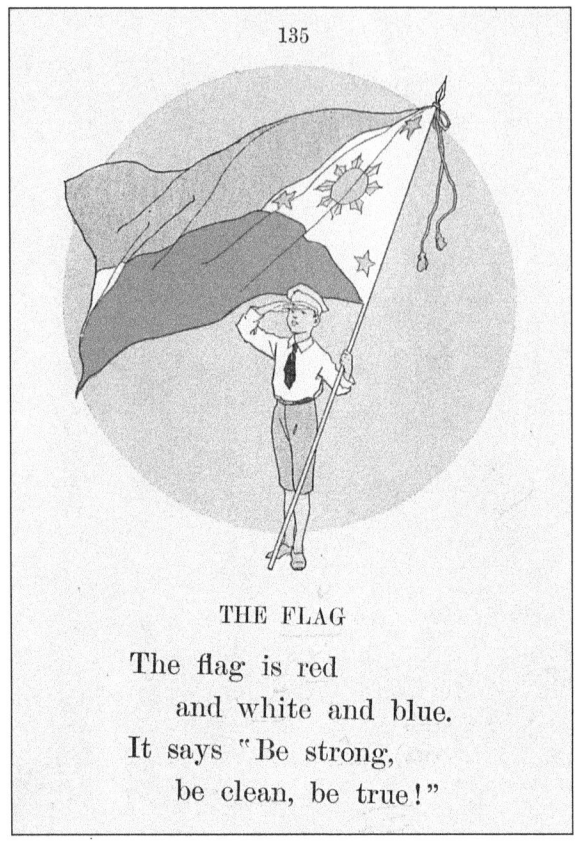

FIGURE 2.9. Saluting the flag of the Philippines. (Camilo Osias, *The Philippine Readers: Book One* [New York: Ginn and Company 1927], 135.)

by strategically misaligning text and image. In book five, for instance, students stand erect, hats tucked under their arms, giving a proper salute as the flags of the United States and Philippines fly in the breeze atop a single flagpole. However, the text instructing students about respecting the flag refers to it in the singular and is preceded and followed by tributes to heroes of Filipino nationalism. The argument by critics that Osias valorizes Filipino nationalists such as Rizal and Bonifacio, who fought for independence against the Spanish, rather than those who continued the insurgency against U.S. rule, thus effectively inuring the colonial regime from critique, is therefore only partially correct. In the revised edition of book five, Osias includes a biography of Mabini, which opens with the announcement that Mabini, who almost until the end of his life refused allegiance to the United States, had been officially honored by the Philippine legislature in 1917–1918—that is, shortly after the passage of the Jones Act. The biography is followed by Edward Everett Hale's "Saluting the Flag," Osias's "The Good Filipino Citizen's Patriotic Pledge," and a translation of "The Philippine Hymn." All of the selections, including Osias's pledge—which includes the sentence, "I want my country to be free and independent"—may have been within the limits of a Filipino nationalism that the colonial authorities deemed permissible (*PR, Book Five*, 276). Indeed, the idea of an eventually free and independent Philippines was an integral component of U.S. colonial rhetoric from the very beginning, and the paradoxical inclusion of Filipino nationalism in schooling in Americanism, became a strategy of colonial schooling. In the 1920s, schools routinely started with "The Star-Spangled Banner" and the Philippine national anthem (R. Thompson, 23). However, in the context of the Woods-Forbes report, which criticized Filipinization and recommended delaying independence, and Osias's own refusal to accept the rhetoric of delayed decolonization, the sentence also speaks to an anticolonial nationalism. Ironically, Hale's credo, which was widely anthologized in readers in the United States, including in the *Wide Awake Reader* series, functions ambivalently as a text accompanying the illustration of two flags that exhorts students to "remember that the flag represents the country to which they owe duties every hour of their lives" (*PR, Book Five*, 275).

As late as the 1960s, Constantino decried the colonial mentality of educational leaders who traced their descent to the soldier-teachers of the American invasion army ("The Miseducation of the Filipino," 2): he felt there was no need for American overseers during the commonwealth period, because a new generation of miseducated "Filipino Americans" had been produced ("The Miseducation of the Filipino," 5). The Filipino linguist Bonifacio Sibayan, in his otherwise fond memories of his rural school, recalls learning English in school in the 1920s, when almost nobody in the town spoke it: "The punishment for speaking the local language was to carry stones from the river to build a fence around the schoolyard" (quoted in R. Thompson, 23). In the very teaching of English, Osias's readers were part of the machinery of colonial rule. But as we have seen, the readers also carried hidden transcripts gesturing beyond the rules of colonial management. The series begins with a volume thoroughly immersed in rural Filipino life. The selections include instructions for making *pinipig* (rice stamped flat); stories about the carabao and fishing; and, of course, lessons on the flag and a story about Rizal's school days. But Osias also uses this first reader to defamiliarize English in order to familiarize it for the student. The very first page uses two everyday Tagalog words that are important in moving the story forward.

Pinipig, which teaches by providing cooking instructions, begins with Juan telling his mother he likes *pinipig*; his mother responds, "First we must have a bundle of palay [unhusked rice]." Spanish words such as *carretela*, *banca*, and *bolo* are also interspersed in the reader. And in a story about linguistic alienation, cultural survival, change, and deterritorialization, students are taught a Tagalog word that is central to the narrative: *putik*. A story titled "The First Clay Pot" narrates the story of a girl who foolishly attempts to cook rice and fish in bamboo tubes, which burn, leaving the family hungry. When she hears a bird singing "Pu-tik," she turns to her grandfather: "*Putik* is *clay*," said her grandfather. "He is trying to say *clay*" (*PR, Book One*, 85). When the girl comprehends why the bird is saying clay, she builds a clay pot and cooks. The question of the loss of language, presented so innocuously here, is dramatized through a story that turns the learning of English into the learning of a Tagalog word. Tagalog, the language of nature and the language the grandfather understands, is thoroughly naturalized; *putik* is a word the young girl should know but does not. Concurrently, the story suggests that the language of survival is English, because only when the word is translated does it change from something unintelligible to something useful and necessary. But the teaching of the story also introduces a defamiliarization of English because the narrative hinges on a Tagalog word's being understood, an objective clearly articulated in a comprehension question at the end of the story: "Does *putik* mean 'clay'?" (*PR, Book One*, 89).

At the same time, Osias's readers are not necessarily at odds with the colonial state. Selections such as Arsenio Luz's "My Early Experiences with Americans," in which Luz describes how fear of occupation soldiers turns into trust and friendship as the soldiers play with children, hand out proverbial candy, and open schools, function as alibis for colonialism. Instructions to students that precede Luz's essay explain the U.S. colonial presence in terms of cultural influence that is similar to British influence on the United States (Osias, *PR, Book Seven*, 308–311). The nationalism that Osias incorporated within the readers was carefully positioned not to function as criticism of U.S. colonial policy or as a radical call to revolt but, rather, as a form of nationalism that could be imagined despite the framework of colonial rule. Thus, in the last two books, selections from Western classics—Cervantes, Shakespeare, Charles Lamb, Tennyson—along with a host of selections from American writers, such as Edward Everett Hale, Phillips Brooks, Bayard Taylor, Washington Irving, and Nathaniel Hawthorne, are predominant. But the celebration of secular heroes includes not simply Columbus and Washington but also Rizal, Bonifacio and Mabini.

In book seven, Bonifacio is hailed as "the father of Philippine democracy": "Now that the greatest Philippine revolution, of which he was the father, has passed . . . now that the story of the Katipunan, of which he was the founder, can be studied without prejudice, we can pay him the honor that is due every true patriot and hero, and hail him as the father of Philippine democracy" (*PR, Book Seven*, 68). The same sketch explains Bonifacio's conviction of the necessity for armed struggle, outlines the formation of the Katipunan, and ends with Bonifacio's Decalogue of the Katipunan. Osias's commemoration of Bonifacio is not singular. In 1929, the state had sanctioned funds for a monument for Bonifacio, and he was being invoked by politicians. However, as Reynaldo Ileto argues, the Bonifacio of the labor and radical movements was not the figure invoked by Quezon, who ignored the Bonifacio who signified "violence, armed insurrection, [and] the people's anger" and instead drew on the "tamer side of Bonifacio, the poor man who succeeded through hard work, who composed the Decalogue of the Katipunan which called for the fulfillment of obligations and love among the brethren" ("The 'Unfinished Revolution' in Philippine Political Discourse," 67). Ileto sees the commemoration of Bonifacio as a cooptation of a potentially subversive historical consciousness ("The 'Unfinished Revolution' in Philippine Political Discourse," 68). In *The Philippine Readers*, Bonifacio is presented as radical and as a quiet sage; his call for armed struggle is not critiqued in either the selection or the questions at the end. Bonifacio is both a seditious figure and an exemplary citizen invoking duties, but his seditious activities are part of a history to be remembered, while his statement of duties is presented as precepts to be followed.

Analyzing textbooks written for Filipino children in the first decade of U.S. rule, Susan K. Harris writes that these books "transform Americans' own desire for a unified American culture into a prescription for nation building in other countries" (100). She argues that the American insistence on a unified Philippines as necessary for independence points to a fundamental flaw in the understanding of a modernity, which, in the United States, was necessarily heterogeneous (Harris, 101–102). Textbooks for subjects that ranged from arithmetic to history attempted to teach republican citizenship, which could be attained only from American Protestant culture (Harris, 91). I suggest that the idea of a unified nation, unfractured by class or race and based on virtues of individualism, thrift, ingenuity, industry, and learning, was central to textbooks written not only by American educators but also by nationalists such as Osias, who in his readers invoked the hard work and education of American and Philippine secular heroes and urged all Filipinos to aspire to middle-class comfort (*PR, Book Seven*, 265–270). Even though he attempted to provincialize America, to use Dipesh Chakrabarty's provocative concept, by articulating in *The Filipino Way of Life* a Filipino ontology—a pluralized philosophy coterminous with, yet different from, a Western modernity—his conception of modernity was racialized. He saw Filipinos as essentially Christian, belonging to the great brown race of Malays, and Tagalog as central to a distinctively Filipino culture (*The Filipino Way of Life*, 14, 251), all of which are reflected in *The Philippine Readers*. While Gibbs's readers included racist depictions of Moros and Negritos, Osias's readers simply excluded non-Christians and non-Malays as representations of Filipinos. The defamiliarization of English via Tagalog (despite Osias's official position on keeping English) in "The First Clay Pot" recognizes the nation-building efforts of contemporary Tagalog writers,[8] but it also rests on an assumed hegemony of Tagalog, which belies the existence of Osias's own native Ilokano.

Toward a Reformist Postcolonial Nationalism

After 1920, when only 325 American teachers were left in the Philippines, the school system functioned as part of the colonial state under the direction of Filipinos, many of whom were themselves products of American schooling either in the Philippines or as *pensionados* in the United States. The school system was part of a machinery of colonial management and tutelage that continued to be used as a metaphor for the colonial state by policy makers and journalists alike, particularly in making the case for delaying independence in the wake of the Woods-Forbes report. Yet even if one argues that schools ultimately support a dominant ideology, they may do so in very different ways and with different consequences for the future. So, for instance, while textbooks in the United States and the Philippines may have reproduced a discourse of exceptional American freedom, there were significant differences between how this exceptionalism was channeled in textbooks written for children in the United States, those written for Filipinos by American educators, and those written by Filipinos. Even so, one cannot simply dismiss the praise that contemporary reviewers of Osias's readers, such as Frederick Starr, bestowed on them for drawing their contents from Philippine sources or recent critics who speculate that the Philippine classroom opened up to Filipino writers due in part to these readers (Starr, 12; I. Martin, "Pedagogy," 120). The Filipino nationalism propagated in *The Philippine Readers* functions within the hegemonic colonial idea of tutelage but questions ideas of gradualism and extended tutelage. The reformism suggested in the readers necessarily demands collaboration with U.S. colonial ideas of benevolent assimilation through the learning of English and the values of freedom, modernity, individualism, and industry, but it also gestures toward a dissent that should not be dismissed. Of course, what Osias's readers resist is the rule of colonial difference, which delayed self-rule for a population seen as yet unfit, not the normalizing mission of the colonial state to produce productive citizens for a unified state. And as long as Osias was part of the colonial machinery, in which textbooks were a prime profit-making industry for U.S. publishing houses, the nationalism of *The Philippine Readers* was, in a sense, coopted for colonial benefit.

3

Unhomeliness and Educational Anxieties in the Neocolonial Philippines

Tiempo and Cordero-Fernando

As I walked through the Faculty Center and the corridors of the English Department at the University of the Philippines, I could not help being struck by the tribute to the esteemed writer N. V. M. Gonzalez. The department was celebrating the centennial of Gonzalez's birth, and a photograph of his genial face and the covers of his novels and short story and essay collections lined the wall. His achievements as a prolific writer in English groomed under the American school system seemed to stand as a testament to the beneficence of U.S. colonial education and to the adoption of English as a language of the Philippines. After all, even though he did not earn a college degree, Gonzalez was solicited to teach at the best universities in the United States. Yet the legacy of American education was by no means straightforward. Gonzalez himself had been painfully aware of the alienness of English to the life he described (62) and continued writing in English only because friends and editors had discouraged him from writing in Tagalog. My colleague Professor Judy Ick was a Shakespearean scholar, a graduate of the University of the Philippines with a doctorate from the United States. She confessed to me that when she completed her education and returned to the Philippines, she felt totally irrelevant. She questioned the value of her training in both the Philippines and the United States. It was her need to understand her own subjectification that drove her to research the writings of the Thomasites and their students. As Ick wrote, "It seems that a hundred years after the fact we are still exorcising that American demon from our classrooms. The specter of colonial education continues to haunt debates about curricula, textbooks, and the medium of education" (268). At the same time, Ick wrote about the "plethora of often contradictory experiences" of American education by Filipinos who exhibited a simultaneity of collaboration with and resistance to it (268).

Gonzalez's robust output of creative works in English and yet his ambivalence about writing in the language exemplify the contradictory experiences that Ick emphasizes. Although Filipinos had started writing in English in the first decade of colonial rule, significant publications in English begun to mushroom in the 1920s, and by the time of independence a healthy group of writers, many of them trained in schools and universities set up by Americans, had made English their own and gained a readership in the Philippines. Yet as Gonzalez's comments make clear, the relationship of this first generation of postcolonial writers in the Philippines to the intellectual legacy of American education was complex. Colonial education in English had at once given them a middle-class readership and stature as intelligentsia in the Philippines even as the decision to write in English distanced them from the masses. The erstwhile American public school system had become a site of cultural contradictions: it was administered by Filipinos, hybridized with the use of local languages, and produced the first generation of Filipino writers in English. Yet Anglo-American culture retained its cultural capital, and the centralized structure of colonialism was maintained.

For Renato Constantino colonial education simply morphed into neocolonialism once direct colonial rule was over. Constantino writes, "And when a Filipino took over [as the head of the Department of Public Instruction] under the Commonwealth, a new generation of 'Filipino-Americans' had already been produced. There was no longer any need for American overseers in this field because a captive generation had already come of age, thinking and acting like little Americans" ("The Miseducation of the Filipino," 5). Filipinos, in his view, had become perfect pedagogical subjects, with the caveat that those trained in English had become American *ilustrados* (18). However, Vicente Rafael's point that Constantino benefited from the very bourgeois structures and colonial education that he so bitterly criticized is an important one (*Motherless Tongues*, 213). Even intellectuals who delivered scathing critiques of colonial education were products of this project. Ick writes, for instance, about being "reared on the dogma of our 'miseducation' by American colonialism" inculcated in her by her education at the University of the Philippines—that is, through a nationalist institution that was started under the aegis of American colonial rule (263).

This chapter examines the anxiety about the legacy of colonial tutelage in the postcolonial Philippines through the figure of the Filipino educator, who stands in for what Constantino called the new captive generation.

Scenes of instruction and disquisitions of literacy become sites of reflection and critique, especially as colonial schooling morphs into the postcolonial. In their short stories, Edith Tiempo and Gilda Cordero-Fernando critique this captive generation by dramatizing the postcolonial alienation fostered by the ingestion of colonialism's culture by embattled educators who are distanced from the folk and forms of community. None of the educators is successful in fostering the individualistic, industrious pedagogical subjects of Anglo-American modernity envisioned by Americans. At the same time, neither Tiempo nor Cordero-Fernando offers a different epistemology or native forms of knowledge as alternatives to neocolonial tutelage. The postcolonial adage about cynicism with the new nation premised on the forms handed to it by the colonial state, and hence doomed to repeat its domination, is particularly apt here. Writing in the first generation after the commonwealth period, Tiempo and Cordero-Fernando register disappointment with the postcolonial state's project of schooling. In Tiempo's "The Dam" and "The Dimensions of Fear" and Cordero-Fernando's "A Harvest of Humble Folk" and "The Visitation of the Gods" (both in her early collection *The Butcher, the Baker, the Candlestick Maker*), the schoolteacher is, in Homi Bhabha's terms, "unhomely," because her condition is necessarily one of the border between Anglo-American and Filipino, (neo)colonial and native—in other words, the unhomely pedagogical subject is caught in a psychosocial limbo. Bhabha writes, "To be unhomed is not to be homeless. . . . In the stirrings of the unhomely, another world becomes visible. It has less to do with forcible eviction and more to do with the uncanny literary and social effects of enforced social accommodation or historical migrations and cultural relocations" ("The World and the Home," 445). Bhabha might have added colonial tutelage to his list of conditions of unhomeliness. Both Tiempo's and Cordero-Fernando's schoolteachers are Anglicized, unhomely figures, the captive generation whose mimicry of Anglo-American culture and estrangement from the community speak to the alienation and epistemic violence of colonial and neocolonial education. Unlike the writings of Carlos Bulosan, Bienvenido Santos, and R. Zamora Linmark discussed in the next chapter, these stories are focalized through teachers of English (both inheritors and transmitters of colonial culture) in specific school settings and are therefore trenchant commentaries on the afterlife of the American educational system for the first generation in the newly independent nation. By Filipina authors who wrote in the Philippines for a Filipino readership, and who remain largely unknown in the United States, these dystopic stories explore the failure of the postcolonial nation's Americanized schooling project through conflicts of race, gender, sexuality, and class.

Tiempo focuses on the inner lives of her educator protagonists and their gendered and sexual turmoil, while Cordero-Fernando focuses on schooling's structures, assessing the workings of the system and its impact on the lives of the community. Tiempo's postwar stories do not directly name colonialism or neocolonialism but present protagonists more comfortable in the imaginative world of Western literature than their everyday lives. These stories address tutelary colonialism by demonstrating how the Anglo American heritage has become elite Filipino heritage, as well. "The Dam" and "Dimensions" feature as their protagonists highly erudite, anxious, lonely, middle-aged male educators repressing their sexuality, unable to connect with colleagues or control juniors and students. School, rather than a site for producing tractable pedagogical subjects, becomes one for exploring the inner torment of educators. It is a place of ambivalence and confusion. Cordero-Fernando's "Visitation" and "Harvest" represent both the faith in education as the vehicle of transformation through the depiction of the earnest schoolteacher Miss Noel and a critique of the American tutelary project as colonial and distanced from the needs of the masses.

Postcolonial Anxiety in Edith Tiempo's "The Dam" and "The Dimensions of Fear"

Edith Tiempo's writing career illustrates the continued impact of American education on Philippine writing in English in the early postcolonial period. Tiempo, a product of English education in the Philippines, continued her writing career when she attended the International Writers Workshop at the University of Iowa, where she studied under Paul Engle and came under the influence of New Criticism. In 1962, after returning to the Philippines, Tiempo, along with her husband, Edilberto Tiempo, set up the Silliman Summer Creative Writing Workshop based on the Iowa model and institutionalized creative writing. Silliman, in turn, has produced many influential Filipino writers of the twentieth and twenty-first centuries. Notably, Tiempo did not encourage bilingualism because she thought it would affect her writing, and Silliman continues a policy of monolingualism, awarding scholarships only to those who write in English. Both of Tiempo's stories about anxious middle-aged educators, "The Dam" and "Dimensions," foreground the vexed psychic life of the protagonists struggling to come to terms with their role as educators and with their sexuality. Both stories are set in the 1950s when the school system had been under Filipino control for more than a decade. "The Dam" was published in 1954 and won second place in the Palanca Memorial Award for Literature; "The Dimensions of Fear" was published in 1959. Neither of the stories is plot-driven nor moves toward resolution of the characters' inner turmoil; instead, the stories dramatize not only the educators' anxieties and doubts but also their estrangement from the community at large. Both are set in schools: the school in "The Dam" is in Bak-ag, and the one in "Dimensions" is a "regional high school deep in the hills of a very inland town" (90).

"The Dam" presents the nervous attempts of Mr. Rosales, the erudite principal of Bak-ag elementary school to discipline one of his wayward teachers, Mr. Conde, whose drunken and disorderly behavior he needs to curb. Rosales, who asserts his authority only with extreme agitation, warns Conde about his conduct and remembers his own discomfiture at Conde's and other teachers' masculinist, homosocial bonding as they lustily enjoy breaking the prohibition against eating mangoes on school property during a dysentery epidemic. Conde, whom Rosales cannot simply dismiss as unruly, triggers in him memories of his youth and his fondness for his cousin's son Nacio, who is a soldier in Korea. The story ends with Rosales being abruptly woken from his sleep by teachers, who report to him that Conde, who had gotten drunk at a local dance and forced his attentions on a girl, was being hunted by the villagers. With difficulty, Rosales reprimands and fires Conde but is beset with guilt and loneliness as he again remembers Nacio.

"The Dimensions of Fear" is a partly gothic tale about the fears and desires of Numeriano Agujo, a schoolteacher in a remote town to which he commutes by bus. Numeriano is a middle-aged bachelor, single by his own accord, and has rebuffed Fidela, who until her death four years earlier, had not forgiven him for the rejection. Unlike Rosales's testiness, which is due partly to the riotous teachers he has to control, Agujo's agitation stems from his conflict with transgressive desires he wants to both fulfill and deny. He yearns to be recognized as more than an inconsequential middle-aged teacher and fondly remembers Rosenberg, his American GI friend. Agujo's outlet from repression is a compulsion to break the law, first by stealing food from La Munda, the owner of the restaurant where he eats lunch, and then stealing fundraising money from the office of the head teacher, Mr. Esteban. Caught between obsessive self-incrimination and a fear of discovery, he writes a confession note and carries it on his person but is afraid to sleep lest it is found. Finally, unable to continue with the anxiety, he attempts to make a dramatic statement by hanging himself, his confession note crumpled in his hand. Instead, he clumsily slips and hangs helplessly from the noose around his wrist as the note falls to the ground and he is discovered by the head teacher.

As the brief outlines of the stories suggest, both focus on the psychic anguish of the protagonists who are overpowered by emotions and compulsions. J. Neil Garcia, who includes both stories in his collection *Aura: The Gay Theme in Philippine Fiction in English*, sees the stories as haunted by a homoeroticism that cannot be named but only hinted at. Tiempo's "sexually repressed and desperately 'uninvolved' characters," he argues "do not seem to be demonstrably aware of the source of their inner turmoil—or at least, what's apparent is that they *do not wish* to confront it—but this repressed 'unconscious' nonetheless haunts and terrifies them" (Garcia, 19). Garcia explains that Filipino local cultures had male gender-crossers (rather than cross-dressers) who possessed "transgenderal characteristics" and enjoyed esteemed status, and "'vestiges' of this egalitarian practice survive and endure in the identity of the effeminate *bakla*" (10, 17). He argues that precisely because Mr. Rosales and Agujo are not frankly effeminate in their gender presentation—that is, they are not *bakla*—they are even more tormented (19). In other words, it is their inability to adopt local forms of homosexual identities that cause the characters increased anguish. Building on Garcia's prescient reading, I suggest that the estrangement of Rosales and Agujo from autochthonous forms of gender and sexual expression is crucially tied to their roles as neocolonial educators, culturally and linguistically alienated from their communities. Sexuality thus not only signifies privatized concerns but also becomes a site of postcolonial estrangement.

Clearly, "The Dam" and "Dimensions" are haunted by a homoeroticism that the characters have difficulty confronting and that surfaces as a return of the repressed. In "The Dam," Mr. Rosales's repressed homoerotic love for his nephew Nacio is triangulated through the obstreperous teacher Mr. Conde, whom Mr. Rosales desires but cannot acknowledge. Even as he is disciplining Mr. Conde, the "thought came once again as something to wonder at: how he looked so much like Nacio . . . the same open look in both faces" (Tiempo, "The Dam," 83). Again after he fails to discipline Mr. Conde, Mr. Rosales wonders, "There was something about the young fellow. One had to grant there was something about him. Even at teachers' meetings while the others remained dumb as statues, Conde's face, once or twice. Importance, though it was more than that, more than that" (85). Crucially, Tiempo presents Mr. Rosales's musings as not only inadmissible and unacknowledgeable but also discursively impossible within the regime of the school. Language itself fails, and grammatical structures flounder as Tiempo records Mr. Rosales's difficulty in articulating his desires. It is only within his dreams that Mr. Rosales is overpowered by his homoerotic feelings, which he cannot reason or name and that Tiempo intimates affectively. Mr. Rosales dreams of being in "a long dark room with all around hanging in rows the wrinkled length of boys' trousers" and realizes he's in the room with Nacio and his brothers. Overcome by desires he cannot admit or recognize, he is nauseous as he grabs Nacio's bedpost. "In the dream a sick feeling swept over him about he knew not what, and he grabbed at one of the thin tubular posts of Nacio's bed; it was made of steel and clammy to his touch. Then it was not a bedpost but Nacio's gun which the boy sent back from Korea" (Tiempo, "The Dam," 86).

In "Dimensions," the protagonist's unwillingness to face his homosexuality is more clearly articulated. A gothic world of "unreasoning and overpowering" fears, the grotesque shapes Agujo fancies seeing "in the dimness of the hall" in the world of "half-twilight" become tropes for a fear of homosexuality (91). Although Agujo attempts to explain his uneasiness and fears as a need to maintain a heteronormative manliness—for instance, not marrying Fidela because she was too bossy—the text questions this heteronormativity through his relationship with his GI friend, Rosenberg, who sends him a volume of poems by the gay poet W. H. Auden. Significantly, Tiempo presents Agujo as reacting viscerally to Auden's famous poem "Canzone," which naturalizes homoeroticism as preceding conscious actions or will. Agujo remembers lines such as, "We cannot choose what we are free to love" (96). But Agujo struggles to find a viable form of sexual expression. He surmises from the poem that "there was no escape, no escape from involvement" (96) and at that moment decides to commit suicide in a dramatic fashion.

These homoerotic anxieties in "The Dam" and "Dimensions" also function as articulations of postcolonial difference and reflect ambivalently on the project of American colonial education. As evident in the cartoon in Chapter 1, schooling was conceived as the masculine task of subjugating resistant Filipinos, the continuation of battle by other means, as evidenced by the soldier striding across a hillside littered with human remains. With the entry of the Thomasites, teachers began to be represented in a less virile manner as suffering missionaries, healers of communities, and cultural diplomats, all representing the benevolent face of colonialism, or what Vicente Rafael has called "white love" or a "civilizing love" that obfuscates the violence of colonialism (*White Love and Other Events in Filipino History*, 21). Popular cartoons that appeared in *Puck* in 1900 and 1901 more explicitly gendered American tutelage as feminine, offering the colonized Filipinos the choice of their fate between the armed soldier ready for combat and the kind female teacher with book in hand (Wesling, 106–107). What this reflected was the early feminization of teaching, despite the fact that teachers, both American and Filipino, were overwhelmingly male. For instance, even by 1910, 67.3 percent of American teachers were men; of Filipino teachers, men constituted 81.5 percent of the national, 68.9 percent of the municipal, and 70.3 percent of the apprentice staff (*Tenth Annual*, 320–321). However, by 1923 these demographics had changed. Seventy-five percent of American teachers were women, and out of the total number of teachers (including

Filipino teachers), 59.45 percent were men and 40.5 percent were women (*Twenty-Fourth Annual*, 15). By the late 1930s, women outnumbered men as schoolteachers. But what these numbers do not capture are the complexities of gendered power relations between American and Filipino teachers and their students, American teachers and their Filipino counterparts, American supervisors and Filipino teachers (and, later, Filipino supervisors and Filipino teachers), and, finally, teachers and the community. As discussed earlier, the colonial system of education remained raced, with American teachers paid more than Filipinos, American supervisors routinely exasperated with their underqualified Filipino teachers, and top positions remaining in American hands so that no matter what, the Filipino male teacher was inscribed within colonial discourses of docility. And memoirs of American teachers, such as William Freer, attest to fantasies about their paternalist, familial relations with people in the Filipino community alongside aggressively dominating visions. Surveyed years later, Filipino teachers had humiliating memories of being "reprimanded in front of their students" by American inspectors (Margold, 389).

By the 1950s, the period that characters such as Mr. Rosales and Agujo begin to populate the world of Tiempo's stories, some of the dynamics of the structure of education had changed. Filipinos were now directors, supervisors, and teachers, with men occupying administrative positions and women doing a majority of the teaching. Yet because the centralized system of education with English as a major language continued, albeit along with instruction in Filipino, vestiges of the raced and gendered hierarchies of colonialism persisted.[1] The male Filipino schoolteacher was thus complexly gendered. Given the feminization of teaching, both literally and symbolically, he participated in a vocation that was arguably demasculinized; he also participated in a system in which Filipino teachers were viewed as docile followers of rules dictated by a centralized Anglo bureaucracy. However, given his role as the conduit of colonial knowledge, he was implicated in the paternalist discourses of colonialism. And as part of a (neocolonial) centralized structure, he was situated within the power structures of the educational apparatus. In "The Dam" and "Dimensions," Tiempo registers these classed and gendered hierarchies and questions them by presenting her protagonists as confused, anxious, unauthoritative, bumbling educators attempting hopelessly to assert power within a symbolic economy in which masculinity is differentially allocated and homosociality is demarcated from homosexuality.

The significance of the school as a site is readily apparent in the opening of "The Dam," where the architecture of Bak-ag Elementary School signifies rationality, order, and the law. The school comprises three buildings "wrapped around a square, a neat space bare of grass reserved for the morning exercises and flag ceremonies . . . sufficiently isolated to render the learning process free of distracting sights, away from traffic and movie houses and food parlors and such" (Tiempo, "The Dam," 81). However, the narrator views the school and its status with ironic amusement, noting that the teachers who are "much regarded as molders of future citizens of Bak-ag" eagerly leave school at dismissal time unless there is a meeting (Tiempo, "The Dam," 81). These molders of future citizens, steeped in the neocolonial order of the school, are inevitably distanced from the country folk. While the school signifies reason, discipline, and modernity, the rural provinces signify a sensuality and community that disturb the Westernized Rosales. If, as Constantino argued, colonial schooling created a wedge between the educated Filipinos and the masses, Mr. Rosales's discomfort with the townspeople demonstrates that. Mr. Rosales "always react[ed] to the portion of the town he had to pass on his way to the boarding house. There were the *nipa* roofs slanted wispily over dark windows, men leaning from the doorways or congregated in the combination store-and-barber shop, the *calamungay* trees sparse-leafed at the fences, children rolling home their water wagons from the artesian well. . . ." (Tiempo, "The Dam," 87). The ellipses at the end of the sentence, which are part of the text, indicate a continuity of the scene as Mr. Rosales perceives the town and townspeople as estheticized, almost in the colonial manner that Mary Louise Pratt has called the "monarch-of-all-I-survey" scene (Tiempo, "The Dam," 201, 204). The people here become part of the scene, without historicity or conflict, in a suspended temporality of the present continuous ("men leaning," "children rolling"), a portraiture that denies the very class discomfort that Mr. Rosales experiences but does not articulate.

However, while dynamics of the distance between the erudite teacher and the townspeople created by unequal (neocolonial) relations are only hinted at and not engaged with, the story dwells on Mr. Rosales's distancing from other teachers and students. Tiempo presents Mr. Rosales as a sentimentalized and demasculinized pedant whose complete immersion in Anglo-American literature renders him comical in the eyes of his fellow teachers. Mr. Rosales keeps his teachers waiting at faculty meetings while he recites Tennyson's "Tears, Idle Tears," a poem about regret, love, and the past that Tiempo renders incongruous in its iteration at Bak-ag elementary school. Tiempo's ventriloquizing of Tennyson's lines through Mr. Rosales is worth quoting here:

> And so the silent audience listened, or half-listened with drooping senses, coming awake by turns, jogged now and then by a word or phrase, but mostly lulled by the gentle graveyard tone, O death in life, the days that are no more, the sick awareness of separation from

the living reality, the casements growing to glimmering shadows, and into the group's collective ears this old boy's droning varied by occasional nervous cackles exploding farcically high and false in the darkening Assembly Room. (Tiempo, "The Dam," 84)

Tiempo not only presents Mr. Rosales's rendition of Tennyson as pathetic and comical because it is misplaced in relation to the teachers, poorly delivered, and symptomatic of his self-absorption, but also suggests the inappropriateness of the poem in the context of the school as she rewrites it in prose form. Mr. Rosales's total immersion in the poem and his obliviousness to the life around him is symptomatic of a colonized mentality that Tiempo represents as farcical. Indeed, Tiempo routes Rosales's failed homoeroticism through his investment in creating perfect American Filipinos. Encountering a group of students reciting Walt Whitman's "O Captain, My Captain," from *Drum Taps*, Rosales is agitated to hear a student recite the poem with a native inflection saying "*captane*, making the vowel a long *a*" and chides him sternly. Significantly, when Rosales jovially claps his hand on the boy's shoulder, expressing a longing, it is rejected by the boy, who shrinks from the principal's touch, and the students stand in sullen silence until he leaves.

Here it is important to emphasize the difference between Mr. Rosales's erudition and immersion in Western culture and the colonial teacher as possessor and dispenser of knowledge. Whereas within the colonial system the American teacher was a visible symbol of the (benevolent) civilizing mission, Tiempo suggests that the native continuing within the colonial structure can become only a pathetic mimic of an Anglo-American man—indeed, one arrested in perpetual boyhood whose poetry recitations ring false. Yet Rosales continually attempts to assert his power over teachers and students, even though he is uncomfortable with the accoutrements of power. As he chastises Mr. Conde and threatens him with the loss of his job, he says, "Understand, I am not just trying to make this a chance to exert my authority. Not at all" (Tiempo, "The Dam," 83). Although nervous and agitated about his control over the teachers "Mr. Rosales wanted Conde to feel this in him, the principal" (Tiempo, "The Dam," 83). Mr. Rosales's inability to discipline Conde also stems partly from his own tenuous grasp on a power his position entitles him to but that he does not feel is rightly his. Attempting to persuade Conde to give up his profligate behavior, Mr. Rosales can only reiterate unconvincing adages about school hierarchy and the need for control: "Authority, understand, must always do its duty. Always" (Tiempo, "The Dam," 84) and "Authority must do its part, or where are we?" (Tiempo, "The Dam," 84.

In "Dimensions," the school as the site of creating docile pedagogical subjects and the teacher as the purveyor of modernity, rationality, and individualism come under question. Ghostliness, as Avery Gordon has suggested, calls attention here to what history has rendered ghostly: colonialism's psychic violence. L. M. Grow suggests that "beneath the apparently solid surface of a world of material objects Tiempo's stories reveal a disturbingly vacant interiority, a cosmic *nada* which can be unsettling to the point of producing angst in the percipient of it" ("The Architecture of the Interior," 79). The ambiguity between inner and outer certainty produces a "general ontological uncertainty" that, Grow argues, pervades Tiempo's stories ("The Architecture of the Interior," 84). I argue that that ontological uncertainty and angst are affectively relayed in "Dimensions" through the school. Tiempo clearly marks the order of the school as a contrast to Agujo's inner landscape. Agujo lives away from the school which is "the rational world of wood-and-cement buildings of vine-smothered trellises and huge leafy trees of flagpole and fluttering flag, and clean dry ground broken by patches of scraggly lawn" (91). Interestingly, Agujo appears to teach geography, a subject in which the world is divided into neat maps. He sees his own inner mapping as affected by ideologies of place and longs for the medicalized order of the United States, where instead of simply being consumed by mysterious fears and longings, he could have them diagnosed and named. "If I were in the States, I'd be running to a psychiatrist," says Agujo to his student, Soledad (Tiempo, "The Dimensions of Fear," 93).

Agujo lives in a gothic world of fear and unreason, imagining shapes in the dark hallways, barely aware of the rows of students in front of him when he goes to teach. Instead of being the symbol of order, authority, and class, he presents a picture of disorder, bewilderment, and confusion. He comes to teach with "burrs in his trouser legs, a dead acacia leaf in his hair, and perspiring profusely" (Tiempo, "The Dimensions of Fear," 92). Instead of reprimanding or disciplining students, he himself is subject to disapproval and stern questioning by Soledad, who confronts him after class, saying, "Why were you staring at me in class sir?" (Tiempo, "The Dimensions of Fear," 92). Agujo is gripped by the desire to disrupt the everyday order of the school by giving in to what Edgar Allan Poe called the imp of the perverse—the need to do something extraordinary, such as successfully committing the perfect crime, yet wanting to incriminate oneself after the success.

Interestingly, Tiempo racializes Agujo's mental topography, thus suggesting that his forays into the world of tribals intersect with colonial anxieties and fantasies of the Other, which have manifested themselves in the diverse forms of colonial racism. If tutelary colonialism was a raced project in which Malays and tribals were sharply differentiated, Agujo has a similar repulsion-fascination with tribals. He wonders about "the existence of an unknown trail through the hills, one perhaps used by the Negroid half-civilized folk deep in the interior; but the sight of the chasm made him forget the half formed intention to explore for a hidden path" ("The Dimensions of Fear," 93). Agujo desires to pursue the hidden, obscure, and different pathways of both sexuality and race. Here he is attracted to people he perceives as outside of rationality and modernity, people viewed as outside the scope of colonial tutelage and who manifest themselves for him as Negrito tribals from whom he is separated yet desires.

While he is drawn to tribals whom he associates with the world of unreason, Agujo, like Mr. Rosales, also defines himself through Western literature. As mentioned earlier, Agujo has a revelation about the uncontrollable nature of his desires and the power of affect when he reads lines from the book of Auden poems given to him by his GI friend, Rosenberg. Agujo has played the part of the eponymous Pierre Patelin in the anonymous French drama and fancies his actions as enacting the lives of two lawyers fashioned from literature—the street-smart Patelin and the brilliant but sentimental Sidney Carton from Charles Dickens's *A Tale of Two Cities*. Using free indirect discourse, Tiempo both endows her protagonist with critical consciousness and humorously presents him as a hapless colonized pedagogical subject doomed to be a mimic, imitating his literary heroes even when attempting suicide:

> Really dramatic he thought; also, it was ridiculous but intriguing, this conflicting combination of Patelin and Sidney Carton! Even now, at this moment, which he could make a supreme one, he was still acting, still the make-believe of make-believe heroes, Patelin and Carton but mimicries of them all his life, the tremendous rogue and the irresolute romantic. ("The Dimensions of Fear," 97)

While the "he thought" clearly designates the enacting of Patelin and Carton as the inner monologue of Agujo, the shift to the third person in the next sentence makes indeterminate whether the lines belong to Agujo or the narrator. Between Agujo's consciousness and the narrator's judgment about Agujo's attempt at mimicry we get the third ambiguously positioned voice, which questions Agujo's awareness of his derivativeness but holds in check our critique of the same.

In both "The Dam" and "The Dimensions of Fear" the school thus functions partly as a site of postcolonial difference, with scenes of instruction that do not function as scenes of pacification or tutelage and where the representatives of the school exude disorder and confusion rather than order and authority. The ambivalent position of the postcolonial pedagogue still operating within the colonial American system of education is dramatized through the clearly nonheteronormative sexuality of both protagonists and, yet, their doubts and uncertainties about accepting native self-definitions that challenge Western gender norms. At the same time, the role of colonial tutelage in estranging Filipinos from their communities is illustrated in the comical and pathetic imitator educators and their distancing from the townspeople. These mimic educators do not produce a subversive mimicry that challenges colonial knowledge.[2] Cultural colonialism distances Anglicized educators from autochthonous forms of expression, and the very being of the Americanized educator is affected by the epistemic violence of colonialism. Yet by not charting emancipatory alternatives to Anglo-American schooling, Tiempo registers the ambivalent position of the postcolonial nation, where the status of colonial knowledge is constantly being negotiated.

Neocolonial Sincerity in Cordero-Fernando's "The Visitation of the Gods" and "A Harvest of Humble Folk"

Whereas Tiempo's stories about tutelage emphasize the interiorized struggles of the protagonists, Gilda Cordero-Fernando's "Harvest" and "Visitation" address the failure of the public school system in the Philippines to address the needs of the masses and the hierarchy within the system. As noted earlier, both stories are included in Cordero-Fernando's *The Butcher, the Baker, the Candlestick Maker* (1962) and are set in the postwar period: "Visitation" shortly after the war, and "Harvest" in the early 1950s. "Visitation" is one of Cordero-Fernando's most popular stories and continues to be assigned as high school and college reading in the Philippines because of its critique of the corruption of the public school system. Interestingly, all readers blogging about the story read it as a present-day indictment of schools in the Philippines, and Sylvia Mendez Ventura, in her book devoted to Cordero-Fernando, connects it to the cronyism and nepotism that she argues pervades all of Filipino society (48–49).[3] However, despite Cordero-Fernando's work on a ten-volume study of Philippine history and culture, her stories have not been seen in relation to colonialism.

Here I focus on "Harvest," the less well-known of the stories, which I read as an allegory of the failure of colonial tutelage. Both stories feature the committed, earnest, and embattled schoolteacher Miss Noel, who is pitted against the country folk in "Harvest" and against the school hierarchy in "Visitation." In "Harvest," she teaches at the rudimentary primary school of Pugad Lawin, while in "Visitation" she teaches at Pugad Lawin High School. "Visitation" is a satiric story that focuses on the frenzied scramble of the teachers of Pugad Lawin High School to impress the school superintendent, Mr. Alava, and Miss Noel's efforts to particularly impress the English supervisor, Mr. Sawit, as the bureaucracy descends on the school for an annual inspection. While the faculty and students rush to prepare the best meals and offer the most extravagant gifts to the inspectors, the feisty Miss Noel frankly discusses her cynical understanding of the farce of the school inspection with Mr. Sawit, who attempts to flirt with her. The story ends with Miss Noel continuing to tolerate the inequities, farces, and gender hierarchies of Pugad Lawin High School. "Visitation" is clearly written as a satire of the school system, with its disengaged teachers and corrupt administrators. Vacationing teachers return from trips abroad with goods to sell; the inspectors arrive in a weapons carrier, like an invading army; the principal presents the prettiest instructors as "offering to the gods" (Cordero-Fernando, 177) as the supervisors take on the trope of the debauched, overfed priest (a common depiction of Spanish corruption) to belch their approval as the teachers wait on them. Set shortly after the war, as evident by the use of a weapons carrier for inspection, and, ironically on Flag Day, the day commemorating a major battle against Spain, the erstwhile colonial master, the story suggests the continuity of colonial and postcolonial histories. The legacy of the colonial centralized school system morphs seamlessly into the corrupt postcolonial state. Significantly, it is the English teacher—in a sense, the perfect pedagogical subject—who fiercely maintains faith in the project of education, despite being the object of derision by her peers.

Unlike "Visitation," with its clear Manichean divisions, "Harvest" is a complex, multilevel allegory about the failure of the tutelary project, as well as alternative emancipatory narratives. Deploying mixed generic modes of local color, magical realism, folklore, and social realism, the story centers on the disruption caused to the villagers by the entry of Lazaro, a stand in for the biblical Lazarus, who awakens the villagers from their somnolent complacency with an exploitative feudal system of tenant farming. Unmindful of the warnings of Miss Noel, who is suspicious of Lazaro's being at once an employee of the landlord and an agitator against the tenantry, the villagers neglect their subsistence vegetable gardens. Lazaro rapes Miss Noel, accidentally sets the villagers' cane fields and homes on fire, and leaves the scene of devastation. The story ends with the indefatigable Miss Noel conducting an English class in a crude nipa hut.

"Harvest" clearly needs to be read within the parameters of Filipino peasant movements and a newly established neocolonial nation mortgaged to the United States in the politics of the Cold War. As most critics have argued, Philippine peasant movements in the 1930s changed from those characterized by mysticism, religion, millennialism, and personality worship to those that were clearly class-conscious and secular (see Sturtevant).[4] The Huk Rebellion, the most important of these peasant movements was formed in 1942 and united with the Communist Party of the Philippines (PKP) to fight Japan's imperial army. Although at the end of the war the Philippine republic pledged to work with the Huks, U.S. Cold War politics dictated that the Huks be thoroughly repressed. The Huks went underground and began an armed rebellion against the Philippine government, which they saw as mortgaged to the United States. Organizing the Hukbong Mapagpalaya ng Bayan (People's Liberation Army), the Huks, supported by peasants, captured villages, redistributed land, and engaged in attacks against the Philippine Constabulary. Starting in the 1950s, the Philippine government, with U.S. assistance, launched a massive counterinsurgency operation, which included both punishing military strikes and soft power strategies and propaganda intended to win over the populace. By the end of the 1950s, many Huk leaders had surrendered, and for all practical purposes, the insurgency ended, although stronger movements, such as the Moro National Liberation Front, emerged and continue until today.

"Harvest" writes the social history of the rural Philippines of the 1950s as conflicted with the hierarchical oppositions that were central to the deliberations of colonial educators: Western modernity and native tradition, individualism and community, rationality and superstition, a quasi-feudal class structure and democracy. But Cordero-Fernando also updates these for the 1950s Philippines by considering the radical alternative presented by revolution. Although the story ultimately rejects this alternative by presenting it as dangerous for the community, it also spurns neocolonial tutelage and the myth of education as the harbinger of a just, democratic social order. It presents the American tutelary project as the civilizing mission at its core: its ability to recruit self-sacrificing workers, its view of the natives as ignorant, its intentions to uplift the populace through knowledge, its social failures, and its distance from the cultural life of the community.

At one level, "Harvest" can be read as a perfect neocolonial Cold War propaganda tale about the success of American expertise and knowledge for simple, rural communities in the Philippines. The "humble folk" of Pugad Lawin are ignorant, unthinking, and easily swayed by uncaring communist troublemakers who disturb their lives. Before Lazaro enters the scene, the *barrio* of Pugad Lawin has been praised as a "Model Barrio." The simple country folk have planted their own vegetable gardens, which yield abundant harvest, thanks to seeds sent to them by the International Cooperative Alliance, particularly the so-called Seeds for Democracy: "The healthy gourds grew longer and fatter than the odd bottles the superstitious folk hung on their trellises for the contour of the fruit to simulate" (Cordero-Fernando, "A Harvest of Humble Folk," 130). Begun in 1951 by the Committee for Free Asia, Seeds for Democracy was a Cold War program designed to enlist ordinary Americans in the battle for hearts and minds in the Philippines. As a Georgia newspaper advertised it, "The people of the Philippines know who is giving them the vegetable seeds. They know they have friends in this nation" ("Seeds for Democracy," 4). The seeds yield such bountiful crops for the humble folk that Pugad Lawin is singled out for emulation by various rural development organizations. Pugad Lawin's model status is clearly procured through neocolonial schemes of benign assistance that promise a limited democracy, shifting the onus of improvement to the individual rather than the massive structural changes conceived by the Huks.

While the Seeds for Democracy scheme had an ethos of individual self-help, Cordero-Fernando shows how neocolonial projects are indigenized differently. For the folk at Pugad Lawin, the fruit of the harvest is communal rather than individual; "Harvest" opens with an organic sense of community reaping the benefits of American benevolence. During the annual feast of the patron saint, the women cook and clean and reinforce their collective bonds. Cordero-Fernando presents the scene as one of mutual harmony: "Several watermelons were cooling in the river. The women boiled rice, gossiped, chopped chicken livers, pounded garlic, washed tender green sugar cane, and lording it over them all was Mang Fausto, the barrio's master cook" ("A Harvest of Humble Folk," 131). The humble peasants here are idealized as they labor contentedly together, each in his or her place, as they talk and incorporate their myths and folklore into their everyday lives.

Similarly, the reforms of the English teacher, Miss Noel, a harbinger of modernity, impatient with the ignorance and superstition of the peasants, are effortlessly incorporated and thoroughly refashioned to blend in seamlessly with the rhythm of the community. The narrator holds Miss Noel in amused regard, representing her as the quintessential pedagogical subject who has absorbed ideas of colonial hygiene, medicine, and a Booker T. Washington bootstraps philosophy that she attempts to impart these to the folk: "Miss Noel was a BSE *magna cum laude* graduate who believed in vaccination, self-help, and septic tanks" (Cordero-Fernando, "A Harvest of Humble Folk," 132). Her speeches to her elders usually begin with "My dear ignorant barrio folk[,] . . . [w]e are saddled with so much superstition" (Cordero-Fernando, "A Harvest of Humble Folk," 135). She heroically sustains the one-room schoolhouse and steps in as judge and church help. Indefatigable in her efforts to educate the community, like the ideal teacher H. C. Theobold outlined in *The Filipino Teacher's Manual* (see Chapter 2), she successfully inaugurates a reading center in the *barrio*. However, although the center never receives the books it needs, it becomes what Michel Foucault would call a heterotopia, "capable of juxtaposing in a single real place, several spaces, several sites that are in themselves incompatible" (Foucault, "Of Other Spaces," 25). The putative library becomes a roaming ground for carabaos, as well as a place for menfolk to gather and discuss the future of the *barrio*. Although the men ruminate about the possibilities of science and modernity that the postcolonial nation-state promises to bring them, they do so in community fashion, "gathering around it at night, sitting on their haunches under the stars" (Cordero-Fernando, "A Harvest of Humble Folk," 133).

Lazaro enters the town resembling an apostle. Wearing a black crucifix, his tattered clothes hanging around him, he seems oblivious to the elements. While Miss Noel has taught the folk to put faith in projects promised by the nation-state, this "man with a cross" (Cordero-Fernando, "A Harvest of Humble Folk," 139) introduces class-consciousness into the minds of the villagers and teaches them to despise the system of structured inequalities on which their lives are patterned. They begin to believe in the redistribution of wealth, hate the landlord and his lifestyle, and are restless for change. Yet, as mentioned earlier, Lazaro is presented as an untrustworthy and scheming agitator, clearly patterned after the propagandistic images of the Huks by counterinsurgency operatives. Lazaro "worked for Don Saturnino yet talked against him, he whispered darkly about sacks of rice rotting in the landlord's bodega; yet in disputes he pretended to favor the plantation owner" (Cordero-Fernando, "A Harvest of Humble Folk," 140). His effect on the barrio is devastating. The once model community lets its vegetable patches rot while the villagers discuss the injustices of tenantry. Recognizing Miss Noel as an adversary who questions his sincerity, Lazaro, in an attempt to dominate, rapes her. In this respect, the representation of Lazaro matches those circulated by counterinsurgency literature. As Vina A. Lanzona writes, these missives argued that "far from being the egalitarian crusaders they claimed, the Huk men were immoral predators who took advantage of young, innocent women and exploited them sexually" (75). Lazaro's cruelty is further reinforced when he sets an injured and dying fawn on fire to put it out of its misery. As the fawn runs through the cane fields, burning them to the ground, Lazaro, the antichrist and bringer of apocalypse, leaves the scene of devastation.

In pitting the earnest Miss Noel, emblematic of the tutelary project of promoting Anglo-American culture and values of personal self-reliance and individualism against the radical social restructuring touted by the dishonest Lazaro, the stand-in for the Huks—and, furthermore, mapping the devastating deterioration of Pugad Lawin from model *barrio* to scorched land—"Harvest" can be read as an allegory of the continued benefits of the legacy of colonial schooling. Miss Noel's rape is also the rape of the community shorn of its pride of harvest. But if Miss Noel is the victim of a rapacious revolutionary masculinity, Cordero-Fernando suggests that the victim can survive through a different, defeminized gendering. The story ends with

Miss Noel resolutely continuing her teaching in a makeshift hut only three days after the fire. Now she is gendered as a strong, masculinized woman and thus able to lead the *barrio* out of its misery. Cordero-Fernando writes, "Miss Noel stood by the blackboard, flat chested and wiry as ever, unfelled by storm or battles, holding high her torch and her aphorisms" ("A Harvest of Humble Folk," 149–150).

However, the reading of the story as an allegory of (neo)colonial tutelary success privileges only the overt teleology of the narrative, ignoring the unresolved issue at the center—namely, that colonial and neocolonial schooling worked for pacification. Cordero-Fernando's rendition of the conflict between Miss Noel and the villagers riled by Lazaro's teachings is worth quoting at length:

> "This," said Miss Noel, bringing a stinging palm down on the textbook she was carrying, "Is progress! Only when these words have shown you the truth and you have learned to think for yourselves will there be true progress!"
>
> Mang Fausto thrust a belligerent face forward. "Why should Don Saturnino own the Land we till—because by an accident of fate he inherited it from his father? With all his wealth and Texas cocks he cannot make a single stalk of sugar cane grow! It is our sweat That has watered the furrows. . . ."
>
> "Don Saturnino has more than he needs—we do not even own the soil in our flowerpots!"
>
> "Or perhaps," said Tino maliciously, "you have finally met your match and here is a savior whose way of life has more meat than the pulp of your books?"
>
> Pale with anger the schoolteacher wheeled upon Tino and struck him full across the mouth. (Cordero-Fernando, "A Harvest of Humble Folk," 143)

Miss Noel's belief in the power of education and in the lone individual as an agent of amelioration cannot address the systemic inequalities of neocolonialism and tenantry; neocolonial tutelage fails to produce the pedagogical subject envisioned by colonial educators. Unable to provide answers or do more than critique the villagers' affinity for Lazaro's teachings, Miss Noel— significantly referred to here through her generic appellation, "the schoolteacher"—can only silence the agitated peasant student and rob him of speech. The confrontation foregrounds the failure of education tethered to Western knowledge and of neocolonial ameliorative schemes to address the needs of the common folk. Here Cordero-Fernando's depiction of Miss Noel as earnest about imparting knowledge, yet ultimately of little use to the masses, resembles Maximo Kalaw's representation of American colonial education in his sententious novel *The Filipino Rebel*. Although teachers such as Kalaw's Mr. and Mrs. Walter are apotheosized as answering "the call to duty" and coming with "the loftiest ideals to help uplift the Filipino people," the revolutionary Don Pedro finds that the poor Fernando who has attended school and studied English for two years cannot perform basic business transactions (Kalaw, *The Filipino Rebel*, 92, 164–165). Miss Noel's students are shown to be similarly unaffected by their schooling. Thus, even though the story ends with Miss Noel bravely conducting her class, the actual lesson is a "weary recitation" of Christina Rossetti's "Who Has Seen the Wind?" Ending the story with a stanza from the poem wearily recited by students suggests the irrelevance of colonial knowledge while simultaneously suggesting its very ubiquity.

In delineating the rupture between neocolonial schooling, albeit carried out by well-intentioned teachers, and the systemic inequalities that rule the lives of the peasants, "Harvest" questions the viability of the tutelary project as a means of progress while also crudely condemning Marxism as an emancipatory narrative. The affirmation of the lives of the peasants comes, as it does in the works of Bulosan (discussed later), in the nonteleological resources of folklore and kinship that here are destroyed by the Marxist teachings of Lazaro. It is only extradiegetically that the story points to revolutionary, anticolonial possibilities. Cordero-Fernando sets the story in Pugad Lawin, the site recognized as the beginning of the Philippine revolution against the Spanish, when Andrés Bonifacio incited people to tear up their *cedulas* (tax certificates), thus declaring their independence from Spain. The very space of the community thus points to the potential of revolution even if it is currently dormant. At present, however, the *barrio* is the site of neocolonial pacification.

Both Tiempo and Cordero-Fernando register the legacy of colonial tutelage through their English instructors steeped in Anglo-American culture, albeit with somewhat different reckonings. Cordero-Fernando's ambivalence about the colonial schooling project is evident in her characterization of Miss Noel, who is both admirable in her efforts to teach the folk and misdirected in imagining herself a heroic figure bringing knowledge to an ignorant populace—indeed, a veritable Thomasite mimic. Tiempo's educators, steeped in Anglo-American culture, are introspective characters who emanate disorder and turmoil and produce schooling as a site of postcolonial difference. Yet both writers ultimately chart the failure of the tutelary project, Tiempo through her tormented and feckless educators, and Cordero-Fernando with the bankruptcy of schooling and neocolonial educators to deal with the needs of the masses. In not charting absolute emancipatory alternatives to the myth of Anglo-American knowledge as a source of transformation, both writers register the stranglehold of colonialism's culture and express the disappointment of the postcolonial nation. Indeed, in the tutelary present of Tiempo and Cordero-Fernando, the colonial and postcolonial are so enmeshed that the appellation "America" itself does not appear in these stories. In the works of Bulosan, Santos, and Linmark, by contrast, the dialectic with colonial schooling is more clearly emphasized, and the struggle to overcome colonial tutelage and offer different forms of cultural memory and community as alternative visions becomes central in marking the subjectivities of Filipinos and Filipino Americans.

4

Articulations of Decolonial Thinking and Collective Subjectivity in Bulosan, Santos, and Linmark

While Edith Tiempo and Gilda Cordero-Fernando focus largely on neocolonial subjectification and use satire and near-dark humor to mock their (post)colonial educators and educational structures, Carlos Bulosan, Bienvenido Santos, and R. Zamora Linmark, writers who have been received as Asian American and Filipino and have had a wide reception in both the Philippines and the United States, engage more sustained polemics with American colonial tutelage. These three writers are positioned very differently in relation to the colonial educational apparatus. Bulosan was schooled in the American colonial system in the Philippines but spent his adult writing career in the United States; Santos first came to the United States as a *pensionado*, a scheme arguably tailored to create mimic men to administer the archipelago, and he continued traveling, teaching, and writing in the Philippines and became a U.S. citizen; Linmark, born in postcolonial Manila, pursued his college degree in Hawaiʻi and divides his time between Honolulu and Manila. Despite these differences, a comparative reading of their respective works lays bare the continued material and ideological force of American tutelage. Writing almost three generations apart, Bulosan and Linmark explore the possibilities of epistemologies and ontologies that offer alternatives to the discourses of colonial schooling and articulate possibilities of creating new collective subjects. By contrast, Santos—in his critique of Filipinos as ideal pedagogical subjects—uses a dystopian estrangement to show how American tutelage severs neocolonial subjects from collectivity and critical consciousness.

I begin this chapter with an analysis of Carlos Bulosan's works. In his short stories "My Mother's Boarders" and "The Education of My Father," in the collection *The Laughter of My Father*, Bulosan undermines the opposition between the literate colonial/elite and the untutored native/peasant by upstaging the status of schoolteachers. In doing so, he destabilizes the teleological narrative of progressive modernity by positing the world of folklore and communal spaces as sites for subaltern resistance. I correspondingly argue that *America Is in the Heart* (1943) charts the movement from a transcendent narrative of socialism to a decolonial mode of thinking (from Filipino subaltern spaces) that renders Filipino Marxism irreducible to a universalist Marxism. I turn next to Bienvenido Santos, whose negotiation of U.S. imperialism and pedagogical subjectivity assumes the registers of a melancholic sensibility. Colonial tutelage produces the conditions under which melancholia flourishes. Santos's *The Volcano* (1965) features the figure of the native who aspires to American assimilation; as the text progresses, this figure transforms into a melancholic mimic subject whose incorporation of colonial pedagogy presages psychic loss, a lack of critical consciousness, and separation from the community. Similarly, in his short story "The Excursionists," Santos explores the native desire to reject the colonial pedagogy that has been forced on Filipinos under the guise of benevolence; as significant, Santos also demonstrates the dilemma of the elite for whom this education brings cultural, social, and economic capital but estrangement from autochthonous forms of collectivity. The chapter concludes with R. Zamora Linmark's *Leche* (2011), a post-postmodern novel that narrates an immigrant Filipino American youth's search for home and identity through a return to the Philippines. *Leche* asks what the legacy of colonial tutelage means in a world connected through circuits of popular culture, consumption, and mobile labor yet striated through neocolonial and militarized power relations. Through a novel that is disjunctive, nonlinear, and multidirectional in its approach to historical memory, Linmark proposes material and discursive forms of unlearning colonial tutelage, decolonizing, and queer collectivity, even as the novel suggests that these are constrained by the diasporic subject's inevitable investment in neocolonial class and culture relations.

Alternative Epistemologies of the Folk and Filipino Labor in Bulosan

Between 1936 and 1938, as he lay in bed at Los Angeles General Hospital recuperating from tuberculosis and kidney problems and educating himself through voracious reading, Carlos Bulosan started writing comic-satiric short stories that would form the collection *The Laughter of My Father* in 1944. Two years later, Bulosan published *America Is in the Heart*, a work that established his literary reputation and occupies a canonical position in Asian American studies. A product of American colonial schooling at a time when Filipinos such as Camilo Osias had begun to occupy high posts within the educational apparatus and were tacitly working with, even as they questioned, aspects of colonial education, Bulosan was well situated to understand the importance of the Filipino pedagogical subject and the project of tutelary colonialism.

The narrative of uplifting Filipinos through education, the project of humanitarian imperialism, had a hegemonic force particularly for the peasantry because it promised, and sometimes provided, social and material betterment, even though that was out of reach for most of them. For Bulosan the Marxist, the narrative of emancipation through colonial education might have seemed to resolve the enduring contradiction between the peasantry and the elite. But for Bulosan the Filipino (Marxist), such a narrative was, in the end, politically limited. Such limitations are evident in *The Laughter of My Father*, the posthumously published *The Philippines Is in the Heart* (1978), and *America Is in the Heart*; despite the distinctiveness of each project (in genre, publication date, and reception history), the question of American schooling remains constant. This emphasis on American schooling in the Philippines makes less stable Bulosan's position as an immigrant writer, a position most scholars (whether dealing with his accounts of racial exclusion, his problematic gendering, or his solidarity work) have assumed.[1] Bulosan has thus been wrenched from colonial history. However, as E. San Juan rightly avers, Bulosan was very much an anticolonial, postcolonial author whose work indefatigably engaged the "power of the negative" in the archive of Western knowledge, questioning its legitimacy ("Introduction," 40).

Such a "power of the negative" is very much tied to a collective resistance to U.S. imperialism and a critique of the contemporary colonial educational system. The postcolonial Bulosan, questioning the legitimacy of Western knowledge through the magical-real world of folklore and subaltern spaces that challenge the rationalist order of colonial tutelage is clearly evident in *The Laughter of My Father*.[2] "My Mother's Boarders" and "The Education of My Father" are characterized by a strategic use of folk humor that simultaneously upstages the status of schoolteachers and blurs the boundaries between colonial (tutelary) and subaltern spaces. To situate the teachers as objects of ridicule undermines a teleological notion of Philippine "progress"; it also renders less credible a reading of institutionalized education as a means of uplift, a viable source of enlightenment, or a fundamental dimension of upward mobility.

Expressly, the stories in *The Laughter of My Father* are organized around trickster peasant figures whose cunning and native ingenuity outwit those who actively facilitate the colonial administration—namely, landlords, the elite, and government functionaries. Even though Bulosan claimed to have no knowledge of Philippine folklore, his use of folklore and peasant ways to articulate subaltern resistance has been noted by many critics (Roseburg, 17; Grow, "The Laughter of My Father"; San Juan, *The Philippine Temptation*, 119). But while these generalized appraisals of the subversive use of folklore are useful, I maintain that this subversion, necessarily fixed to a historically specific moment of U.S. colonial rule, delivers a complex indictment of colonialism and its project of schooling. As historians have noted, the 1920s were a period of retrenchment from the promises of imminent independence made before World War I. The Woods-Forbes report of 1921 had diagnosed a failure of public health projects, a corrupt judiciary, and irresponsible banking resulting from the policy of Filipinization. On the basis of the report, Leonard Woods, the governor-general of the Philippines, urged greater Americanization and a postponement of independence (Kramer, 388–389). Filipinos, it seemed, still needed American tutelage. In contrast, Bulosan's stories set after World War I, when the grand experiment of schooling had had almost two decades to establish itself, suggest the ineffectiveness of colonial education.

Bulosan challenges the American project of schooling by deploying a familiar figure from Filipino folklore: Juan Tamad, the comic, proverbially lazy boy who finds ingenious ways to avoid work. The Juan Tamad figure of Father as illiterate and perennially slothful, yet with a cunning that enables him to outfox the educated elite, allows Bulosan to satirically challenge the value of literacy and question the temporal narrative of betterment through colonial schooling.[3] The stories engage with and contest colonial tutelage by interrogating the binaries of teacher-pupil, learned-unlearned, and order-disorder by working through pivotal scenes in which literacy has dubious value and subaltern spaces interrogate the order of the school. The illiterate Father is able to sell his carabao by simply marking legal documents ("The Soldiers Came Marching"); repel onslaughts by his avaricious neighbors, who use their literacy to cheat peasants ("The Tree of My Father"); and even open a school of music ("The Wisdom of Uncle Santor").[4] However, although many stories question the value of literacy, "My Mother's Boarders" and "The Education of My Father" center on schooling as a technology of governance.

The plots of both stories are deceptively simple. In "My Mother's Boarders," a gendered narrative of desire, attraction, and repulsion, three female teachers from the city, who have recently been hired to teach in the new village school, come to board in the narrator's house. Although disliked by the villagers because of their sexual promiscuity, they are housed by Mother, who needs their money to buy a mourning cloak. Eventually, they so corrupt the morals of the town with their drinking, dancing, and lewd clothing that the elders decide to evict them. The story stands as an allegory of cultural debasement brought about by mimicking American mores. In "The Education of My Father," the principal, Mr. Occo, recruits Father to ring the bell at school in exchange for educating the young narrator. Father agrees, using a trumpet instead of a bell, and continues to play music sporadically all day. Meanwhile, the narrator spends his time teaching a delighted Mr. Occo card tricks and never acquires literacy. The story ends in confusion as the district superintendent of schools, aghast at Mr. Occo's gambling, comes to reprimand the teachers, at which point Father's trumpet playing, mistaken as a fire alarm, causes a stampede. The district superintendent, furious at being disrespected and injured in the commotion, fires Mr. Occo, who subsequently becomes a professional gambler.

Both stories interrogate colonial tutelary oppositions of discipline and disorder, learning and ignorance, civilization and savagery. "My Mother's Boarders" begins with a description of the disarray of the narrator's provincial town that matches the classic naturalism of works such as Michael Gold's *Jews without Money*. The life of the community is disrupted from the outside when soldiers come home from a war and "produce[d] children left and right. ... The children grew rapidly and stayed in the street, in the way of carts and other vehicles, like their fathers who stayed out most of the night" (Bulosan, *The Laughter of My Father*, 14). Significantly, the town is composed of "tribals," so named via an in-text reference to the rural town council. It is these tribals, deemed primitive by the colonial government, who now decide how to regulate the disarray brought about by colonial recruits. This rural council body does so in mimic fashion, establishing a new school for the children of the soldiers by hiring three teachers from the city. Bulosan makes clear the class and cultural differences between the Americanized city teachers and the tribals. The teachers, immodest in their gender presentation, overtly displaying their sexuality, strut around with their "bobbed hair, painted lips and cheeks ... wearing short skirts [and] tight fitting blouses and sweaters" as the townswomen look away or spit contemptuously when the teachers are out of sight (Bulosan, *The Laughter of My Father*, 14).

What ensues is a comic satire on colonial miseducation, the order of the school, and the temporal narrative of uplift exemplified through the school. Father is both enamored of the school, with its promise of literacy and upward mobility, and irreverent of it as institution. Having tricked school officials into enrolling his son, the picaro figure of Father, a virtual Pied Piper, upsets the regimen of the school by not accepting its boundaries. He coarsens the urbane world of the teachers by introducing an earthly masculinity—dancing with them while reeking of onions; his refusal of work challenges the discipline of capitalist modernity; and his actions dramatize a defiance of the spatial order of the school. Humorously enacting the colonial argument that problems in the Philippines would be solved if Americans dealt "with natives of mature years as they would deal at home with school-boys" (Becker, 745), Father invades the space of the classroom as he sits in the back, mischievously attempting to distract the teachers. On the playground he attracts the attention of children as he marches in his old military uniform. Told by the principal to leave the premises of the school, he stands at the fence and successfully commands the students to follow his orders to march as he renders porous the boundaries of the school. In turn, the education of the students by the teachers is comically registered as a corruption of sexual mores rather than learning. The teachers give the youth lessons in dancing to jazz music, ironically succeeding in this part of tutelary colonialism, as the natives respond well to it; however, this Americanization leads to a degeneration, including flirtatious behavior that debases the youth, who become "loose with their morals" (Bulosan, *The Laughter of My Father*, 19), until the town elders are compelled to oust the teachers. Colonial education has succeeded in its stratagem but not its results. Indeed, Bulosan uses the language that Americans had used to racialize Filipinos to describe the teachers in their frenzied dancing as "monkeys."

Yet the story is not simply a comic inversion of the paradigms of tutelary colonialism. The vernacular world of Bulosan's story is at once the self-contained and autonomous realm of peasant culture described by subaltern studies scholars (Guha, 13), one that can withstand the onslaughts of the colonial modernity and that engages with the history of American colonialism. The occasion for the story is one that Bulosan turned to several times in his fiction: the return of Filipino soldiers from World War I. *America Is in the Heart* opens with Allos's brother, Leon, coming home from the war; "The Day the Soldier's Came" registers the loss of local soldiers as a massive disruption that shatters the narrator's childhood.[5] World War I had occasioned an intense outpouring of loyalty from Filipinos, with Manuel Quezon offering 25,000 Filipino soldiers (to be called the Philippine National Guard) as proof of the colony's loyalty. In his book advocating self-government for the Philippines, Maximo Kalaw wrote, "No greater proof can be found of the success of America's policy in the Philippines than the loyalty and friendship the Filipino people have shown her during the great war" (*Self-Government in the Philippines*, 59). Hopes for a speedy independence to the Philippines were, however, quashed as the war rendered matters in the colony less significant. Meanwhile, the Philippine National Guard, although mobilized, was called to service only on Armistice Day and never left the islands.

Bulosan imaginatively transforms this history not by challenging the narrative of Filipino loyalty—indeed, in Bulosan's stories the soldiers "demonstrate" their loyalty by going to war—but by subtly contesting this narrative as a celebration of Filipinos as colonial American subjects. The soldiers who come back from the war in "My Mother's Boarders" are fornicators and drunks who "produce children left and right . . . shouting out loud at the presidencia and laughing hysterically at the wine store across from the church" (Bulosan, *The Laughter of My Father*, 14), thus necessitating the discipline of a new school for their wayward children. Two decades after U.S. colonial rule, both the military as an apparatus of domination and the school as hegemonic apparatus fail hysterically. Contesting the temporal narrative of progress, Bulosan has Father, who disrupts the order of the school and lures the students to march to his instructions, wear emblems of the Spanish-American War, a war that preceded American colonization. Between the two wars is, of course, the Philippine-American War and the beginning of U.S. colonialism, which Bulosan never explicitly names in his works but is always the absent present, or the Real.

"The Education of My Father" is a multilevel satire of the school as disciplinary apparatus. It contests the claim of the colonial school to civilize and teach; it questions the specific movements toward industrial education that had gained traction by the 1920s; and it interrogates the tutelary narrative of racial difference and progress. Bulosan evokes the contradiction between the discipline of the school and the world of the peasantry by beginning the story with Father agreeing to play his trumpet to mark the timed divisions of the school day; however, the narrative moves forward through events that demonstrate that Father's subjection into modernity is at best superficial and fails to render Father or the narrator as docile bodies that can be subjected or transformed.[6] The communal spaces of the cockpit and gamblers and the magic of Father's music prevail over the temporal and spatial order of the school.

The story begins with Mr. Occo, the principal, undertaking the project of educating the narrator if Lacay Simeon, the Father, will play the trumpet to mark the beginning, middle, and end of the school day. He says to the mother, "If your husband takes the job, I'll attend to the education of this boy personally. He looks like an Igorot, but I'll make a gentleman out of him" (Bulosan, *The Laughter of My Father*, 135). The promise of "book learning" the mother desires is one of social and class mobility. "See to it that he'll learn to write his name," the mother orders (Bulosan, *The Laughter of My Father*, 136). The narrator is not actually an Igorot, but Bulosan emphasizes that he looks like one to highlight the gap between the boy and the privileged principal, the ostensible functionary of the colonial order who promises to uplift not just the peasant boy but, as Joel Slotkin points out, a boy who "straddles the boundaries between peasant and Igorot" (Slotkin, 862).[7]

Bulosan's use of the Igorotized narrator with the potential to acquire literacy and learn English (which is revealed to be the language of the school) is particularly significant. As discussed in Chapter 3, when the young Camilo Osias had pleaded for independence, he did so by reassuring Americans that their pedagogical subjects were Christian and Malay and not savage Igorots. If the most controversial display of the St. Louis World's Fair of 1904 was the Igorot exhibit that, Filipino intellectuals argued, demeaned them, the most visible symbol of educational uplift was Antero, the English-speaking Igorot. Part of a group of people from the Igorot village who were taught English by Leonora P. Vandaveer, a stenographer at the Igorot village, Antero was interviewed by officials from the Department of Education and continued to be an object of wonder years after the World's Fair had closed. He was part of the Lewis and Clark Centennial and American Pacific Exposition in 1905 and the Panama-Pacific International Exposition in 1915, where, like the Igorots in 1904, he was measured by anthropologists from the University of California, Berkeley (Fermin, 177, 187). Whether or not Bulosan was familiar with Antero's history is beside the point. What is important is that he deliberately evokes an Igorot-"like" narrator to engage with the narrative of uplift at its most triumphant—the ability to educate the most "savage" of tribes.

In "The Education of My Father," however, the Igorot-like boy never acquires literacy because instead of being the ideal pedagogical subject, he teaches the principal gambling tricks. Through language that moves from magical to real, Bulosan associates the narrator with the subaltern world of his peasant father: "He could not believe what he saw on the table. The cards danced and leaped invisibly between my fingers" (*The Laughter of My Father*, 135). Instead of the Igorot-like boy being subject to the colonial order of the school, the principal is lured to the subaltern world of the cockpit and gambling. While many Americans saw cockfighting as evidence of Filipino primitivism and wondered how a people playing such a barbarous sport could govern themselves, Mr. Occo constantly takes his student to the cockpit.[8] "Let's go to the cockpit, son," says Occo, "We've got to win, with some of your tricks" (Bulosan, *The Laughter of My Father*, 138). Mr. Occo blurs the boundaries between the communal world of the cockpit and the neocolonial order of the school by using his office to learn card tricks from the narrator.

Not only does the illiterate Igorot teach the principal; Father once again disrupts the order of the school. Called on to mark the order of the school day and the colonial order by playing the national hymn when the flags of the United States and the Philippines are raised, Father negotiates the encounter between the world of the peasantry and that of tutelage and colonial modernity. Bulosan represents this encounter as a comic breakdown of colonial authority, albeit brought about unwittingly through a figure belonging to a world of spontaneity and instinct and hence outside ideological critique. Although Father follows his regulatory job, his obstinate and continual trumpet playing beyond the boundary of the school, blurring work and nonwork, beguiles the students away from their learning. By contrast, the district superintendent of schools who comes to chastise Mr. Occo for his negligence is himself weak, ineffectual, and unmanly, "a small man with a wooden leg" (Bulosan, *The Laughter of My Father*, 138). As the superintendent pounds on the tables, significantly speaking English as he delivers his harangue to the teachers, he is literally castrated as his prosthetic leg gets stuck in the bamboo floor and detaches. The students and teachers rush out, erroneously imagining a fire when they hear Father playing "Reveille." Inverting the gender dynamics of colonialism, a vibrant collective world of disorderly peasant masculinity reigns over an anxious, demasculinized colonial order.

Yet this comic incident also engages with American educational experiments with industrial education that had been used to deal with Native Americans and African Americans following the Tuskegee model. Father's prodigious musical abilities are central to the story. He flawlessly plays Schubert's "Ave Maria," "Serenade," Sibellius's "Finlandia," "Reveille," and the National Hymn. An undisciplined figure, he wanders from one classroom to another, sitting at the back, entranced with the teachers: "He went home with enchanted eyes" (Bulosan, *The Laughter of My Father*, 136). It is significant that only once do we learn what is taught at the school: when the narrator's brother, Berto, recognizes the tune his father is playing as "Ave Maria" because he has heard it in the classroom. Bulosan's decision to endow Father with an aesthetic sense that transcends literacy both speaks to the limits of colonial uplift and engages with the paternalistic conviction of American educators that industrial education was of paramount importance in the Philippines and that the school system needed to be organized "to promote the material welfare of the country" (*Tenth Annual*, 24). This focus on industrial education was also a model in which schools were seen as producing goods appropriate to the colonized nation.[9] In defiance on the emphasis on practicality, Bulosan emphasizes the aesthetic and immaterial in what Father knows and has learned.

In both stories, the colonial order is challenged—in the first through the teachers, the mimic women, who are unstable neocolonial representatives, and in both through Father, who transgresses the spatial and cultural order of the school. E. San Juan suggests that the stories in *Laughter* depict the "life-world of plebian rebels and outcasts, outlawed subalterns who [bear] the stigmata of inhabitants from a dependent economy" ("Introduction," 7). But to pose Gayatri Chakravorty Spivak's question: how does the subaltern peasant paradoxically represented through signifiers of aestheticism, speak in the story? I suggest that Bulosan, acutely aware of the problems of subaltern representation, chooses to have his peasant characters "speak" in ways that are nondiscursive and with effects that are not always clear. Father speaks not only through his music (in ways that the principal, who blows into the trumpet but emits only a cracked sound, cannot) but also through his body, his "enchanted eyes," which learn what the school cannot teach. The Igorot-like narrator speaks through his magical card tricks.

But while both stories demonstrate the power of everyday subaltern acts to resist the peasants' becoming normalized pedagogical subjects, they also leave undetermined the nature of their challenge to colonial modernity. After all, the mother in "My Mother's Boarders" is a shrewd capitalist who takes in the teachers to make money to buy her mourning cloak. Reflecting the hypocrisy of the civilizing project, she pretends a righteousness about the morality of the teachers that belies her own business dealings with them. Mimicry in this case challenges the symbolic bearers of colonialism in the realm of culture but also, paradoxically, enacts a capitalism from below. Her shrewd business is a conscious subversion, as well as a use, of capitalist modernity. Father lures the students away from the school wearing a tattered uniform of the Spanish-American War, reflecting his disconnection from historical consciousness but also Bulosan's willed erasure of the Philippine-American War. Father's professionally played music that disrupts the disciplinary apparatus of colonial schooling is a critique of the paternalistic conviction of many American educators that industrial education was the model for the Philippines, but the militaristic tunes played by Father also point to his enchantment with the very disciplinary technologies that his comic actions undermine. Bulosan's stories thus point to the resources as well as the limits of everyday, often nonrational forms of communal resistance.

In *America Is in the Heart*, Bulosan discards the roguish Juan Tamad Father and the magical, carnivalesque imaginary of the folk for the angry figure of Allos and the naturalistic world of the Filipino peasant and the migrant worker on the West Coast. But while the short stories in *Laughter* attest to the hegemonic appeal of schooling while simultaneously rendering colonial schooling ineffectual, *America Is in the Heart* seems to valorize the promise of education even as it presents a severe indictment of the actual workings of the colonial system. Bulosan resurrects the figure of the lone artist in search of knowledge (after all, one of his mentors, Alice Odell, reads aloud to Carlos the classic American Kunstlerroman: Thomas Wolfe's *Look Homeward Angel*), but insofar as the knowledge Bulosan needs has to be commensurate with the hopes and aspirations of colonized Filipinos, it is a dialectically generated decolonial knowledge, emerging from the experiences of Filipinos. This knowledge is a contrast to the colonial project of mapping, charting, and quantifying, as well as to a linear, teleological Marxism, and constantly resists completion.

Part one of the text, set in the rural Philippines, where schools were beginning to make inroads, demonstrates the infiltration of schooling into the life of the community, the alienation it fosters, and the harsh toll it takes on the peasants, even as they are beguiled by the promise of tutelage. *America Is in the Heart* begins with a denunciation of education appropriate to elite ends. It is "men with ample education" who exploit the movement for national independence "to their own advantage" (Bulosan, *America is in the Heart*, 5). As opposed to this elite education is the American democratic promise of education for all. As the narrator summarizes, "Popular education was spreading throughout the archipelago and this opened up new opportunities. It was a new and democratic system brought by the American government into the Philippines, and a nation hitherto illiterate and backward was beginning to awaken" (Bulosan, *America Is in the Heart*, 14). Here Bulosan explicitly uses the rhetoric of benevolent tutelage to justify the colonial occupation of the Philippines but places it squarely within a depiction of a system that extracts payments from the peasantry as harsh as that of *caciquismo*. As Allos painfully recollects in the very next paragraph, "We had free education, but the school was in Lingayen. . . . Going to school in Lingayen, in those predatory years, took plenty of money. . . . My father sold one hectare of our land and gave the money to my brother Macario. Then we worked even harder on the farm" (Bulosan, *America Is in the Heart*, 14). Indeed, Macario's relationship to the family is represented as almost usurious: "We had deprived ourselves of any form of leisure and simple luxury so that my brother could finish high school. But even then he kept asking for more money, threatening that he would stop if we did not send him enough. The thought that he would really stop terrified us" (Bulosan, *America Is in the Heart*, 14). The family sells the last hectare of land to enable Macario to finish his education, but Macario's subsequent job as a schoolteacher fails to help the family regain its land.

Although the idea of school is invested with promise, the narrator's personal experiences with the school suggest that it is a site that reinforces race and class hierarchies. As in "The Education of My Father," the narrator is Igorotized, but here his appearance provokes racial abjection. As a child, the narrator undergoes the taunting of other schoolchildren when, for a short period, he enters a school three miles away from his home and his poor, unkempt appearance racializes him as Igorot and subjects him to ridicule: "The other children taunted me in the school yard and threw stones at me, laughing at my long hair and bare feet" (Bulosan, *America Is in the Heart*, 48). While this incident draws attention to the contempt of the villagers toward Igorots, it also demonstrates that the school, as a technology of governance, reproduces colonial racial hierarchies. The narrator's second chance for formal schooling comes in the village of Lingayen, where he goes to work with fishermen. Bulosan's rendition of this experience is central to understanding the text's critique of the tutelary system and demonstrates how the institution of the American school stands as a synecdoche for a colonial order benefiting the elite, a corrupt system worth only maneuvering to one's ends. The incident is worth considering in detail:

> My cousin's English teacher was a man who had been in America. He wore American shoes and clothes, and came to class smoking a pipe. He sat on a small chair which he tilted backward, putting his feet on the table so that we could see his silk socks.... There he wrote out a credit card which made it appear that I had been going to school regularly for two years, graduating from one grade to another with excellent marks. "These fat sons and soft daughters of the sons-of-bitches think they are smart," he used to say to me, referring to the children of the crooked politicians and land grabbers in Pangasinan.... "I will show them!"'... It seemed that he had gone to America as a boy, had worked as a houseboy, and in fifteen years had finished his course. His parents were poor peasants; they had died by the time he returned to the Philippines.... Instead of using his experience as an inspiring example to other peasant children, he had turned inward and used it as a weapon of revenge.... But he was kind and considerate to me. When a general intelligence test was given to all the students, he gave me a copy of the examination paper in advance.... There were one hundred thirty questions and I had correctly answered one hundred twenty-seven in thirty minutes.... My fame spread far and wide. I saw my teacher regularly and we had fun laughing at the joke that we had played on the school. (Bulosan, *America Is in the Heart*, 83–84)

The schoolteacher, the former peasant, is uplifted from his condition of poverty and ignorance not into humanist knowledge, the justification for American colonization of the Philippines, but into a superficial adoption of American class signifiers—the pipe and silk socks. His education in the United States, acquired under the racial system of colonial occupation through an unfair extraction of labor, comes, as Macario's does earlier, at enormous cost to the family. With his new status, the schoolteacher challenges the elite by refusing them privilege but maneuvering the system to benefit the young Allos. Schooling can thus promise class mobility for the narrator, but only when the system is cannily rigged to benefit him. The teacher, a resistant subaltern, is the unruly pedagogical subject who refuses the rhetoric of uplift; he participates in the system of colonial tutelage only by cynically manipulating it and thus refusing absorption into an American colonial order he views as equally corrupt as that of the landed elite.

Yet the status conferred by being part of the system of institutionalized education proves illusory at best. As a national (but not a citizen), Macario is able to go to the United States, but despite his education, gained at enormous cost to the family, he is able to find work only as a cook and houseboy. The colonial status of Filipino education is made evident in the statement by the lady of the house, who explains to one of her guests, "'He is an educated servant.... He was a schoolteacher in the Philippines. And he went to college here'" (Bulosan, *America Is in the Heart*, 140–141). Even climbing the ladder within the system of colonial education does little to ensure dignity or quality, and distinguished educators visiting the United States are treated no better than colonial exhibits performing for their fellow American educators. As the narrator describes it:

> The party was held at the back of a restaurant on First Street; only men were invited because it would be *primitive*. When we were seated at the table, I noticed that there was no silverware. Then I understood what was meant by *primitive*, which was, of course, to eat with bare hands.... The prominent educator put on his ribboned glasses and began balling the steaming rice with his hand.... He told brilliant anecdotes . . . recalling his youth with the poor peasants of Luzon where, it seemed, he had learned to eat rice with bare hands. (Bulosan, *America Is in the Heart*, 306)

Through incidents that expose the poverty of the institution of schooling, Bulosan questions the justification of empire based on what was propounded as the unique American experiment in education. What Bulosan does not repudiate in *America Is in the Heart* is the liberatory potential of education. Unlike the stories in *Laughter*, which celebrate the loafing figure of Father and the world of the cockpit over the world of learning, America reveres the possibilities of book learning despite the indictment of the actual system of schooling. In the only reading of *America Is in the Heart* as a text concerned with the tutelary project in the Philippines, Meg Wesling writes, "It is precisely because the text vacillates between a valorization of the institutionalized, formal education used to justify the imperialist occupation of the Philippines on the one hand, and the challenges Carlos faces living within the racist logic of that occupation on the other, that the reader is forced to confront the contradiction between these two paradigms and acknowledge the hollowness of liberal humanist justifications behind the occupation of the Philippines" (159). Although Wesling's analysis fruitfully brings Bulosan's classic text within the ambit of empire studies, and specifically within colonial tutelage, it does not distinguish between the peasants' reverence for formal education as a means of social mobility and Carlos the writer and organic intellectual's search for a decolonial knowledge as a possible means of liberation. This contrast is evident once *America Is in the Heart* is read alongside the stories in *Laughter*, where the peasants' veneration of formal education is both registered and subjected to disdain. But the decolonial knowledge that Bulosan seeks, a knowledge different from formal education, is adumbrated only in the longer work.

U.S. educators well into the late 1920s viewed schooling in the Philippines as an evolutionary racial project, the purpose of which was to "integrate native and minority peoples into a new social and economic order" (Cook, 571). As discussed in Chapter 2, the Monroe Report of 1925 advocated teaching Filipinos models of individualism and property that they lacked. Bulosan, however, searches for a knowledge for Filipino workers integrally woven into the needs of the community. Carlos looks for literary forebears from whom he can fashion what Frantz Fanon termed a "fighting literature, a revolutionary literature," in which the native, "after having tried to lose himself in the people and with the people, will on the contrary shake the people" (*The Wretched of the Earth*, 222–223). In the vast panoply of poets and novelists from whom he seeks inspiration, he turns repeatedly to figures such as José Rizal, Walt Whitman, and Hart Crane, who saw themselves as writing epics for a people. For Carlos, the learning of English is a path toward producing a fighting literature. "They can't silence me anymore! I'll tell the world what they have done to me!" exclaims Carlos when he gains fluency in English (Bulosan, *America Is in the Heart*, 180). His end is to use the knowledge culled from literary figures and Marxist writings to liberate the peasants from poverty and reveal "the philistinism of educated Filipinos and the petty bourgeoisie, and the arrogance of officials of the Philippine government in Washington" (Bulosan, *America Is in the Heart*, 243). Indeed, Carlos figures his writing as battle. As he starts to write poems, he feels he can "fight the world now with [his] mind. . . . My weapon could not be taken away from me anymore" (Bulosan, *America Is in the Heart*, 224).

What Bulosan idealizes in his reading and writing is thus not learning as a means of rising from peasantry to individualism through the world of capitalist modernity ushered in by colonialism but, rather, radical learning to unite the working classes. It is for this reason that San Juan rightly sees *America Is in the Heart* as a collective autobiography and as a "popular-front allegory that articulates class, race, nation (ethnicity), and gender in a protean configuration" ("Introduction," 12).¹⁰ *America Is in the Heart* dramatizes the incomplete project of formulating what Walter Mignolo, following Anibal Quijano, explains as decolonial thinking, a "geo and body politics of knowledge," "epistemic embodiments [both] geo historical and body graphical" that emerge from the Other of modernity and coloniality ("Delinking," 269, 282). The Other of modernity can be seen in the struggles of the Filipino peasantry, the memories of Binalonan, cast in woman's time, and the lives of Filipino immigrants whose "body graphical" speaks the logic of colonial racial difference (San Juan, "Introduction," 13). The text speaks subalternity through the bodies of Filipinos hurtled in trains, huddled in the cold, crowded in dance halls, sleeping dozens to a small room, hunted by police. What the narrator struggles with is his desire for a universalist Marxist narrative that connects, for instance, the labor-ridden, rough hands of Marian to those of his mother in Binalonan and the constant fracturing of this narrative with the irruptions of racial difference that refuse encapsulation in the narrative of class.

Filipinos arrive on a ship like the cargo of middle passage, "sold for five dollars each to work in the fish canneries in Alaska" (Bulosan, *America Is in the Heart*, 101).¹¹ Faced with the constant violence and prejudice against Filipinos that the narrator strives desperately to stave off from affecting him, the narrator is introduced to the world of labor solidarity as he works for the socialist, Pascual. However, it is Jose, an organizer of a union of Filipino laborers who questions the undifferentiated subject of Marxism. As he explains to Carlos, "This is a war between labor and capital. To our people, however, it is something else. It is an assertion of our right to be human beings again. . . . He began to tell me the story of his life, which was similar to mine" (Bulosan, *America Is in the Heart*, 186). Yet it is through the realization of a common class oppression between him and Alice Odell, the daughter of a poor farmer who "directs [his] education' (Bulosan, *America Is in the Heart*, 232) and Eileen who continues it, that he discovers the world of Engels, R. Palme Dutt, Lewis Morgan, and Robert Briffault.

Bulosan describes his narrator as having found an absolute knowledge of history as a struggle against tyranny. "I trembled with excitement and a feeling of superiority. Here within my grasp was one of the great discoveries in the life of man" (*America Is in the Heart*, 235). But it is visceral experiences of colonial racism—being denied entry at Los Angeles County Hospital and to rental properties—that push the narrator into the realization that he needs to integrate Philippine folklore and history, the memory of community, into his struggle for liberation. That this constant pattern of the narrator attaining a final knowledge based on labor solidarity that is then fractured by the narrative of colonial racism continues until the end of the text suggests that Bulosan means to call attention to the limits of conventional Marxism, although he is unable, at this juncture, to theorize a modern world system of racial capitalism. Years later Fanon would write, "In the colonies the economic substructure is also a superstructure. The cause is the consequence; you are rich because you are white, you are white because you are rich. That is why Marxist analysis should always be slightly stretched every time we have to do with the colonial problem" (*The Wretched of the Earth*, 40).

America Is in the Heart dramatizes the process of articulating a decolonial knowledge that does not seek to replicate either the totality of Enlightenment humanism or the colonial knowledge project but is constantly changing as it emerges from the embodied material experiences of Filipino laborers. Here it is important to emphasize that the numerous white women who facilitate Carlos's education, and who stand in as figures for the project of tutelage as benevolence rather than the harsh school system that inflicts misery on the narrator's family in Binolan, often replicate a colonial relationship with the narrator that Bulosan implicitly critiques. Indeed, this gendering of benevolent tutelage mirrors the gendered, feminized visual representations of colonial schooling in popular magazines such as *Puck* that supported colonization.[12] Mary Strandon, the daughter of an American soldier in the Spanish-American War who settles in the colony as an artist and a librarian, takes the young Allos under her wing and gives him books to read and access to the library in Baguio. Allos works for her as a cook and houseboy, a little brown brother whose greatest delight is to deliver books to the wealthy. Years later, Carlos inscribes his knowledge on Strandon's archive when he visits Strandon's hometown library in Iowa and donates an autographed copy of his book. For Marian, who donates money toward his education, the narrator is like a household pet. Explaining her desire to help him, Marian explains "I would be happier if I had something to care for—even if it were only a dog or a cat. But it doesn't really matter which it is: a dog or a cat. What matters is the affection, the relationship between you and the object" (Bulosan, *America Is in the Heart*, 212).[13] Significantly, the narrator's relationship with Marian develops after the narrator, having been renamed by comrades in the labor movement, introduces himself for the first time using his deracialized, American name, Carl. Thus, although Carl attempts to interpellate Marian under the category of undifferentiated labor, noting that her rough hands remind him of his mother's in Binalonan, he, even as Carl, continues to be differentiated as household pet. With the Odell sisters Alice and Eileen (modeled on the socialist writer Sanora Babb and her sister Dorothy), both of whom educate him through books, Carl is the infantilized object of care, of Eileen's "maternal solicitude" (Bulosan, *America Is in the Heart*, 234). However, as the narrator recuperates in the hospital, he no longer receives tutelage but turns literary critic, pointing out the crudities of the proletarian writer Laura Clarendorn's novel and advising her to delve more deeply into the lives of Filipinos in the United States. Thus, if at one level *America Is in the Heart* buys into the gendered trope of benevolent tutelage symbolized by the female teacher, the instrument of colonial pacification, it also critiques the trope by spelling out its ideological investments and inverting it.

While it might seem odd to read a work titled *America Is in the Heart* as a text in search of decolonial knowledge because it seems, at crucial moments, to reiterate a narrative of American exceptionalism, it does not rehearse this narrative uncritically or in the service of empire. The most cited apotheosis of American democracy, taken as evidence of Bulosan's faith in American exceptionalism, comes at the end of part two and includes statements such as, "We must live in America where there is freedom for all regardless of color, station and beliefs" (Bulosan, *America Is in the Heart*, 188). It is crucial to remember that the America interpellated here is not, in fact, the nation "America" but a decolonial imagined community of exploited labor and racial minorities "not bound by geographical latitudes" (Bulosan, *America Is in the Heart*, 189), a utopia. It is "in the heart of men that died for freedom; it is also in the eyes of men that are building a new world" (Bulosan, *America Is in the Heart*, 189). This decolonial imaginary can come into being only through the material experiences of the wretched of America who cannot be left unnamed: "We are all that nameless foreigner, that homeless refugee, that hungry boy, that illiterate immigrant and that lynched black body. All of us, from the first Adams, to the last Filipino, native born or alien, educated or illiterate—*We are America!*" (Bulosan, *America Is in the Heart*, 189). But calling for America to live up to its democratic promise is also a critique of hegemony that works through the language of hegemony, asking the society to live up to its promises, a weapon of the weak, as James Scott would put it (*Weapons of the Weak*, 337–338). It is a utopian rhetoric in the tradition of Langston Hughes's "Let America Be America Again" and written, furthermore, in the context of a popular front solidarity against fascism in Europe and Japan.[14]

Yet it is undeniable that the language of exceptional democracy is also the language of American empire and that the grand experiment of colonial schooling in the Philippines was showcased as an example of this unique democracy. In reiterating the idea of America as a metonym for democracy writ large, even if to claim the rights of a democratic subject, Bulosan repeats the language of empire. Perhaps, then, the paeans to America in *America Is in the Heart* ask to be read as both decolonial knowledge and an acknowledgment of the difficulty of decolonizing the mind. Curiously, it has escaped the attention of critics that in the celebrated passage above, Bulosan chooses to distance his authorial voice from the narration. The narrator, in his interpellation as Carl, writes the passages as he remembers them from his former schoolteacher brother, Macario: "His words seized my imagination, so that years afterward I am able to write them almost word for word" (Bulosan, *America Is in the Heart*, 188).

I suggest that Bulosan has Carl ventriloquizing Macario at this juncture to indicate the hegemonic power of American tutelage even as the text has offered a powerful indictment of the system of colonial education and has enunciated a decolonial knowledge for a collectivity rather than knowledge as an individual pursuit. After all, Carlos continues to be tutored by the colonial textbook, remembering close to the end of the text his reading of English primers with Macario, particularly the story of Robinson Crusoe. In all likelihood, the primer was one of the series by the American educator Orlando Scheirer Reimold, who had served as division superintendent of schools in Tarlac Province and returned home to become the eastern manager of the World Book Company, with which the Philippine government entered an exclusive contract in 1908. Reimold's *Second Primary Language Book*, written specifically to teach English to Filipino children and adopted as a required textbook for ten years for grades 3–5, was organized around the figure of Robinson Crusoe, the courageous and industrious shipwrecked survivor who of necessity becomes a builder, carpenter, and potter—a demonstration of self-sufficiency, individualism, and industrial education.[15] But the primer also depicts Friday as grateful and willing servant. Crusoe seems to appear for Carlos, as he did for most of the West, not as slave owner and colonizer but as the lone figure who overcomes adversity through inner resources. However, by including Macario's tutoring of Carlos through the Robinson Crusoe primer at the end of the text, Bulosan encourages us to read the narrator's growth through the difference between this and the very same scene of instruction when Carlos is a child in the Philippines. Whereas in the earlier scene Macario reads Crusoe's story as a blueprint for self-sufficiency in a strange land where Allos might have "nothing to protect you expect your hands and your mind" (Bulosan, *America Is in the Heart*, 32), Macario now chooses to read the story metaphorically and as implicitly not translatable for the narrator: "We are cast upon the sea of life hoping to land somewhere in the world. But there is only one island, and it is in the heart" (Bulosan, *America Is in the Heart*, 313). Instead of the story being a parable of survival, control, and success in a strange land, it suggests that for the raced other there are no hospitable enclaves except in the imagination.

Colonial Knowledge and Melancholic Incorporation in Santos's *The Volcano* and "The Excursionists"

Unlike Bulosan, who was schooled in the American colonial system but spent most of his writing career in the United States, Bienvenido Santos went to the United States first as a *pensionado*, then traveled between the United States and the Philippines and worked within the American and Filipino educational systems. By the time he came of age, the first generation of *pensionados* had already returned to the Philippines and acquired positions of influence in education and politics. As discussed in Chapter 3, Osias was a prime example of the influential *pensionado*-turned-nationalist. Like Bulosan, Santos was a product of colonial education. A precocious student who started writing poems in English when he was ten, Santos was already a published writer by the time he left high school teaching to go to the United States as a *pensionado* in 1941, when the Philippines was a commonwealth. Santos thus joined the *pensionado* program conscious that his education was meant to prepare him to be part of an intellectual elite of a putatively independent country. Unable to return to the Philippines when the United States entered World War II, he became an emissary of the United States and was assigned by the U.S. Office of Special Services to lecture in schools, colleges, and civic and religious clubs, informing largely ignorant audiences about Filipinos and the Philippines (Santos, *Memory's Fictions*, 95). Santos himself attained elite status upon his return to the Philippines in 1946 when he became the vice-president of Legazpi College. Most of his writing career spans the years he spent in the United States—his student years at the University of Iowa Writer's Workshop in 1958; the transit years in the 1960s, when he traveled between the United States and the Philippines; his forcible exile in the United States because of the Marcos regime's banning of his book *The Praying Man*; and the last years of his life in the 1980s and 1990s, when he once again divided his time between the two countries. Santos thus moved from being a colonized subject to becoming a postcolonial elite and then a minority subject in the United States.

Santos was acutely conscious of the colonial implications of being a Filipino writer working only in English. At the symposium "Asian Voices in English," held at the University of Hong Kong in 1990, Santos explained the position of the Filipino writer in English as being that of both a storyteller and a translator thus: "As storyteller, he is our connection with the past, as he hearkens back to an oral tradition and a heritage of songs; as translator he is our link to the future, as he brings his culture forward to new audiences" ("The Filipino Writer in English as Storyteller and Translator," 36). He suggests that the Filipino writing in English is vitally connected to and part of an oral culture of the Philippines, a collective tradition incontrovertibly different from that of (white) America. In contrast to nationalists who decried English as a colonial tool, Santos invented the Filipino writer in English as storyteller.

However, while in his address Santos sees the colonial language as a gift that the Filipino can retool, his fiction on American schooling registers the melancholic state of being the pedagogical subject of U.S. imperialism. In his little-known allegorical novel *The Volcano* (1965), set in the Philippines both during and after U.S. colonial rule, he uses the mimic native who aspires to assimilate Americanness as a melancholic figure whose incorporation of colonial knowledge promises empowerment but also brings about psychic loss, splintering, and a lack of critical consciousness. In the short story "The Excursionists," also set in the Philippines, Santos uses class differences to critically render the effects of colonial pedagogy on both the educated elite and the poor tribal native. Through the figures of elite students and the native who holds up a mirror to the elite, Santos allegorizes the need to violently reject the colonial pedagogy that has been forced on Filipinos under the guise of benevolence while simultaneously demonstrating the dilemma of the elite for whom this education brings cultural, social, and economic capital. At the same time Santos makes clear the importance of collective cultural memory. My analysis of Santos follows the trajectory of critics who have focused on postcolonial readings of his work—most notably, Augusto Fauni Espiritu, who sees Santos as dramatizing "the ambivalence at the heart of colonialism, postcolonialism, and nationalism" (177), and Victor Bascara, who examines Santos's stories as "expressions of the transition from the older practice of colonization to an emergent neocolonialism" ("Up from Benevolent Assimilation," 61).

In describing Santos's pedagogical subject through the lens of melancholia, I am using Anne Anlin Cheng's compelling deployment of Sigmund Freud's explanation of the dynamic of mourning and melancholia to characterize the process of racialization in the United States. In "Mourning and Melancholia," Freud distinguishes between melancholia that is unhealthy and continual because the melancholic internalizes and consumes the lost object, refuses substitution, and is therefore stuck, and mourning that is a healthy response to loss because it accepts substitution and enables one to move on. In a powerful psychosocial theorization of race, Cheng uses Freud's concept of melancholia to explain racial identity: "The racial other (the so-called melancholic object) also suffers from racial melancholia whereby his or her racial identity is imaginatively reinforced through the introjection of a lost, never-possible perfection" (xi). Santos's major characters, marked by the social and material effects of colonial tutelage, unable to relinquish the ideology of benevolence and substitute it dialectically with a postcolonial consciousness, and under the shadow of colonial tutelage, which they introject, demonstrate a melancholic colonized subjectivity; by interrogating this subjectivity and its loss of cultural identity, Santos marks a nascent protest. He sees the melancholia of colonial tutelage as a powerful descriptor of Filipinos but also the very condition of neocolonialism, which nevertheless needs to be resisted and overcome. As Chapter 7 shows, the Japanese filmmaker Masahiro Shinoda also dramatizes the melancholic "group memory" of American tutelage as the basis for protest.

The Volcano, as critics have argued, is a thesis-driven novel spanning thirty years in the lives of Paul Hunter, an American missionary doctor, his wife, Sarah, and their children, Florence and Junior, who arrive in the Philippines in 1928 and are accepted in the community at Albay, until 1958, when they leave because of rejection and resentment by Filipinos.[16] During the thirty years, Filipinos move from colonized to independent status and suffer the hardships of Japanese occupation. The Hunters form a close friendship with the Barrios, a Bikol family with two sons—Badong, who is satisfied with American colonial rule, and Tito, the nationalist, who joins the resistance against the Japanese and ironically serves as a role model for Junior. Intersecting with this political narrative is the interracial romance between Badong and Flor, who are permitted to marry but not to enter the United States together. The remnant of Spanish colonialism is represented through Don Vicente, a close friend of the Hunters and a flamboyant and aristocratic figure of noblesse oblige, loved by the Filipinos. The novel follows the lives of the Hunters, Barrios, and Vicente as the Hunters set up their mission, flee Legazpi when the Japanese land, and attempt to resurrect the mission after the Japanese are defeated. Meanwhile, Tito and Junior suffer through the Bataan Death March, and Junior is killed; Tito, a guerrilla leader, is in turn hunted down and badgered by former collaborators who assume positions of power after the war. Don Vicente develops gangrene and is slowly dying, and the Hunters become the object of local hatred and decide to return to the United States. In the backdrop is the volcano, Mount Mayon, the eruptions of which, with its cycles of destruction and regeneration, represent the permanence of the Philippines beyond colonialism and postcolonialism.

Regarding the novel, Santos maintains, "The entire story hinges on the change of attitude toward the Americans and the Americans' inability to understand why it was so, why the Filipinos are not grateful after everything the Americans have done" (quoted in Bresnahan, 121). Critics similarly have focused on the novel's critique of colonial relations but have not paid attention to its engagement with colonial education.[17] I argue that in the novel the major act of magnanimity is that of tutelage, a gift that is not unconditionally accepted. The novel allegorizes the lure and destructiveness of becoming the perfect pedagogical subject on several levels: through Badong's absolute love for American education and his faith in America; his distancing from other Filipinos; his relationship with his American teachers, the Hunters; and his body, which marks his subjection. Badong is a melancholic who has so introjected colonial teaching that his subjectivity is constantly formed by colonial identification and lack. Paul Hunter, by contrast, suffers from what Paul Gilroy has termed "postcolonial melancholia," an inability to relinquish the idea of the perfect pedagogical subject, grateful for American benevolence.

Santos begins the novel with the Hunters preparing to leave and by setting up the major allegorical elements. If Mount Mayon and its eruptions represent the ungovernable aspect of the Philippines, Junior's cardboard replica of the volcano, unmoving in its concrete foundation, represents the material force of colonial tutelage that situates itself in the local but has its firm foundation in imperialism (Santos, *The Volcano*, 3). Juxtaposed with this image of an unyielding American resolve are two forthrightly thematized incidents: the Hunters' vain efforts to donate their belongings to the natives and Tito and Badong's argument about their different perceptions of Americans. The Hunters reveal their alienness to Filipino contractual morality and system of exchange when they attempt to give their clothes as gifts to native children. The children ignore or actively spurn their offers until the Hunters aggressively dazzle the children and adamantly insist on plying them with clothes. The Hunters seek to perpetuate colonial relations. As Mary Douglas explains in her foreword to Marcel Mauss's brilliant analysis of the gift, "What is wrong with the so-called free gift is the donor's intention to be exempt from returning gifts from the recipient. Refusing requital puts the act of giving outside any mutual ties" (vii). But the Hunters as colonialists refuse to recognize mutuality or the importance of the ability to reciprocate the gift.

The contrast between Tito, the bellicose nationalist, and Badong, the agreeable native, is starkly rendered in the first description of them. When Junior plays tennis with the American principal, Mr. Peterson, his friend Tito joins Junior's friends in cheering him, but Badong also acts as ball boy, a task Tito deliberately rejects. Taunting his brother, Tito says, "Do you know what you look to me running after that ball and throwing it back to these Americans? A dog. A trained dog" (Santos, *The Volcano*, 8). When quizzed about his antagonism toward Americans Tito replies, "They're masters. I don't like masters" (Santos, *The Volcano*, 8). Badong, however, cheerfully acts as ball boy: "He panted and sweated and didn't mind doing it again and again" (Santos, *The Volcano*, 8). Tito's remarks demonstrate that critical consciousness emerges only through nationalism. Tito and Badong are thus represented early in the novel as figures allegorizing a resistant nationalism and an acquiescent colonial subjecthood.

Santos presents Legazpi as a classic colonial outpost flanked on one side by the constabulary and army headquarters and on the other by the provincial high school and normal school. As in the Fanonian Manichean world of the colony, American teachers and government officials live in cottages of wood and cement under a row of coconut trees while the high school students board in rooms rented in nipa shacks; while the cheap homes of natives are dark during the rains, the cottages of American teachers are bright with electric lights. Poor boarders walk far to school and live in small thatched houses while they run errands for wives of officers who play mahjong in their palatial homes (Santos, *The Volcano*, 148). Tito resents the superior attitude of teachers who are forever saying, "In America . . . ," and expostulates, "Heck, if they loved it so much there, what were they doing here?" (Santos, *The Volcano*, 149). The teachers celebrate Quezon's announcement of a special holiday recognizing the American occupation of Manila, and a longtime American resident writes a laudatory column in the *Saturday Evening Post* hailing the American pioneers who have falsely been dubbed imperialists (Santos, *The Volcano*, 149–150).

Badong, unlike Tito, does not apprehend the fault lines in this Manichean world. In his work as a librarian at the Christian center, surrounded by books donated by libraries and schools in the United States, Badong imbibes American culture and, when alone, reads English texts aloud. Introjecting American culture as part of his subjectivity, he ironically recites pieces such as "Give Me Liberty or Give Me Death" and poetry by Longfellow, whose epic poems were required readings for high school students during U.S. colonial rule. Badong's embrace of English is so absolute that even when he is spoken to in the vernacular, he responds in English. As the narrator puts it, "He always spoke in English. His classmates made fun of him for this, but he didn't mind them" (Santos, *The Volcano*, 43). Despite Tito's harsh derision, Badong is fascinated with America and his attraction is fueled by the stories Miss Wendt, the English teacher, reads to the class. "If I were an American, Badong said to himself, I would stay there" (Santos, *The Volcano*, 48). Indeed, the narrator obliquely comments on Badong's uncritical reverence for Miss Wendt by signifying on a key pedagogical moment Santos has analyzed in his own memoir, *Memory's Fictions*—the reading of John Greenleaf Whittier's "Snow-Bound" to Filipino students. In *The Volcano*, the narrator scorns Miss Wendt's disregard for the students' lack of response to a topography to which they have no connection. Badong's melancholic identity, by contrast, is intimately bound up with this pedagogically engendered colonial geographic fantasy of America, with "the snow on the ground, the frozen rivers and pools where one could go skating in the moonlight, the many-colored mufflers around the neck, flying in the wind" (Santos, *The Volcano*, 90).

In his visions of America, Badong fancies himself as the perfect tutelary subject who has learned so well that he excites the wonder and amazement of Americans. Santos represents Badong's fantasies through internal monologues rather than dialogue, thus emphasizing these fantasies as an integral component of his identity. What Badong longs for and never gets in the novel is acceptance by Americans. Like Freud's melancholic for whom the response to the loss of an abstraction is a withdrawal into the ego and an attempt to "establish an identification of the ego with the abandoned object" ("Mourning and Melancholia," 249), Badong attempts to secure an identification with an Americanness he has learned from teachers such as Miss Wendt. Although aware of his subaltern status in relation to Americans, Badong longs for a oneness with them, to bridge the unbridgeable gap, as it were, between mimicry and the original. Tito, however, uses the knowledge of subalternity to forge a postcolonial identity. Americanness, as inculcated in Badong both by the school and by the Hunters' missionary activity, causes him to lose a sense of his self through wishful identification. As Freud so powerfully put it: "Thus the shadow of the object fell upon the ego.... In this way an object-loss was transformed into an ego-loss and the conflict between the ego and the loved person into a cleavage between the critical activity of the ego and the ego as altered by identification" ("Mourning and Melancholia," 249).

Badong introjects the colonial gaze into his consciousness and strives constantly to bridge the contradiction between being interpellated as the good pedagogical subject of empire and envisioning himself as a potential American, a rights-bearing citizen. Santos's representation of Badong's fantasies about going to the United States and being the object of curiosity for Americans is worth quoting at length:

> The Americans would wonder how well he spoke. Where did you learn it? They would ask. How long have you been speaking it? Imagine their surprise when he could have the chance to show them his knowledge of American history: Custer's last stand, fifty-eight, forty or fight, taxation without representation ... the Mason-Dixon Line, Jim Crow, the underground railway.... Then when they sang *The Star-Spangled Banner*, he would add his voice to theirs, and they would look at him, a strange little brown man, standing on his toes to reach the high notes, singing the words and the music as if he had been doing it all his life. Which was the truth. (Santos, *The Volcano*, 90–91)

Badong envisions the astonishment of Americans at his mimicry of perfect English as he pictures himself singing "The Star-Spangled Banner." Echoing and internalizing William Howard Taft's condescending labeling of Filipinos as little brown brothers, a phrase that was widely circulated by the 1930s, Badong thinks of himself as "a strange little brown man" who literally and figuratively needs to reach high to be at par with white America. At the same time, he craves a complete identification with mainstream America because colonial tutelage has formed him as a putatively patriotic American. However, most of the American history lessons Badong longs to tout belong to the archives of anticolonial indigenous resistance (Custer's last stand) or to the annals of African American struggle. Badong cognitively maps these raced struggles seamlessly with Anglo-American battles against Britain, thus entering a discursive tradition in which U.S. history is a color-blind one of constant revolution and revolt.

The Volcano dramatizes Badong's inability to effectively use this knowledge of revolutionary and anticolonial America to nurture a critical consciousness because American schooling, in which he is immersed, disallows it. Instead, Badong's melancholic colonized subjectivity simply sutures the schism between anticolonial resistance and uncritical accommodation through a constant identification with the colonial pedagogy of American teachers and the paternalistic ideology of Dr. Hunter's missionary colonialism. Unlike Tito, who joins a guerrilla unit to fight the Japanese, and Junior, who waives his American citizenship to join the fighting, Badong stays with his family and the Hunters, who are in hiding. His ambition is to study in the United States and work in the ministry like Dr. Hunter, a role model he admires despite the fact that Hunter constantly proselytizes a Protestantism that many peasants resist. If, as Augusto Fauni Espiritu suggests, the Hunters' "arrogant relationship to the natives" reflects "the doubled character of U.S. imperialism itself—as sentimental imperialism and as white racism" (172), Badong is the melancholic native who sees only the sentimental imperialism.

The culmination of Badong's attempted assimilation into colonial white America is his romance and subsequent marriage to Florence, the daughter of the missionary doctor. Santos uses the trope of the inaccessible white woman who symbolizes America in its generosity and kindness, a trope also used by Bulosan, to register Badong's simultaneous inclusion in and exclusion from the world of the colonizers. Although the Hunters profess racial equality, the novel signals the impossibility of the romance by describing the couple through images of abjection. When Badong and Florence have sex in a cave, bats dart toward them, and "they [feel] the rocks under them slimy with filth. They gagged with the foulness in the air." Even as they continue their secret meetings at the cave "they [feel] filthy with the droppings from the bats, which went right through them, staining their blood, coloring their souls black" (Santos, *The Volcano*, 116). The couple literally becomes filth, their bodies inseparable from the dirty leakiness that surrounds them. For Julia Kristeva, the place of the abject is where boundaries between subject and object, self and other, human and animal begin to break down. The horror of this breakdown is elicited by filth such as vomit, shit, and sewage; leaky bodily fluids such as pus; and corpses (Kristeva, 12–13). Abjection is the state of the "in-between, the ambiguous" (Kristeva, 4) that poses a threat to the wholeness of the subject. Santos evokes a similar abjection here, but most important, the abjection, as with Fanon (who anticipates Kristeva), is racially engendered (*Black Skin, White Masks*, 109).

Crossing the racial border at a time that Filipinos in the United States were increasingly being perceived as threats to white womanhood, the couple is represented as experiencing a heightened state of abjection. Internalizing the abjection attributed to breaking the boundaries between American and Filipino, white and brown, colonial civilizer and native, Badong and Florence, instead of challenging racial hierarchies through the ambivalence of abjection, see themselves as animalistic, filthy, impure, shitty, and abject. If Badong was already a melancholic subject for whom the shadow of American tutelage was central, his sexual relationship with Florence further defines his melancholia as he introjects the racial Manicheanism of American colonial rule. In other words, Badong buys into racial paternalism and the narrative of American beneficence. He is grateful to Florence for marrying him and idolizes her whiteness. As Badong ruminates, "Florence was an American girl, and who had ever thought of anyone like him marrying an American girl.... When the war was over, he would still be ... Badong Barrios, a farmer's son, a Protestant, small and dark-skinned, a mere high school student.... And look at Florence. In a lovely dress, she would be lovely.... Her tan would disappear and she would be as she really was, a white girl, an American" (Santos, *The Volcano*, 119–120). Badong sees Florence's whiteness as a perfection he cannot hope to attain.

The Volcano allegorizes Badong's inability to apprehend and critically engage with his position in the colonial order through the metaphor of sight. Badong loses sight in one of his eyes after being beaten by the Japanese while being interrogated on the whereabouts of the Hunters, the Americans to whom he maintains complete loyalty. He manages to protect the Hunters but only by performing the part of a local madman, Kayas. He is literally one-eyed when he marries Florence, symbolically continuing his earlier lack of awareness when he had "closed his eyes to everything except the books he loved to read" (Santos, *The Volcano*, 64). When he is blinded, local children taunt him with quips about his association with Americans. "'*Butang kino, agom ay cano*,' . . . they kept repeating like a deadly refrain. Involuntarily, he walked faster, away from the jeering voices, calling him a blind mouse wedded to an American" (Santos, *The Volcano*, 214). Blindness and sight are central metaphors through which Santos thematizes cognizance or the lack thereof of the exigencies of American colonial rule. Sarah Hunter suffers from "dull, myopic eyes," reflecting, as Tomas Santos points out, her inability to appreciate the distance between her and the postwar generation (Santos, *The Volcano*, 128; Santos, "Introduction," vi). When Paul Hunter cannot see change, he becomes "blind to other things, say, how the country itself is growing in a changing world" (Santos, *The Volcano*, 221). Similarly, the English teacher, Miss Wendt, cannot appreciate a Filipino nationalism that is different from the "ward" status assigned to the Philippines during the commonwealth period. For her, there cannot be a Filipino nationalism apart from U.S. nationalism: "When she raised her head towards the high school building where the two flags flew from the same pole, the distance and her poor sight [blurred] their differences" (Santos, *The Volcano*, 49–50). If Miss Wendt is blinded being a sentimental imperialist, Badong's lack of critical insight causes him to lose all viable connection to native agency. The volcano is an active and visible symbol of the materiality and agency of the Philippines, capable of destruction and renewal, but Badong who has forgotten about it cannot locate himself. It is only when he looks at the volcano and gets his bearings that he sees the Japanese soldiers who have landed in Legazpi.

Interestingly, the character Santos chooses to consistently voice an oppositional critical consciousness is a Spanish aristocrat, Don Vicente, whose rotting body, infested with gangrene, Paul Hunter is trying to fix. Hunter represents rationality, a singleness of purpose, and a sincere belief in the mission of curing Filipino culture of both its native superstition and Spanish feudalism. But as Don Vicente reminds Dr. Hunter, Americans cannot hope to install a culture free of the dis-ease of colonial imposition. Don Vicente indicts the forcible tutelage of Filipinos and predicts the impermanence of the pedagogical subjects that Americans have worked so hard to create:

> You gave them your songs and your speeches, and what did you get? A generation of parrots singing your America and The Star-Spangled Banner, thinking it's their county they are singing about. . . . Watch out when they get their independence after this war. They'll drive all of us away. They'll try to unlearn everything, almost everything, you have taught them, even the language you have tried to force down their throats. (Santos, *The Volcano*, 167)

He indicts the mimic Americans created through colonial education. The novel, however, refuses the simple narrative of learning and unlearning that Don Vicente presents. Tito, who returns from the war embittered about many of his comrades, voices the vexed nature of postcolonial identity when he expresses frustration with his inability to mark a history and identity that is purely Filipino or to celebrate the postcolonial present as a marked improvement from the colonial past. As a figure for postcolonial disenchantment, he ponders what is truly his own, including the language that has been forced down his throat, which he can never master but which is nevertheless part of his identity. Badong, by contrast, remains the melancholic subject oblivious to his own ingestion of American nationalism. Although Paul Hunter, sincere and benevolent colonizer par excellence, ultimately cannot accept his daughter's miscegenated marriage to a Filipino and decides to leave Badong in charge of the mission while the family moves to the United States, Badong continues to believe in the idealized vision of America that has been taught to the natives. Clinging to the prospect of going to the United States, even as he intuits otherwise, Badong is hopeful that the country will restore his vision "Maybe in the States, I can have a real eye.... Or perhaps I can see again with this eye. Everything is possible out there" (Santos, *The Volcano*, 241). Blinded to the limits of inclusion within American civil society, Badong remains to the end a deluded melancholic native who cannot relinquish the promise of America as endless possibility.

While *The Volcano* is a narrative about the melancholic subject whose ingestion of American pedagogy renders him blind to the very workings of colonial racism, "The Excursionists" dramatizes the process of ingestion as a thoroughly misplaced, even brutal process of feeding that sickens the pedagogical subject and must be ejected. Santos registers the alienation engendered by Western pedagogy on multiple levels: it separates the native elite from the masses, culture from the nation, memory from history, English from the vernacular, city from backcountry. The story takes its title from Wordsworth's *The Excursion*, an epic poem about the changes wrought by industrialism and the redemptive function of historical memory in recapturing an agrarian, preindustrial past. Santos transposes the antitheses presented in the poem to the postwar Philippines of the 1940s to comment ironically on educated Filipino estrangement from the natives by presenting his excursionists not as thoughtful characters, like Wordsworth's wanderer, the solitary, the pastor, and the poet, but as a group of arrogant, swaggering city students oblivious to their surroundings.

The action of the story involves a number of students, the "excursionists," leaving an unnamed city to go to the countryside, where they flirt, picnic, flaunt their knowledge of Western literature, and accost a young, naked tribal boy, whom they taunt and derive amusement from as he sings and dances for them and swings from tree branches. They are somewhat discomfited by the misery they cause the untutored native, who cannot digest the food they hand out to him, but they distance themselves from this temporary encroachment of empathy and return to the city almost as self-absorbed as they were at the outset. As with most of Santos's stories, this one is told by an omniscient narrator and relies for its impact on an unspoken series of affects and the sedimented histories of colonialism that are gestured to through what King-Kok Cheung has aptly termed "articulate silences." The story is told from the perspective of Oscar, interpellated ambiguously by the narrator as "a friendly 'outsider'" who looks with wry amusement at the students as perfect colonial pedagogical subjects and yet is ultimately also unable to forge a connection with the native boy (Santos, "The Excursionists," 159).

The story begins with Oscar positioning the excursionists as effete pedagogical subjects who are estranged from the business of daily living. The students are taught Wordsworth's *The Excursion* by a professor with a Harvard accent and enact the journey to the country not with the weight of history or the material nostalgia of the Wanderer whose lines are quoted in the story but like residents of a metropole delighting in the charms of the countryside. They are distanced from the poor woodcutters who peer at them from their nipa-thatched huts and are conscious of their difference. Santos mocks the pretentions of the students as they liberally sprinkle their innocuous conversation with references to American and British writers, "throwing water and quotations at one another" (Santos, "The Excursionists," 162).

With the entrance of the naked tribal boy, the focus of the story shifts. The American education of the students has tutored them not only in Anglo-American literature but also in the racial discourses of white America, as they refer to the unnamed boy as "Sambo." The story dramatizes the distancing between the students and the native, as the students, through a crude display of economic and cultural power, initiate a morally and affectively unequal exchange:

> Somebody had started a game with the boy. Several hands were stretched towards him, each filled with meat or bread as bait while everybody talked, at the same time asking the boy to do something for them.
>
> The boy didn't know what to do. His eyes ran all over the extended hands, filled with food. One girl rose from the ground and walked over to him.

> "I will sing and you dance, then I'll give this to you," she said, showing a fistful of sandwiches.
>
> The girl sang "El Bobo de la Yucca" and the others joined in. The boy did not move, but was listening. He moved his head a little, then he smiled and broke into a dance, that was as crazy as the song and, for the audience at least, as hilarious. . . . The girl . . . beckoned the boy with the food in her hand for him to claim his prize. The boy ran towards her, snatched the food and filled his mouth, almost choking in his hurry. (Santos, "The Excursionists," 166–167)

Just as *pensionados* had roamed the St. Louis World's Fair of 1904 as ambassadors of an Americanized and modern Philippines while the Igorots were being displayed as primitives, the students of "The Excursionists," now part of an emergent *ilustrado* class, enact their neocolonial position by making the native boy an exhibit for them as they interpellate him as illiterate and unintelligent ("El Bobo de la Yucca"). The story makes it clear, however, that the native, well aware that his survival depends on performing primitivism, is ready to comply. Like the young Carlos of Bulosan's *America Is in the Heart* who passes for Igorot and poses naked for American tourists in Bagio, the native boy readily understands the injunction to perform as colonial exhibit when asked to climb and swing like Tarzan.

Through the tribal boy the story dramatizes the linguistic and cultural alienation of the students: "The boy was singing. He was standing in front of the group giving out with a song, perhaps a ballad well-known in the locality. They could not catch the words, but the boy could sing" (Santos, "The Excursionists," 168–169). Those who cannot comprehend the boy include the students, whose primary hermeneutic codes derive from their American schooling; Oscar, who we know has earlier spoken to the boy in dialect; and the limited narrator, who can only guess that the boy is singing a popular ballad. Santos underlines the estrangement of the students from local culture by having a female student pedantically attempt to understand the boy through the ruminations of her American teacher, Professor Brion, about American families in the South. Through the ruse of interrupted conversation, Santos deliberately leaves the student's connection between American southerners (who we can only presume are African Americans, although Santos leaves this ambiguous) and the village boy incomplete, so that no student explicitly racializes the tribal. But as readers, we are invited to both explore the appropriateness of the analogy and share the narrator's ironic mockery of the colonized student, whose relationship with her own culture has to be mediated through an American lens.

For the students, the constant display of erudition that they attempt to clumsily integrate into their lighthearted day excursion—quotes from Longfellow and Wordsworth to Shakespeare—is essential for them in maintaining their position as mimic Americanized subjects fluent in English, steeped in Anglo-American and British literature that they have introjected, a class of the native elite. Like Americans who were simultaneously fascinated and repulsed by Igorots and Negritos, the students in their neocolonial positions anthropologize and codify the boy as savage. Fetishizing his performance of savagery distances them from recognizing their own complicity, as members of a native elite ruling class, in the exploitation of poor tribals. But while the story demarcates the native as exhibit and students as neocolonial spectators, it also draws lines of affect and suggests that the native functions to the students as a mirror of their own, indiscriminate ingestion of colonial knowledge. Freud describes the melancholic subject through metaphors of ingestion. The melancholic wants to "incorporate this object into itself, and, in accordance with the oral or cannibalistic phase of libidinal development in which it is, it wants to do so by devouring it" ("Mourning and Melancholia," 249–250). Commenting on Freud's description of melancholia as consumption, Cheng writes, "The melancholic is not melancholic because he or she has lost something but because he or she has introjected that which he or she now reviles.... He or she is stuck—almost choking on—the hateful and loved thing he or she just devoured" (9). Santos literalizes the students' ingestion of American learning by positioning them as uncomfortable spectators of melancholic consumption. While they throw food at the boy who performs for them, the boy frantically gorges himself on the store-bought Western biscuits and sandwiches. Although aware that the physical gratification he derives from the food is enmeshed with his own personal humiliation, he continues to stuff himself voraciously until he chokes on and vomits out what has been fed to him. At this point, Santos makes evident the affective relationship between the students and the boy:

> The boy went into spasms, the veins standing on his forehead, and the tears in his eyes. But he was not crying. Then he made water which formed a trail at his feet and joined the grime spread on the sand like the map of a lost city.
> Nobody was laughing now. Everybody fell silent.
> A few had taken shelter behind rocks and trees and changed into dry clothes. A stray dog began to feed on the left-over food under the trees. Where Maneng had left him, the boy sat quietly looking at the flies swarming over his vomit.

Vanity cases snapped open and the women began to paint their lips and powder their faces. Young serious eyes peered into tiny mirrors. Time to go. (Santos, "The Excursionists," 170)

To this point the story has been built on the juxtaposition of two different pedagogical subjects: the students who devour the culture as it has been fed to them through their Americanized schooling and introject it to the extent that it takes over their very beings and the boy who hungrily devours the offal of the students, willingly becoming the butt of their ridicule by performing the primitivism they as putative teachers demand and reward. The dark humor of the situation depends on the students' being able to maintain the separation between themselves and the boy, who represents a native savagery from which the students as neocolonial subjects seek distantiation. However, when the body of the boy resists the engorging and performing, a resistance prefigured in his earlier singing that the students cannot comprehend, he becomes the Althusserian bad subject who cannot easily be interpellated as compliant, teachable native (Althusser, "Ideology and Ideological State Apparatuses," 181). He becomes instead a figure of abjection, surrounded by vomit and urine, the despised products of bodily waste, marking a primitivist disorder from which they want separation. Yet the boy's visceral expelling of what he has greedily devoured mirrors to the students their own melancholic introjection of a tutelage they cannot yet disgorge. Repelled by, yet strangely cathected to, this abjected figure, the students effect their dissociation through an abrupt departure and a silence that feigns absolute separation.

Santos ends the story with Oscar, the sentimental neocolonialist who desires a more equitable relationship with the boy, attempting to be solicitous as the rest of the students leave. Oscar is a liminal figure whose class status and cultural capital position him as part of the American students, yet one with a critical consciousness capable of reflecting on the contradictions of neocolonialism that perpetuate conditions of economic, cultural, and psychic oppression. Yet Santos refuses to allow his story to be balanced through what Mary Louise Pratt has termed "the mystique of reciprocity" (78–85). Oscar can revel in guilt and imagine his relationship with the boy as equitable rather than exploitative, but he cannot completely step out of his social, cultural, and class position, bequeathed by colonialism, and relate to the boy outside the neocolonial order in which the poor tribal can, at best, perform at the behest of the native elite. In other words, he cannot move from critical consciousness to critical intervention. Instead, Santos chooses to end the story with a final gesture that confirms the commodification of the tribal. Realizing that he cannot forge affective solidarity, Oscar instead chooses to acknowledge the uneven exchanges that take place between the tribal and elite and marks this unevenness with an acknowledgment that, in the putatively postcolonial Philippines, relations between the Americanized elite and the tribal natives operate through a logic of colonial exchange rather than affective value. Attempting to negate the surplus of affect the tribal boy has afforded them, and unable to sever his ties to an American tutelary culture, Oscar tosses a silver coin to the boy and leaves the scene "in anger over a lot of things he was helpless to do anything about" (Santos, "The Excursionists," 171). Oscar's ruminations here exceed the narrative events of the story and point to a paralysis engendered by the melancholic ingestion of a colonial tutelage he cannot simply expel and his need for an identification he cannot forge with the tribal boy. By dramatizing the divide between Badong and Tito and Oscar (and other students) and the tribal boy as one generated by the consumption of American teaching—and, further, by emphasizing the alienation of Badong and Oscar—Santos points to the force of American tutelage that delimits critical consciousness and affect while simultaneously gesturing to the need for a collective identity as a means of resistance.

Unlearning Colonial Tutelage in Linmark's *Leche*

To see how Filipino Americans register American colonial schooling in the contemporary moment I turn to *Leche* (2011), a novel by R. Zamora Linmark, another Filipino American writer who travels between Manila and the United States. In the 1970s, as structural adjustment programs were being foisted on the Third World by the International Monetary Fund, the Marcos regime coined the term *balikbayan* to exploit Filipinos' attachment to their homeland. *Balikbayans*, or Filipinos living abroad, were touted as vital to the nation and encouraged through tax incentives and bargain airfares to visit home and bring an influx of dollars as the failure of the nation to employ its citizens was turned into a neocolonial bargain. The American education of Filipinos would become an asset for the exportation of cheap labor to the United States and other English-speaking countries, leaving in its wake tens of thousands of separated families. In this world of what Mignolo calls "global colonialism," *balikbayans* became simultaneously providers of low-wage services for new colonial centers and the conduits of capital remittances to, and consumption in, the homeland (*Local Histories/Global Designs*, x). Linmark's *Leche*, a post-postmodern novel that narrates an immigrant Filipino American youth's search for home and identity through a return to the Philippines, examines the legacy of colonial tutelage in a neoliberal, neocolonial world connected through circuits of popular culture, consumption, mobile labor, and militarization. It attempts to articulate possibilities for a collective subjecthood through an intersection of personal and collective historical memory that questions the pedagogy of Americanization, self-help, and capitalist individualism, as well as the notions of the subject in postmodernism.

Leche is set in the 1990s. Vince De Los Reyes, a twenty-three-year-old Filipino American from Honolulu, wins a runner-up prize in the Mr. Pogi pageant sponsored by the U.S.-Philippines Friendship Society and is awarded an all-expense-paid trip to the Philippines and an invitation to party with the rich and famous in Malate, Manila. When he returns to the Philippines after an absence of thirteen years, Vince is jolted out of his "Filipino" identity, accosted by the contradictions of an anthropomorphic city that defies classification, and haunted by the personal memories of his grandfather, as well as the collective memory of the colonial Philippines. Told through a third-person narrator who is privy to Vince's innermost thoughts and thoroughly familiar with Philippine history, the novel is broken into short sections, interspersed with satirical tourist tips, colonial postcards with Vince's musings, and dictionary entries from Bonifacio Dumpit's book *Decolonization for Beginners: A Filipino Glossary*. In his six days in the Philippines, Vince is thrust into contact with a kaleidoscopic variety of characters—movie directors, actors, taxi drivers, maids, shopkeepers, drag queens, and tourists—as he wends his way through Manila and finally reaches his ancestral home, only to find it stripped clean of all signifiers of familial history. In this minimally plot-driven novel, propelled by the twin imperatives of a quest for ethnic identity and sexual desire, the legacy of colonial teaching increasingly occupies center stage.

The novel begins with a dictionary entry from *Decolonization for Beginners*, thus intimating at the very start the potential of Filipinos to decolonize by turning the anthropological gaze into autoethnography. Yet the first term defined is "balikbayan," a cynical neocolonial coinage. "Leche," the common expletive that Linmark chooses as the title of the novel, is also a place Vince constantly hears about, is invited to, and finally encounters close to the end of the narrative. Founded in the 1870s as a milk distribution center by wives of Spanish government officials, Leche was converted into an orphanage for children whose parents were killed in the Philippine-American War, served as the headquarters for the Japanese Imperial Army, and, later, as housing for Ferdinand Marcos's mistresses. Leche functions as a sex club during the night and museum during the day. When Tita G, the hostess of Leche, guides Vince on a short tour of the place, he takes Vince to the museum that houses a classroom built at the turn of the twentieth century and shows him a primer, *The First Philippine Reader*, printed in 1903. As Vince curiously opens the textbook, he is struck by the first lesson, which illustrates children learning first- and second-person pronouns through identification with the

U.S. flag (Linmark, *Leche*, 274). That the textbook is preserved at the heart of a building emblematic of the Philippines as a nation, having served Spanish, American, and Japanese colonial powers, as well as the neocolonial Philippines under Marcos, speaks to the importance of American colonial instruction for Linmark's analysis of the present-day Philippines.

In this section, I tease out the multiple meanings, tensions, and contradictions attached to Leche, the space of the colonial textbook, as a way of negotiating a complex set of questions about the legacy of colonial tutelage in a hyperexperiential world in which neoliberal globalization and neocolonialism coexist. How does the legacy of colonial tutelage manifest itself in such a culture? What are the possibilities of resistance and decolonial thinking when neoliberalism reproduces itself through forms of cultural hybridity and multiplicity? What might it mean to unlearn colonial tutelage, and what are the forms of collectivity that can be adumbrated through unlearning? I contend that *Leche* uses a disjunctive, nonlinear, and multidirectional approach to historical memory not to acclaim a decentered subject, but to posit the possibility of a decolonial collectivity through the communal making of history.

From the very beginning of *Leche*, it is clear that the novel is saturated with many of the markers of globalization. It is a world of global flows, as theorized by Michael Hardt and Antonio Negri, in which the music of the Mr. Pogi pageant in Honolulu circulates smoothly between Honolulu and Manila, as do designer goods. If, as Jeffrey Nealon argues à la Frederic Jameson, postmodernism functioned according to the logic of late capitalism, the post-postmodern, globalized world functions according to the logic of globalization. In such a world where the economic logic is "in fact dedicated to the unleashing of multifarious individual desires," postmodernist political moves celebrating the transgressions of hybridity and multiplicity against a putatively normalized, repressive order are problematic because (1) this normalization is not the primary danger in contemporary capitalism; and (2) they also replicate the world of marketing in neoliberal capitalism (Nealon, 21, 23). The Deleuzian desiring machine is, in fact, a model for global capitalism. In such a scenario, Nealon argues, "You don't so much consume goods as you have experiences where your subjectivity can be intensified, bent and retooled.... You are offered opportunities for doing work on yourself (experiencing, seeing, feeling) rather than opportunities for confronting, overcoming, purchasing, or otherwise consuming some 'other'" (31). Following Hardt and Negri, Nealon argues that in this post-postmodern world of global capital, surveillance, discipline, and control do exist but not to overcome a threatening Other, because difference is no longer that to be overcome but rather to be intensified (23).

Nealon's explanations of global capitalism are useful in relating the cultural and economic landscapes of globalization, as well as in questioning the premium cultural theories still placed on the radical potential of hybridity and multiplicity in thinking about subjectivity; however, Nealon's theories fail to explain the realities of postcolonialism and neocolonialism. In *Leche*, Linmark boldly represents urban Manila both as a hyperexperiential post-postmodern world where all desires are circulated instead of repressed and culturally, politically, and economically as neocolonial and a strategic base for the United States. Neocolonialism, in other words, is perfectly capable of reproducing itself in the affective world of post-postmodernity. Through Vince, a somewhat naive, picaresque hero in search of his Filipino identity, Linmark attempts to provide a cognitive mapping of this hyperexperiential neocolonial world where Vince locates himself in relation to the collective memory of Filipino colonial history and its neocolonial present. In the process of this mapping, Linmark provides possibilities of a decolonial epistemology grounded in a collectivity and an unlearning of colonial education adequate to the present moment that circulates desires and fetishizes hybridity and multiplicity. At the same time, Linmark complicates these possibilities by pointing to the lure of the neocolonial position for overseas Filipinos.

If all roads in Manila lead to Leche, it is because Leche is both a repository of colonial histories and a decolonized space where heterogeneous desires are circulated and where Vince is promised epicurean fulfillment. "Wet dreams come true at Leche. Check it out. It's in Pasay City," writes Vince's best friend and former lover, Edgar (Linmark, *Leche*, 58). Leche serves as a condensation of the contradictory and conflictual affects of the Philippines that the narrator has registered through Vince: the complication of colonial oppression with desire. If Filipino *komiks* stage imaginary resolutions to the contradictions of colonialism by having the *bangungut* (killer nightmare that can cause death) prey on greedy and unscrupulous American businessmen, such as Mr. Smith, who destroy the environment through illegal logging, Vince as a boy sexualizes his attraction for comprador rewards of neocolonialism. He fantasizes sexual encounters with Mr. Smith each night before bedtime even as his nightmares chasten him with reminders of anticolonial resistance: Mr. Smith "proposes" to him under the statue of Rizal. Leche points to the haunting legacy of colonialism and collective history amidst and beneath the energy of present-day Manila and urgently explores ways to unlearn colonial education.

Vince is issued a membership to Leche by the drag queen host, Tita G, who guides him, Virgil-like, through historical Leche, the colonial hell of the Philippines. "Leche is the gatekeeper of secrets and Yermaphrodite is the three-headed dog," says Tita G. Like Cerberus guarding Dante's third circle of hell, Yermaphrodite watches over Leche, a monument to colonial and neocolonial excess. Tita G guides Vince to a classroom signifying colonial benevolence, as well as power. Representing the multilayered colonial past of the Philippines, it has walls covered with alphabet charts, grammar plans, and other instructional material in Spanish, English, and Japanese, "the language of the colonial masters, which Filipinos spoke at one point or another in their history," as the third-person narrator reminds us (Linmark, *Leche*, 274). Linmark juxtaposes the complex and multiple linguistic colonialisms of the Philippines with the material presence of an American primer, *The First Philippine Reader* published in 1903, thus situating American instruction in English in the archipelago in its properly colonial context. As discussed in Chapter 2, flag politics were central to colonial governance, and primers participated in this. In David Gibbs's *Revised Insular Primer*, published three years later, in 1906, the innocuous lesson on first- and second-person pronouns through the objects fan and flag, identical to the lesson recounted in Leche (I have a flag / You have a fan), is preceded by an undisguised lesson in colonial authority in which a flag is defined as the U.S. flag. But if America's tutelary relationship with the Philippines needs to be read as a sign of colonial power, Linmark suggests, neoliberal capitalist relations do little to alter the relationship. Imelda Marcos appropriates the primers, now valuable commodities, for her private collection hidden behind a wall. In turn, Tita G, hostess of Leche, negotiates with canny middlemen to acquire the collection. And in the 1990s, American postcolonial studies scholars come to Leche hoping to trade sex for a bargain price for the primers in what Tita G sees as a neocolonial attempt to pillage Filipino history: "What do those Kang-Kang Kanos take me for? I told them off. . . . Go pillage somebody else's history. Mine is already on reserve. Leche!" (Linmark, *Leche*, 275)

While Leche as American classroom and, later, as headquarters for the Japanese signifies colonial Filipino history, Leche in the current day is a decolonized space known both to celebrities, such as the famous film director Bino Boca, and to cab drivers and passersby. Open to a plurality of meanings, just like the word "leche," it is a place proposed as a tryst by a potential lover Vince names "the postcard thief" and a bar frequented by Lita, a stranger who gives Vince directions to the place. It is a space where queerness is welcomed. Leche is open to transvestites, bisexuals, and gays; it stages a variety of sexual performances, and houses porn tapes catering to the sexually diverse population of Manila. Unlike the colonial classroom, Leche serves multiple purposes and invites multiple readings. For Lita, Leche is *leche* as in *lecheng laway* (devil's spit) but also just a bar for her Japayuki (Filipina entertainers working in Japan) friends; for Tita G, it is the "gatekeeper of secrets" for the closeted population of Manila and a repository of histories; for those, such as

Edgar, who have simply heard of Leche, it is a fulfillment of fantasies; for Jonas, tour guide and potential lover, Leche typifies Manila, a city where anything can happen (Linmark, *Leche*, 201, 265, 273).

Yet if in Leche what was once a colonial space is now where queerness comes together, it is also an expensive commodity, a capitalist space. Dante, the taxi driver to whom Vince is irresistibly attracted, is a worker excluded from the high-priced club-cum-museum that he has been able to afford just once. Tita G is adept at marketing exorbitantly priced lifetime memberships to Leche. Bino Boca pays homage to the memory of Filipina comfort women by filming his movie about them at Leche, former headquarters of the Japanese Imperial Army. He enters the struggle with historical record by narrating Japanese colonialism from the point of view of the colonized, thus creating what he calls "reciprocating memory" (Linmark, *Leche*, 281). Yet his movie, *In the Name of Shame*, circulates as cheap melodrama and as marketing publicity for Kris Aquino, the legendary "Massacre Queen" of Philippine cinema and talk-show hostess who features *balikbayans* on her program. The movie is also a major commercial success, winning both awards and profits for Bico Bino and shown to *balikbayans* aboard the aircraft coming back home. Vince ruminates that "Bino has achieved nothing except to exploit the Lolas' ordeal, cheapen their suffering, capitalize on their sorrows by turning their victimization into a two-hour melodrama" (Linmark, *Leche*, 281–282).

The erstwhile colonial space is now capitalist and neocolonial, but at the same time it generates possibilities for resistance through history and collective memory. Vince, whose potential love trysts with his chauffeur, Dante, as well as with the postcard thief and Jonas, have been thwarted, finds some fulfillment, and a promise of more, with a waiter at Leche. More importantly, it is only after leaving Leche that Vince speaks his first Tagalog words in years, saying, "I- metro mo" as he haggles with the cabdriver. The physicality and materiality of the colonial tutelage Vince encounters at the heart of Leche releases in him, the colonized subject, the affect of decolonized language that he feels intensely. As the narrator describes it, "It catches him off guard: the grin of the *i* followed by the fold of the *m*, and then the trill of the *r*, and finally, the half-opened *mo*.... The mother tongue that's been silenced by years of assimilation and school-enforced laws is waking up, waiting for him to transform a simple phrase into music" (Linmark, *Leche*, 295–296). The assimilation referred to here is that of schools in Hawai'i that erase Filipino cultural difference, but Vince experiences the moment of linguistic decolonization, his unlearning, once the collective memory of American colonial tutelage in the Philippines intersects with his personal memory of linguistic assimilation in Hawai'i.

Subsequently, Vince's dreams begin to include a colonial past in which the personal and collective intersect. Vince's deep connection to the colonial history of the Philippines and the bifurcated strategies of conquest—the sword and the book—emerge through his unconscious. He dreams about seeing a photograph of his great-grandfather, who in his unambiguous racial and national positionings represents colonial white America, "*a blond, blue-eyed man, square-jawed, broad shoulders, wide forehead, trimmed moustache, a pronounced widow's peak. He is Vince's great-grandfather who went to the Philippines at the turn of the twentieth century to fight the Filipino revolutionaries in the Philippine-American War*" (Linmark, *Leche*, 299). Vince's ancestor appears in a dream that expresses his guilt at not going to his grandfather's funeral, a guilt that speaks to Vince's positioning as a Filipino. Vince's dream is both a reminder of his fraught colonial family history and an unlearning of colonial tutelage, in which the Philippine-American War has been erased from historical memory. At the same time, Vince dreams about his great-great-great-aunt "*wearing a Mother Hubbard gown with long sleeves and high neck . . . one of the first American teachers, to arrive in the islands and introduce public education to the natives*" (Linmark, *Leche*, 299).

Linmark also uses the form of the novel to experiment with ways of unlearning. As noted earlier, the novel begins with an entry from *Decolonization for Beginners: A Filipino Glossary*, a book written by Vince's University of Hawai'i teacher Bonifacio Dumpit, signaling both the decolonization that Vince, the character, has been learning and the decolonization of form that Linmark, as writer, is proposing. Anibal Quijano has suggested that colonialism was a repression "above all, over modes of knowing, of producing knowledge, of producing perspectives, images and systems of images, symbols, modes of signification, over the resources, patterns and instruments of formalized and objectivized expression, intellectual or visual" (169). Linmark decolonizes the linear narrative structure of a tourist novel or the journey back home by relating Vince's six-day adventure in episodic form, with nine books broken into short sections and subsections that switch between Vince's present and past, individual memory and collective memory, history and legend, fantasy and reality, movie screenplay and individual journey. He suggests instead, by including an epigraph from Dante's *Inferno*, that Vince's journey, presented to us in nine books (like Dante's *Inferno*, in which hell is depicted as nine circles of suffering), must be seen as a modern-day epic that is as important as the canonical Western narrative, *Inferno*, which describes the soul's recognition and rejection of sin. Yet Linmark invites us to relearn this canonical text by playfully and deliberately jumbling the key characters in the allegory. Vince, the putative Dante, is actually guided through the city by the chauffeur named Dante whom he desires, and Manila is "hell" only to tourists.

Leche as an antitourist text also aims to expose the flaws in touristic modes of perception by dispelling any anthropological nostalgia for cultural difference. Interspersed in the novel are satirical tourist tips that serve the purpose of disinviting the (colonial) tourist from Manila and thus function to reeducate the tourist mind-set, turning it from cultural consumption to cultural outsiderism and panic. Linmark's tourist tips exaggerate the noise, heat, and diseases of the Philippines ("The Philippines is a very loud country: bring earplugs" [23]) while presenting local foods and greeting habits as unattractive ("If you want to be accepted into the tribe, you have to eat balut [hard-boiled duck fetus], dinugan [pig's blood stew], or bayawak [monitor lizard]" [149]). Similarly, Linmark also includes postcards in the novel but estranges these commonplace tourist items from their traditional context. The thirty-four postcards in *Leche* are taken from a coffee-table book, Jonathan Best's *A Philippine Album: American Era Photographs, 1900–1930*. Best's book, a visual cultural history, contains both photographs taken by Americans and postcards sent by Americans to the United States, along with quotes from Americans living in the Philippines during the colonial era. The online Popular Bookstore markets it through colonial nostalgia as "bringing back an era which was swept away by the Second World War and subsequent modern development."[18]

Postcards promoted through colonial tourism are attempts to simultaneously exoticize and taxonomize. Best's *A Philippine Album* reproduces comments that reveal the confidence and certainty with which American colonial residents wrote their knowledge about the Philippines. Maud Huntley Jenks, for instance, normalized Igorot labor for American colonial officials by providing a distanced, anthropological description of Igorots carrying her husband's belongings: "Men carry from sixty to one hundred pounds. They always have a bolo fastened to their gee string, and carry a long stick to use as a staff in climbing a steep rough trail" (Best, 141). Linmark, by contrast, rewrites the colonial archive by including these postcards in *Leche*, where they function as extradiegetic historical memory, but replaces colonial-era comments with Vince's, thus marking an unlearning of colonial knowledge. Vince's postcards suggest an anticolonial sensibility, as he often chafes at the neocolonial relations through which Pagsanjan Falls becomes the setting for Francis Ford Coppola's *Apocalypse Now*, a film that is critical of the Vietnam War but erases the colonial history of the Philippines and uncritically swaps the Philippines for Vietnam. Vince writes, "Can I blame it on Holly-fucking-wood? . . . The jungles of Mindoro and Isabela? Postcard-perfect river of Pagsanjan? The Philippines as the prime location for a silver-screen war zone. Stand-in for Cambodia; Xerox of Vietnam" (Linmark, *Leche*, 69).

It is in the inscribing of these postcards, where Vince's thoughts are unmediated by the narrator, that Vince articulates the hyperexperiential yet anticolonial aesthetic of *Leche* and discovers a form of voicing that one might associate with "unlearning." The writing on the postcards, unmediated by a narrator and without the free indirect discourse that characterizes much of the novel, represents the most direct thoughts of Vince, the postcolonial subject. Vince ends several of his postcards not simply with his signature but also with a postscript, and sometimes with two postscripts, often using the P.S.es to reveal his most significant thoughts. If Vince cannot simply unlearn his position as an "American" reared in Hawai'i, even though his parents' migration is part of a neocolonial compact, Linmark suggests that Vince cannot escape from the collective history of American colonial tutelage, either. Vince's encounter with the colonial textbook appears as uncanny, or *unheimlich*, something familiar that needs to be repressed. Vince is fascinated with, and purchases, a postcard titled "Thomasite Schoolteacher Being Carried in a Chair by Igorots," but he uses the main text of the postcard to write to his brother Alvin about his frustration with shopping misadventures in Manila. However, in the second postscript (the P.P.S.), as if decentering the narrative of colonialism, Vince connects the extradiegetic with the diegetic, individual history and collective history, by commenting, "*The schoolteacher reminds me of our great-great-aunt. Didn't she take a similar photo?*" (Linmark, *Leche*, 187).

Through Vince's postcard writing, Linmark suggests the postscript as an appropriate, decolonizing form. The postscript exists outside, yet in relation to, the main script, adding and commenting on it even as it disrupts its closure. Like the postcolonial, the postscript comes temporally after the main narrative yet exists alongside it in productive tension. The postscript is an after-writing, announcing its belatedness, a writing that decenters the writer and the body of the letter. It is an alternative, reeducating act, at once apologetic and aggressive, a supplement.[19] The postscript, like the endnote that has been used by novelists such as Junot Diaz to write an alternative history, proclaims itself as outside and marginal, yet insistent, a form, Linmark intimates, as particularly appropriate for writing the postcolonial. As both accretion and substitution, as Jacques Derrida suggests of the supplement (145), the postscript marks itself as a text that must necessarily exist alongside and after the script. When Vince asks whether the great-great-aunt had taken a similar photo, he is marking the great-great-aunt (who was a Thomasite teacher) as similar to the woman in the picture, who, in a quintessential colonial posture, is seen triumphantly posing atop a palanquin being carried by two abject Igorot men. Clearly defined in the foreground with a backdrop of the Philippine countryside, the woman looks squarely at the camera while the Igorot men look down and ahead at the path they have to traverse. Yet the Igorot men, like the postscript, question ideas of margin and center, text and supplement. Similar postscripts in which Vince attempts to understand his position in the Philippines—why people call him "Sir," why he feels caged, why he dreams about his grandfather—appear on other postcards.

While colonial tutelage offers ways to define, demarcate, and order the objects of knowledge, Linmark presents us with a city that, emblematic of a people, resists definition or the colonial gaze where the viewer has the power to possess and evaluate the scene (Pratt, 201–206). For Vince, an anthropomorphic Manila "breathes, belches, farts, grabs, and begs . . . burns stings, licks, laughs, rains, boils, bleeds, honks, barks, dances, chants, until your dreams bust" (Linmark, *Leche*, 133). But while Vince testifies to the inexhaustible heterogeneity of Manila through the post-postmodern aesthetics of the hyperexperiential, he, as Western tutelary subject, has also learned to "divide the world," as John Willinsky would put it. At once an American and a neocolonial Filipino schooled in Western-style "Good Guidance & Manners," he recoils at the dirt, disorder, pollution, and poverty of Manila, the "Motorcycles speeding on sidewalks / People living off garbage / People living in garbage," a place where "Brownout is blackout" and "Diarrhea is an acronym" (Linmark, *Leche*, 183). As he writes to Edgar, he is living "in a shithole" (Linmark, *Leche*, 180). Indeed, Vince's renditions of Manila to his friends in Hawai'i are often so vituperative that they share with standard Western touristic representations of encounters with the Third World the depiction of the Westerner heroically suffering poverty. In his very obsession with dirt that Mary Douglas has argued is simply matter out of place, Vince reveals his need to control and classify (*Purity and Danger*, 44). It is also interesting to think about the audience for the narrator's jokes about the disorder of Manila. Readers are invited to laugh but one wonders whether the very reality that Vince narrates as a joke would not ring as humorous to people living in Manila. So is the humor directed to a non-Filipino, perhaps largely Filipino American, or American readership? The very fact that *Leche* itself—at 10,000 pesos for a paperback—is too expensive for most Filipinos to buy should give us pause.[20]

Vince's relationship with other Filipinos in the novel also reflects his neocolonial status as a Filipino American visiting the native country. From his very first encounter with the taxi driver, Dante, Vince exoticizes and desires him. Dante's arm is tattooed with a cockfight, the very symbol that marked Filipinos as primitive in the eyes of American colonial reformers. Vince is mesmerized by the tattoo, which reappears to him as he daydreams about Dante. He is, as the narrator satirically suggests, a voyeur in relation to Dante: "Voyeurism, like meditation, requires great concentration. And Vince has mastered it. Nothing distracts him from drinking the man in with his eyes"

(Linmark, *Leche*, 73). He tips Dante double the fare to lure him back and is fascinated by the earthiness of this taxi driver "with a wife, three kids, [who] wears a crucifix medallion, has a cockfight tattoo on his arm" (Linmark, *Leche*, 111). Vince, the American, can afford to repeatedly hire Dante and play out his fantasies about Dante as the object of his desire. For Vince, Dante is not simply a potential lover but someone whose ethnicity and working-class background he exoticizes and Orientalizes.

Yet it is the colonial dream/nightmare that interpellates Vince as Filipino. As he tells his housekeeper and clairvoyant Burrnadette, his dreams have been about his grandfather, a Bataan Death March survivor, and his great-grandfather and sister: "They came to the Philippines almost around the same time. He was a soldier and she a Thomasite teacher" (Linmark, *Leche*, 313). Vince's ancestors literally embody the technology of U.S. colonial rule in which schooling was a necessary, if different, arm of empire, an adjunct to military operations. Pronouncing his dream "bangungut," Burrnadette defines Vince as a Filipino who has now been asked to return to complete the unfulfilled task of burying his grandfather. Linmark complicates this Oedipal return to Filipino origins by simultaneously coding it as providing possibilities for decolonial thinking and collectivity and pointing to the persistence of Vince's liminally neocolonial status as Filipino American.

Whereas most of the novel uses a third-person narrator who holds Vince at an amused, arms-length distance even as he is privy to Vince's innermost thoughts, when Vince travels back to his grandfather's home, Linmark registers his thoughts through an interior monologue. Through this monologue, in which he alternately identifies and disidentifies with Filipinos, he distances the natives as "them," the benighted undisciplined ones who need colonial lessons in social manners and hygiene "How to file in a single line. . . . How to cough in public" (Linmark, *Leche*, 318). However, this distancing is complicated when Vince remembers his own tutelage: "Things they already learned in Good Guidance & Manners in elementary school. I took this class in second grade" (Linmark, *Leche*, 318). Although Vince still maintains a separation between "they" (the natives) and himself, he also suggests a kinship with them as he remembers being molded into Western respectability.

Vince's journey back home is marked by a frenetic intersection of neocolonial and anticolonial politics. Bino Boca, the acclaimed director Vince has met at Leche, dies in a car crash, his demise becoming an instantaneous occasion for vendors to sell copies of his films, such as *P.S. U.S.A.: My Brother Is Not a Pig*, a movie based on a true account of an American soldier who accidentally shot a Filipino boy he mistook for a wild pig. By choosing as a title for Bino Boca's film the famous line from *Minsa'y isang gamu-gamo* (dir. Lupita Aquino-Kashiwahara [1976]), which was highly critical of U.S. military presence in the Philippines, Linmark connects the film extradiegetically to the present-day events of *Leche*, as well as to Vince's postscripts. Vince, Linmark suggests, is potentially a radical postcolonial subject questioning the militarized neoliberal, neocolonial order. However, in the contemporary neocolonial Philippines, the presence of U.S. soldiers at Subic Bay is a matter of debate. Riding on the bus, Vince witnesses the withdrawal of U.S. troops—a political move that in the 1990s was widely seen as a victory against the remnants of U.S. colonialism—and becomes party to the passengers' heated disputations about the necessity of a U.S. Army presence in the Philippines. Ironically, Linmark has Vince agreeing with proponents of both sides before symbolically marking him as Filipino. Fulfilling Bonifacio Dumpit's jocular pronouncement that "a Filipino is not a Filipino until he has climbed into a jeepney and paid his share of the ride" (Linmark, *Leche*, 152), Vince gets off his bus and, "stuttering in Tagalog" and unlearning colonial education, manages to find his way to a jeepney called "Killer Pogi," which will take him to San Vicente, his ancestral home (Linmark, *Leche*, 343). On the jeepney he is immediately recognized and interpellated as Don Alfonso's grandson, reborn, so to speak, as Filipino as he "clambers his way out of the hole, like a baby crawling out of a womb" when the jeepney stops in front of his grandfather's house (Linmark, *Leche*, 350).

Vince is linguistically and metaphorically reborn as Filipino, but Linmark ends the novel by refusing to provide him with the signifiers of home he has been thinking and dreaming about. In a characteristically postmodern questioning of the stability of ethnic identity, Linmark confronts Vince with an empty house, devoid of furniture and the family photographs of the colonial ancestors who have haunted his dreams. "Why did Lolo Al do this—erase all dust and dirt of my past?" asks Vince. "Why did he renounce everything? Nothing salvaged" (Linmark, *Leche*, 354). However, if ethnic identity here is unstable, it is not singular. Linmark has made clear that his hero is not the privatized, decentered individual of post-postmodernism because Vince's memories are not simply his own but those of many others. The locals "resurrect scenes, events, and snapshots of a young Vicente, his grandfather Don Alfonso, Yaya Let, and the rest of Vicente's clan, alive or dead. They surrender their tongues to the past, interrupting each other now and then to insert an aside or correct each other's memories" (Linmark, *Leche*, 345). Bill Ashcroft's explanation of the use of postmodern strategies and collectivity in postcolonial literature is useful here. Commenting on the tension between the individual and collective in postcolonial literature, Ashcroft argues that, although the decentered subject is central for writers such as Édouard Glissant and Aimé Césaire, "such a subject is relentlessly drawn back by the urgency of resistance, the material effects of the colonizing process into identification with the cultural collective" (11). Vince fears that his past has been lost, but what Linmark suggests is that Vince's past, his history, and his memories are also the past, histories, and memories of all others in the community. Colonial history creates the collective subject.

Vince's anguished musings also deploy the language of Filipino doublespeak in which, as we are reminded in an earlier tourist tip, the colonial language, English, has been deformed, refashioned, and resignified, because for Filipinos "language is like a machine that can be taken apart, tinkered with, reassembled, decorated, and given a face-lift" (Linmark, *Leche*, 131). As Linmark explained in an interview, "How leche devolved from 'milk' to 'merde' I don't know, except to say Filipinos constantly play with the language of their former colonizers."[21] Thus, because English words in the Philippines often take on opposite meanings, Linmark writes in one of the tourist tips, "to salvage" is also "to kill" or "exterminate" (131)—a word that became particularly sinister during the Marcos regime but the roots of which go back to the Philippine-American War, where "to salvage" was a euphemism for clandestine executions (Wyatt-Brown, 137). So despite the empty house, nothing has been destroyed and ethnicity can be reimagined. By ending the novel with a retelling of the narrative of individual ethnic identity as collective, Linmark connects it to the larger narrative of colonialism and offers his hero the possibility of rewriting, reimagining, and relearning the colonial past afresh.

More than a century after the institution of educational programs premised on teaching the values of individualism, self-reliance, industry, and democracy to a backward people, crippled by Spanish feudalism and without a viable native language or culture and unfit for self-government, the legacy of colonial schooling continues to haunt the imagination of Filipino American writers. It is a testament to the power of this tutelage that writers as different as Bulosan, Santos, and Linmark register the attraction of this legacy at the same time as they wrestle with the politics of this legacy, reimagine the past, and attempt to envision forms of collectivity that resist the desiring pedagogical subject of U.S. empire.

5

Mapping the Japanese Tutelary Subject in the Classroom and Brides Schools

In a secret radiogram to the Adjutant-General of the War Department (AGWAR), dated February 1, 1942, Douglas MacArthur, incensed at the treatment of Americans and the British in occupied areas in the Philippines, urged the War Department to consider restrictions on the Japanese in the United States. In his view, the comparative rough treatment of the British and Americans by the Japanese in contrast to the relatively moderate handling of "metropolitan Filipinos" was dangerous because it was "designed to discredit the white races." Decrying the "negligible restrictions apparently applied in the United States to the many thousands of Japanese nationals there," he stated: "The only language the Japanese understand is force and it should be applied mercilessly."[1] Soon thereafter, the State Department echoed MacArthur, stating that, if Americans in Japan and the occupied Philippines would not be treated well, "it may be necessary for this government to reconsider its policy of according to Japanese nationals on its territory the most liberal treatment consistent with the national safety" (quoted in Hayashi, 83).

MacArthur had served in the Philippines periodically since 1903, first as part of the U.S. colonial forces, and finally during World War II. His father, Arthur MacArthur, having fought against Native Americans at home, had forcibly occupied the Philippines and, as noted in the Introduction, had requested funds for schools as a necessary complement to military operations (Forbes, 423); Douglas MacArthur had waxed nostalgic about this work of colonizing the Philippines through education. Decades later, Douglas Mac-

Arthur would be executing the overhaul of the educational system in occupied Japan. My point is not to suggest that one figure orchestrated the tutelary social engineering of the Japanese and Japanese Americans but, rather, to suggest that despite the vast differences between the colonization of the Philippines and the occupation of Japan, the construction of the Japanese pedagogical subject during occupation was generated by perceptions of the Japanese in the United States, in Japan, and in the Philippines. The racialization of the Japanese Americans in the United States was related to events in the Philippines, and ideas of the Japanese during occupation, in turn, were affected by the management of the Japanese American population at home. More importantly, American educators participating in the overhaul of Japanese education praised the occupation as a major colonial endeavor. As Joseph J. Trainor, who served in the education division of the Allied Command's Civil Information and Education Section (CI&E) for the entire occupation period, reflected in his memoir:

> A prostrate Japan was taken over by an occupation force which, for all its Allied Powers legal basis, was essentially and for all practical purposes, an American Occupation. Thus representatives of one of the world's newest cultures, a special type of western culture, took charge of affairs in a land of one of the world's oldest cultures, one distinctly Oriental. . . . Never have east and west met with such impact, not even in the long history of colonization and domination of Asian areas by western powers during the nineteenth and twentieth centuries. (390)

Trainor's characterization of the occupation as colonial was justified given the power of U.S. authorities and the nearly complete control over the system of education. The office of the Supreme Commander of Allied Powers (SCAP) maintained authority over all divisions, including the CI&E, and in the course of occupation established rules about school conduct, purged dissident teachers, authorized curricula, deleted objectionable portions of textbooks, mandated textbook selections, changed the school system to a 6-3-3 structure (six years of elementary school, three years of middle school, and three years of high school) and coordinated with educators about changes. As in the Philippines, where American schools were opened almost immediately after the military invasion, schools in Japan were reopened shortly after the ending of wartime destruction. Atomic bombs had devastated Hiroshima and Nagasaki, and incendiary bombs dropped on heavily populated areas of Tokyo killed more than 100,000 people and destroyed sixteen square miles of the city (Staaveren, 8). On the day of surrender, eighteen million students were idle, four thousand schools were destroyed, and thousands more were heavily damaged (Beauchamp, "Reforming Education in Postwar Japan," 67). Similar to the Philippines, schooling was viewed as an adjunct to military operations, though obviously not for the purposes of quelling an insurgency but for ensuring a populace compliant with a postwar Pax Americana. But whereas Filipino education for pacification became tethered to a vision of the benevolent colonial uplift of a backward people, Japanese education for democracy was envisioned as a curbing of dangerous, imperialist mind-sets and the teaching of an already learned people, aspects of whose culture needed drastic changes. A policy document of the U.S. Army Staff written a year before the occupation (and in anticipation of military occupation) reveals long-standing ideas about the Japanese, as well as about the importance of "reeducation," a term repeatedly used by occupation officials. The document determines salient aspects of Japanese character as including "glorification of the military," "subservience to authority," and an imperialist mind-set connected to emperor worship (quoted in Beauchamp and Vardaman, 46). Advocating an integration of economic policies of the military government with reeducation, it affirms the centrality of education to the project of occupation: "The program of education cannot be restricted to formalized education or to a mere reform of the educational system. It must be aimed at re-educating not only the youth but the whole population." Ironically, the document suggests that the very traits deemed undesirable—"obedience to authority and uncritical acceptance of the teachings of their leaders"—could be harnessed toward changing them (quoted in Beauchamp and Vardaman, 47).

Despite the differences in conceptions of Filipinos and Japanese, Americans' sense of having accomplished something unprecedented through schooling was similar. As Trainor wrote, after six years of occupation:

> Japanese education was in a healthy condition, its schools rehabilitated and the war damage remedied.... It had built into its fabric the essentials of a democratic system of education and had developed a teaching force that deserved the characterization of professional. It was a masterly achievement and perhaps unparalleled in the history of education. (ix)

Of course, in the half-century between the colonization of the Philippines and the occupation of Japan, the conditions of the world system had changed. Direct colonial occupation of foreign lands was over, and the United States was emerging as world hegemon, exercising power through an informal empire of military bases and strategic alliances, buttressed through soft power, in which education was central. According to Victoria de Grazia, it was a "market empire" based on a democracy of consumerism that challenged the bourgeois hierarchies and civilizing mission of Europe (2–3, 5). The Japanese, particularly after the Reverse Course of occupation (generally after 1948), were seen as crucial to this empire and viewed as subjects of a misdirected and incomplete modernity who needed to change from fealty to the state to fealty to capitalism, although, in contrast to de Grazia, I would argue that the Orientalism of an older colonialism was still visibly present in anxieties about the alienness of Japanese culture to Western modernity. As John Dower argues, there was a messianic fervor to Japanese occupation unlike that of Germany, and according to MacArthur, the occupation was unequivocally a Christianizing mission, as well (*Embracing Defeat*, 23). MacArthur repeatedly told visiting Christian ministers about the need for more missionaries and had ten million Bibles translated into Japanese. As MacArthur reminisced about his evangelization, "Gradually, a spiritual regeneration in Japan began to grow" (*Reminiscences*, 311).[2] However, while Filipinos had to be educated as subjects of a U.S. colony because they were unfit for self-government, the Japanese had to be reeducated and reformed to eventually be subjects of a new American hegemony, with Japan was a strategic Pacific outpost.

In the early years of occupation, mandating changes that restored such liberties as the right to assembly and freeing political prisoners who had opposed the Japanese military regime produced unlikely bedfellows for the United States, such as leftist teachers and union activists, who were later purged during the Reverse Course. The contradiction of occupation was that many democratic reforms undertaken in the early days of occupation were through the direct military command of Douglas MacArthur, who bore the distinctly colonial title of Supreme Commander of Allied Powers and who also issued strict directives on censorship, banned books, suppressed textbooks, ordered the removal of Shinto shrines from schools, and disallowed emperor worship. It was, in many ways, a democracy from above, whose suddenness alarmed some in the education establishment. Yoshishige Abe, the Japanese minister of education, worried that "liberals, who had been under the pressure of militarism during the war, took the Allied Powers for their saviors and fell under the illusion that suddenly their best days have come."[3] My purpose is not to assess the democratic or undemocratic nature through which reforms were carried out or the changes during the Reverse Course when Red purges were implemented.[4] Most scholars have noted the contradiction between the authoritarian nature of occupation and the "freedoms" it introduced (see Eiji, 393; Nishi, 109). Rather, I am interested in how major documents instituting educational reform imagined the Japanese and the pedagogical subjects they hoped to produce for a nonmilitaristic, nonimperial, capitalist, putatively democratized, pro-American Japan. The centrality of culture to education is evident everywhere in these documents, where culture is seen as a central component of Japanese imperialism. These reports constantly formulate ideas about essential Japaneseness, such as conformity and obsequiousness; evaluate Japanese social norms; and call for changing behavior to be amenable to a peaceful democracy. Concurrently, the documents do the work of informal empire by assuming, either implicitly or explicitly, Anglo-American cultural practices to be normative. Of major importance are tenets of Deweyan progressive education, such as deemphasizing formal learning, fostering active participation of the individual child, and gearing education toward the interests of children rather than imposing adult standards. Victor Kobayashi points out that Dewey had argued for the inclusion of an explicit social ideal in a philosophy of education (52). U.S. educators linked progressive pedagogical practices and educational reforms to an ideal of American-style democratic individualism, with freedoms, as with Filipinos, on a personal rather than a social/national level. And theories of recapitulation, in which progressivists believed, made American social ideals the goals toward which the Japanese were to be guided.

Yet the reeducation of the Japanese also assumed a certain kind of culturally constructed pedagogical subject that leaked beyond the boundaries of postwar political exigencies, theories of progressivist education, or the needs of Japanese students. Here, Edward Said's powerful delineation of Orientalism as a discourse that depends for its strategy on the "flexible positional superiority" of the Westerner is useful (7). Orientalism as a hierarchical discourse that both enabled and justified Western colonialism was logically anomalous in relation to Japan, because as an Asian colonial power Japan had challenged the power dynamics of Orientalism. Indeed, the Japanese had justified their rapacious colonization as a necessary safeguard against Western colonialism and racism. But in light of Japanese fascism, a specific kind of Orientalism was marshaled to explain Japanese deviance. It was argued that Japanese cultural practices, more feudal than modern, despite the nation's rise to industrial power, lent themselves to totalitarianism rather than democracy. Policy documents related to educational reform reflect the deployment of this kind of Orientalism while simultaneously promoting progressive pedagogies. This chapter teases out the contradictory constructions of the Japanese as conformist, obsequious, and uninventive people, feared as potentially threatening non-Western moderns and seen as pedagogical subjects capable of overcoming their dated rituals and becoming individualistic and desirous of an American-style capitalist democracy in the key occupation documents: *Report of the United States Education Mission to Japan* and the bestselling and widely read required high school history volumes published under the direction of SCAP, the *Primer of De-*

mocracy. It then analyzes the self-Orientalization by Japanese officials in the widely disseminated *Guide to New Education in Japan* and briefly examines the critical registering of the contradictions of democratic reforms and the subjectification of the Japanese in the memoir of the education officer Jacob Van Staaveren. Finally, it examines the construction of a different kind of pedagogical subject emerging from Brides School texts produced by the American Red Cross—the Japanese wife ready to unquestioningly occupy her class position in a racially stratified United States and thereby function as racial capital for the nation. My analysis of these texts moves from the *Report*, written in 1946 during the initial stages of occupation, to the *Primer*, one volume of which was published at the end of the first stage and the second at the start of the Reverse Course (1948), to the Brides School texts initially published during the Reverse Course. During this period, the policies of the United States changed from demilitarizing and controlling the population to ensuring Japan as a Cold War ally against communism and a strategic Pacific military base. Yukiko Koshiro sees the change as one from where race was used to impress on the Japanese "a proper sense of relations between the white conqueror and the colored vanquished" during the early stages of occupation to the Reverse Course, where the status of Japanese was upgraded to that of "honorary whites and an ally" (16). My readings of the texts of occupation, particularly the Brides School texts, reflect this shift but also make clear the persistence in the neocolonial racialization of the Japanese, who would continue to be seen as better than Filipinos but subordinate to whites.

Popular Cultural Visions of the Japanese

Despite the very specific aegis of educational overhaul during occupation under which the texts under discussion were produced, the cultural construction of the Japanese tutelary subject was heavily influenced by popular culture representations of the Japanese as, in turn, clever, dangerous, unscrupulous, family-oriented, superstitious, conformist, and militarist. While the racialization of Filipinos during the early colonial period was mapped onto existing racial categories at home—those of Indians and African Americans—the Japanese during occupation were racialized as the powerful Oriental threat. On the West Coast, "yellow peril" Orientalism predicated on the unsuitability of Asians, their Otherness to American culture, had been inflected to deal with the particular threat of the Japanese. In Wallace Irwin's *Seed of the Sun* (1921), the crafty Baron Tazumi, a former officer in the Japanese Imperial Army, gives rousing speeches about "America, ever-generous giver" coming with "the gift of all science" and instructing Japan "to learn that [it] may teach" (36). The novel demonstrates how the opening up of Japan to Western knowledge (without Western guidance) had been a dangerous gift, producing the likes of Tazumi, an immoral polygamist who cleverly instantiates a plot to take over California farmlands. In Gene Stratton-Porter's novel *Her Father's Daughter*, published the same year, Linda Strong, who cannot countenance the academic success of Oka Sayye in her school, reflects on the Japanese by saying:

> Take them as a race—of course there are exceptions, there always are—but the great body of them are mechanical. They are imitative. They are not developing anything great of their own in their own country. They are spreading all over the world and carrying home sewing machines and threshing machines and automobiles and cantilever bridges and submarines and aeroplanes—anything from eggbeaters to telescopes. They are not creating one single thing. (116)

Stratton-Porter counters fears of Japanese ascendancy by reverting to Orientalist ideas about the essential inability of Asians to match Anglo intelligence and creativity, a notion that had also been applied to Filipinos.[5] The technological modernity of the Japanese is an incomplete modernity, based on a superficial mimicry. Yet this mimicry is potentially threatening, even if it is derivative. In other words, conceptions of the Japanese—as ambitious and technologically modern but morally culpable and intellectually inferior—had been circulating in American popular culture before World War II and were part of the cultural imaginary before Occupation authorities began constructing the Japanese as subjects suitable for a new American Pacific hegemony.

With the onset of the Japanese invasion of the Philippines, Orientalist conceptions of the Japanese were, for a short while, combined with more primitivist stereotypes to represent the peculiar nature of Japanese power, especially in comparison with Germany. While both the Germans and the Japanese were apprehended as brutal, the cultural-racial logic of Eurocentrism dictated that there be a differentiation between European and Asian ferocity, though both were to be soundly condemned. They were equally morally culpable, but vis-à-vis civilization, Japan was considered backward compared with Germany. A wartime *Washington Post* cartoon published in 1942, for instance, explains the heinousness of the Japanese invasion of the Philippines by commenting on the inhuman and monstrous nature of the Japanese compared with Hitler, a cruel human (Dower, *War without Mercy*, 182). Three years later, when the Japanese surrendered, the *Detroit News* published a cartoon (later reprinted in the *Sunday New York Times*) of the

Japanese as a puzzling species to be studied, analyzed, and presumably reformed and educated (Figure 5.1). However, as Dower points out, such cartoons of the Japanese appeared alongside their representations as fierce supermen, "possessed of uncanny discipline and fighting skills," particularly as the Japanese were gaining victories early in the war (*War without Mercy*, 9). Representations of Japanese before occupation thus included some primitivism but generally worked through Orientalism. Propaganda films such as Frank Capra's *Know Your Enemy—Japan* located the causes of Japanese brutality in the history of the samurai and included commentaries on "the Japanese mind" ruled by the "Shinto-emperor amalgam ... of racial superiority" (Dower, *War without Mercy*, 20). In contrast to German fascism, which was seen as an anomalous and dangerous moment that had surfaced only in recent history, Japanese military aggression was seen as embedded in Orientalist metaphysical and unchanging cultural traditions rooted in emperor worship and Shintoism. Robert Ballou's *Shinto, the Unconquered Enemy* (1945), which U.S. officials took seriously, argued that, in contrast to the war against Germany, the war against Japan was "also against an ideological force which was more than a thousand years old when Pan-Germanism was born ... and which is more powerful in conditioning a people than Nazism could ever be, because it has behind it the strength of an ancient and undying religious reverence" (4). In contrast to the material manifestations of German ultranationalism, Japanese ultranationalism was seen as ontological, rooted in an ancient, eternal, and unchanging past. It was part of the very being of Japaneseness and hence more stubborn and difficult to challenge.

Thus, even though Deweyans criticized Kantian pedagogy as a contributor to German totalitarianism, and officials such as Assistant Secretary of State William Benton argued for the need to reeducate the Germans away from authoritarianism, the U.S. Education Mission to Germany (USEMG) was sent a full year after the German surrender (Shibata, 118). Although the USEMG saw the elitist system of German education as a potential cause of the country's fascism, it hesitated to condemn the structure of a country with a culture so central to Western civilization. "The virulent disease of Nazism," the report states, "developed in a culture of very profound dimensions. No country ... has contributed more generously to the common treasures of our civilization. No approach to the German educational problem dare be blind to this achievement."[6] John Taylor, chief of the Education and Religious Affairs Branch of the Office of the Military Government of the United States (OMGUS), expressed the difference between Japanese and German reeducation most clearly when he stated, "Japan is an oriental country, the culture of which never reached a level comparable to that of Germany, the Nazi in-

FIGURE 5.1. "Another Puzzler for World Scholars."
(*Detroit News*, August 15, 1945.)

terregnum notwithstanding. . . . Hence, the situation in Germany is not analogous to that in Japan" (quoted in Shibata, 126). The conflicted attitude of the USEMG, combined with German educators' acute offense to the idea of being reeducated and their lack of admiration of American pedagogies, resulted in virtually no changes to the German educational system. In contrast, Japanese education was viewed as in need of complete overhaul through both immediate directives and long-term cultural and pedagogical changes.

SCAP Educational Directives

As in the Philippines, the occupation of Japan under the operatives of SCAP deemed education as a complement to the military victory, albeit with a rhetoric more about effecting cultural modifications than uplifting a race. Yet like the Philippines, Japan would be viewed as a social science and pedagogical laboratory where American educators could change the Japanese mind-set. Douglas MacArthur, for instance, wrote about being deeply affected by the lessons his father had taught him, "lessons learned out of his experiences as military governor of the Philippines." For MacArthur, Japan was "the world's greatest laboratory for an experiment in the liberation of a people from totalitarian military rule and for the liberalization of government from within" (*Reminiscences*, 282). MacArthur's analogy of the colonist as scientist is particularly interesting given David Barrows's anthropological study of Filipinos, as well as sociologists and anthropologists who were sent to systematically analyze the behavior and traits of Japanese Americans in internment camps in the United States. Japanese education officials were acutely sensitive to the imperialist implications of their country's being conceived of as a laboratory for political reform. In his address at the first meeting of the U.S. Education Mission, Japanese Minister of Education Yoshishige Abe requested that Americans "not ... deal with us simply from an American point of view" and criticized those who "tend to use Japan as a kind of laboratory in a rash attempt to experiment on some abstract ideals of their own, ideals which have not yet been realized even in their own country" (*Education in the New Japan*, 2:263). At the beginning of occupation, however, a key to bringing about cultural changes was the elimination of traits seen as responsible for Japanese aggression and the rise of Japan as a major military power—ultranationalism, conformity, and militarism—which were seen as interrelated, deeply embedded in the culture of Shintoism, and hence unique to the Japanese. Most importantly, the Japanese had to relearn and rethink their own history, particularly that of the twentieth century, as a narrative of moral decline concomitant with the country's rise as an imperial power.

Yet Allied documents, as much as Stratton-Porter's novel, also displayed an Orientalist anxiety about Japanese modernity. Japanese imperialism was sometimes viewed not as a culmination of reasoned (if evil) deliberation, because the capacity for rationality was a condition of modernity that Japan had not yet entered. The Potsdam Declaration, for instance, stated that the time had come for Japan to decide whether to be controlled by "those self-willed militaristic advisers whose unintelligent calculations have brought the Empire of Japan to the threshold of annihilation, or whether she will follow the path of reason" (*Education in the New Japan*, 2:6). That a highly public, international declaration delivering an ultimatum to the Japanese to surrender would be framed by the logic of colonial difference in which the division between reason and unreason is central speaks volumes about the perceived alterity of the Japanese to received ideas of civilization. But what was clear was that, unlike the Filipino—who had to be educated, for example, to be a Jeffersonian yeoman (in David Barrows's vision) who could do simple calculations—the Japanese had to be reeducated and decivilized. And this reeducation, conceived of as a continuation of military action, was partially articulated through the rhetoric of combat. As the CI&E's 1948 report made clear, "Demobilization of the Japanese Army and destruction of the Imperial Navy were initial reforms, but basic and permanent reforms would require changes in thought and behavior that could hope to be realized only by re-education" (*Education in the New Japan*, 1:135). The Potsdam Declaration dictating conditions of surrender was framed in the rhetoric of absolutes: "Following are our terms. We will not deviate from them. There are no alternatives. . . . There must be eliminated for all time the authority and influence of those who have deceived and misled the people of Japan into embarking on world conquest" (*Education in the New Japan*, 2:6–7). The Japanese government read this as a call for reeducating students and officials hurriedly acted to ensure compliance. Between surrender in August 1945 and the formation of SCAP in October, the Japanese government ordered that militaristic phrases be blacked out of school textbooks (Thakur, 24). SCAP continued, expanding the censorship to encompass all media, including film and radio, and prohibiting any criticism of its policy. However, the SCAP directive of October 1945 mandating the removal of all nationalism and militarism from textbooks was so sweeping that, had it been strictly followed, schools would be left without textbooks. The compromise was to use textbooks with massive deletions made by inking out, cutting, or pasting pages together to remove offensive material.

Educational reforms were directed at changing ideological conceptions of nation and practices associated with affirming Japanese nationalism; at cultural practices associated with a fierce, warlike spirit; and at what was perceived as the essentially conformist and imitative nature of the Japanese. All were important because it was a sense of superior Japanese nationalism that had challenged the supremacy of the West. It was imperative, therefore, to sever children from rituals through which, to use Homi Bhabha's term, the nation as pedagogical was affirmed: "The people are historical 'objects' of a nationalist pedagogy, giving the discourse an authority that is based on the pre-given or constituted historical origin in the past" (*The Location of Culture*, 145). What Bhabha views as constitutive of any nationalism, U.S. authorities in Japan saw as uniquely and dangerously Japanese. Helen Mears, who came to work for the occupation forces, critiqued this Orientalist logic and suggested that "the notion that the Japanese went to war because their Shinto gods commanded them to put their Emperor on the throne of the world is a tall story of the same credibility as Paul Bunyan's Blue Ox" (114). She saw the institution of the emperor and state Shinto as part of an "emotional nationalism" common throughout the world, including in democracies (115). Her view of Japanese military aggression as a mirror of Western colonialism provoked the ire of the U.S. government, and her book *Mirror for Americans: Japan* was banned during the occupation.

For SCAP, affecting what it viewed as deep-seated, cultural roots of military aggression was essential in schools. Central to maintaining ultranationalism was the practice of obeisance before portraits of the emperor. SCAP moved swiftly to prohibit this practice in schools because it had contributed to Japan's "militant nationalism" (*Report*, 25). SCAP not only viewed rituals of emperor worship as unhealthy and potentially fascist, commemorating an ideology of superior Japanese nationalism, it also viewed with suspicion any recreational activities that it saw as contributing to militarism (*Education in the New Japan*, 1:328). Therefore, sports such as judo, kendo, kyudo, jujitsu, fencing, and archery were deemed military arts and eliminated by order of the Ministry of Education, even though students resented not having their sports and demanded them back. A 1947 State Department directive declared, "Classical sports, such as *kendo*, which encourage the martial spirit, should be totally abandoned. . . . Greater emphasis should be placed on games and other recreational activities than on pure calisthenics and drill" (*Education in the New Japan*, 2:10–11). The assumption that Japanese imperialism and military belligerence were the result of a metaphysical warlike spirit meant questioning all classical cultural practices that could be construed as promoting militarism. Interestingly, despite the competition inherent in them, group sports, presumably due to rules of fairness and play, were deemed benign. That Americanization and democracy were synonymous was evident in the choice of the alternative sport: baseball was considered democratic and thus promoted (Staaveren, 46). Regular school inspections ensured compliance with directives and punishment for violations.

While some of the educational reforms were articulated as complementary to the military actions of subduing a warlike, superhuman foe with an inbuilt strain of militarism, others were directed at ideas of the Japanese as belonging to a feudal culture that needed to be brought into modernity through the introduction of individualism, capitalism, and democracy. Here the Japanese were seen in stereotypical Orientalist terms as backward, underdeveloped, eternal, and uniform (Said, 40, 300–301). In a sense these two attributes were not necessarily at odds with each other. As Said pointed out, the Oriental was viewed both as fanatic warrior and as denizen of a monarchical tradition in which democracy could not be imagined (317). Similarly, the Japanese could be seen as fierce and formidable fighters who, although defeated, had a militarism that needed to be destroyed, and at the same time a people whose culture demanded nothing less than absolute conformity. What needed to be effected were not simply changes in a few jingoistic practices but changes in the culture itself. Joseph Ballantine, a Japanese specialist involved in the premilitary planning of the occupation, put it most succinctly when he stated, "We do not believe that Japanese militarism had its roots in the emperor, or in any other single institution. . . . We believe that it is grounded in the habit of thought and in an [ideology] which have persisted among the Japanese for many centuries, which can be eradicated only by the sufferings of defeat and by long drawn-out and gradual processes" (quoted in Iriye, 386).

Education Reform: *Report of the United States Education Mission to Japan*

The most important document related to education reform in occupied Japan was the *Report of the United States Education Mission to Japan*. Prepared in March 1946, it became "a veritable 'bible' for all military and civilian officials, whether they were engaged in the civil education task in Tokyo or on military government units" (Staaveren, 44). The idea of an education mission was proposed shortly after the formation of SCAP, with the list of members being revised as the objectives changed from nominating distinguished university educators to a more nationally representative group that included educators with public school backgrounds. The final education mission, consisting of twenty-seven American educators and headed by George D. Stoddard, who was selected by the Department of State and vetted by General Headquarters (GHQ), included an eclectic mixture of leading educators, including some who would become victims of McCarthyism. There were followers of progressivist education, such as Harold Benjamin and Alexander J. Stoddard, who chaired the Educational Policies Commission of 1938; leftist critics of progressivist education, such as George S. Counts, whose *Dare the School Build a New Social Order?* (1932) promulgated a social reconstructionism at odds with the child-centered subjective experimentalism of the progressivists, and Isaac L. Kandel, whose commitment to common values also put him at odds with aspects of progressivism; important feminist educators, such as Virginia C. Gildersleeve and Pearl A. Wanamaker; and Willard E. Givens, head of the National Education Association. Many members of the mission had considerable international experience, but only one, Gordon Bowles, had long-standing familiarity with Japan. The members stayed in Japan for barely over three weeks, visiting schools and colleges and consulting with local educators, in addition to visiting tourist sites. At the end of the month, they submitted their report. In keeping with MacArthur's slogan, "Education for Democracy," these educators formulated guidelines to inculcate "liberalism" and "democracy," both of which were preconditions for learning and growth. They wrote:

> We believe in the power of every race and nation to create from its own cultural resources something good for itself and for the whole

world. That is the liberal creed. We are not devoted to uniformity; as educators we are constantly alert to deviation, originality, and spontaneity. This is the spirit of democracy.... The best capacities of teachers flourish only in an atmosphere of freedom.... The unmeasured resources of childhood will bear rich fruit only under the sunshine of liberalism.... [I]t is the responsibility of all in authority to find out how much can be allowed rather than how much can be forbidden. That is the meaning of liberalism. Where that spirit is, democracy has already taken root; it needs only time and patience to become a representative government. (*Report*, 4)

These statements about liberalism and democracy clearly reveal the influences of new racial and educational theories in the United States. Philosophers such as Horace M. Kallen proposed cultural pluralism and opposed nativists who argued for Americanization programs for immigrants.[7] These thinkers shifted the focus from race to culture and argued for changes facilitating a democratic vision, albeit an American one rooted in capitalist individualism rather than community. Randolph S. Bourne admired the Gary Schools of William Wirth for educating the illiterate immigrant

not into a New Englander, but into a socialized American.... I do not believe that this process is to be one of decades of evolution. The spectacle of Japan's sudden jump from medievalism to post-modernism should have destroyed that superstition.... Let us cease to think of ideals like democracy as magical qualities inherent in certain peoples. Let us speak, not of inferior races, but of inferior civilizations. (95)

As discussed in the Introduction, such progressivist ideas of education at once disputed racist ideas about inherent mental capabilities and emphasized the superiority of Anglo-American culture. Although the beginning of World War II reinvigorated biological racism in the arena of social policy—as evidenced in the interning of Japanese Americans—Bourne's ideas about educating immigrants into a culture of democracy were reflected in the *Report*. Kallen and Bourne, along with intellectuals such as Jean Toomer, saw possibilities in changing group behavior through education.[8]

The *Report* reveals the influence of a variegated legacy of progressivist, cultural pluralist, and antinativist meliorist thought, all of which were different from assimilationist theories of ethnicity. At the same time, the *Report* valorizes and universalizes American ideas of individualism, Anglo-American modernity, and freedom through capitalism and consumerism and retains distinctly racialized ideas of the Japanese. The educators began their report by acknowledging their vexed positions as agents of quasi-colonial occupiers but distancing themselves from the state and expressing a progressivist, universalist belief in the inherent possibilities of each individual: "We do not come in the spirit of conquerors but as experienced educators who believe that there is unmeasured potential for freedom and for individual and social growth in every human being" (*Report*, 3). To effect democratic reforms, the educators felt they had to influence and modify aspects of Japanese culture that were inimical to democracy. However, they identified not only social features that had contributed to Japan's military aggression but also, in Orientalist fashion, aspects that put Japan "behind" in the teleology of civilization. The struggle of schools was threefold, against "obscurantism, feudalism, and militarism" (*Report*, 6). Militarism spelled the evident political structure, the ethos of fascism it was the business of the occupation to dismantle. Obscurantism and feudalism, however, indicated civilizational aspects drawn from the rhetoric of colonial difference. Although Euro-American eyes saw Asia through Orientalist lenses, Japan's defeat of Russia in 1905, while viewed with alarm by Western nations, had also confounded civilizational hierarchies. Indeed, in Britain, writers admired the simplicity and moral training of *bushido* that had made possible Japan's victory (Wolff et al., 388). The label of feudalism, however, relegated the Japanese to the middle ages of Europe. Finally, obscurantism signified the racialization of the Japanese in particularly Japanese-Orientalist terms. Unlike Filipinos, who had been conceived of through a tropicalist Orientalism as indolent and contented (except for those who had acquired some learning through contact with the Spanish), the Japanese were seen as heirs to a respectable though antiquated system of learning, one outside of and possibly inimical to Western systems of rationality. The epitome of this learning was *kanji*, which became a major object of the mission's language reform, and which I discuss shortly.

Japan's militarism had indeed affected its intellectual milieu and educational policies. When John Dewey visited Japan in 1919 and 1920, he had found it a mixture of political ferment and militarism. A "returned student" told him that when he landed "just a year before it was not safe to utter the word democracy, as it might send you to prison, but now everybody was talking it, even coolies and ricksha-men" (Feuer, 124). Dewey was excited about journals such as *Democracy* and *The New Society* being published by students every month but worried about government repression of intellectuals (Feuer, 129). Militarism, he despaired, was destined to win the day because liberal intellectuals could not deny the importance of a heavily armed Japan in thwarting Western imperialism and keeping the country from being colonized like the rest of Asia (Dewey, *Characters and Events*, 182). However, Deweyan thought had been the motor of the "New Education Movement" of the interwar years, the period of Taishō Democracy which saw the publication of twelve books on Dewey, with Nagano Yoshio's *Jyon Dyui kyoikugakuestsu no kenkyu* (A Study of John Dewey's Educational Theory [1920]) going through its seventh printing in 1926 (Kobayashi, 49). By the 1930s, the educator Obara Kuniyoshi estimated that about three hundred schools were following the New Education, with half of elementary schools attempting to use progressive ideas (Kobayashi, 71). Many of these schools avoided the military drills and chauvinistic songs that had become standard in public schools in the 1930s (Kobayashi, 77).

Absolute and binaristic separations between American and Japanese cultures and pedagogical practices, in other words, had been rendered untenable by the very imperialist "opening up" of Japan almost a century earlier. Progressivist educational thought had been disseminated in Japan decades before the U.S. Education Mission delivered its report, a fact that was probably clear to the American educators, because the Japanese Education Committee, which worked with the mission, included many progressive educators of the interwar years. The report abjured this history, however, save one acknowledgment that some Japanese educators had "managed to attain an admirable degree of flexibility in their teaching," despite heavy restrictions (*Report*, 32). The result was a document of benevolent (colonial) liberalism written by educators convinced of their advanced methods and presenting them to their Japanese colleagues as strategies for moving from unthinking autocratic control to enlightened freedom. The numerous disagreements of the eclectic group of American educators (see Hochwalt, 378) and the advice from their progressive Japanese counterparts were excised from the official document, which served as a technology of tutelary governance envisioning itself as advancing Japanese education from a hierarchical culture mired in the past to a new equality predicated on American-style individualism: "In the older pattern education was organized from the top downwards; its essential characteristic was authoritarianism. In the new pattern, for which we have discovered a deep-lying support at all social levels, the starting point must be the individual" (*Report*, 8).

Such an optic, which precluded any consideration of divergent pedagogical styles resulting from different cultural patterns of respect for teachers, made it possible to write the difference in classroom patterns in terms of a Cold War politics of totalitarianism versus democracy. Furthermore, in keeping with a style of colonial paternalism, Japanese educators were presented as natives awaiting leadership and direction from Americans. As the

Report put it, "They [Japanese educators] demand and require of us some positive guidance. They state freely that they know the words 'liberalism, democracy, science, and humanism,' but that they do not always sense the fundamental meaning and may be unable to chart the painful road toward implementation" (4). The document, that is, not only provided guidelines for reeducation based on a narrative of progress from tyranny to freedom, feudalism to modernity, but also cast Japanese educators as grateful recipients of a new educational order they could scarcely comprehend. This was an ironic narrative given the formation in 1876 of the University of Hokkaido as a "frontier spirit" university under the aegis of William S. Clark, founder of the Massachusetts Agricultural College. Educational interaction between Japan and the United States had been long-standing, a fact that the *Report* simply did not acknowledge. And despite collaboration with, and helpful input from, the Japanese, the published *Report* drew on the colonial trope of enlightening the Japanese, as well as on the well-worn Orientalist trope of Asiatic despotism. Japanese educators, eager to dispel ideas about their status on the ladder of democratic intellectual evolution, depicted the New Education of the occupation years as a continuation, albeit interrupted, of their own, progressive education in the interwar years and resented statements by members of the commission, such as those of Isaac Kandel, that denied any such connection (Kobayashi, 6–7). In accordance with the stringent censorship of references to the atomic bombings early in the occupation, the *Report* made no mention of the material devastation to schools or the human casualties.

Ironically, the educators saw possibilities of an incipient democracy in formal Japanese manners, which, they argued, could function in egalitarian fashion. Noting that Japanese civilians were renowned for their gentility, the *Report* suggested that skeptics of "the consummate art of face-saving" might well wish "that they knew as well how to save human feelings from daily hurt." It reinterpreted the practice of bowing, often seen as a mark of submission, as a marker of social equality. Deference, the educators argued, was overdone "only when it [was] invidiously done: make bowing universal, and you make it democratic. Indeed, whatever forms of politeness can be applied by all men to all men will ease the path of democracy" (12). Of course, the Americans noted only the universality of bowing, not the social gradations acknowledged in the practice. But in arguing that customs such as bowing could, in fact, be the basis for Japanese democracy, the Americans were expressing their commitment to cultural pluralism and distancing themselves from arguments about civilizational hierarchies such as those made by Douglas MacArthur. Yet by not acknowledging the democratic practices of the politically charged Left, such as the protests of teachers' unions, which were allowed in the early days of the occupation, the educators denied the existence of modern democratic movements in Japan.

The recommendations for the reconstruction of education also revealed ideas about the inherent conformity of the Japanese. While ideas about Filipinos as mimics contained anxiety about insurrections and the intransigence of native subjects (they were more than the partial mimics needed for colonialism and could rebel) or the need for a schematization that would categorize Filipinos as undeveloped, pronouncements about the Japanese as imitators pointed to the inherently obedient, mechanical, and potentially imperial mind-set of the Japanese. In keeping with popular representations of Japanese as copiers, capable of little imagination or innovation, members of the mission sought to make recommendations designed to cultivate creativity. The mission commented on the very real restrictions on course content and evaluation in the Japanese system and commended the few who undauntedly challenged the system but saw the Japanese as largely bound to mechanical learning. "Japanese teachers need no one to tell them how to conduct memory exercises or to develop skill of hand," they wrote. "They are masters at this art." What their teaching might shut out is "the development of curiosity and originality" (*Report*, 32). This perception of East Asians as imitators was an eighteenth-century phenomenon, when ideas of memorization and imitation as intellectual tenacity changed to critiques of mimicry (Lucken, 10), a critique that continued in Hegel's pronouncement of Chinese artists as imitators who could copy European pictures but who could not portray the Exalted, the Ideal, and Beautiful. Similar arguments were made by nineteenth-century British scholars who, unable to comprehend different epistemological traditions, were perplexed by what they perceived as Indians' prodigious capacities for parrot-like memorization without the ability to understand what they had learned (Cohn, 51–52). Arguably, by the early twentieth century the faculty of imitation was condemned to the lower rungs of the civilizational hierarchy and became a means of colonial demarcation.

Thus, ideas of Japanese as unoriginal, committed to rote memorization, and blindly following authority coalesced in initiatives to reform language that, despite the well-meaning intentions of the mission, were problematically implicated in conceptions of the inherently democratic or undemocratic nature of languages and reiterated earlier debates about the characters of English and Tagalog in the Philippines. Of course, ideas about language reform did not originate with the mission, and the question of script reform has generated ample critical controversy. Some scholars view script reform, particularly the promotion of *kana* (syllabic Japanese script) and *romaji* (Japanese sounds written in English letters), as inherently democratic, designed to increase literacy among the masses. They see the suppression of script reform in the decades before World War II as reflective of the authoritarianism of the government and the reemergence of script reform after Japan's surrender as exemplary of a commitment to a more egalitarian social order. However, these scholars also problematically see the movement to phonetic script as a civilizational advancement over the logographic and hence view script reform as a step in the necessary teleology of a Western-determined progress toward modernity. Nanette Gottlieb sees the proposal presented by Japanese societies for romanization (Nihon Romazikai) and the Kana society (Kanamojikai) to SCAP in December 1945 as indicative of a period when "sovereignty was passing into the hands of the people." It was a time of "revulsion against xenophobia, reactionary conservatism, and ultranationalism of the war period; the people had a yearning for that which was modern, Western, and rational" (1178). J. Marshall Unger similarly lauds Japanese advocates of romanization because they were "willing to push tradition aside [and] examine their own culture in the cold light of objectivity" (7). While Gottlieb rightly observes the reactions against ultranationalism, she automatically assumes the democratic nature of moves toward romanization and the adoption of *kana*. More blatantly Eurocentric, Unger takes for granted that modern, rational thought will reveal the superiority of and necessity for romanization. Gottlieb and Unger both accept hierarchical, binaristic divisions between West and East, present and past, rationality and superstition as given. Despite the earnestness of the members of the U.S. Education Mission in wanting to help the citizens of a nation defeated in war become a democratic and sovereign nation, the *Report* buys into these civilizational divisions.

At the root of Japan's linguistic problems, the educators felt, was the inordinately difficult nature of *kanji*, a demanding script that impeded literacy and therefore hindered democracy. Although aware of the close relationship between language and culture and the colonial implications of the desire to change a native language, the mission proposed a wholesale adoption of *romaji*. Because "language is so intimate an organism in a people's life that it is hazardous to approach it from without," they reasoned that they were simply giving the reform a "friendly stimulus" and stated, "From a deep sense of duty, and from it alone, we recommend a drastic reform of the Japanese written language" (*Report*, 20). As discussed in Chapter 1, the imposition of English in the Philippines was justified on grounds of unifying the archipelago and on the traits of Anglo-Saxon culture—individualism and sharpness, among others—transmitted through the language. Literature in native languages such as Tagalog was so devalued by the colonial administration that it received scarce attention in school and university curricula, even after the commonwealth period. Discussions about *kanji*, however, were different. The literary merits of *kanji* or its inherent capacity to change and grow were not significant issues, as they were in the Philippines. Instead, the attempt to overhaul *kanji*, the Chinese-based script in Japan, stemmed from a sense of the logographic system's utter dissimilarity from phonetic Latin languages that had always posed difficulty for foreigners and from an Orientalist anxiety about difference. But now *kanji* was portrayed as intimidating for Japanese children and inimical to their learning and growth. Europeans had developed forms of *romaji* as early as the sixteenth century, but it received a boost only after Commodore Perry's gunboat diplomacy in the 1850s, when J. S. Hepburn published his Japanese-English dictionary using *romaji*. As Trainor of the CI&E put it, "*Romaji* was invented by foreigners primarily for the use of foreigners," and the Hepburn romanization was "conceived as an aid to Christian missionaries who came to Japan," even though some Japanese groups later advocated different forms of *romaji* (313–314).

The educators of the mission, however, conceived it as their duty to ease the burden of what they saw as obscurantist learning. "Clearly the question of language reform," they earnestly wrote, "is basic and urgent. . . . If no satisfactory answer can be found to this problem, the achievement of many agreed upon educational goals will be rendered most difficult. For example, the promotion of an understanding of other nations and of democracy at home will be hampered" (*Report*, 20). The assumption was that *kanji* could not possibly be learned easily enough for a population to be literate. It was a language too difficult for democracy, a concern repeatedly raised in the *Report*. The educators argued that the memorization of *kanji* placed "an excessive burden on the pupils," and despite the "inordinate amount of time allotted to recognizing and writing *kanji*, . . . pupils may lack the linguistic abilities essential to democratic citizenship" (*Report*, 20–21). To carry out "the elementary duties of citizenship," students needed to "understand the meaning of simple statements of fact touching social events," a skill apparently not possible because of the difficulty of *kanji*.

If the slogan "Education for Democracy" was being followed here, it is difficult to understand why these educators would not see the lack of knowledge of democratic citizenship simply as a result of stringent wartime controls over educational content rather than as something inherent in language. Interestingly, despite the fact that many members of the United States Education Mission had credentials in education research, the group did not rely on such studies in reaching its conclusions about the constraining effects of *kanji*. Having simply consulted a few *romaji* advocates, they assumed that a logographic script could not but hinder learning. Data that the Education

Division collected in 1947 revealed, in fact, that elementary schools in Japan devoted less time to language learning than did elementary schools in the United States, and high literacy rates could be deduced from larger circulation of newspapers in Japan than in the United States (Trainor, 320). The problem with *kanji* was not simply that of linguistic proficiency but also the nature of the script, which required more of a different pedagogical skill and epistemology: memorization. My point here is not to critique the mission's report for inadequate research but, rather, to analyze the cultural assumptions inherent in the recommendations and to see how the *Report* imagines and maps out ideal pedagogical subjects.

Most progressivist educators had been clear about democracy as a precondition for cooperative learning. Dewey's fierce critique of education being a handmaiden to the state, beginning with Fichte's and Hegel's emphasis on the state and continuing in early twentieth-century Germany, had been familiar reading for educators before the postwar period (*Democracy and Education*, 56). Little wonder that American educators enthusiastically participated in the opportunity to help reform a system that had formerly been under the control of a repressive militarist government. At the same time, ideas about rote learning as creating a populace receptive to doctrines of Japan as Asia's leader also entered into reports about the stultifying effects of instruction by memorization. Reflecting on a visit to a classroom where students shouted in unison to answer a question asked by a teacher, Staaveren wrote, "American educationists considered this pedagogical method as a mind-numbing exercise that stifled creative thinking. They believed it contributed significantly to the susceptibility of students in prewar and wartime period to government propaganda about Japan's 'destiny' and the importance of its 'Greater East Asia Co-[P]rosperity Sphere.' Thus all military officers and civilians . . . had been counseled . . . to discourage, if possible, the practice of learning by rote" (52–53). While the facility of memorization had denoted intellectual/civilizational limits for Filipinos, ideas about rote learning as creating an imperialist mind-set are reflected in Staaveren's recollections. Consequently, conceptions about Japanese as rote learners, while reflecting a racialized Eurocentric teleology, were also imbricated in anxieties and fears about Japan as an Asian colonial power and of an Asian geopolitical order outside the system of Western colonialism. Conceptions of Filipinos as imitators incapable of originality and the Japanese as dangerous mimics were both strategic racial formations, but whereas one was civilizational and used the rhetoric of uplift, the other used the rhetoric of democracy.

The language of the *Report* also suggests the need for students attuned to an efficient, capitalist modernity, without wasting time in unproductive channels. Japan had to become an organized, Taylorist producer of goods without expending energy in obscurantist learning. Lamenting that "the memorization of *kanji* . . . places an excessive burden on the pupils," who "continue to labor at the unending task of mastering the symbols of the written language," the U.S. Education Mission asks, "Can any modern nation afford the luxury of such a difficult and time-consuming medium of expression and communication?" (*Report*, 20–21) Robert King Hall, who advocated *katakana* (the simplest syllabic form of Japanese), argued clearly for the channeling of productivity more efficiently. Instead of spending time learning *kanji*, "Children would . . . reach a productive level at an earlier age and would increase the labor supply without reducing the educational standard of the country" (quoted in Nishi, 200). Similar arguments were raised when calligraphy, which had been compulsory in Japanese schools and seen to foster tenderness and grace, was declared optional (Nishi, 206). Perhaps most revealing of the mission's belief in the inherently liberatory bases of Western language systems, rather than simply the relative ease of learning, is their belief that "there are more advantages to *romaji* than to *kana*" because the former "would lend itself well to the growth of democratic citizenship and international understanding" (*Report*, 22). Evaluating three possible options—reducing *kanji* characters, abandoning *kanji* for a form of *kana*, or dropping both *kanji* and *kana* for *romaji*—the mission recommended completely discarding *kanji* and adopting a phonetic system, preferably *romaji*.

Behind the educators' recommendations for a language that would facilitate democracy lay anxiety about the radical difference of the logographic script, a marker for an imperial nation that had attained industrial modernity by selectively adopting Western technology but rejecting a wholesale adoption of Western culture. Roland Barthes's veneration of Japan as a culture with an "unheard of symbolic system . . . detached from our own" is simply the reverse of this anxiety (3). The U.S. Education Mission therefore argued that "wherever possible linguistic supports of the spirit of national isolation and exclusiveness need breaking down. The adoption of *romaji* would constitute a major contribution to the transmission of knowledge and ideas across national boundaries" (*Report*, 23). As a sign of absolute difference, contributing to "the spirit of national isolation and exclusiveness," *kanji* seemed also to be a marker of an Otherness that is often Orientalized as inscrutability. The attempt to instantiate linguistic change in the effort to democratize and modernize Japanese education revealed not only what the historian Kenneth Pyle has called a fostering of a "wholesale adoption of the American educational system and its philosophy" (163) in Japan but also, more importantly, ideas about the Japanese derived from a system of Orientalist difference that leaked beyond the earnest mission of demilitarizing education. Although a Romaji Educational Committee was formed subsequent to the U.S. Education Mission's recommendations, and the Ministry of Education began experimenting with the introduction of *romaji* for the grade 3 and higher in 1947, misgivings about a wholesale change, which Japanese members of the committee and other Japanese educators expressed, and MacArthur's view that language change ultimately should be the decision of the Japanese, meant that *romaji* was never mandated and *kanji* was never banned. Yet the very proposal for language change, Toshio Nishi writes, created a long-term fear of Americanization and cultural colonization because it "in effect invited the Japanese people to commit cultural suicide" (206).

The Ministry of Education's *Primer of Democracy*

While the U.S. Education Mission envisioned pedagogical subjects freed from a cumbersome script and Shinto-inspired nationalism, and ready to embrace a capitalist modernity that centered on individualism, production, and efficiency, with the United States as hegemon, textbooks on democracy for the school curriculum and guides for teachers created by the Ministry of Education attempted to further the task of tutelage by offering lessons in history and civics. Written by Japanese scholars in the Ministry of Education, which was disproportionately composed of Christians and vetted by the SCAP's CI&E, these texts taught democracy through an appreciation for Western culture and capitalism. Two volumes of textbooks called *Primer of Democracy* were published, the first in 1948, to be used by grade 9, and the second in 1949, to be used by grade 10 and in adult education. The foreword to the first volume states as its purpose the teaching of democracy as a way of life directed especially at children, because "the job of reconstructing Japan falls particularly on the shoulders of the young boys and girls of today" (*Primer*, "Foreword," 1:n.p.). The *Primer* then goes on to define democracy:

> What then is democracy? Many will answer that it is a form of government that permits the people to elect their representatives who will govern for them. True, that is one manifestation of democracy. But it is wrong to consider democracy as merely a form of government. . . . It is rooted in the minds and hearts of individuals. It is essentially a spiritual thing. It is a disposition and willingness to deal with all human beings as individuals having worth and dignity of their own. (1:n.p.)

This resurrection of the spirit of democracy, interestingly, was seen as the job of "reconstructing Japan," echoing the reformism of the United States a century ago. But if democracy was inherently spiritual, involving a disposition to respect human dignity, its manifestations could presumably take different political forms, including socialism. It is here that the occupation as largely a U.S. undertaking, rather than an Allied occupation, manifests itself, with the Ministry of Education using Cold War rhetoric. The chapter titled "The Story of Democracy" begins with the Norman invasion of Britain, discusses the final construction of the British constitutional government, and turns to North America. Writing a narrative of American exceptionalism, it contrasts the atrocities of Spanish colonialism on the American continent with the democratic colonialism of North America, harking back to contrasts made between U.S. and Spanish colonialism in the Philippines. During Spanish colonialism, motivated by a "quest for gold" and marked by "exploit[ation] of the labor of natives, . . . not even a spark of democracy was visible in the new land called New Spain" (*Primer*, 1:n.p.). The beginning of liberty starts with the landing of the *Mayflower*: "It was not until the English settlers arrived to colonize [North America] that the first glimmer of democracy began to dawn over the New World" (*Primer*, 1:n.p.).

Central to the task of the *Primer* was the demonstration of American capitalism as a just social system, expressive of democracy. Given the poverty of postwar Japan, addressing the issue of economic equality was urgent. Here the *Primer* danced a fine line between denouncing all aspects of socialism and critiquing the ills of unfettered capitalism by embracing the reformism of the New Deal as democratic capitalism; at the same time, this democracy (realized in Japan to an extent through MacArthur's land reforms) had to work within capitalism and be dissociated from socialism. Thus, paradoxically, under a section titled "Advantages of Free Competition," the *Primer* underscored the importance of "democracy in economic activities" through a "guarantee [of] fair economic distribution." Readers were assured that although "people often talk today about the evils of capitalism . . . [i]n the advanced capitalist states of today[,] . . . various measures are invented to democratize [*sic*] economy without altering the basic system of capitalism" (2:57). The *Primer* thus condemned the excesses of capitalism, lauded the policies of the New Deal, and contrasted the totalitarianism of communism with real practices of democracy. It sought to squelch possible sympathies for teachers' unions that had been banned by MacArthur by recognizing the importance of labor unions in general but condemning the "communist" connections of these particular unions.

But despite its publication and dissemination during the Reverse Course of occupation, when, Koshiro argues, Japanese were seen as honorary whites, the *Primer* assessed Japanese cultural practices through the lens of colonial difference and found them distinctly unmodern, survivors of a mode of living long surpassed in the West. Assessing Japanese familial practices in a chapter titled "Democracy in Social Life," the authors trace the decline of feudalism in the West and argue that, "in the minds of the Japanese people, there still remain traces of feudalism." Exemplary of this feudalism is the tradition of respect for age that the *Primer* holds in utter contempt: "There is no valid reason why a father should impose unreasonable restrictions on his children merely because he is a father. . . . Parents do not have great worth and dignity merely because they are parents. Pigs, for example, are parents" (1:chap. 8 [n.p.]). Working through an ontologically singular, stagist conception of history, the writers see Japanese political modernity as a survival of an earlier mode rather than a different kind of modernity in which kinship is central.[9] They argue vociferously for a change in Japanese family relationships because these are incompatible with democracy, but the possibility of a modern Japanese subject comprising multiple, incommensurable practices is not considered, and Japanese familial practices are simply seen as nonrational.

Similarly, sections titled "Respect for the Individual" and "Individualism" underscore the key feature of American social life as integral to democracy. "The philosophy of respecting human beings as individuals is 'individualism.' Therefore, the fundamental spirit of democracy is founded on individualism" (*Primer*, 1:chap. 8 [n.p.]). Thus traditional Japanese practices, such as the performance of humility in public life, are shown to be antithetical to individualism and, hence, democracy. The *Primer* suggests that protestations such as "I am such a worthless person" disallow human dignity and deny the democratic "respect for individuality," in contrast to "advanced democratic nations of the West[, which] are determined to defend to the last their human freedoms and individual rights" (1:chap. 8 [n.p.]). Simultaneously, in keeping with the Reverse Course of occupation, the Japanese pedagogical subject is constructed as one useful for capitalism. As the *Primer* categorically states, "Property is indispensable for the maintenance of orderly human life" (1:chap. 8 [n.p.]). The *Primer*, resting on a Lockean notion of property as a guarantor of individual liberty and a Protestant belief in acquisition as a sign of individual industry, as theorized by Max Weber, was thus an American version of the Japanese *shushin*, or course in morals that was banned by SCAP, filling the gap left by removing state Shintoism (Trainor, 334).[10]

But if the *Primer* substituted democracy for *shushin*, it also assumed the primacy of not only American political institutions and civil structures, but also everyday American culture. A section titled "Democratic Education," for instance, touts the Deweyan premise of school being a kind of society and promotes spontaneity, cooperation, and egalitarian relations between teachers and students. The section begins with a baseball analogy for education:

To know baseball, you must study its rules. But, however hard you may study baseball rules[,] . . . these things in themselves, will not enable you to play genuinely good baseball. To be able to play baseball well, it is absolutely essential that you play it yourself. . . . In order to learn the true ways of social living[,] . . . the shortest cut, therefore, is to practice them in the society of the school. (*Primer*, 2:25)

Clearly, in addition to the colonial apparatus of SCAP, the soft weapon of culture was deemed a necessary component to effecting subjectivities conducive to U.S. hegemony. Democratic education was a means of not only furthering equitable, nonmilitaristic relations among people but also breaking down "the Oriental tradition of obsequious master-disciple relations" characteristic of Japanese culture (*Primer*, 2:26). The *Primer* was soundly criticized by the Japan Communist Party, as well as by the Japan Teachers Union, for its anti-labor spirit but was supported by many newspapers, circulated in women's clubs, parent-teacher associations, and became a best seller, with five million copies in circulation by 1950 (Trainor, 338–339).

The Japanese Ministry of Education's
Guide to New Education in Japan

The origin of Japan's wartime militarism as inherently cultural was soundly vetted by the Japanese Ministry of Education's *Guide to New Education in Japan*, 436,020 copies of which were published, in May 1946, amidst an acute paper shortage, to be distributed to elementary and secondary school teachers. The book was written by experts outside the Ministry of Education and revised by officials in the ministry in consultation with SCAP. Although the *Guide* was ostensibly not mandated for teachers but to be availed by them through "free investigation" and intended to "encourage teachers to exercise initiative and critical thinking with regard to educational problems" (*Guide*, "Foreword," n.p.), it was read by most schoolteachers. It was a document steeped in Orientalism, convinced about the superiority of Western civilization, and it urged teachers to "embrace and assimilate and take in the fundamental principles of western civilization, digest these principles and be able to use them as [their] own" (*Guide*, 1:pt. A [4]). The problem was the essential nature of the Japanese. Attributing the problems afflicting the nation to the inherent character flaws of the Japanese, the document answered the question "How did Japan come to be in the condition she is today?" by providing five answers that are worth quoting: "Japan is not yet sufficiently modernized"; "The Japanese Nation does not sufficiently respect Humanity, Character, nor Individuality"; "The Japanese lack critical skill and are prone to obey authority blindly"; "The Japanese people are scientifically backward and have a poor sense of logic"; and "The Japanese are self-satisfied and narrow-minded" (*Guide*, 1:pt. A [3–4, 6–8]). As Nishi put it, the *Guide* "combined the victor's propaganda with the loser's self-abasement" (237).

What is particularly interesting is the analysis of Japan's relationship to modernity. The *Guide* suggested that modernity in Japan was superficial and incomplete. It argued that Japanese culture had adopted the material trappings of modern civilization, such as the use of electricity and gas in homes and large-scale production, but stubbornly continued to maintain superstitious practices, such as palmistry and backward familial relations in which mothers-in-law maintained unjust power over daughters-in-law. Again, the possibility of the coexistence of the secular and spiritual in Japanese modernity is not considered, and as in the Philippines, teachers are encouraged to attempt to change family structures. It is commonplace among historians, political scientists, and cultural studies scholars to point to the strategic Westernization of Japan as a means of resisting colonization. "Wakon Yosai" (Japanese spirit, Western technologies) was a slogan of the Meiji Restoration (Iwasbuchi, 54–55).[11] In his classic analysis of the growth of anticolonial nationalism under British colonial rule, Partha Chatterjee argued that Bengali nationalists declared freedom by dividing the world into inner and outer spheres and preserving a sphere of the inner/spiritual/traditional inviolable to the encroachments of the British (6). By selectively appropriating aspects of modernity in the domains of statecraft, science, and technology, where the West was superior, and maintaining an "'inner' domain bearing the 'essential' marks of cultural identity,' anticolonial nationalism declared that the West had "failed to colonize the inner, essential identity of the East, which lay in its distinctive, and superior, spiritual culture. Here the East was undominated, sovereign, master of its own fate" (Chatterjee, 6, 121). Chatterjee suggests that this inner-outer division, which also ended up creating its own hierarchies, was a principal feature of anticolonial nationalisms in Asia and Africa.

No doubt the idea of a Japanese essence/spirituality could lead down the slippery slope of exceptionalism and discourses of racial purity. However, the authors of the *Guide* see complete Westernization as the only alternative to Japanese imperialism. They recognize the selective modernity of the Meiji Restoration and impute the sorry situation of postwar Japan precisely to this particular appropriation of Western modernity: "Since the Meiji Restoration, Japan has been eagerly adopting and imbibing western civilization. . . . But it was principally the materialistic side of Western Civilization" (*Guide*, 1:pt. A [3]). According to the *Guide*, therefore, the modernization of Japan was incomplete and superficial. The *Guide* suggested it was, in fact, the failure to adopt completely the attributes of Western modernity that contributed to the downfall of Japan. The critique is worth quoting at length:

> The modernization of Japan was only half-measure, especially the substance of modern spirit.... In spite of this, it was thought that the same level of civilization as that of the occidentals had been reached—on the contrary, there were some people who even thought that insofar as the spiritual side was concerned the spirit of the orientals, especially the Japanese spirit, was better. People with wrong ideas such as these became leaders of the nation who gave little thought to Western culture, underestimated their power, and plunged the nation into war.... We must make better use of our abilities to embrace and assimilate and take in the fundamental principles of western civilization, digest these principles and be able to use them as our own. (*Guide*, 1:pt. A [4])

At one level, the advice that teachers embrace and adopt all aspects of Western civilization to instill them in students and effectively create a thoroughly Westernized Japan can be seen as a strategic attempt to regain power in the world arena or to mollify the victors who were convinced of the feudal nature of Japanese culture and the superiority of the West. As MacArthur stated, "Supposedly, the Japanese were a twentieth-century civilization. In reality, they were more nearly a feudal society, of the type discarded by Western nations some four centuries ago" (*Reminiscences*, 283) The *Guide* also affirms the chronopolitics of Western temporality in which the non-West lags "behind" the West in terms of culture, development, and human rights and needs to "catch up." At another level, the guide is an interrogation and indictment of Japanese colonialism. Yet the authors seem unable to critique Japanese fascism without buying in to the hierarchical binaries of Orientalism, in which Eastern civilizations cannot be seen as at par with the West.

What Chatterjee identified as a strategy of strategic (anticolonial) nationalism Japanese educators saw as ultranationalism and the cause of Japanese totalitarianism. Not accepting the superiority of Western civilization, being strategic imitators rather than proverbial mimic men, was the downfall of the Japanese. For these educators, there is no room in this binaristic formulation for the construction of alternative or counter-modernities. Modernity is seen as simply Western, and an embrace of this modernity is an embrace of egalitarianism. What the *Guide* does not address is the fundamental contradiction of Western modernity: that modernity and colonialism were coterminous. Instead, the *Guide* suggests that it was Japan's attack on Western colonialism and its attempt to become a colonial power that were inherently misguided.

The Japanese were taught that "because the countries of Europe and America had invaded and exploited East Asia, they must now be driven away; they asserted that it was to realize the way of the Empire to lead and rule the peoples of the Greater East Asia with the characteristic spirit of Japan" (1:pt. A [20]). Thus, while the *Guide* closely analyzes and critiques the ideological justifications for Japanese imperialism and the concomitant belief in the superiority of Japanese culture, there is no critique of Euro-American colonialism and imperialism.

The pedagogical end of the *Guide* was a reeducation of students into realizing the excesses of Japanese ultranationalism, the oppressiveness of its kinship structures, and the promises of Anglo-American culture, with its unitary subject and capitalist democracy. Each chapter ends with "problems for discussion" crudely designed to foster admiration for the principles of Anglo-American civilization and a repugnance for Japan's recent militarism. Among the discussion points are "Let us discuss the forms in which the weak points in the Japanese national character appeared in Education"; "Let us study and criticize the fundamental thoughts which were used to justify the war"; and "Let us inquire into the development of democratic government in the histories of America and England" (*Guide*, 1:pt. A [10, 23, 57]). Significantly, other than a gesture that the Japanese acknowledge responsibility for the war and apologize to the world for their sins, there is no mention of Asian suffering caused by Japan or for this suffering to be part of collective memory.

That the object of the *Guide* was to prepare students to emulate the United States is made clear in the chapter on democracy, which has as its hero Abraham Lincoln. The first subheading of the chapter, "Government of the People, by the People, and for the People," explains popular government and the safeguarding of human rights through Lincoln's remarks and continues to endorse the U.S. narrative of exceptional North American settler colonialism: "The Americans who sought a land of freedom on the new continent away from the old conventions of Europe, pushed their pioneering work with courage and enterprise, and got independent after fighting English oppression, are full of the spirit of freedom and independence" (*Guide*, 1:pt. A [44]). The "Americans" identified here are clearly white, and the *Guide* eschews any reference to American colonialism, slavery, segregation, or even racism—criticism of which had been public during the war. It suggests that the new nation follow the guidelines of the Potsdam Declaration and encourages teachers to "embrace and assimilate and take in the fundamental principles of Western Civilization" (Nishi, 233). Such a path would help a nation that was backward, narrow-minded, without an understanding of character or individuality, and given to blind obedience. Indeed, the *Guide*'s insistence on the need for Japanese students to follow Western civilization, particularly its North American variant, is so strong that it suggests a pragmatic embrace of the winner's ideologies as a way of staving off future defeat as much as it does what Nishi describes as a loser's self-abasement. Little wonder, then, that despite riots that had to be squelched and censorship of any criticism of SCAP, official and popular representations of the Japanese under occupation were those of a defeated populace, adulatory of occupation authorities and eager to learn a new way of living.

Jacob Van Staaveren's *An American in Japan*

When we turn away from official documents to accounts of educational officers during occupation, the narrative of a largely quiescent population eagerly receiving the benefits of democracy is troubled. In his "autobiographical account of the occupation of Japan 'from below'" (x), Staaveren, who served as civil information and education officer of the Yamanashi Military Government Team from late 1946 to late 1948, reveals the contradictions in the occupation project of democratizing education and notes the authoritarian nature of U.S. military personnel and their opulent lifestyles. Staaveren is by no means a reluctant occupation recruit—indeed, his juxtaposition of the actions of prejudiced and imperious officers with his own, more considered responses might work as a means of soft-pedaling occupation decrees—but his more ingenuous accounts of school inspections, based on his diary entries, reveal the excesses of occupation power, the wartime destruction of Japan, and, ironically, the scripted nature of democratic education.

From 1946 to 1948, Staaveren's job involved both inspecting schools for compliance with SCAP guidelines and assisting officials and citizens of Yamasashi Prefecture with "how to democratize their educational system, adult organizations, and labor unions" (x). In his visits to schools, Staaveren, like many such officials, was both a punitive occupation representative and a teacher of democratic pedagogies. He attempted to ensure SCAP injunctions against emperor worship, the demolishing of Shinto shrines on school property, and the prohibition of martial sports such as judo and kendo and tried to steer teachers away from rote learning toward individual discussion. He recounts being greeted by enthusiastic students and demonstrating the American teaching method (asking individual students to respond to questions instead of having the class respond in chorus), but his account of his visits reveals a more complex picture than the received Orientalist one of Americans bringing Western methods of democratic education to a rigid Eastern culture. Staaveren's visits to schools illustrate the basic contradiction of democracy by decree, undergirded by prohibitions, censorship, and occupation, on one hand, and, on the other hand, attempts to foster a democratic culture. These encounters also interrogate the basic assumption about new pedagogical techniques being inherently egalitarian.

Staaveren describes a school visit as a "fairly stereotyped event" in which the principal rushes out to meet him and he is surrounded by hundreds of students, the desirous subjects of occupation, who greet him with shouts of "Hello!" "Hello!" (75). He then meets with the faculty to check compliance with SCAP directives, observes teachers, and compliments the occasional teacher who instructs according to the "American way" (Staaveren, 75). Each school visit includes a demonstration of the "democratic method" of teaching, in which students are instructed to raise their hands without shouting. Staaveren's notes about this practice reveal less enthusiasm for the method than polite acquiescence or a genuine questioning of its efficacy. Staaveren writes about one meeting, "Did all the teachers understand this better teaching method? All murmured their assent. Were there any questions? There were only two or three. It was a very stilted meeting" (53). At another time, teachers wonder about the fairness of the new teaching method. They ask, "Should only students who raised their hands be asked to reply? With forty to forty-five or more students in some classrooms, how could each student have an opportunity to recite?" (Staaveren, 77). The teachers, that is, interrogate the myth of a completely democratic pedagogical method. Staaveren concludes that his responses to these queries are not satisfactory to those accustomed to rigid directions, but the omission of his own responses in the narrative also suggests the troubling nature of the questions.

Ironically, his teaching presentation illustrates the limits of occupation democracy and reeducation. The "American" (democratic) method allows students to reply individually rather than collectively, but it also presumes a didactically correct response. Staaveren writes, "I would test their knowledge of the new Constitution: What is the role of the Emperor? (Answer: He is now the symbol of the nation). . . . What is the role of public officials? (Answer: They are the servants of the people)" (76). That the reeducation of students in democracy is also a valorization of American culture is evident from his interaction with students. As Staaveren stops to talk to students while on an inspection tour, attempting to gauge their compliance with SCAP directives about eliminating militarism and militarist sports, he questions them: "What is your favorite sport? 'Baseball!' they replied in unison. Can you name a famous American baseball player? 'Babe Ruth!' they replied" (58). Staaveren's depiction of this interaction in the manner of rote learning and collective response he has thus far decried is an ironic commentary about the redemptive tutelary value of American culture that SCAP was actively promoting.

Indeed, Staaveren notes the unintended consequences of attempting to promote American culture through cinematic representation. While baseball (as democratic sport) is apparently welcomed by students, no doubt because of the popularity of baseball in Japan since the Meiji era, the reception of documentary films about America's democratic lifestyle is unexpected. Staaveren gives two films about "how young students in the United States lived, played, and studied, and presented 'democratic' teaching methods used in their schools" to the education section of Yamanashi Prefecture, with instructions for their free screening (64). However, while students politely state that the documentaries are helpful, most are struck by the wealth and prosperity of their American counterparts while teachers recall with envy the smaller class sizes (Staaveren, 65). Material inequalities rupture the ideological narrative of American democratic learning. A similar reception is accorded the documentary film *Tuesday in November*, an illustration of the process of U.S. elections at both national and local levels. Students note the "large homes, the lawns, the modern kitchens, the beautiful schools, and other common items of an affluent society," and the "democratic message" is overshadowed by the "contrast between 'rich' Americans and 'poor' Japanese" (Staaveren, 130). Staaveren's account complicates easier Orientalizing narratives about democratizing a feudal Japan by being astute to the power dynamics of occupation and recognizing Japanese awareness of this power, but not necessarily the idea of fundamental cultural differences that incline the Japanese toward rigid pedagogies and mechanical rote learning. Yet in Staaveren's account, Japanese students refuse to be simple beneficiaries of American tutelage, the ideal pedagogical subjects, as they both question the egalitarianism of the new educational methods and point to the economic disparities of occupation.

The Other Other as Pedagogical Subject

Although my focus is on the mainland Japanese pedagogical subject of occupation because the bulk of education reforms were directed there, it is important to briefly point out the different subjectification of Okinawans and of Koreans in Japan. Not surprisingly, while mainstream Japanese were viewed as subjects to be reeducated politically from militarism, superior nationalism, and a familial ethos into that of individualism, democracy, and capitalism, Koreans and Okinawans were viewed differently. Official representations of both served the end of turning mainland Japan into an ally of U.S. capitalist democracy and a strategic Pacific base. As Koshiro suggests, the United States and Japan had a "mutual dependency on each other's racism" (12). Thus, Koreans, who as subjects of the Japanese empire were second-class denizens in Japan, found themselves in an anomalous position after the Japanese defeat. Although occupation authorities encouraged and enabled many Koreans who had been living in Japan to go to Korea, more than half a million chose to stay rather than leave their possessions. Possibly emboldened by SCAP's directives on teaching democracy and encouraging decentralization, Korean educators, backed by the left-leaning Japan Teachers Union, refused Japanese personnel screening their teachers and demanded the rights to use their own textbooks and Korean as a language of instruction. When in 1948 a number of Korean schools refused to use the mandated Japanese textbooks, as was required of private schools, the Ministry of Education ordered the closure of these schools.

For some U.S. education officers, such expressions of autonomy were not examples of cultural individualism but, rather, markers of a destructive Korean exclusiveness. Trainor criticized the Koreans' "tendency to isolate themselves from Japanese society[, which] was neither sound nor conducive to adjustment" and commended those who "lived in quiet adjustment and acceptance with their Japanese neighbors" (352). Trainor was clearly taken aback by Korean educators who "loudly claimed that they were entitled to complete autonomy for their schools since they considered themselves allies of the Americans (a strange notion)" (355). The desirability of a unified mainland populace, suitably democratized under U.S. tutelage, following racial anxieties in the United States and ironically reiterating Japanese discourses on racial purity rendered all Korean teachers who resisted Japanization as subversive communists who needed to be controlled (Trainor, 354). Here Naoki Sakai's argument that occupation forces encouraged Japanese nationalism because it furthered the aims of U.S. imperialism is apropos insofar as nationalism was conceived of as homogeneity (240–268). Thus, Koreans' expressions of cultural difference were read either as markers of ethnic provincialism or as dangerous sedition, and their position as racialized, marginalized subjects of Japanese imperialism who had suffered under Japanese rule was ignored.

While Koreans as minorities within the mainland were seen as threats to the creation of a unified, democratic, and capitalist Japan, Okinawans (Japan's first colonized subjects) were the Other of Japan. As many scholars have noted, the more benign rule over the mainland, where SCAP ruled through the Japanese government, contrasted with the direct military rule over Okinawa (Molasky, 15). Whereas the mainland was technically occupied by the Allies, Okinawa was occupied by the United States and continued to remain in U.S. hands until 1972.[12] By serving as a massive military base and a colony with far more repression than the mainland, Okinawa met the twin U.S. goals of maintaining a strong military presence in the islands and having Japan as a postwar ally, because mainlanders would not see the uglier face of U.S. occupation. The colonial status that the United States accorded Okinawa was facilitated by existing Japanese colonial discourses on Okinawans, which, as Michael Molasky suggests, constructed them as slow, simple-minded islanders belonging to a premodern paradise (13).[13] U.S. discourses on Okinawans resembled what Paul Lyons has labeled "American Pacificism," a way of thinking about islander peoples as simple, carefree, sexually uninhibited, without history. This was a tropicalism different from that assigned to Filipinos, which, although characterizing them as carefree and indolent, was also Orientalized. Americans who wrote about Okinawans routinely began with descriptions of the island as a lush space, which implicitly tropicalized its peoples. Daniel D. Karasik, staff writer for the *Chicago Daily News*, who had served as an intelligence officer during the war and participated in the Battle of Okinawa, characterized Okinawans as people "who greatly resemble the Japanese but do not value exactness, orderliness, and cleanliness to the same high degree as do the Japanese" (255).

Educators similarly thought of Okinawans as a special tutelary challenge, partly due to their tropical nature. In a conference on education in 1950, Arthur E. Mead, CI&E director of the Ryukyus Command, corrected the impression that Ryukyu people were primitive because 85 percent of them were literate (19). They were, however, slow island peoples, outside of history. On the positive side of working with Ryukyuans, he wrote, "The people are intelligent, but it takes time for them to grasp ideas which are completely foreign to them." The negative aspects of working with them were "inflexibility of a culture which has not changed for 4,000 years," and "their conception of time, which makes it impossible for them to hurry" (Mead, 20–21). Such discourses both justified and facilitated the government of Okinawa under more direct and brutal military rule; concurrently, they allowed a more paternalistic view of Okinawans as minorities suppressed under Japanese rule and as members of a special culture whose difference from Japan had to be emphasized (particularly after the establishment of the U.S. Civil Administration of the Ryukyu in 1950) to continue the occupation long after the end of occupation in Japan.[14] Indeed, in 1946 English became compulsory in the first year of elementary school in Okinawa, unlike on the mainland, where it where it was required from junior high school on (Uehara, 4, 6).[15] In addition, U.S. magazines were more widely available than on the mainland (Rabson, 24). However, the fundamental postwar education system followed that of the mainland. Like the mainlanders, Okinawans were subject to the Basic Education Law of 1947, with stipulations about the teaching of democracy and the prohibition of teaching Japanese imperial nationalism.

This is not to suggest that Okinawans and Koreans in Japan did not benefit in any way from the educational reforms of the occupation or that they uniformly opposed them. There is much evidence to the contrary, including the establishment of the University of the Ryukyus, the first institute of higher education in the island, in 1950. What I am arguing is that American educators' constructions of Okinawans and Koreans borrowed from and reinforced preexisting Japanese racial hierarchies rather than challenged them and that these hierarchies were, in their different ways, necessary for the governance of the mainland and Okinawa. Japanese racism and U.S. occupation were thus complicitous in molding an order necessary for creating Japan as an ally for postwar U.S. hegemony and Okinawa as a strategic military base. It is in keeping with this hegemonic alliance that none of the educational documents discussed here pays attention to the violence Japanese imperialism inflicted on Asian nations. Instead, the focus is on presenting Japan's colonization and invasions as tragic because they resulted in defeat and suffering for the masses of Japanese (*Primer*, 1:chap. 1 [n.p.]). The Japanese are thus taught to see themselves mainly as victims, rescued from the brink of ruin by the Potsdam Declaration (*Primer*, 2:11) and as forward-looking pacifists (*Primer*, 1:chap. 1 [n.p.]).

Continuing Cold War Education: Schooling Brides in Americana

Although this chapter has been concerned with the many-pronged attempts to change the character of Japanese people through different educational channels during the occupation years, here I briefly analyze the ideological function of post-occupation Brides Schools for Japanese women marrying GIs and moving to the United States to suggest the continuity of the educational project in other forms. These American Red Cross schools, begun at the behest of the U.S. government in 1951, increased at the request of the U.S. Army (Nakamura, 122). In demand by soldiers who wanted their wives to have cooking lessons, and staffed by volunteer American wives of occupation officials, the Brides Schools were unique educational spaces inflected with multiple power relations. There American and Japanese women could potentially interact through the shared experience of being wives of American soldiers, albeit through interpreters: American housewives were simultaneously engaging in altruism, in civilizational missions continuing the tradition of benevolent minority uplift, and in a State Department agenda; Japanese women were at once students whose graduation from these schools was marked by a formal ceremony and participants in a state machinery whose "schooling" was filmed multiple times by the Department of Defense and by several broadcasting networks and shown in propaganda movies.

Brides School texts produced under the aegis of the American Red Cross can thus be considered, like the project of reforming Japanese schools, part of a biopolitical technology of governance and reproduction, but one that had moved from occupation control to Reverse Course and post-occupation hegemonic alliance. Whereas the Japanese subjects of language reform were viewed as incomprehensible racial-cultural Others who needed to be brought into the orbit of American discursive legibility, GIs' Japanese wives in the early 1950s were seen as racially assimilable mimics who could, in Bhabha's classic formulation, be almost the same but not quite American. The specifics of the authorship of the Brides School texts remains unknown. They could have been written partly by volunteer housewives, officials of the Red Cross, and officers in the GHQ's Information section. The authors could have relied on their impressions of Japanese women based on casual or intimate contact or simply lay anthropology or on ideas about the Japanese from American popular culture. My reading of these texts, while cognizant of the multiplicities of their authorship, focuses on their circulation and propagation. Given the fact that Red Cross workers landed in Japan with the first occupation troops, that their headquarters were attached to GHQ, and that the military asked the Red Cross to set up schools near U.S. Navy, Air Force, and Army bases, the texts lend themselves to being read as part of what Michael Omi and Howard Winant call a state racial project "that connect(s) what race means in a particular discursive practice and the ways in which both social structures and everyday experiences are racially organized" (56).

Unlike the projects of schooling in the Philippines and Japan under occupation, both of which attempted to create willing subjects of the U.S. empire, albeit through different means, Brides School texts were designed to help Japanese brides' entry into American society. They reflected the enthusiasm of the volunteer wives who ran the schools, their contradictory idealization of a multicultural nation and a hegemonic narrative of white U.S. history, and their optimistic view of the Japanese brides as ultimately assimilable in American society. However, the American society depicted in these texts was normalized as white and middle class, as reflected in instructions on dressing and housekeeping. Here a fundamental contradiction appears: the brides are urged to aspire to middle-class whiteness but to be content with less than middle-class status. Race and class discourses diverge to construct the Japanese immigrant wife as one who will unquestioningly occupy her class position in a society of structured race and class inequality but idealized as a melting pot.

In these texts, the Japanese bride functions as racial capital both domestically and internationally. At a time that skeptical nations, which repeatedly pointed to racist structures in the United States, were questioning the country's stature as a beacon of freedom against a totalitarian communist bloc, the Japanese immigrant bride could be evidence of American racial pluralism and equality, the ability of the nation to absorb nonwhites. The manuals for the "schools" thus continue the project of constructing the tutelary subject of U.S. empire, but one who is now an immigrant and, as such, will both buttress domestic racial hierarchies as a model minority and function as racial capital for U.S. Cold War politics. Thus, while the bride, like the Japanese schoolchild and sometimes infantilized as such, is still a pedagogical subject to be schooled in the ways of American culture, she is also a potential ally and exhibit in the Cold War project of corroborating the United States as a multiracial nation and hence suitable hegemon. At the same time, essentialist Orientalist ideas about Asian women's inherent meekness and respect for elders, as well as the fundamental frugality of the Japanese, combined with an American ideal of motherhood and domesticity, are summoned to mold her into what later metamorphosed into the model minority subject. Ironically, the same womanly qualities of meekness and sacrifice were touted as essential for women trained in "continental brides schools" initiated by the Japanese government for wives of Japanese soldiers in Manchuria as part of Japan's colonization program.[16]

In an analysis of the imperial power dynamics in the emancipation of Japanese women during occupation, Mire Koikari demonstrates the paternalist and Orientalist views of them held by U.S. feminists working on women's issues during occupation and the role of the enfranchised Japanese woman as necessary for the stability of a country being transformed as a U.S. ally. Beate Sirota Gordon, a member of the Civil Rights Commission, for instance, wrote about feeling responsible for liberating oppressed women (Koikari, 25, 29, 31). However, "because of the union activism of working-class Japanese women through Fujin bu, or 'women's sections,'" occupation authorities saw them as suspect and ordered them to disband (Koikari, 36). In other words, only a certain kind of liberation was tolerated. For Douglas MacArthur, the liberation of Japanese women from the clutches of feudalism was precisely to make them better guardians of the home, a role valorized for their middle-class white counterparts in the United States (see Coontz; E. May). As MacArthur wrote, enfranchisement would aid Japanese women to wield "the noble influence of womanhood and the home which has done so much to further American stability and progress."[17] The lessons offered the women in Brides School depend on this figure of the noble housewife, even though, ironically, most of these women, often forced to work outside the home to help support their families after wartime devastation, met their American husbands at the workplace.

Scholars working specifically on Japanese war brides have also noted how reporting on the brides in popular journalism and film reveals that the brides became important figures in the national discourse on cultural pluralism. Caroline Chung Simpson traces the change in the representation of the war bride from the sexual, mysterious, possibly opportunistic alien in the early 1950s to the exemplary middle-class housewife in the late 1950s. She sees the transformation of the war bride from inadmissible into the nation in James Michener's *Sayonara* (1953) to the bride who fits in happily in the film version in 1957 as emblematic of this shift (Simpson, "Out of an Obscure Place"). Studying the functioning, reception, and student-teacher interactions of Brides Schools, Masako Nakamura also concludes that these schools turned Japanese brides from the racially inassimilable to integrated in the national family (133). Ayaka Yoshimizu sees these brides accepted as model minorities and as good-will ambassadors, teaching the United States about Japanese culture (117, 124). Both Nakamura and Yoshimizu see brides functioning as model minority citizens affirming the racial tolerance of America.[18] However, neither Yoshimizu nor Nakamura sees the important function of the Brides School as a continuation of the biopolitical technology of creating suitable tutelary subjects during occupation or as subjects who will unquestioningly take their raced place in class society

Brides Schools were started to serve the needs of Japanese women who had married American GIs, just as they had been for European women earlier.[19] Permitted by the War Brides Act of 1945 to enter the United States as the wives of American soldiers, about fifty thousand Japanese war brides immigrated to the United States during and after World War II (Crawford, Hayashi, and Suenaga, 251). By 1952, eight thousand women had attended these Brides Schools (Crawford, Hayashi, and Suenaga, xx). Each Brides School had its own text in both English and Japanese until in 1959 the Red Cross authorized a text prepared by the Far East Asia American Red Cross to be used in all schools. Brides Schools typically met for two hours a day, three times a week, for a month, with the first hour and a half devoted to teaching, followed by a half-hour of coffee time, during which brides could socialize with one another and the American housewives. Topics ranged from U.S. culture, history, religion, social life, and fashions to instructions on hygiene, childcare, and travel to and within the United States. Sessions were led largely by American housewives married to occupation soldiers or by officers and served as an outlet for volunteerism and charity. The few sessions that required expert information, such as those on passports and visas, were led by Army officers.

The Brides School texts I analyze here are *Camp Kokura Brides School* (1956) and *Far East Asia American Red Cross Brides School* (1959).[20] The texts of both Brides Schools are indeed testimony to the earnestness of Red Cross volunteers, who show an appreciation for Japanese culture and a sincere desire to assist Japanese brides in their smooth entry into American society. The women are specifically told, "Do not make the mistake of belittling things Japanese. In this country there is the custom of speaking disparagingly of one's own possessions and belongings. Don't make that mistake for Americans are very apt to take you at your own evaluation" (*CK*, "Culture, Customs, and Manners in the United States," 3). At the same time, it is clear that the brides function as racial capital for America and its proxies abroad. Nancy Leong has defined racial capitalism as "a systemic phenomenon" that describes "the way that white people and predominantly white institutions derive value from non-whiteness" (2154). Leong sees this phenomenon as occurring post-civil rights, when nonwhiteness has acquired a status value for whites who can claim diversity while displacing issues of continuing systemic racism. I suggest that racial capital works on institutional, as well as national and transnational, levels, where it began to function much earlier—in the Cold War period, shortly after the end of World War II. It was precisely because the mechanisms to marshal racial capitalism at an institutional and individual level had not been put into place that the need to acquire it at the national level, and thus gain legitimacy internationally, was paramount.

It is not surprising, therefore, to see that both Brides School texts use the session on American culture to present the United States as a nation welcoming all immigrants, including nonwhites. The *Camp Kokura Brides School* text begins with the conventional trope of the United States as a young nation, not, as customarily invoked, as an exceptional Western nation, but as a virtual color-blind tabula rasa awaiting the cultural imprint of all immigrants. Interpellating the women as contributors to U.S. culture, the text states, "America is young and so has no old culture and customs of its own. It is a blend of cultures and customs of people from all over the world, so each of you can be an important contributor. Americans are eager to learn about culture, customs and manners of other people. Give all your knowledge and talents, for you have many" (*CK*, "Culture, Customs, and Manners in the United States," 1). In contrast to occupation educators who had decried aspects of Japanese culture because they contributed to its militarism, the women are asked not to belittle their origin or country (*CK*, "Culture, Customs, and Manners in the United States," 1). Similarly, the section on history and geography sees U.S. history as a multicultural one, "made by the people of Europe, Africa, Asia, of all the countries of the world, who came to the United States to establish new homes, to find freedom of speech and religion, to build new careers, and to achieve happiness and a worthwhile life" (*CK*, "History and Geography," n.p.). Clearly this attempt to derive international racial capital for the nation is predicated on a hegemonic narrative of the nation, which erases histories of settler colonialism, slavery as well as Chinese exclusion. Even more significant for Japanese brides, the history is haunted by the absence of any reference to Japanese American internment camps, which had closed just a decade before. The section functions through the erasure of all histories of people of color at the same time that it attempts to acquire racial capital through them. For instance, the travel section directed by Commander J. T. Sullivan in the midst of Jim Crow segregation presents rail and bus travel as simple and inviting and ends by exclaiming, "You will like America. It is a wonderful land and offers abundant opportunities to everyone" (*CK*, "Travel in the United States," 2). Arguably the women would not be prepared for the racism they would encounter, and wives of African American GIs would be particularly unprepared for segregation.

Brides functioned as not only racial capital but also model minority subjects discursively constructed out of stereotypes of Japanese culture. Just as the U.S. Education Commission stereotyped the Japanese as rote learners without originality, Brides School texts negatively stereotype Japanese as lacking spontaneity and being fatalistic and imperturbable; simultaneously, they stereotype Japanese positively as methodical, courteous, respectful of authority, and with a penchant for "ignoring the unpleasant" (*CK*, "Culture, Customs, and Manners in the United States," 2). The Brides School texts use both types of stereotypes, along with the gendered figure of the 1950s housewife, to create the ideal subject of Cold War capitalist America: the model minority subject who does not question her position in class society and on whom the smooth functioning of capitalism and racial difference depends. If the Brides Schools manuals purport to guide Japanese women to assimilate to capitalist American society, it is to the structured inequalities that are part and parcel of racial capitalism. The very first advice given to the women is not to expect too much material comfort. The culture section, led by Mrs. E. D. Mulvanity, cautions brides to "be on guard against being carried away by rosy dreams of luxurious comforts, expensive smart fashions and ideas of life in America [they] may have acquired from American movies" (*CK*, "Culture, Customs, and Manners in the United States," 1). Ironically, the section warns the brides not to fall prey to the ideological work of American propaganda movies shown in occupation Japan—movies in which freedom, democracy, happiness, and material acquisition are coterminous. As mentioned earlier, such movies discomfited many, who compared their own postwar deprivations with American plenty.

However, the text's exhortation is not a critique of capitalism but, rather, a means of recruiting Japanese brides to take unquestioningly take their assigned (raced) positions within class society. In a manner foreshadowing William Peterson's commendation of Japanese Americans for being satisfied with wages at or below their qualification level in his well-known article "Success Story Japanese-American Style," which constructed Asians as model, the Camp Kokura Brides School manual urges the brides to not desire the material fruits of liberal capitalist democracy even as it prevails upon them to assimilate to it. Here, facets of Japanese culture are marshaled to create the ideal model minority pedagogical subject. The Japanese are lauded for being "very frugal and resourceful in adapting their way of living to their economy" (*CK*, "Culture, Customs, and Manners in the United States," 2). In contrast to the Lockean theory of the individual who comes into being through the right to life, liberty, and property, the Brides School strives to produce subjects whose happiness does not, in fact, derive from acquisition. The women are instructed to spend evenings with the family instead of going to movies, eat at home instead of a restaurant, take the streetcar instead of the bus, and avoid "keeping up with the Jones" (*FE*, 49).

But lest we read the Brides School text as a Left critique, the lessons on civil rights suggest otherwise. Beginning with epigraphs from the Declaration of Independence that define the nation through ideas of freedom, equality, and the pursuit of individual happiness (which echo John Locke), the section proceeds to outline for the brides their duties as U.S. citizens using a civic republican model of citizenship as participation and obligation rather than a rights-based model of contract derived from Hobbes and Locke (see Marshall, 71–134). The section suggests to the women that this model of civic duty is an extension of, and coterminous with, their duties in the home: "You cannot separate your citizenship and the exercise of your civic duties from the rest of your life. . . . If your life is noble and rich, your citizenship will express that nobility" (*CK*, "Civil Rights," 2). Yet this very invocation of the legal language of minority rights in the title of the section—begun with the Civil Rights Act of 1866—functions simply to displace questions of race and rights in 1950s America, when questions about civil rights were again burgeoning in the public sphere. Minorities were staging their citizenship through struggles to attain their rights, an integral component of citizenship, as T. H. Marshall argued in his famous essay "Citizenship and Social Class" (1950). Arguably, then, Japanese brides here function as proxy vehicles for disciplining unruly African Americans who were demanding their rights.

The brides, however, are offered civic and moral instructions meant to integrate them as citizens into the body politic of the nation. Yet both the content and context of the instructions suggest a view of the women less as potentially rights-bearing citizens than as infantilized beings in need of moral training. The section on civil rights includes a part titled "The Code of the Good American," eleven laws that the women should follow: self-control, good health, kindness, sportsmanship, self-reliance, duty, reliability, truth, good workmanship, teamwork, and loyalty. Written anaphorically with the beginning pledge "I will . . ." to further recitation, all the laws except the law of truth are taken verbatim from William J. Hutchins's "Children's Code of Morals for Elementary Schools," for which the author won a competition offered by the National Institute of Moral Instruction in Washington, DC, in 1918. Hutchins's codes enjoyed great popularity and were widely reprinted in the 1920s in educational journals and manuals for teaching schoolchildren, such as *The Good American Vacation Lessons* (1920). Their inclusion in the Brides School lessons, however, begs the question of audience, given the standard trope of the colonized as children. Although the women are encouraged to be active citizens who take an interest in local government and can therefore exercise their political rights—particularly voting—responsibly, the insertion of the laws at the end of the section interpellates the brides as juveniles, obediently reciting laws of good conduct, reminiscent of Staaveren eliciting uniform responses from students during his school inspection tours.

Interestingly, by the 1950s ideas about the basic values to be taught to American youth had changed. In 1953, the National Congress of the Parent Teacher Association, in conjunction with the Educational Policies Commission (EPC), had published *Moral and Spiritual Education in Home, School, and Community*. Based on a 1951 EPC document on moral values in public schools, the PTA identified some of the values as moral responsibility, institutions as the servants of man, pursuit of happiness, and spiritual enrichment (Hunt and Mullins, 168). Noticeably absent from these values were the 1920s ones of self-control and duty. The inclusion of these values in the Brides School text is therefore egregious. Coming at a time that citizen training classes in the United States had become simply language instruction and the teaching of basic national history, the lessons in Brides School suggest a greater investment in the creation of appropriate minority pedagogical subjects: obedient, respectful, and childlike. Significantly, *Camp Kokura Brides School* lists the law of self-control as the first law, ironically a law appropriate both for elementary school children, who were its original subjects, and Japanese brides conceived as model minority subjects. It urges restraint even under unreasonable conditions: "I will control my TEMPER, and will not get angry when people or things displease me. Even when indignant against wrong and contradicting falsehood, I will keep my selfcontrol" (*CK*, "Civil Rights," 4).

By 1959, Brides Schools had become so popular that the Red Cross produced an authorized textbook to be used thereafter. Much of it followed the topics covered in *Camp Kokura Brides School* and repeated the information verbatim, though in a different order, foregrounding practicality by offering first information about visas and travel and later lessons in history and culture. The authorized text infantilizes the women to a lesser degree, although the progress from specific instructions on how to shampoo hair in the Camp Kokura textbook to simply telling women to bathe daily and wash hair as needed is perhaps dubious (*FE*, 29). What is significant, however, is that the "Children's Code of Morals for Elementary Schools" is omitted, possibly reflecting the input from Japanese Red Cross members who were participating in the running of Brides Schools and the public acceptance of the brides and the media coverage of them as models of assimilation. The cover of the 1959 text, for instance, was designed by Kidehiko Shinohara of the Japanese Red Cross, who chose for the image two ducks after the term "Mandarin ducks," which was applied to American couples and reflected the equality of couples who were often seen together. The foreword makes clear that such public equality is absent in the "Orient" (*FE*, Foreword, n.p.). The authorized text continues binaristic distinctions between America and Japan, particularly traits associated with the Orientalist construction of the Asian woman as meek and obedient. The women are urged to maintain their "Japanese womanly qualities of gentleness, patience, thoughtfulness for [the] husband's comfort" and to maintain "respect for him as the head of your little household" (*FE*, 27). Yet the fact that most of the brides had, in fact, worked outside the home is effaced in the manual, which reiterates the creation of the middle-class 1950s housewife, who keeps an orderly home and serves dinner with appropriate place settings and whose "primary role in life is now being [her] husband's helpmate" (*FE*, 26).

Japanese brides were ideal subjects for a postwar U.S. empire because they could simultaneously serve as racial capital, potentially be testaments to the values of middle-class (white) America, and function as model minorities for Black America. They could be proof of American egalitarianism and multiracialism. At the same time, exhortations to assimilate also reveal the concern of American housewives that their Japanese counterparts might be subject to prejudice. In the strongest statement acknowledging anti-Japanese racism, the text states, "In some communities in the States, the very fact that you are Japanese will make you different. It is best, therefore, to dress conservatively, and not cause unfavorable comment about your appearance"

(*FE*, 35). While this advice is clearly an attempt to shield Japanese women from the brunt of racism, the solution to racism, problematically, is to attempt to appear racially unmarked and assimilate to the model of the (white) 1950s housewife. In other words, the women are advised to make a cultural compact with white America. Indeed, the sections on makeup and good grooming and those on food preparation and housekeeping are a veritable 1950s version of Ford's 1920s melting pot, which churned out identical immigrants in suits. The women are specifically instructed not to wear bright colors or the combination of colors common in Japan but to play it safe by never wearing more than two colors at a time.

However, it is the sections on food preparation that the desire to transform Japanese women's cultural practices into the norm of white America, albeit under the guise of assimilation, is dominant. Probably reflecting the desire of many soldiers that their wives learn American cooking, the food preparation and housekeeping sections tutor women in cooking stereotypical American foods, such as macaroni and cheese, spaghetti, hamburgers, and meatloaf, and in laying appropriate place settings. The assimilation is proposed not simply as a safeguard against racism. It also reflects the idea of a non–Asian Americanness that must be imbibed by erasing markers of Japaneseness even within the home. Sample breakfast, lunch, and dinner menus contain no trace of Japanese food habits: rice, the staple food in Japanese homes, for instance, is simply missing. If food is a metonym for culture, the menus here work biopolitically in urging the women to expunge culinary traces of Japaneseness: chopsticks, soy sauce, rice, and fish. However, such sections are also a vindication of the triumph of culture over race, signaling the fact that being (white) American is a function of cultural practices that can be learned, thus diminishing the power of whiteness. Yet the emphasis on culture as the defining aspect of national belonging pays short shrift to a rights-based citizenship. It is significant that the civil rights section is noticeably absent from the authorized version and that the short section titled "Citizenship" is merely a practical guide to the paperwork required for naturalization. These attenuated sections, however, are in keeping with the construction of the Japanese wife as a model minority pedagogical subject and as a gendered subject representing ideals of 1950s womanhood rather than a subject exercising rights in the public sphere.

Thus, within a few years after occupation the project of reeducating the Japanese to produce Americanized subjects amenable to U.S. imperialism (rather than to an ultranationalist, militant, and feudal order) had been fused seamlessly into the project of educating the Japanese to become invisible minorities in a racially charged America seeking to suppress Black unrest. Simultaneously, the immigration of thousands of these brides could function as racial capital in a country seeking to change its international image as a society of deep racial divisions. It would remain for the 1960s to flesh out an Asian American model minority that found its early inception in the U.S. imperial enterprise to create suitable pedagogical subjects: the assimilated and undemanding wife of the American GI as exemplary immigrant.

6

Mourning, Nationalism, and Historical Memory in Kojima, Shinoda, Albery, Houston, and Otsuka

Educational reforms in occupied Japan and magnanimous tutelary projects such as Brides Schools embodied biopolitical reproduction aimed at influencing social, cultural, and political spheres in postwar Japan. The goal of these Civil Information and Education Section (CI&E) projects was to engage the Japanese elite in collaboration over control of ideological sectors of society through education and culture, engineer a Gramscian consent for occupation, and enlist the Japanese into a Pax Americana. The Japanese, like Filipinos, were to be grateful subjects of U.S. reform. Japanese educators, like their American superiors, largely agreed on the importance of democracy, learning through participation, and creativity, and, as suggested earlier, some engaged in self-abasement by buying wholesale American denigrations of Japanese character. Others expressed solidarity with Supreme Commander of Allied Powers (SCAP) directives, particularly the urgency of negating militarism and ultranationalism, but saw the implementation of democratic measures as a renaissance of essential Japanese values. For instance, when Japanese Minister of Education Yoshishige Abe addressed the first meeting of the U.S. Education Mission, he strongly condemned the ignominy of occupation and countered SCAP presumptions about absolute contrasts between American democracy and Japanese totalitarianism. Lamenting SCAP's agenda to control all facets of Japanese life, he stated, "We are to be under the control of your countrymen in everything, in our politics, economy, culture, and education. . . . [W]e cannot call it an honor for us" (*Education in the New Japan*, 2:258). While acknowledging the need for democratization in social, political, and educational spheres in postwar Japan, Abe questioned the occupation's rhetoric of paternal tutelage, insisting on the inherent democracy in Japan, as well as the importance of Meiji modernity. He was convinced about the importance of democracy "not simply because this was the principle forced upon us by America, but because this derives from a fundamental principle of the universe" (*Education in the New Japan*, 2:261). What Abe challenged was the occupation mandate to rewrite the pedagogical narrative of nation as one of occupation-bestowed democracy for culturally premodern subjects. Hinting at the ill effects of censorship imposed by SCAP and looking back nostalgically to the Meiji era—arguably, one when Japan began its own imperial expansion coincident with the European scramble for colonies—he argued that, "as a result of her defeat, Japan is now placed in the most absolute state of isolation ever experienced since the beginning of the Meiji Era" (*Education in the New Japan*, 2:262). So while he questioned the colonial imperatives of occupation, Abe repressed Japan's own colonial past by evoking Japan's inherent investment in democratic thinking.

Japanese and some Japanese Americans have similarly registered the implications of SCAP's tutelary imperatives in their fiction, film, and personal reminiscences within the complexities of the occupation period. With its entanglements of wartime devastation, postwar hope, imperial occupation, mistrust of militarist nationalism, the ignominy of defeat, and faith in cultural resilience, Japan was an ideological landscape of cognitive dissonance. If for Japanese writers SCAP signified colonial dominance and native humiliation, Japanese imperial nationalism signified wartime hardships and the horrors of unquestioned national allegiance. Little wonder that the dominant strain of occupation period narratives is the "literature of humiliation," tropes of which continue well after the period of formal occupation (see Orbaugh, 481–482).[1] Of the array of Japanese texts about occupation, I focus on two that center on schooling during occupation: Kojima Nobuo's short story "The American School" (1954), and Masahiro Shinoda's film *MacArthur's Children* (1984)—and briefly examine Nobuko Albery's *Balloon Top* (1978), in which occupation tutelage functions as a springboard for searching for different forms of identity. Deploying gender and race as dominant axes of social relations, these texts upset the popular narrative of loving, democratic tutelage by representing the United States through a racialized imperial masculinity. But while all of the texts, like those of Filipinos discussed earlier, delegitimize this masculinist power by offering alternative forms of gendered agency and by questioning racialized American assumptions about Japanese conformism and militarism, they also distance themselves from nostalgic constructions of Japanese imperial nationalism. Unlike in Filipino texts, a (selectively) critical attitude to the nation's history is a central part of these narratives even as they largely avoid representing the suffering of Japan's Asian colonies.²

Japanese writers positing forms of subjectification that critique occupation tutelage are invested in different forms of kinship and community; however, they reject identities founded in dominance. Kojima formulates a unique conjuncture of emasculation and resistance in the Bartleby-like figure of the schoolteacher Isa, suggesting a complex idea of power in defeat, while Shinoda postulates a feminized nationalism, mourning, and historical memory as alternatives to capitalist individualism, predatory or militaristic masculinities, and Americanization. Albery dramatizes the continuity of occupation tutelage and post-occupation U.S. power in her novel's heroine, Kana, who through her communist reeducation struggles to formulate a radical gendered identity resistant to the Cold War compact of Japanese tradition and American individualism and capitalist democracy. Finally, I briefly examine how the Japanese American writers Jeanne Wakatsuki Houston and James D. Houston (in *Farewell to Manzanar*) and Julie Otsuka (in *When the Emperor Was Divine*) use intersectional historical memory to challenge the singular narrative of democratic occupation; this memory links the tutelage of internment camps to occupation but remains problematically uncritical of Japanese imperialism.

Published in 1954, "The American School" (Amerikan Sukuru) partly draws on Kojima's liminal position in relation to occupation forces. Kojima, who had a degree in English literature and worked as a linguistic decoder and translator during World War II, taught English at a high school in Japan after the war and worked as a translator for the American occupation force in Okinawa. The story hinges on the interactions of three groups: Japanese teachers of English who have been invited to observe a school for the children of U.S. occupation personnel; U.S. military officers, who drive along the six-kilometer road next to the Japanese teachers, who come on foot; and the American teachers at the school. The principal characters of the story are Japanese: Shibamoto, from the Office of Education and a judo expert; Yamada, a former company commander who is proud of his command of meager English and eager to demonstrate his pedagogical skills; the attractive Michiko, who is fluent in English; and the pathetic, bumbling protagonist Isa, who is least interested in the American school and terrified of speaking English. Isa, emblematic of the enfeeblement and humiliation of Japanese men that Kojima parades in many stories, including those in the aptly titled collection *Long Belts and Thin Men*, is the comic object of concern; his feet are injured by the ill-fitting shoes he has borrowed for the occasion (see Rogers, vii). American soldiers give him a ride, and an American teacher, much to Isa's embarrassment, insists on treating his feet. The Japanese teachers, eager to prove their worth, propose demonstrating their teaching skills for the Americans but are not permitted to do so because Michiko accidentally slips while wearing Western high heels, screams, and upsets the class routine. Dismissed by the principal, Mr. Williams, who forbids them any further visits to the school, the Japanese teachers leave, humiliated. Kojima's occupation story is thus structured to explore questions of power and powerlessness, authority and survival, victory and defeat, masculinity and emasculation within a narrative that literalizes the idea of a reeducated Japanese pedagogical subject.

The title of the story refers to the school for the children of Americans, but the story is not so much about the school as it is about the kind of schooling Japanese teachers need to be viable in postwar Japan. Metaphorically, the American School is also occupied Japan, which was a pedagogical experiment for Americans—or, as Douglas MacArthur put it, a laboratory (*Reminiscences*, 282). The subjects of the story are not Japanese children but adult Japanese teachers, who are infantilized and feel compelled to prove their competence and knowledge.[3] In other words, the story dramatizes assumed relations of filiality under colonial occupation that are undermined by the Japanese teachers through interrogation and shows of bravado. If occupation rhetoric constantly reiterated the adage of teaching democracy to a hitherto craven and authoritatively ruled population and stressed the teaching of individual expression, the story ironically comments on and questions the benefits of unrestricted expression by students. Moreover, the comic tone of the story, directed particularly at the efforts of Japanese teachers, suggests the futility of such attempts to attain status in the eyes of Americans. Kojima structures the story's basic plot through the colonial psychodynamics of identity so powerfully articulated by Frantz Fanon, in which the white gaze—"the attitudes, the glances of the other"—fix the Black into objecthood, as captured by the insistent reiteration, "Look, a Negro" (*Black Skin, White Masks*, 109). The Japanese teachers of the story, aware of their status as tutelary subjects, are instructed to act appropriately to extract adult valuation from the Americans, who act as social mirrors. To that end, the administrator at the Office of Education admonishes them to "assemble promptly," "dress impeccably," and "maintain a solemn silence at all times" (Kojima, 120). Once on the road, they are told not to walk in rows, clearly to avoid the appearance of militarism, and yet to move closer: "You mustn't look so straggly—there are Occupation personnel all around you" (Kojima, 124). Yamada, the most eager to attain recognition from Americans and optimistic about the possibility, urges his peers to avoid sloppiness: "They despise us as a defeated people . . . and when they see the clothes we wear[,] . . . they just look the other way" (Kojima, 121).

Yamada is outfitted in neat clothes and shoes that attract particular attention because there is "scarcely another pair of leather shoes in sight" (Kojima, 121). Leather shoes, regularly worn by occupation soldiers but unaffordable for natives, become markers of American affluence and, along with the stock figure of the American GI handing out chocolate, gum, and cigarettes, signify U.S. material power. Indeed, shoes mark status in many of Kojima's stories, including his novella *Kisha no Naka* (On the Train), in which they signify the difference between the authoritative train inspector and the timid teacher, Sano.

English, in Kojima's story, functions as a symbol of occupation. While English was not imposed on the Japanese as it was on Filipinos (although there were attempts to impose the English script through *romaji* and, as discussed in Chapter 5, English began to be required as a subject in junior high school), SCAP authorities and educators viewed it as a language inherently suitable for modernity and democracy. The paradox, of course, is that acceptance in the colonial symbolic economy is premised on an acknowledgment of American authority, an acknowledgment that none of the players—the fluent Michiko, the eager Yamada, the resistant Isa—is fully willing to grant. At one level, Isa is seemingly eager to gain adult recognition in the material economy of occupation. He borrows leather shoes from a friend and literally gets bruised and blistered from his effort to fit into them: "It came to Isa by slow degrees that his shoes hurt.... He began to regret having worn these ill-fitting genuine leather shoes; and when he reflected that he had put them on to please Yamada, to speak the foreign tongue in the right style—simply to hold down his job—his regrets gave way to anger" (Kojima, 125). Kojima uses objects of a well-worn Freudian symbology (Freud, *A General Introduction to Psychoanalysis*, 129) to mark not an ahistorical sexual desire but questions of power. Isa's efforts to empower himself through the norms of adulthood and masculinity normalized by Americans and his inability to embody those norms—not being able to fit into the shoes the way the Americans can—accentuate an inaccessible American phallic power. This racialized demasculinization of the Japanese remains a major trope in texts about Americans and the occupation. For instance, Nosaka Akiyuki structures "American Hijiki," a story about a Japanese family hosting a former occupation journalist named Higgins and his wife, as a narrative of competing masculinities. Toshio, the narrator, remembers his teacher explaining Japan's wartime defeat as a consequence of the Americans' body sizes: "A basic difference in physical strength is invariably manifested in national strength" (Akiyuki, 447). Higgins literally demasculinizes the famous Japanese porn star whom he has paid to watch and who is unable to perform. And the unnamed narrator of Kojima's "The House of Hooligans" continually hides under bedcovers and crouches behind bushes to escape the rowdy children of his midwestern host.

"The American School" similarly dramatizes the disempowerment of the Japanese through a loss of masculinity. The near-comical drama of Isa's shoes resonates with Orientalist ideas about Asian men's effeminacy that are readily available in American popular culture, yet Isa's bruised and blistered feet also point to the painful bruising of the Japanese male psyche in occupied Japan. As the story progresses, Isa's demasculinization and infantilization persist as he is placed under the protective and benevolent mantle of the white woman. As Isa painfully attempts to walk without his shoes in the school, the attractive American teacher, Miss Emily, forcefully removes his socks and examines his feet. Miss Emily and Isa virtually play parent and child roles as Miss Emily locks the obdurate Isa in her office while she goes to search for medication and Isa attempts to escape through the office window.

Although Isa attempts to painfully don the accoutrements of occupation and attain phallic power, he resists speaking the occupier's language; he also fails to follow the injunctions of the authorities. While the other teachers wait for an official to take them to the American school, Isa turns his back to the group and starts eating lunch; the group walks ahead while Isa struggles; given a ride by an American, Isa runs to the playground to hide; and told to stay in the teacher's room, he slips out at the first opportunity. This display of rebellious, quirky behavior meets the sanction of neither the American authorities nor the Japanese teachers. The contradictory dictates of occupation require the abandoning of militaristic group behavior but also demand obedience to the idea of a superior American tutelage. The teachers have been invited to the American school to learn both American pedagogies and behavioral norms, and Isa's idiosyncratic behavior only renders him pathetic in the eyes of both Americans and Japanese.

However, Kojima uses Isa's refusal of English to signify a resistance against American power. Here it is important to stress that language has occupied a central place in asserting colonial and imperial control. Ngugi's passionate statement, "The choice of language and the use to which language is put is central to a people's definition of themselves in relation to their natural and social environment" (4), is a statement not only about the intimate relation of language to culture and identity but also against linguistic and cultural imperialism. Although English was not summarily imposed as it was in the Philippines, the adoption of *romaji* was viewed as essential to modernizing and democratizing the nation, as was English in the Philippines, and English was the language of power.

As the language of occupation, English signified a realigned status in which preexisting hierarchies were eschewed. As Sharalyn Orbaugh suggests, "The Japanese did experience . . . a sudden and complete shift in the balance of epistemic power and centrality. The language spoken on the streets of Tokyo was still Japanese, but it was no longer the 'native tongue' of the centers of power" (87). To wit, the new constitution, commonly referred to as the MacArthur constitution, was written in English and then translated to Japanese. As Mark Gayn observes, "Any Japanese high-school student simply by reading it [could] perceive its foreign origin" (23, quoted in Orbaugh, 87).The Japanese themselves popularized the learning of English by associating it with optimism, humor, and the lifting of wartime restrictions. February 1946 saw the inception of a Hirakawa Tada'ichi's wildly popular *Come, Come, English*, a fifteen-minute English conversation program that aired on Japan's national radio station, NHK, every weekday; the show was NHK's top-rated broadcast, boasting an audience of 5.7 million families by 1947, with the accompanying textbook selling more than half a million copies (Eiji, 400, 402). The show began each day with an invitation to listeners (Eiji, 400):

> *Come, come everybody—*
> *How do you do, and how are you?*
> *Won't you have some candy?*
> *Let's all sing a happy song—*
> *singing tra la la.*

Belying the nation's defeat and postwar poverty, the childlike ditty evokes the iconic image of the GI, symbol of authority and plenty, handing out candy and gum. It solicits listeners to interpellate themselves as happy and carefree through the learning of English (which was banned during the war), a marker of occupation democracy. As Takemae Eiji writes, for her generation *Come, Come, English* was "our first genuine encounter with American democracy," and "Hirakawa remains indissolubly associated with the early reform phase of the Occupation, when English briefly was an instrument not of ideological domination but of personal discovery and social liberation" (403–404). Similarly, in her novel *Twenty-Four Eyes*, Sakae Tsuboi registers the excitement of schoolchildren discovering concepts such as "democracy" and activities such as "peekneek."[4] By contrast in "The American School" and "American Hijiki," English is associated with domination, defeat, and personal humiliation.

Kojima represents the introduction of English into Isa's life as a visceral, infantilizing intrusion that puts him in the position of a nervous student. At the thought of speaking English, Isa is at once panic-stricken, nauseous, tired, and close to fainting; his knees quake; his weakened body trembles, and his face tingles. As he hides near the school, his eyes shut to ward off the anxiety he feels in the presence of Americans, Miss Emily interrupts and jarringly addresses him, her body bespeaking "an ample diet, material well-being, and pride of race" (Kojima, 133). Nodding dumbly to her questions, Isa follows her "like a timid servant with his mistress" (Kojima, 133). Adulthood, Kojima implies, is not possible for Japanese tutelary subjects, even if the subjects are ironically Japanese teachers of English.[5] Yet in light of the power wielded through English, Isa's refusal to speak it bespeaks the strength of a nonhegemonic masculinity. Just as Edith Tiempo's narrators articulate postcolonial difference through homoerotic anxieties, Kojima's Isa rejects the equation of manhood with dominance and proffers instead a passive resistance.[6] Isa, like Melville's Bartleby, a figure Giorgio Agamben has seen as offering the "strongest objection against the principle of sovereignty" (Agamben, 48), practices in his refusal of English Bartleby's reiterated position: "I would prefer not to." When Isa does speak English, he does so literally at the barrel of a gun when a GI threatens him. The soldier points a pistol at Isa's head and commands, "Speak English man. Let's hear it again. 'I am truly very sorry to have kept you waiting'" (Kojima, 141). Forcing Isa to repeat the only sentence he has spoken in English, the GI reminds Isa that the position of the Japanese in relation to English is that of imitators, a popular stereotype of Japanese as submissive rote learners.

In his analysis of politicized language in "The American School," Michael Molasky critiques what he sees as essentialist and mystical ideas of language in which "agency is attributed to language, allowing it to empower and thereby transform the speaker" (37). The idea all three teachers—Yamada, Michiko, and Isa—share, that speaking English makes them less authentically Japanese, argues Molasky, "situates us in the realm of *nihonjinron*, which is to say an ideology of Japanese cultural authenticity" (38). While Molasky aptly points out that the characters' attitudes toward English reveal an investment in Japaneseness, his analysis soft-pedals issues of imperial power and militarized force.[7] When Isa, forced to serve as interpreter for the occupation team, apologizes in English for being late and repeats his apology thrice, the GI's refusal to admit comprehension, even though he demonstrates later that he clearly understood Isa, is a display of his domination over Isa.

The compound of the American School where the teachers are to be instructed is also a sign of U.S. material power. By surrounding the school with spacious houses where "Japanese maids [are] attending to the needs of American babies" Kojima productively accentuates Japan's poverty. Once inside the compound, the teachers are made painfully aware of their lowly status in the material economy of occupation. The principal informs them that the school is shoddy and overcrowded according to American standards, even though it has one-third the number of students in a Japanese classroom; he is therefore not surprised that Japanese classrooms are regimented and militarized. Confirming a divide between Americans and natives, the teachers are subsequently informed that their American counterparts have salaries ten times higher, which is justified because "the standard of living which American teachers had to maintain was, after all, extremely high" (Kojima, 139). In calling attention to American luxuries, albeit in crudely sententious form, Kojima brings to light postwar realities while accessing popular resentments against them. As Jacob Van Staaveren candidly noted in his memoir, the frayed clothes of teachers and students bespoke their "severe economic straits" and the luxurious lifestyles of Americans made Tokyo "the Occupationaire's Utopia" (20, 55).

Once in the classrooms, the teachers as observers have the opportunity to perform adult roles; nevertheless, they are once again given circumscribed agency. While the Japanese teachers think the students' artwork is simply mediocre, they realize—to their collective horror and humiliation—that the children have caricatured them. Expressly, Shibamoto has been transformed into a sea devil; Yamada into a shark; Isa into a flying fish; and Michiko into a goldfish. Kojima's use of the classroom not as ideological battleground but as a site for unequal power relations where Japanese teachers are subjectified as children speaks to schooling as a metonym for the dynamics of occupation. More importantly, the children's uninhibited and humiliating caricaturing of the Japanese teachers critiques American educators' fetish for individual expression. In addition, the refusal of colonial mimicry by Isa, rendered as a pathetically comic figure, and the relatively empowered positions of the militarists Yamada (he constantly revels in his wartime valor) and Shibamoto, who are willing to follow occupation directives, suggest a critique of the occupation compromise with Japanese imperialism and the ostensibly democratic and pacifist goals of reeducation.[8]

Like Kojima, Masahiro Shinoda uses the classroom to affectively register the epistemic trauma of occupation reeducation. *MacArthur's Children*, released in 1984 when Japan was at the height of its postwar economic power, testifies to the intergenerational importance of this legacy of reeducation. Shinoda, a prolific filmmaker recognized as a major director of Japanese New Wave cinema of the 1960s, shifted his focus in the 1980s via a trilogy about postwar Japan seen through childhood perspectives: *MacArthur's Children* (*Setouchi shonen yakyudan* [1984]), *Childhood Days* (*Shonen jidai* [1991]), and *Setouchi Moonlight Serenade* (*Setouchi munraito serenade* [1995]). Shinoda was himself a teenager when the occupation started, about the same age as those featured in the trilogy. *Childhood Days* dramatizes the upheaval in schoolchildren's lives during the war as Shinji is sent from Tokyo to the countryside in Kazodomari; *Setouchi Moonlight Serenade* focuses on adolescent sexual awakening; and *MacArthur's Children*, the first in the series, is most concerned with the project of reeducation under occupation.⁹

Shinoda has talked extensively about the importance of emperor worship in molding Japanese national character, the shock people experienced when listening to Hirohito's momentous renouncing of his divinity in 1946, and the difficulty of suddenly undergoing a "complete psychological gear change" (Okamura, 49, quoted in Koble, 2). *MacArthur's Children* registers the aftermath of such changes by foregrounding both the materiality of the project of reeducation and tutelage as a trope for occupation. Shinoda's explanation of the film's English title is worth quoting: "There is a famous photograph of General MacArthur standing with the emperor and that made it absolutely clear that the emperor was no longer a god, and also it was obvious that that was conscious effort on the part of the Occupation to make that statement. And that was one of the reasons that the English title for the film was called *MacArthur's Children*. They were no longer the emperor's children."¹⁰ If the emperor as god was revered as father of the nation, Shinoda suggests, a similar divinity has been bestowed on MacArthur. Although the title interpellates all Japanese in a filial relationship with MacArthur, the film's overall focus on schoolchildren suggests the formation of a new social order through schooling. It reclaims what Homi Bhabha calls the performative and everyday narrative of nation, paradoxically through the past and memory (*The Location of Culture*, 145); like "The American School," the film offers alternative forms of gender agency and lays bare a mode of "cultural melancholia" wherein the grief of cultural colonization is not substituted by a different narrative but simply retained as grief, an affective counter to occupation narratives of individualist reeducation.

MacArthur's Children is set in the immediate aftermath of the war in Awaji, a small island that escaped large-scale bombing and is spatially, though not cognitively, distant from the war. Indeed, Shinoda's decision to center three children—Ryuta and Saburo, who are war orphans living with their grandparents, and Mume, who is orphaned in the course of the film—makes palpable the profound losses suffered by the Japanese prior to occupation. The film consists of four loosely related storylines: Komako, the children's fifth-grade schoolteacher, whose husband, Masao, has been (incorrectly) presumed dead and whose degenerate brother-in-law attempts to coerce Komako into a sexual relationship; Mume and her father, a Navy captain, who have come to Awaji to await the father's fate as a designated war criminal, his subsequent execution, and Mume's departure from Tokyo; the relationships among the three children and Saburo's exhortations to all to become *baraketsus* (gangsters) because, as Saburo says, "We no longer have a country"; and, finally, Masao's determined change from returning soldier to horticulturalist.

Despite these plot differences, the fifth-grade classroom serves as a central through line. The film repeatedly foregrounds the topos of schooling by returning to the school—the classroom, the corridors, and the playground. The most recurrent shot is one in which a corridor perspective is used to look outside, which reiterates the notion of tutelage as an optic into occupation Japan. The film also ends with a long shot of the school corridor, first without any sound, then with Glen Miller's band playing "In the Mood" as the credits roll, and then again with silence until the final fadeout. Shinoda's decision to sever the English title of the film from the Japanese one also suggests an emphasis on the imperialism of occupation and on MacArthur as the new phallic father. The Japanese title of the film is *Setouchi shonen yakyudan* (Setouchi Boys Baseball Team). Keiko McDonald, who views baseball as the controlling metaphor of the film—about the Japanese learning the rules of a game that will change their culture—sees the English title as inadequate in capturing the significance of baseball (159). I suggest, however, that the English title clearly speaks to the importance Shinoda places on the imperialism of occupation in the transnational circulation of the film and on MacArthur as a paternalist, tutelary figure in occupation Japan.

Referring to the corridor camera angle, Shinoda says, "What I most wanted to do with this film was to shoot the school ground. And I wanted to do it from the vantage point of the corridor that connects the classrooms" (quoted in Phelps). The schoolyard is a metonym for Japan at large. *MacArthur's Children* opens with the moment of national humiliation—a black screen and the voice of Emperor Hirohito solemnly announcing the surrender of Japan: "We have decided to effect a settlement. . . . On August 15th, 1945[,] Japan lost the war." The film then cuts to the clock on the schoolyard wall noting the precise time of the radio address, followed by a long shot of grade-school children standing at attention, listening to the address on a radio. This black-and-white shot connects visually with the historical black-and-white montage that follows: MacArthur's display of casual masculinity as he steps off the plane, a phallic corn cob pipe in his mouth; the arrival of occupation troops; the skeletal dome in Hiroshima; soldiers on crutches and orphans sleeping in the street; and the signing of surrender aboard the battleship *Missouri*. Interspersed between the emperor's announcement and the montage is a color sequence that details the perplexed and horrified reactions of the two schoolboys, Ryuta and Saburo, and that of their teacher, Komako, who serves as an outlet for their bewilderment, shock, and grief. All are joined in communal affect.

Thus, even before the scene shifts to the classroom, the children have been visually connected to the larger history of wartime and occupation Japan. The historical montage that opens the film ends with footage from MacArthur's famous speech aboard the *USS Missouri* just before the signing of the surrender documents. As we see MacArthur speak into the microphone about "the hope of all mankind" for a world dedicated to the "wish for freedom, tolerance and justice," the image dissolves into that of the fifth-grade classroom, where rows of boys are insistently rubbing their brushes onto inkpads in accordance with a Ministry of Education directive to delete all militarist content, references to militarist nationalism, and references to the emperor's divinity.[11] Meant as an ironic commentary on MacArthur's speech about freedom, the shot, like the footage that precedes it, begins in black and white and gradually moves to color as the camera moves to a close-up of children's hands rubbing the brushes on the inkpads.

What follows is a seriocomic yet grave commentary on the project of reeducation. As agents of reform, teachers follow the occupation-inspired pedagogical script of the nation, instructing students to ink out all references to the imperial shrine, wars, and soldiers, effectively erasing chunks of Japanese history. They guide students to effect modifications, such as changing a story about an uncle commanding a troop abroad to one about an uncle working overseas. When Saburo shouts, "My father went to warrior's heaven," the supervising principal slaps him, reinforcing a reading of occupation reeducation as discipline but also suggesting a breakdown of the authority of occupation schooling and of the power of Japanese men. As in Edith Tiempo's "The Dam" and "The Dimensions of Fear," school exudes disorder and confusion. Children use brushes to smear one another with ink; Saburo shouts at the principal, and mayhem ensues as the boys run out of the classroom. Alternatively, Shinoda uses Komako, the war widow whose body stands in for the nation and who functions as the films' moral compass, to capture the affect of occupation reform, particularly the task of asking students to ink out textbooks that Yoshiko Nozaki suggests was psychologically conflictual for teachers (Nozaki, 125). Accompanying a close-up of hands methodically inking entire textbook pages from right to left and top to bottom is Komako's voice saying, "What we're doing today you must remember all of your lives." In this performance of melancholic incorporation, Komako does not specify what particularly is lost; nor does she define the significance of "what we're doing today." Instead, the shot (consumed with the destruction of what had previously been written) and the narration (focused on remembrance) interrupt an idealized occupation narrative by making an unnamed collective loss part of their subjectification and historical memory.

As the film progresses, occupation is represented as a landscape of conflicted—often gendered—ideological tutelage, reflecting postwar Japan's complex social alignments. The film rejects the patriarchy to which Komako as a daughter-in-law is subject, the predatory maleness of her brother-in-law, and the aggrandizing masculinity of American soldiers. Correspondingly, *MacArthur's Children* suggests possibilities in the gentle masculinity of Masao, who is not possessive about Komako, whose acceptance of his amputated leg bespeaks less castration than a peaceful fortitude, and who looks forward to gardening rather than soldiering, and in the intrepid, melancholic nationalism of Komako. Early in the film, the schoolchildren listen with rapt attention as Ryuta's grandfather, a patriot though also a policeman for the occupation, stands erect and delivers an emotional address as distraught, emasculated returning soldiers weep loudly in the arms of friends and family. He acknowledges defeat but urges fortitude in building a new Japan, his upright body bespeaking a resilient masculinity in contrast to the soldiers. Yet Shinoda complicates the lure of epochal nationalism by making the epitome of a dignified, nationalist Japanese masculinity, Captain Hitano (Mume's father), a war criminal. Hitano always appears upright, well dressed in a white suit, clearly a class above the villagers, acknowledges his crime and awaits his almost certain imprisonment with fortitude. Shinoda elicits sympathy for Hitano by affectively reporting his death through the grief of his daughter and her empathetic classmates. However, he also makes clear the violence at the heart of Japanese imperial nationalism through Hitano's own admission of having failed to rescue injured prisoners of war on his ship and leaving them to a certain death. At the same time, Americans embody a raced and gendered (though benevolent) multicultural imperialism. The American soldiers, while respectful of local customs, also epitomize absolute difference and power. The children's speculations about "Yankee" penises being as big as beer bottles reflect the gendered and racialized power of the Americans. Shinoda represents the crude authority and wealth of Americans through the iconic picture of the well-clad, well-fed, jeep-riding soldiers who throw fistfuls of gum and candy at the scrawny children who surround them. An extreme close-up of the packets of Wrigley's gum and Hershey's bars lying in the dirt calls attention to the United States as market empire and the American capitalist culture of heedless consumption, consumerism, and waste. While most of the children scramble for the junk, Mume and Ryuta stand stiffly at a disapproving distance. Shinoda parallels this scene with that of Saburo's black-marketeering brother and sister as they interrupt Komako's classroom. The gaudily dressed siblings, their garish clothes emphasized by close-ups, enter the classroom with aplomb and disrupt it by throwing candy to the children. While texts of occupation tutelage such as *Guide to New Edu-*

cation in Japan proposed individualism as a moral doctrine, Shinoda depicts its excesses through Saburo's older siblings. Caricatures of individualism run amok, they see themselves as embodying democracy and opportunity: "I'm just handing out a bit of my good fortune." "You should teach them to desire until they get it," says the brother, to Komako's consternation, and the sister reiterates, "The people's desires come first."

The alternative tutelage is provided by Komako, who teaches the schoolchildren, contra General Headquarters (GHQ) propaganda, that occupation is domination rather than democracy and based on destroying traditional kinship and community. Yet for Shinoda, occupation Japan is not just a Manichean dynamic of American power over a defeated Japan; it is more. Awaji comprises not simply moral patriots and misled dandies but also what John Dower has referred to as Kasutori culture—a culture of illicit drugs, alcohol, and prostitution—named after "Kasutori shochu," a particularly dangerous form of moonshine that was rampant in postwar Japan (*Embracing Defeat*, 107–108, 149–150). Komako's brother-in-law, Tetsuo, embodies this culture and is shown taking drugs and drinking heavily. Impatient that Komako will not accede to his advances soon enough (her husband, Masao, is presumed dead, and tradition would dictate that she marry Tetsuo), Tetsuo rapes her. In using a common colonial trope—the rape of the woman standing for the rape of the land—Shinoda accesses an obvious gendered hierarchy to demonstrate the degeneracies of postwar Japanese society. At the same time, Tetsuo's rape of Komako reflects the colonial logic of occupation. Komako is raped in a room adjacent to one in which Komako's in-laws and community members entertain occupation troops; such scenes of merriment are juxtaposed with images of Komako's prostrate body and wide-eyed face reflecting pain and shock.

The scene discussed here ends with a high-angle shot of Komako's body; the next scene opens with an immediate cut to Komako in the classroom, confirming through visual cue the political and social violence of occupation. Komako displaces her rape onto occupation and offers her students an alternative tutelage of cultural pride. As the bewildered students wonder about Komako's tearful demeanor, she reminds them that the nation is under occupation and emotionally exhorts them about this, saying, "Japan is under occupation. The army of occupation is on this island. But our souls are not under occupation. Therefore, don't have low opinions of yourselves. Don't sneak around. . . . Our spirit will never be occupied." While Komako's speech reverses the occupation mandate of reeducation into individualist capitalist democracy and urges an identification with national spirit, it nevertheless refuses to name Japanese complicity, patriarchy, and violence.

Komako's critique of the occupation narrative is reiterated in a scene redolent of the raced nature of colonial hygiene in which children running from the school are sprayed with the pesticide dichlorodiphenyltrichloroethane (DDT) by soldiers. Referencing MacArthur's overly zealous campaigns against malaria, along with the marketing of DDT in the United States via jingoistic appeals to the necessity of a bug-free country (DDT was never recommended for human application in the United States, and studies in 1945 were already pointing out potential health hazards), the scene establishes the racist dimensions of occupation (see Schmitt, 18). "It's General MacArthur's idea. You Japanese are so dirty," says an occupation officer, "infested with lice." Significantly, Mume, who up to this point has been characterized as precociously well-informed and intelligent, screams her refusal to put up with DDT spraying and plunges into the river. This resistance to accepting the tutelage of occupation is made even more evident later when Shinoda includes shots of the United States testing an atomic bomb on Bikini Atoll. The camera focuses on Ryuta's sober face; in the accompanying voiceover, Ryuta asks Mume, "Do you know your father's ship was used as a target vessel during a recent U.S. atomic bomb test at Bikini Atoll?" Mume, whose face is superimposed on the battleship *Nagato*, whispers "yes." Ryuta's somber reporting of the explosion looks ahead to 1954, two years after occupation when hydrogen bombs were tested, and calls attention to the questionable moral imperatives of occupation.

Nevertheless, despite registering occupation as domination, Shinoda does not view American and Japanese cultures as completely discrete. The last two-thirds of the film focuses on the children forming a baseball team and playing games against both Japanese and American teams. The team, coached by Komako's husband, Masao, a former baseball champion who has returned from the war crippled but with an unbroken spirit speaks to cultural deterritorialization, reterritorialization, and indigenization. Popularized by Hiroshi Hiraoka, a railway engineer who studied in New York, baseball was an established sport in Japan by the 1870s. To wit, Japanese fascination with the sport predates Hiraoka's return; an 1874 primary school reader (*Shogaku Tokuhon*) includes a description of the game (Nakagawa, 23–24). The culmination of the team's success is a game it plays against American soldiers, which tellingly ends in a draw. The outcome presages McDonald's contention concerning Shinoda's balanced view of Japanese and American relations (160), a reading supported by the fact that the game occurs at the nostalgic request of an American soldier who speaks some Japanese and has good memories of his stay in Japan. Even so, the children attending the game do so as a way to avenge the execution of Mume's father, which undercuts a purely sentimental reading. This lack of sentimentality with regard to occupation (as a relationship between equals) is further substantiated in the film's final sequence, in which the classroom is central.

As the story moves to its sorrowful close with the orphaned Mume returning to a war-devastated Tokyo, the film juxtaposes scenes of Mume's somber leave-taking from the Awaji community with Komako's classroom. The children continue their lesson, painfully aware of Mume's departure as they hear the ship's horn. In a close-up shot, Ryuta reveals his distress but resists leaving the class; Saburo, however, gives in to his emotions, leaves the classroom, and joins the villagers gathered to witness Mume's departure. This communal tearful farewell lays bare the collective (rather than simply the privatized) grief of the Japanese, who, like Mume, are faced with an uncertain postwar future. The film closes with two performative possibilities of nation. Komako's husband, Masao, idealistically envisions Awaji as "an island of flowers" to which he hopes Mume will return. In contrast, the classroom powerfully registers the epistemic violence of the project of reeducation. A close-up of the children's Japanese readers reveals the sentences "Tom is a boy" and "Mary is a girl" while the sentences "I am a boy. I am an American boy" are transcribed in English on the blackboard. Both sets of sentences clearly mark the disconnect of occupation tutelage from the students' lives while critiquing their Americanized subjectification. As the film cuts between the English lesson and Mume's farewell, the pathos of postwar mourning is fused with the losses of Americanization. Saburo runs alongside the ship, crying and singing to Mume, while the class chants in English, "I am an American boy." The camera reveals a close-up of Ryuta, a tear trickling down his face as he listens to the chanting, then cuts to Komako, whose eyes brim with tears as she brokenly repeats, "I am an American boy"—the final sequence thus bespeaking a melancholic performativity.

However, while both Kojima and Shinoda offer different affective mappings—passive resistance and mourning—as alternatives to the idea of the postwar Japanese subject newly re-formed through American tutelage and masculinities that are gentle and vulnerable in contrast to masculinities grounded in dominance, the ideological function of these mappings and subjectivities needs careful scrutiny. As Yoshikuni Igarashi suggests, the demasculinization of Japanese men in the postwar period, metonymically represented through the feminized emperor, speaks not only to the crisis of male identity but also to a strategic victimhood that disavows Japan's colonial legacy (14). To an extent this is true of Kojima's and Shinoda's texts. Isa, the moral center of Kojima's story, is a victimized though resistant figure; Komako's melancholic nationalism excludes an acknowledgment of Japanese colonization; and Masao is presented simply as a wounded soldier without a wartime past. Yet both Kojima and Shinoda complicate and triangulate these alternative subjectifications by suturing together wartime and postwar Japan vis-à-vis figures such as Yamada (who boasts of having killed American prisoners of war) and Hitani (who has let prisoners drown on his ship). Taken together, demasculinization and feminization do not evacuate Japanese wartime violence (even as they heavily foreground the humiliation of occupation) in either "The American School" or *MacArthur's Children*.

Although less overtly focused on postwar schooling, Albery's *Balloon Top* maps the contours of an alter-education that destabilizes narratives of benign occupation. Through the protagonist Kana, Albery dramatizes the search for a radical female identity that refuses Japanese gender norms, occupation culture, and the imperialist compact of a Pax Americana. Like *MacArthur's Children*, *Balloon Top* commences with the wartime evacuation of a wealthy family, the Todas, to the village of Shitsukawa. Both family and neighbors register bewilderment and shock as they listen to the emperor's surrender speech, which simultaneously marks the arrival of U.S. troops. As the novel progresses, occupation tutelage is scorned even as some of its aspects are absorbed and hybridized. The Todas, who have undergone wartime deprivation, are forced to move out of their house to accommodate overbearing, lewd, and satiated Americans. Colonel Bridgewater arrives with his "corpulent pink wife" and runs an establishment staffed with houseboys and maids, guarded by soldiers with "wet fleshy lips" (Albery, 25). The colonel's children travel to the American school in a shiny station wagon; by contrast, the Todas' children attend a school that lacks notebooks and pencils. After seeing Kana's homework, Mrs. Toda declares, "Just look at these New Chinese characters. Simplified, yes, but ugly, bare and without image. However, I'd better be quiet. General MacArthur probably knows best what is good for you young people" (Albery, 41).

The bulk of *Balloon Top*'s plot follows Kana's struggle as she negotiates her political and gender identities in a Japan irrevocably affected by occupation. Sent to a prestigious private institution (Faith College) outside the co-educational strictures of post-occupation public schooling, Kana is subject to the complex dictates of a bourgeois Cold War compact; within this compact, feminine decorum and respectability are intimately linked with the acceptance of American power. Faith College, a combined high school and two-year college founded by American missionaries in the 1890s, is a monument to American opulence, with its lush, manicured lawns, gymnasium, fountains, and marble benches. Despite its Christian origins, Faith College, by the time the novel opens, has branded itself: "The higher the fees soared, the more applications poured in" (Albery, 78). It is a spectacle to the populace who come to take photographs of the foreign teachers and declare the paradise, "Just like in a Hollywood film" (Albery, 79). In addition to their Christian indoctrination and English language learning, Japanese women are taught the exotic yet decorous arts and other skills that will make them attractive for elite marriage: piano, batik wax dyeing, oil painting, and French embroidery.

It is in this unique gendered and classed space of American capitalism, Westernization, and feminine propriety that Kana ironically begins her alter-education. If the sentence "I-am-happy" that Kana learns in Miss Cobb's English class is emblematic of a complacent post-occupation Pax Americana Japan, Kana's friendship with Misa signals a critical education in U.S. imperialism. Kana, who has been taught to believe that "it's brazen bad manners" to protest against Americans who are the protectors of Japanese, is horrified to see Misa joining student protests against U.S. nuclear testing on Bikini Atoll (Albery, 94). However, Kana is soon introduced to the world of Zengakuren (ZGR), the student activist group of the Japanese Left formed in 1948 and opposed to GHQ's attempts to privatize universities. Zengakuren had played a major role in demonstrations against the San Francisco Peace Treaty, which gave Japan its putative sovereignty but maintained U.S. military bases, limited Japanese autonomy, and pulled Japan firmly into the U.S. Cold War orbit. Albery's heroine moves from the world of her upper-class Japanese family (whose members surreptitiously arrange meetings for her with rich prospective husbands) to the revolutionary ZGR, which baptizes her "balloon head" for her bourgeois education. Finally, once the ZGR deems her without "capitalist sin," the group offers to her the undifferentiated body of the laboring worker as the revolutionary group travels the coast performing political drama.

As Kana is reeducated through the writings of Arthur Miller, Anton Chekhov, and Konstantin Sergeyevitch and histories of the Russian Revolution, as well as the music of Art Blakey and Thelonious Monk, she severs her capitalist attachment to American tutelary paternalism and angrily pronounces the former prime minister, Yoshida, a "pig" who "turned Japan into a brash American boom town" (Albery, 158). Joining demonstrators against Anpo, Kana plunges wholeheartedly into ZGR activities.[12] She defaces posters of the smiling crown prince, whom she designates "the war criminal's brat," thus directly challenging SCAP's support of the continued role of the emperor and the decision not to try him for war crimes and emphasizing postwar Japan's continued investment in its colonial past.[13] Yet although the novel deploys a narrator who keeps an amused distance from Kana, often commenting cynically on her intoxication with the slogans of the ZGR derived from European and Russian intellectual traditions to the neglect of autochthonous ones, Albery also suggests that through her alter-education Kana formulates an identity outside of both American capitalist individualism and Japanese cultural nationalism. While the women of Faith College combine the individualist designated agency that their teachers have given them—for instance, not wearing uniforms or walking instead of taking the train—with markers of elite European and Japanese womanhood, Kana joins the ranks of protesters storming the Diet, where her body is simply one of a mass. Battered on the head with a truncheon, her knuckles flattened, flung into the crowd with a water-spray hose, Kana's body is degendered; she is subjectified through solidarity.

Until this point, Kana had been unable to position herself outside a normative heterosexuality in which women must mark themselves as objects of men's desire and only men are subjects. Even as a performer with the ZGR-sponsored theater group Kana repeatedly casts her revolutionary ardor as a displaced yearning for Ken Otani, a student leader with whom she has been infatuated and whose attention she constantly tries to win. Witnessing a display of intimacy between Otani and Denim (a ZGR member), Kana decides to begin seeing the prospective husband, Akio Masuda, whom she had earlier dismissed. However, after her participation in the break-in of the Diet in protest of Anpo, Kana rejects traditional ideas of women's chastity and purity along with conceptualizations of masculinity and power. Ken appears to her not simply as manly and strong but also as debauched and flabby, a springboard for what Alison Jaggar calls "outlaw emotions" (166–167), as Kana has sex with Ken only as "a body matter" (Albery, 250) and rebuffs his entreaties for her to see him again. Kana's radical identity is thus intimately tied to her resistance to the legacies of occupation and to her solidarity with ZGR.

Glimpses of Occupation in Internment Literature

The Japanese were occupied; Japanese Americans were interned. While the two histories are temporally, spatially, and materially distinct, they are also inextricably connected. After all, social scientists assigned to Community Analysis sections at the camps were instructed to use internees as informants on Japanese culture and such information would be used during occupation. On the basis of their findings, social scientists made predictions about the Japanese, such as their need for paternal symbols, a notion used during occupation to rationalize keeping Hirohito as emperor (see Simpson, *An Absent Presence*, 44, 69). Conflated as the Japanese enemy, Japanese Americans were enjoined to sign loyalty oaths and enlist to prove their Americanness; many were sent to be part of occupation forces. And incontrovertibly, tutelage was central to both occupation and internment. It is not surprising, therefore, that while novels and memoirs written several years after internment make visible its suppressed history of internment, some of these writings also speak to occupation (along with the contemporaneous reeducation of the Japanese).

But while historians and social scientists have studied the links between internment and occupation (see Hayashi, 1–12; Minear; Spicer; Starn, 700–720), internment literature has largely been considered alongside Asian American racial exclusion, Japan-U.S. relations, memory, and trauma.[14] Asian American literary critics have also discussed how memory work guides cultural identity through spatialization (see Palumbo-Liu, 218–219), how memory work functions as an alternative site for reclamation (see Schlund-Vials, 17–20), how mixed-up memories militate against narratives of progress (see Cho, 53–54), and how just memories challenge singular narratives of victimhood (see Nguyen, 17, 283). In my brief analysis of *Farewell to Manzanar* and *When the Emperor Was Divine*, I suggest that these works use a mode of "intersectional memory" that connects, splices, and bridges different collective remembrances. When such memories come together through chronological temporality because of commonalities, their convergence subverts official memory, which relies on problematic compartmentalization and strategic omission.[15] As the remainder of this chapter argues, Jeanne Wakatsuki and James D. Houston and Otsuka creatively use intersectional memory to conjoin internment and occupation; such combinations challenge and re-vision the tutelage of both. For Houston, the dignity-in-defeat narrative of occupation bespeaks a nurturing Japanese identity that internment has proscribed; for Otsuka, the "remembered" emperor becomes a complex figure of oppositional (though not idealized) memory.

Farewell to Manzanar opens with Houston reviewing her 1944 yearbook from Manzanar High School. This rhetorical review practice allows Houston to maintain the fiction that her internment narrative can be divorced from "political history" and simply be a "story, or web of stories," presumably apolitical. What the yearbook does not capture, and what Houston documents later, are the humiliations her father endures as he is labeled *inu* (collaborator), the discontent at Manzanar over food and loyalty oaths, the revolt of crowds shouting "Banzai" at the guards, and the shooting by guards that leaves two dead and several injured. As a technology of normalization, however, the yearbook defuses the contradiction of internment and citizenship through its portraits of students in bowties and jackets. If camp is reeducation writ large for Japanese Americans, schooling in the camp performs the vexed function of creating national subjects out of a population deemed unnational and seems to succeed admirably. Camp schooling is first introduced in *Farewell to Manzanar*'s part two; what precedes it (in a section ironically titled "Manzanar, USA") is an account of the rioting and anguish caused by the loyalty questionnaire. At school, students not only identify with and perform a white American identity; they also refuse to register the racial exclusion white America has imposed on them. For example, the camp's young internees belong to Glee Clubs, where they sing patriotic songs and stage plays concentrated on the trials of "typical" white American homes, with the children playing white characters. Houston's older brother, Bill, leads a dance band in which he sings popular tunes, such as Cole Porter and Robert Fleischer's "Don't Fence Me In." As Houston clarifies, her brother expressly "didn't sing *Don't Fence Me In* out of protest, as if trying quietly to mock the authorities. It just happened to be a hit song one year, and they all wanted to be an up-to-date American swing band" (101–102). Despite occupying a position outside mainstream America, children "at camp" are inducted into nationalism through schools named after U.S. presidents, singing the national anthem, and hearing War Relocation Authority (WRA) officials talk about the importance of signing loyalty oaths. This reeducation does little to prepare the camp population for the outside world where, after the closure of camps, they are viewed as foreign and suspicious.

The memoir also counters ideas about militarism and ultranationalism being inherent to the Japanese, suggesting instead alternative possibilities in a quintessentially Japanese aesthetic and a nurturing, feminized cultural identity. National allegiances in camp are complex and conflicted. Houston's father is a "yes yes" boy, labeled *inu* by other internees, but he is emotionally invested in Japanese nationalism, as evidenced by his tearful singing of "Kimigayo," the Japanese national anthem, at camp. *Farewell to Manzanar* problematically attempts to deny this allegiance by suggesting that, unlike other anthems, "Kimigayo" is not a military or victory song, effacing in the process its mandatory use by the Japanese in the occupied Philippines. Ironically, it is near Hiroshima, in postwar Japan, that the strongest moment of national and racial identification takes place through Houston's brother, Woody, who is stationed there as part of the U.S. occupation army. As a *nisei*, on task to both prove patriotism and reclaim the manliness of *issei* men, Woody explores different possibilities of subjectification, not in a nostalgic masculinist militarism or an abject humiliation but through identification with his great-aunt Toyo, who embodies "an ancient inextinguishable dignity" and whose once elegant home, though bare, is clean and immaculate (Houston and Houston, 145). This section, italicized to note a temporal and spatial break, simultaneously establishes the occupation as separate from internment yet integral to it. The aunt's ancient dignity belies both the humiliation of occupation and the militarism of wartime. Subjectified by family, community, and culture, Woody is connected bodily to Toyo through her tears, which he touches and which move him. It is tellingly through an Americanness bestowed by occupation that Woody experiences feelings of loss and guilt: "Being an American is hard enough; being a Nisei among these occupying forces is sometimes agony" (Houston and Houston, 144). Tayo's house, with its "immaculate rock garden, its sand white and freshly raked" (Houston and Houston, 145), bespeaks an aesthetic that evokes in Woody a sense of Japanese national pride, despite defeat. Although the familial past evoked by Woody's visit to his family home is aristocratic, it is not, contra occupation rhetoric, imperial or militaristic. However, unlike Kojima's, Shinoda's, and, to an extent, Albery's works, Houston memorializes an idealized version of the past, shorn of its relationship to Japanese imperialism.

Otsuka's *When the Emperor Was Divine* speaks most persistently to issues of occupation through Japanese American internment. The novel's title refers literally to the time before January 1, 1946, when Hirohito addressed the nation and renounced his divinity. By then Japan had surrendered, and most internment camps had been closed. The emperor was regarded as divine during the internment period, but believing in his divinity was seen as fealty to Japan; hence, forswearing allegiance to the emperor formed part of the loyalty questionnaire. The use of past tense in the title nostalgically evokes a simpler time when the emperor's divinity was unquestioned and immigrant loyalty to Japan was not viewed as subversive but simply cultural. As Eiichiro Azuma has brilliantly demonstrated, prior to the war *issei* thought it imperative that the *nisei* be educated in Japaneseness and lay claim to an imperial Japanese heritage to paradoxically belong to mainstream (white) America (14). Monica Sone's depiction of the unveiling of the emperor's picture on his birthday and the reading of Kyoiku Chyokugo (the Imperial Rescript on Education) in her internment memoir likewise attempts to demonstrate the routine nature of the ritual even as she critiques the disciplinary obedience demanded by the practice (67–70). Nevertheless, the significance of the emperor's divinity to a novel about internment becomes clearer if internment is seen in relation to the politics of occupation, in which such beliefs and practices affected the everyday lives of Japanese.

Otsuka's novel follows four years in the lives of an unnamed Japanese American family from Berkeley, California, in the aftermath of Executive Order 9066; the arrest of their father; their removal to Tanforan, California; their internment in the Topaz camp in Utah; their return to Berkeley after the closure of the camps; the release of their father; and their attempts to piece their lives together. Structurally, the novel contests the idea of internment as an easily apprehensible or a unitary experience. It repeatedly rewrites the scene of patronymic trauma when the father is arrested and forced to leave the house in his slippers. It is also divided into five sections, seen from the perspectives of different family members, as well as a first-person plural section and a direct address to the reader, thus belying the idea of a singular Japanese American voice. The first two sections, written from the point of view of the mother and daughter, respectively, replete with childhood associations with U.S. popular culture and the mother's fascination with European opera, engage an omnivorous ethnic identity not rooted in nativism. Significantly, the third and longest section, told from the viewpoint of the son and covering the period of internment in Topaz, also bears the title of the novel and is the segment in which the emperor repeatedly enters the narrative. For analysis, I focus mainly on this section.

Camp, in Otsuka's novel, looks ahead to the dynamics of occupation. It is a space of interdictions and a site for reeducation. Surrounded by barbed wire and watched over by tower guards, internees are subjected to both written and unwritten rules. Early in the section, the boy's mother counsels him for his safety to stay away from the barbed-wire fence and avoid fraternizing with the guards. Above all, he is cautioned never to say the emperor's name out loud. Camp rules dictate the flow of information and designate the allowable and forbidden. The father's censored letters, rendered unintelligible because of expunged sentences, underscore the psychic violence of internment while laying bare interdictions of occupation. As the narrator reveals, "Sometimes entire sentences had been cut out with a razor blade by the censors and the letters did not make any sense" (Otsuka, 59). Such crude methods of censorship, poignantly memorialized in *MacArthur's Children*, were carried out en masse in the classrooms of occupied Japan. The education specialist Nakamura Kikuji writes, "The inked-over school books impressed indelibly on youthful minds the harsh finality of defeat. For many pupils, that moment of truth had a lasting influence on their lives" (quoted in Eiji, 362).

Educating the Japanese in modernity, capitalist democracy, and individualism through new pedagogies, abolishing emperor worship, and censoring militarist histories became ways of creating new subjects for a nation that had been dangerously powerful but culturally alien. Baseball rather than karate, *romaji* rather than *kanji*, a new constitution, and exposure to American life through documentaries ostensibly created a population receptive to U.S. interests. Japanese Americans in camps were similarly seen as subjects of reeducation. Although over half the internees were *nisei* Americans and most *issei* were long settled in the United States (though they were denied naturalization rights), the WRA cast them as foreigners in need of Americanization through reeducation. The final report of the Amache camp, for instance, identified that the primary purpose of adult education was "to promote understanding of American ideals and loyalty to

American institutions which would enable the individual to become a more effective and functional worker and citizen" (Garrison, 146). WRA officials, in turn, proposed training qualified Japanese Americans "in the fundamentals and workings of the democratic way of life so that they might go back to Japan after the war as missionaries of such doctrines to the Japanese people" (Garrison, 146).

Otsuka critically registers the reeducation at camp by juxtaposing the quotidian school routine with a barrage of standard justifications for internment. Presented through the boy's consciousness, the numbing familiarity of arguments for internment is dramatized anaphorically:

> *It was all in the interest of national security*
> *It was a matter of military necessity*
> *It was an opportunity for them to prove their loyalty. (70)*

Otsuka immediately follows these spurious justifications with a description of schooling at Topaz, where these same children are made to daily profess their loyalty to the nation-state: "Every morning, at Mountain View Elementary, he placed his hand over his heart and recited the pledge of allegiance. He sang 'Oh, beautiful for spacious skies' and 'My country, 'tis of thee'" (Otsuka, 71). "Americanization" includes being inculcated into the settler colonial version of North American history, such as Christopher Columbus's narrative of discovery, the grateful Indians exemplified by Squanto, and the valor of the Massachusetts Bay pilgrims as they establish religious freedom in the new colony. "The first week of school they learned all about the *Nina* and the *Pinta* and the *Santa Maria*, and Squanto and the Pilgrims at Plymouth Rock" (Otsuka, 71). Otsuka emphasizes the contradiction of children being groomed into becoming hegemonic national subjects while they are denied entry, as racialized subjects, into the national symbolic.

Postwar schooling under SCAP would perform a similar paradoxical education for democracy for a population under occupation. As historians and cultural critics assert, the *Primer of Democracy*'s history lesson was predicated on a morality that would serve as a counterpart to Japan's "Way of the Subjects" (*kotukai*) proscribed by the occupation (Trainor, 338). But what centrally conjoins internment and occupation is the question of the emperor's divinity. After the father returns home, broken and befuddled following his arrest and long detention, the children wonder whether his changed demeanor reflects an inability to cope with the transformed postwar landscape, where real events have the aura of the fantastic. The boy muses, "It is possible he was troubled by something he'd read in the paper earlier that morning— *Lend Lease Diapers Used as Turbans by African Sheikhs!* Or *Jap Emperor Re-*

pudiates Own Divinity!—and he'd had about as much news as he could take for one day" (Otsuka, 136). By juxtaposing the news of the emperor's divinity repudiation alongside the "diaper cloth being used as turbans," Otsuka uses the sensational register of the former to emphasize the incredulous nature of the latter. Although the subject of diaper cloth being sent to North Africa amidst an in-country shortage, and reports of diaper cloth being worn by Arabs and African sheikhs circulated widely in newspapers, it was also the object of satiric and humorous pieces precisely because it stretched notions of reality. For the father the repudiation of the emperor's divinity falls into the same category. On the other hand, the concurrence of the two news items in the text also points to a critique of both the Japanese and the occupation's investment in the emperor as a figure to be saved. As mentioned earlier, SCAP had clearly banned such sovereign worship before the emperor formally renounced his divinity. To many Japanese the September 1945 photograph of a diminutive Hirohito standing at attention next to a tall MacArthur with his arms tucked casually behind his back bespoke a national humiliation associated with the emperor's fall from status; not surprisingly, Japanese authorities moved swiftly to ban its circulation. While MacArthur quickly rescinded the ban in the name of freedom of the press and cultivated his own ruler persona, he was well aware of the potential havoc in dethroning the emperor or accusing him of atrocities. Occupation authorities ensured that Hirohito kept his monarch status and made such efforts to dissociate him from war crimes that he was turned, as Dower suggests, into a saintly figure (*Embracing Defeat*, 326). Textbooks such as *Primer of Democracy* explained Hirohito's status as comparable to the status of European constitutional monarchs and compatible with democracy.

Analogously, in the central section of Otsuka's *When the Emperor Was Divine*, written from the perspective of the boy, the emperor is repeatedly invoked as a talismanic figure, associated with the otherworldly. In contrast to the harsh material realities of camp life—inclusive of barracks, sweltering heat, dust storms, curfews, and omnipresent barbed wire—the emperor is configured vis-à-vis dreams, magic, and fantasy. To many Japanese, the emperor was so godlike that when he announced the surrender, the popular radio commentator Tokugawa Musei recollected, "The jade voice began to be audible. The physical sensation when I heard the voice for the first time. Every cell in my body shook" (quoted in Keene, 102). The emperor in Otsuka's novel is similarly omnipotent. Told not to say the emperor's name aloud in the camp, the boy whispers it as a sign of defiance against camp restrictions: "He said it quietly. Quickly. He whispered it" (Otsuka, 52).[16] In dreams, the emperor promises freedom from the space of internment and is associated with mobility and the white color of dresses and parasols of girls playing outside as the trains take the internees to camp. The emperor sends ships across the oceans: "Their sails were white and square and filled with wind and their masts were straight and tall" (Otsuka, 53). While camp rules disallow emperor worship, the boy can hear the man next door chanting in defiance, "Kokyo ni taishite keirei," which the author immediately translates, as if to make the rebellion clear, "Salute to the Imperial Palace" (Otsuka, 83).

Yet Otsuka makes clear that the answer to the racial politics of internment is not an unreconstructed imperial nationalism. Like Kojima, who points to Yamada's problematic militarism, Otsuka complicates the boy's resistance to reeducation, particularly the denial of the emperor's power and divinity. Although dreams about the emperor transport the boy away from the camp, it is not always to an uncomplicated freedom. As the boy dreams about the emperor whose inaccessibility and godlike status is signified by the closed doors behind which he is hidden, he is overcome by the emperor's power. As the omniscient narrator asserts, "For the Emperor was holy and divine. A god. / You could not look him in the eye" (Otsuka, 73). Yet the dream of the emperor, whose divinity embodies the exceptional nature of the Japanese, is also complicated. The emperor as sign of a special nationalism does not fulfill the fantasies of cultural omnipotence but, rather, portends a breakdown of the national-cultural order. In a classic Freudian dream of disorder in which the boy cannot open the door to see the emperor because his shoelaces become untied, he hears instead the clash of heavy fighting in Peleliu and Saipan, sites of heavy Japanese losses. The emperor's divinity is disturbed. Neither the schooling in American patriotism nor the alternative tutelage in Japanese cultural nationalism, signified through the divinity of the emperor, promises a viable cultural identity.

Instead, like Kojima and Shinoda, who reconfigured masculinity for occupation Japan, Otsuka's boy maps an alternative identity through his father, thus emphasizing the importance of kinship. In the boy's dreams, his father, arrested under suspicion of aiding the enemy, evades race and gender definitions and by implication the singular identity imposed on him by camp authorities. He appears wearing a pinstriped suit, a kimono, a grass skirt, or a cowboy hat (Otsuka, 104). The pathetic father, unceremoniously hustled away by the police, and who signifies patriarchal loss, transmogrifies in the boy's dreams as a complexly powerful figure: "And then he'd raise his hand slowly into the air, as though he were Jesus, or the man with the withered arm, or even Douglas MacArthur. 'I have returned,' he'd say" (Otsuka, 104). The narrator, ventriloquizing through the boy, offers him different imaginative possibilities for a subjectification that challenges the docile, grateful pedagogical subjects that both camp and occupation authorities envision. The father is multiply figured: he is Jesus, a savior figure; the biblical figure with the withered arm whose healing prompted questions about Jesus's heresy and whose literary incarnations often involve prophecy, miracle, ghostliness, and doom;[17] and the *gaijin shogun* person of MacArthur referenced here in relation not to Japan but to the Philippines, where he landed victoriously in 1944 and whose figure connects colonialism and occupation. But precisely by offering the masculinist MacArthur as only one of the incarnations of the father, alongside Jesus, who is commonly portrayed as pensive and gentle, and the diseased, often mysterious man with the withered arm, Otsuka rejects constructions of imperial virility and power as the only alternatives to the Japanese as tutelary subjects and simultaneously undercuts MacArthur's commanding persona and his cultivated image of remote, inaccessible ruler. Indeed, it is when the boy is portrayed as childlike that MacArthur is portrayed as unambiguously heroic: "We used to play war. I'll be MacArthur and you be the enemy" (Otsuka, 125–126).

Taken together, occupation thus functions as a supplement, in the Derridean sense, to *Farewell to Manzanar* and *When the Emperor Was Divine*, two texts traditionally seen only as part of internment literature. Both texts critically register the schooling in Americanness devised for internees and for postwar Japan as a technology of imperial governance and see possibilities in resistance and community. While Japanese American narratives about the camps are more invested in the injustice of internment than Japanese texts are about the excesses of occupation because occupation was a reprieve from the hardships of war, all of the texts nonetheless demonstrate the refusal of interpellation into the subjects envisioned by occupation: docile subjects ready to embrace the individualism and capitalist democracy taught to them under the aegis of SCAP. From the comical linguistic resistance of Kojima's Isa to the melancholic nationalism of Shinoda's Komako, the radical womanhood of Albery's Kana, the feminized cultural nationalism of Houston's Woody, and the transgressive figure of Otsuka's father, these texts offer a range of alternatives to the idea of a newly created postwar Japanese subjecthood under the tutelage of the United States.

7

Occupation Tutelage and the Pragmatics of Individual Memory

> Maybe I have a very good impression about American people. Maybe that was the effect of education. Teachers praised America very much and thanked that the American people helped us [and teachers said] America is a country of democracy. American people are very good, something like that.
> —Shigeko Kitani

> Many . . . have trouble resolving their memories of the occupation not because they feel resentment . . . but [because they feel] something closer to a guilty conscience for being seduced too easily.
> —Sodei Rinjiro, *Dear General MacArthur*

The institution of English as the lingua franca of the Philippines, despite the recent propagation of Pilipino and the steady migration of Filipinos to the United States, has resulted in a continued awareness of the legacy of colonial education. Whether this consciousness culminates in panegyrics to the project of schooling (as in the 2001 celebration of the arrival of the Thomasites) or the anguish of R. Zamora Linmark's complex fictional imagination in 2011, the memory of the American pedagogical project circulates in multiple cultural registers. The shorter though arguably significant period of American occupation and educational reforms in Japan has understandably found comparatively fewer cultural renditions for both temporal and sociopolitical reasons. Although the occupation enabled an easy if sudden shift in the narrative of nation from an imperial to a pacifist nationalism (stripped of the memory of Chinese, Filipino, and Korean suffering), this shift necessitated an acceptance of defeat that has been a dominant subject of occupation literature. In addition, as I point out in the Epilogue, although Japan was economically and politically successfully recruited into a Pax Americana, the cultural and epistemological changes sought by educational reform did not materialize and many reforms were discarded after occupation.

Yet as Shinoda's film reminded me, MacArthur's children, the objects of educational reform, still survived and carried with them their histories, stories, and memories. Convinced that their oral narratives would be invaluable cultural registers, I sought to interview Japanese about their experiences of schooling under occupation. Despite barriers of language and the constraints of age, I was able to exhaustively interview five subjects in November 2015. All were highly educated products of elite schools, with varying levels of competency in English; some had traveled to the United States for higher education or as part of their professional careers. To be sure, such subjects are by no means representative of something as varied as "the Japanese experience." Instead, their narratives—indicative of a privileged, intellectual group status—lay bare a reflexive relationship to historical memory as subjects fully aware of their interviews becoming part of this book. Accordingly, I look at these oral histories not as correctives to the fictions of occupation but as texts that are similarly complex, messy, and ambivalent. As was the case in previous chapters, I read these histories—which include reflection, performance, and memory—symptomatically through a postcolonial lens that uncovers connections to racial politics and U.S. hegemony.[1] To that end, I purposefully situate interview narratives within the discursive context of occupation initially aimed pedagogically at stripping Japanese ultranationalism and later at creating strategic allies and permanent U.S. military base sites.

What the testimonies of these subjects of reeducation revealed, more than the literary and filmic texts discussed in the previous chapter, was a stark disjunction between remembering occupation schooling as a welcome reprieve from enforced wartime nationalism or as a return to normalcy and therefore unremarkable and reflecting on it with skepticism or ideologically significant elisions and omissions. The subjects' self-identification as pacifists paradoxically allowed them to both distance themselves from the violence of Japanese colonialism and recollect occupation tutelage fondly. Importantly, such identitarian engagements enabled them to fashion a new Japanese nationalism skeptical of U.S. hegemony and outside the purview of this tutelage. As this chapter illustrates, benevolent reeducation had done its job but nevertheless failed to produce docile subjects.

My approach to these oral histories follows some of the trajectories of scholarship in the rich field of memory studies, which has complicated ideas of individual, historical, and collective memory, and scholars of oral history who point to the self-consciousness of subjects as they position themselves in relation to history. Theorists of memory usefully suggest the collective mediation that takes place in any individual memory, with Michael Schudson arguing that "there is no such thing as individual memory. . . . Memory is social." Even when memories are located in individual minds, he argues for their social and cultural qualities (346–347). Memories function through language, are often triggered through social cues, and can be shared by groups. Barbie Zelizer similarly sees memory as an activity generated through shared consciousness with others and points out the importance of historicizing the process of memory creation and focusing on why people construct their memories in a particular fashion at a particular moment (215, 217). This constructedness, as well as the social, cultural, and communal need for memory, is starkly evident when people have memories of events in which they have not participated but with which they want to ally themselves.[2]

Memory is therefore not simply a ready, standing, and stable archive to be retrieved but a means of connecting with the past, understanding it, bringing it to bear on the present, and connecting oneself with history, a process heightened in the process of the interview when subjects are encouraged to consider personal events in relation to larger historical trajectories.[3] My readings of the oral histories below are therefore guided by the assumption that the memories of occupation schooling that my subjects offered were not simply individual but also cultural and political, deeply invested in the process of cultural interpretation and self-fashioning. In different ways they were modes of what has been called "history-telling" (Portelli, 25). Indeed, nothing illustrates the constructed nature of the individual stories more than the fact that most of the interviewees had either come prepared with written timelines or had brought photographs and other artifacts to supplement their stories. While some of these additional materials, such as class photographs, report cards, and drawings, were personal, others, such as precise dates of Japanese surrender and the firebombing of Tokyo on March 10, 1945, clearly demonstrated the consciousness with which the interviewees placed themselves as part of a larger, important historical narrative. My questions to the interviewees were designed to see how they had perceived occupation schooling and the extent to which it had affected modes of thinking, behaviors, and attitudes. The interviews ranged from my simply listening to subjects tell their stories to urging them to reflect on certain events in the manner of what Alessandro Portelli calls "thick dialogue" (30). Our conversations involved specific memories of the inking of textbooks, the reeducation into democracy, the changed role of the emperor, and the learning of *romaji* to gestalt feelings about occupation and schooling.

All of the interviews took place in Tokyo in November 2015, either at my hotel room in the center of the city, with magnificent views of the rebuilt metropolis, or at a university campus. Below I narrate and discuss the oral histories of couples in the order in which they chose to do the interviews, with the aim of being faithful to their self-presentations.

"Can we make this silence speak? What is the unspoken saying? What does it mean? To what extent is dissimulation a way of speaking? . . . Speech eventually has nothing more to tell us: we investigate the silence, for it is the silence that is doing the speaking" (Macherey, 96).

It might seem problematic to begin an analysis of oral histories by valorizing the role of narrative gaps and silences which Pierre Macherey saw as central in reading literature. However, the role of silences has also been crucial for Freudian psychoanalysis, as well as cultural anthropology. As mentioned earlier, I am indebted to James C. Scott for his brilliant riposte to theories that posit hegemony as impenetrable through his idea of hidden transcripts, which underlie what might be seen as routine submissions to power (*Domination and the Arts of Resistance*, 1–15). I correspondingly read the interview of my first subject, Norio Ogura, an emeritus professor of agriculture and technology, at Tokyo University, in large part for its elisions and hesitancies in relation to reeducation, where it points to interesting reworkings and reroutings of the tutelary project. Ogura was a wiry, bespectacled, earnest seventy-five-year-old, highly educated like the rest of my interviewees. He had prepared a timeline of his schooling and family history and carried copies of his class photos from 1946 and 1947. When I explained my project to him and offered to send him the published manuscript in the future, he retorted, "I expect no less." Ogura was born in Tokyo, the son of a botany professor at Tokyo University. As with the characters of Shinoda's films *Childhood Days* and *MacArthur's Children*, he, along with his siblings and mother, evacuated Tokyo but moved to Sendai City, rather than the countryside, after the massive bombing of Tokyo in March 1945. (Sendai City was also bombed in July.) By April, his house in Tokyo had been destroyed by the aerial bombing. Ogura studied at an elementary school in Miyagi Prefecture for three years before returning to Tokyo in 1948.

Ogura greeted me in English and was able to converse haltingly in the language but preferred to answer my questions through a translator, Sachie Kawaguchi, a young woman working as a secretary for Sakae Shibusawa, a professor at Tokyo University of Agriculture and Technology. Shibusawa was too young to have been in school during the occupation and was not part of the interview, although he intervened to translate and interject his voice. Ogura traveled at least an hour by train to meet with me in Shibusawa's private office but looked none the worse for wear. He was keen to go through his prepared timeline and show me his diary, with drawings and report cards. Ogura began by directing me to his timeline, which documented the air raids and his evacuation to Sendai, as well as the names of his schools. He mentioned among the list of subjects he learned that he had studied *shushin* (moral education) only in his first year and not after occupation, but he did not dwell on the change. Similarly, when he pointed to his drawing of children playing baseball, he omitted the fact that baseball was deemed American and therefore proscribed by the Japanese from 1940 to 1945. Shibusawa, clearly more politically minded, intervened to point out the prohibition.

Ogura focused on materiality rather than affect throughout most of his narration. He showed me drawings of the food he ate and only after being prodded mentioned enduring the lack of rice, being forced to cook radish leaves, picking up grasses to eat, and suffering hunger pangs. He proudly flourished a crayon drawing of a bright red car carrying a man waving a hat alongside a boy and girl also waving. In response to my query about the children's excitement, he explained that it is was a special, "fancy" car for the emperor, that the children were happy to see it and were saying "Banzai." Curious about Ogura's inclusion of the emperor being greeted with banzai cheers, which for Americans had signified the deranged nature of soldiers and their unthinking fealty to the emperor, I interjected to question Ogura about his feelings about the emperor. Ogura was noncommittal, noting only that his family taught him that the emperor was respectable but that the school avoided any mention of the emperor. Ogura was singularly uninterested in questions about censorship and textbooks being erased, emphasizing that his major want was the lack of food. He remembered learning *romaji* but attached no significance to it. His recollection of attending a GHQ-run Sunday school, even though he identified himself as Buddhist, was similarly void of any connection with the proselytization promoted by General Douglas MacArthur. Ogura's memories of being a subject of the education for democracy program were particularly vivid, and his answer to how democracy was taught in school was forthright. As Kawaguchi translated it, he said, "The teacher taught to the student that America occupied Japan and America introduced democracy and Japanese thought democracy is important so the Japanese government made the constitution. . . . [T]his is what he was told." Although the Allied occupation was ultimately a U.S. one, with MacArthur given sovereign power (Dower, *Embracing Defeat*, 73), I wondered about the elision between "Allied" and "American" in Ogura's account, but when questioned, he deemed these issues insignificant for him compared with mathematics and science. For the son of a botanist who would later become an engineering professor at a prestigious university, this statement, though perhaps forged in hindsight, did not seem surprising.

For most of the interview Ogura seemed uninterested in issues of freedom, democracy, and pedagogical subjectification during occupation. With further questioning he recollected being taught about the changed role of the emperor from manifest deity and head of the nation to a symbol and remembered feeling more "comfortable." As Kawaguchi put it, "He thought it's more free now; he felt more comfortable; he was told it [Japan] is more free." Ogura did not recall MacArthur's being mentioned in school but remembered vividly seeing Gaetano Faillace's iconic photograph of the emperor beside MacArthur and thinking of the United States as being stronger than Japan. However, when asked about the difference in schooling after occupation, Ogura's recollections were suddenly tinged with affect and presented a different narrative. He spoke more emphatically, stating that he felt inexplicably freer. This shift from his earlier reticence from affect and his seeming lack of interest in the politics of occupation suggested the divergent ways he needed to negotiate his past. When I urged him to think further about his feelings, Ogura remembered his teachers intimating the changes after occupation: "Teacher didn't say occupation ended, but they say you can speak more freely and act freely; but they didn't say occupation is end." But it was also clear that Ogura was deeply affected by the change. As Kawaguchi explained, "Since he had in mind that America is in control, he was thinking that in his mind, so he was not truly free, but after occupation he . . . felt very free." Speaking animatedly, Ogura reminisced about what he sensed. As Kawaguchi translated it, "He thinks the family was thinking that way, too. He didn't actually talk directly. He thought the family was thinking they were free."

Close to the end of the interview, Ogura chose to narrate his strongest memory of occupation by reiterating the constraints he felt. Kawaguchi explained, "He was thinking that he was not free; [he was] occupied by the alliance he was feeling that; he thinks his friends were thinking the same way and the teachers too." As Kawaguchi finished translating, Shibusawa, who mostly had been quiet until this moment (except to confirm Ogura's statement that no details about the atomic bomb were mentioned in school and to add information about the testing at Bikini Atoll) eagerly supplemented Ogura's personal narrative with a historical one by detailing the anticommunist purges initiated by occupation forces. He declaimed spiritedly about the shift in perception of the GHQ from being harbingers of democracy to Cold War McCarthyites who fired left-leaning teachers, and he remembered his teachers characterizing GHQ as undemocratic. Shibusawa clearly wanted to articulate an anti-imperial collective memory he found wanting in Ogura.

Ogura's meticulous records of his schooling and his willingness to travel and share his experiences, despite his hesitance with English, suggest that the occupation period and occupation schooling were significant memories he wished to narrate. His carefully preserved diary, written under the guidance of the teacher and explicated through his own commentary, was a historical palimpsest. The teacher clearly encouraged students to record their wartime and postwar deprivation by asking them to document their daily meals; she also engaged them in nationalism by motivating them to cheer for the emperor and document the visit in drawings, even though it was a nationalism associated with a changed view of the emperor. Ogura, however, conjoined autobiographical and collective memory when he discussed an entire society affected by food shortages but attempted to keep personal and social memories discrete when broaching the politics of occupation. While the use of "Banzai" in his drawing spoke to the complex negotiations of individual and national identity, Ogura displaced these social tensions by explaining the excitement of the children as analogous to that over a new toy—the children were enthusiastic "because the car was shiny and red."

However, the stark contrast between Ogura's preliminary recall of occupation schooling and his later comments bears scrutiny. Ogura initially remembered his schooling in the context of the war, the destruction it wreaked, and the privations his family suffered. The printed timeline he had prepared accentuated the precise dates of the war: the U.S. declaration of war against Japan on December 8, 1941; the firebombing of Tokyo on March 10, 1945; and the surrender of Japan—glossed only as "End of the War" by Ogura—on August 15, 1945. Clearly illustrating the point that memory is always social, Ogura meant the personal account of his schooling to be seen in the context of the war, even though he was at pains to dissociate his private anecdotes from any structural analysis. Interestingly, occupation was occluded in the timeline, possibly suggesting Ogura's desire to distance his individual narrative from the politics of occupation, a curious omission, given his knowledge that occupation schooling was central to the interview. Yet it became clear at the end of the interview that this initial dissociation functioned as a ruse that allowed Ogura to reimagine his schooling outside of occupation. If the object of the tutelary project was the biopolitical one of producing grateful subjects who were benignly reeducated into democracy, this object did not succeed with Ogura. As he reconstructed his memories, he sought to present occupation first as irrelevant to his schooling and later as inexplicably oppressive as he sought to articulate a nebulous nationalism by ventriloquizing the collective voices of his teachers and his family.

Ogura's noncommittal and, later, critical views of occupation schooling contrasted with the largely fond memories of Shigeko Kitani and her husband, Osamu Kitani, whom I interviewed on a sunny afternoon at the Shinegawa Prince hotel in the heart of Tokyo. We began the interview in the hotel's coffee shop, as the Kitanis had wanted, but soon moved to the quiet of my hotel room. Osamu was a thin, intense, energetic eighty-year-old, and Shigeko was a vivacious seventy-eight-year-old. Shigeko was a graduate in American studies from the University of Tokyo; Osamu had a long career as an engineer, culminating in a professorship at the prestigious University of Tokyo. Like Ogura, Osamu, the son of a landowner, was born in Tokyo but moved during the war and spent several years in Takamatsu, his ancestral town on Shikoku island. He was exceedingly modest, and I learned only by circuitous questioning that he had earned his doctorate at the University of Michigan in just two years. Osamu was earnest about the interview and had taken the occasion to read books on educational reform in occupied Japan. Even though Shigeko and Osamu bashfully apologized for their poor English, they were obviously fluent. Both interrupted their conversations with nervous or polite laughs.

Osamu was older than Ogura, and his memories of schooling during occupation were affected by recollections of his wartime experiences. Like one of Komako's students in *MacArthur's Children*, he vividly remembered being asked to erase parts of textbooks with black ink because, as he laughingly explained, the printing system was destroyed. What he inked out were portions related to the history of Japan, "and also the ancestors and gods of this country especially as they related to the emperor system," as well as changed national boundaries. Unlike Komaki, who in Shinoda's film marks the event as momentous, Osamu saw it as relatively insignificant: "We thought there will be very big change in the future, you know, so compared to what we thought, erasing part of the textbook is small thing, you know." This is when I learned that the aerial bombing of Takamatsu had killed Osamu's mother and two of his brothers and permanently injured another brother. Only two siblings survived unscathed. Thus, when occupation started, Osamu was expecting the worst. As he said, "Three of my family was killed in the war, so compared to this kind of things [inking textbooks], you know, we thought more serious things could happen."

Osamu remembered schooling under occupation as a welcome relief and freedom from the militarism of imperial Japan. He vociferously denounced the mandatory, martial-like athletic drills and the daily ritual of repeating the Imperial Rescript on Education, which stressed loyalty to the emperor and love and sacrifice for the country. As Osamu said, "In the morning during the war we had to repeat it.... I didn't like it very much, and many pupils didn't like it." He recalled with distaste standing erect, waiting for the schoolmaster who carried the rescript on a tray and being told not to lift his head or he would be blinded. The children hated the ritual and created their own parody of it, mocking the emperor farting. He had a similar dislike for *shushin* and the inculcation of values such as hard work through parables. Above all, he was highly critical of the "forced nationalism" of Japan that "led to the very big war." But while Osamu felt gratitude about the food aid given by Americans, he was cynical about his teachers who, formerly critical of the United States, suddenly took to praising the country during occupation. However, he dissociated this suspicion of teachers from the politics of occupation or the project of reeducation. Given Osamu's distrust of nationalism I was curious about the impressions he gathered of the United States during his stay at the height of the Civil Rights Movement. However, Osamu was disinclined to discuss his thoughts about U.S. racial politics, remarking only that he had traveled south and, although he noted apparent differences, he felt "they are progressing." He moved on to talk about gun control.

Shigeko Kitani was an intelligent woman who was eager to talk about the war and occupation and, unlike Osamu, attested to remembering the change in schooling after occupation very vividly. Shigeko talked animatedly about her schooling and described the wartime nationalistic and militaristic practices of her school in great detail. The schoolmaster came in "gravely holding the black tray covered with purple cloth. Inside it [was] the emperor's rescript..., and we [had] to bow to the tray and we are ordered not to lift head; if we lifted we would be blind." She recalled hating these practices and feeling freed from these constrictions once occupation started. Her memories of schooling during occupation were tinged with relief from militarism and were more affective than material. She laughed excitedly as she described how "liberalized" she felt, how she had a "feeling of freedom." She remembered blacking out her textbooks in third grade but did not recall attaching any significance to it. Similarly, when asked about one strong memory of occupation, she said, "We are only just students, so we didn't feel anything about the operation of the occupation, especially in the regional city. We are very free."

But while Shigeko's account of occupation schooling largely echoed that of American educational officers, she was also deeply suspicious of the teachers whose perspectives suddenly changed: "I was very much surprised that, you know, the teachers turned 180 degrees around.... [T]hey switched sides [talking about] American and England very viciously, but after the war they praised those countries with smiles on the face. Oh, I couldn't believe it." As her synchronic memory of schooling intersected with her diachronic historical reflection years later, she gave voice to a counterdiscourse that circumscribed the freedom she had just described. She remembered that her teachers praised America: "America is a country of democracy. American people is very good ... something like that.... I think they are ordered to praise America before schoolchildren.... [T]hey don't think to discuss about America because they didn't know anything about America." Her ruminations suggested a missing narrative that was not allowed voice during occupation and that Shigeko was just beginning to consider, partly through the process of the thick dialogue of the interview, which triggered memories she had chosen not to prioritize earlier. She said, "Maybe I have very good impression about American people. Maybe that was the effect of education. Teachers praised America very very much and thanked the American people for giving us food . . . so when I met American people on the street, [I thought,] 'Oh, how nice.'"

Osamu's and Shigeko's interviews posed problems of cognitive tension. While I was interested in their experiences of occupation schooling, they were largely intent on recounting the horrors of Japanese wartime militarist education, an emphasis totally understandable, particularly given Osamu's emphatic denunciation of Japan's forced nationalism, which had led to the war and the traumatic loss of his family members. Occupation schooling spelled a relief from the strictures of fascism but was not significant in itself. Only Shizuko Tsuchiya, a professor of English literature at Tsuda College, whom I interviewed in August 2016 and whose memories of occupation schooling were scant enough to merit little or no mention, came close to the Kitanis' noncommittal responses. I mention her very briefly because her memories were only of the war and the martial schooling during the war rather than later. Shizuko remembered being made to write comfort letters to soldiers during the war and singing militarist songs while being shocked at the move to coeducation during occupation. Osamu's and Shigeko's narratives were testaments to the success of benevolent reeducation and to the strategic ends of securing Japan as a site for major military bases, for if the dominant impression of "American people on the street," most of whom were military personnel, was "Oh, how nice" (Shigeko) or thankfulness for food aid (Osamu), the suturing of the pedagogical project with the Cold War project of occupation and permanent militarization was complete. At the same time, Shigeko's very memory of teachers praising America and encouraging a subjectification of gratitude questioned the narrative of education in individualism, freedom, and democracy.

My last two interviewees were Emiko Miwa and Kimitada Miwa, an elderly cosmopolitan couple living in Tokyo who sometimes supplemented each other's recollections. We met in my hotel room and talked over green tea and cookies. Emiko Miwa was a cheerful woman who frequently broke into laughter, her salt-and-pepper hair and smart clothes giving her a youthful appearance. Kimitada Miwa was a short, portly man, impeccably dressed in a dark suit, with an amicable disposition and a friendly round, smiling face that habitually beamed. Both were in their mid-eighties—Kimitada was eighty-six and Emiko was eighty-three—but were sprightly, eager to talk, and had a good sense of humor. Emiko Miwa was a graduate of the University of Tokyo, had taught English at Sacred Heart Elementary School, and had raised their three children; Kimitada Miwa held a doctorate from Princeton University and was a former professor of international relations at Sophia University in Tokyo. Kimitada was very well published in Japan-U.S. relations and possessed a wealth of information. Both were well traveled, committed to the idea of a pacifist Japan, and fluent in English.

The Miwas were part of the 1 percent minority of Japanese who are Christian and descended from generations of Catholics. Kimitada grew up in Matsumoto City, which has a fairly large Christian population, and attended Matsumoto Middle School, the oldest and most renowned middle school in Japan, where he continued to learn English even during the war. During the occupation, he was at Sophia University. Emiko presented herself as someone who had incorporated aspects of American and British culture into a Japaneseness that she cherished. Her mother was born in the United States, but even though she returned to Japan as a child and chose Japanese citizenship, she taught her children English. Emiko had lived in Tokyo most of her life and attended Sacred Heart school, an institution run by Catholic nuns where English was taught from the start. Like many others, Emiko's family evacuated to the countryside during the war. The family followed many Western customs, such as sitting at a dining table, and her mother found sitting on a tatami floor uncomfortable.

Like Ogura, Kimitada came prepared with a handout, but one that was as much historical and political as personal. It was clear that for him, autobiographical, historical, and collective memory were consciously linked. Kimitada began by showing me his essay, which an editor with poor English had incorrectly revised, thus establishing himself as having fluency in English that was more advanced than that of most Japanese. His next handout was labeled "16 year old boy's reaction." Unlike the previous interviewees, Kimitada consciously conjoined personal memory with a larger historical narrative of the racial politics of occupation. He began by explaining a postwar news item prohibiting Japanese from producing salt because of a study correlating salt intake and sexual drive and saw it as a proposition to stop Japanese procreation. He commented, "The very America that fought Hitler [was] proposing to do what Hitler did against the Japanese." He moved next to talk about the demilitarization of his hometown, Matsumoto City, where American soldiers disarmed his middle school of rifles.

The most startling of Kimitada's written memories was his early encounter with American GIs: "A couple of GIs riding the street car showed us a condom, saying they were going to the Yokota legally open brothels. They were 17 years old who had fought in Okinawa. They were from North Dakota." Kimitada's narrative was part of a larger history of prostitutes being made available for American GIs almost immediately following occupation, but this episode had so many of the markings of a well-worn trope of gendered domination that I wonder how Kimitada would translate it. Kimitada explained that he and his friend were riding the streetcar in Matsumoto when he met the two young American GIs, who were returning from Asama Hot Springs, where they had visited Yokota, a legal brothel specifically opened for American soldiers, a practice Kimitada cynically referred to as "Japanese hospitality." He remembered one of the soldiers triumphantly showing them a condom. To my question about how they reacted to the soldiers, Kimitada simply stated, "We are much younger than them," which surprised me, because Kimitada was then sixteen. Kimitada, however, explained the difference as cultural:

> Well, we were brought up in such a nice family atmosphere, and that's all the boys we know; we didn't know about these things as yet . . . two Japanese boys of sixteen years old and two American GIs of seventeen years old who came through the killing fields of Okinawa. . . . [S]o I saw them get off at the Yokota to visit this brothel, so that was something you understand . . . opening up of a new vista for a growing up boy of sixteen.

Kimitada characterized the soldiers as having been toughened by Okinawa and laughingly added, "And besides, they are the farmer boys of North Dakota. North Dakota, I assume it's one of the poorest states."

As a cultural response to occupation, Kimitada's account is interesting on many levels. Clearly, he had turned the GIs' vaunting of masculinity and American power into an account of his own moral superiority. As discussed in Chapter 6, Meiji modernity, which involved incorporating European technology and habits into a specifically Japanese worldview, was constructed on similar grounds (Ivy, 71). Although Kimitada was highly critical of wartime Japanese imperial nationalism, as became evident later in the interview, he was simultaneously skillfully deploying an anticolonial (if elitist) protective cultural nationalism to ward off the soldiers' show of power. Even though they were just a year apart in age, Kimitada marked himself and his friend as children, different from the putatively adult soldiers, which in turn contrasted the innocent Japanese youth with corrupt and debauched Americans. They had the swagger of an occupying force while he belonged to a more righteous culture and could claim Japanese moral high ground. Kimitada also used the category of class to jettison the arrogant strutting of the soldiers by contrasting the sophisticated respectability of his family with that of the uncouth, rustic soldiers, who at this point arguably stood for the United States. Kimitada concluded by ironically characterizing the episode as one of misplaced education. It was "the opening up of a new vista for a growing up boy of sixteen."

Indeed, it seemed as if Kimitada was using the strategic oppositions of anticolonial nationalism and Meiji modernity to characterize U.S. culture through vulgar materialism. I asked Kimitada about an incident described in his handout in which he was working for a young American in Matsumoto and received a box of Whitman chocolates at Christmas. He had glossed this encounter with the cynical written statement, "We all felt very much obliged at a tell-tale glimpse at the American civilization." When asked whether he was being ironic, Kimitada evaded the question and explained that American soldiers offered children gum, not chocolate, and that the first encounter of young Japanese with Americans was through chewing gum. "But the chocolate box," he said, "Whitman chocolates—I've never seen such a big box. This was really American civilization: beautiful box, decorated." I had heard Kimitada pepper his conversation with references to Sartre and Plato, so his remark did not seem to be anything but a critique of the culture of consumption. My impression was confirmed later in the interview when Kimitada compared his dormitory at Sophia University with the heated classroom for U.S. soldiers and their wives: "The sound of the radiator: that's American civilization, I thought."

But despite Kimitada's satirical, if jocular, characterization of American culture as consisting of creature comforts and gaudy displays of wealth, he, like Osamu, saw aspects of occupation tutelage as a welcome relief from wartime militarism. Indeed, he used the term "occupation" to refer to wartime Japanese control and wrote in his handout, "People felt liberated from the Japanese military's 'occupation' of Japan to the vast possibility of [the] American form of liberalism and democracy." He remembered inking out parts of history textbooks, particularly references to the divinity of the emperor, and linked autobiographical to historical memory when he recalled parts of Japanese history being incorrectly erased. His remembrance of this event was intellectual rather than affective, and as a historian he wanted to set the record straight. However, occupation tutelage generated not an unambiguous Americanism but, rather, an intense skepticism of the apparatus of schooling. As Kimitada put it, "My generation, sixteen years old, became very skeptical; not believing in anybody, especially authorities." Kimitada was contemptuous of his teachers because "the same person who said 'Fight this war to a bitter end. Sacrifice your life for the glory of the nation,' etc., now came back and said, 'Democracy, you are free.' We couldn't believe that."

When asked whether there were any other memories of occupation he wanted to rehearse, Kimitada recalled Father Johnson, an American chaplain who came to Sophia University to teach conversational English. Unlike the other interviewees, Kimitada had experienced being taught by Americans. He quickly pointed out that Johnson was not qualified to be a university professor. He remembered Johnson as a colonial figure—arrogant, insensitive, and derogatory toward the Japanese; Johnson, he explained, had a "certain attitude to Japanese culture and the Japanese way of living; he was so proud of American civilization, . . . American standard of living." Johnson attributed the high rate of tuberculosis among the Japanese to their poor diet and their practice of shutting windows at night while heating their homes. He said that, in the United States, "we keep heater up and windows open during the night when we sleep," according to Kimitada. "Therefore, we have no tuberculosis; air is clean. . . . We have so much surplus of milk and eggs; we eat so much [and are] so well nourished. That's another reason we don't have lung tuberculosis." Clearly, Kimitada was still affected by this memory. "What an awful thing you can say to a poor defeated people," he reflected. "Isn't that terrible?" He hastened to add that most American teachers were amicable and that the Japanese liked MacArthur and were surprised when he was recalled by President Harry Truman. He praised MacArthur's astuteness in keeping the imperial institution, thus winning the trust of the Japanese.

Kimitada informed me that by the end of middle school, students were already divided into "political" and "nonpolitical," and he belonged to the latter category. "Nonpolitical" really meant not being part of *ming se* (democratic youth organizations), which Kimitada described as "communist-tainted." He reported the atmosphere in his classes during occupation as corrupted by the leftist students, who insisted on unjustifiably introducing political matter into the classroom. Referring to political students presumably introducing Trofim Lysenko's Lamarckian ideas about evolution, which contradicted Gregor Mendel, Kimitada related his impatience with the students:

> My classmates are so concerned about Mendel's natural selection as contradicting Soviet biologist, some Soviet biology of evolution. They were arguing with the nonpolitical if they are ready to accept the challenge, so it wasn't a very good academic atmosphere. It's a political thing; the teacher is a balanced scientist, but the students were political or nonpolitical and introducing something the teacher is not elaborating on. . . . So being a nonpolitical, I wasn't interested in this argument at all.

Unlike Nobuko Albery's heroine, Kana, Kimitada was horrified when one of his classmates, Takezawa Masao, joined in the "violent" student demonstrations against the U.S.-Japan security treaty on May Day in 1952, days after the occupation formally ended. Kimitada saw the uprising as one against American occupation because of the protests outside the GHQ headquarters and the continued physical presence of Americans. He described himself as uninterested in the activities of political students and invested in the idea of a pacifist culture for Japan.

Kimitada's account of education under occupation and shortly thereafter suggests schooling as a site of conflict, tension, and contradiction rather than a simple site for the project of reformation. The overnight political shift of teachers from Japanese loyalists to cheerleaders for the United States left students with no faith in teachers' authority and suspicious about their knowledge. In his recounting of events, Kimitada articulated a postcolonial subjectivity that questioned and critiqued the hegemony of the U.S.-led occupation, the racism and arrogance of soldiers and teachers, and the putative value of American culture. Indeed, Kimitada's continual use of the term "American culture" to refer to crass behavior or consumer goods suggested a conscious critique of the arrogance of occupation. Kimitada's memories also suggested that, rather than generating an Americanized pedagogical subject, the classroom generated skepticism and distrust—or, as in the case of his friend, fomented leftist resistance. At the same time, his relief at being liberated from militarism and his repeated stating that he had had "a good impression about American soldiers and American culture" suggested that benevolent reeducation was at least partly successful. Indeed, Kimitada's alarm at student protests against the U.S.-Japan treaty (which maintained the United States' right to military bases in Japan) and his characterization of these protests as "violent," although it was students who were attacked and one was killed, suggest an accommodation to continuing U.S. military presence, made palatable through the process of reeducation. The pacifist culture he envisioned precluded an overthrow of U.S. military presence; it may even have needed this presence.

My last subject, Emiko Miwa, was keenly interested in the interview, although she sometimes deferred to her husband when answering questions. Emiko was thirteen when the war ended, so like Kimitada she had memories of her schooling both before and during occupation. Like her husband, she was a pacifist and resolutely opposed to the removal of Article 9 of the Japanese constitution, which prohibits war as a means of settling international disputes. She gave me a music sheet in an envelope marked "Song for a Peaceful World by Father Peter Junichi Iwakashi who passed away last year." A student of elite Sacred Heart institutions from kindergarten through junior college, she learned English as a child and used English readers and books shipped directly from the United Kingdom. Emiko explained that with the onset of the war, English instruction was suspended, and children were prohibited from speaking the language, including words such as "mama" and "papa." Emiko mimicked the teacher: "We are all Japanese, and we fight for the emperor and empress." She had unpleasant memories of mandatory lessons on how to use a *naginata* (sword) and made hissing sounds as she imitated the teacher and laughed. Emiko's school was bombed during the war but rebuilt later. Her overriding memory of occupation was of relief at the end of the war and the onset of peace. She remembered kind American soldiers and American nuns helping at the school after the war. Asked about the American nuns, Emiko was politely noncommittal, saying, "We had wonderful people, and we Japanese are wonderful . . . same as Americans. We are same human beings. Why should we have war?" To my question about what she thought of MacArthur, she responded, "Nothing special. Douglas MacArthur came to do good things, as we thought. But maybe not." However, on being asked to explain her mixed feelings about MacArthur, she hesitated and simply stated she was not a specialist.

An interesting modification in the school curriculum after the war was the change of textbooks, which clearly signified the central role of the United States in the occupation. Although the Sacred Heart school was an international institution, it was, as Emiko described it, affected by the politics of occupation. After the war, Emiko's school began using American instead of British textbooks, which, she said, felt very different because "American culture is written in the reader—history and everything." Emiko's school had started using the *Cathedral Basic Reader*, a Catholic version of the Dick and Jane series readers popular in the United States from the 1930s until the late 1960s. These readers, with their hegemonic and homogeneous vision of a white, middle-class, capitalist, suburban America, were heavily criticized for their racial insularity. Emiko also remembered *St. Mary's Messenger*, a weekly publication that was shipped from the United States. I was curious about the history taught in these texts, but Emiko simply stated that they, and other new books, taught children "the American way, cowboy things." What Emiko meant by "cowboy things" is perhaps illustrated in her narrative about Americans' casual attitude toward violence. Incensed with the normative American version of the righteous war with Japan that discounted human suffering, Emiko was eager to narrate her encounter with a former veteran when she visited a friend in a nursing home in the United States. The soldier accosted her and regaled her with an account of his difficulty in bombing Tokyo because of the smoke the incendiary bombs had created. Emiko mimicked him saying, "It was so crowded, it was horrible. But it's history, you know, he said. How can I answer? I was there in convent school; our place didn't burn but it came close to burning. . . . So many died, and he's so happy telling me it's a horrible thing. It was terrible, I thought."

The Miwas, Kitanis, and Ogura were a heterogeneous group in many ways, even though they were all highly educated and elite. The Kitanis and the Miwas had traveled extensively outside Japan, spoke English fluently, and had pursued advanced degrees in the United States. All of my interview subjects had endured hardships during the war, but Osamu Kitani had suffered the most devastating losses, with half of his family killed. Ogura's homes in Tokyo and Sendai were destroyed in aerial bombings, while the Miwas' homes were relatively untouched. The Miwas were among the small minority of Catholics in Japan and consciously cosmopolitan. Emiko Miwa was unusual in having gone to an international school and received English instruction from the outset. Because the Kitanis and the Miwas were older than Ogura, they had particularly strong memories of the militarism and nationalism coerced by the wartime government. Only the Miwas had had direct encounters with American teachers and soldiers.

To some extent, the memories of the interviewees corroborated the two dominant strains of institutional memory recorded in occupation documents: that of a democratic nation reeducating a populace out of a hitherto conformist and militarist culture, and that of a filial, paternalistic occupation helping a downtrodden people. All of my interviewees expressed relief at not having to follow militarist wartime rituals in the classroom, and many expressed gratitude for U.S. aid. Emiko Miwa presented the jingoistic wartime restrictions on schools as comic and absurd, while Osamu and Shigeko Kitani simply reported hating them. In that sense, these oral histories did not contest hegemonic narratives produced by occupation authorities, including MacArthur's publication of the adulatory letters written to him. These memories of relief are also what Cathy Caruth would call the belated address of trauma—that is, continuation under a different form of memories of war (4). Thus, what might be represented as a docile subject of occupation might be a subject at the intersection of the contradictory forces of wartime trauma and the welcome respite from the war.

However, while the beginning of occupation was welcomed by the interviewees because it meant the end of aerial bombing, a reprieve from intense food scarcity, and relief from forced militarism, occupation schooling was viewed with skepticism precisely because teachers had been instructed to follow a script and tutelage had become an alibi for a colonized mentality. (The interviewees were understandably not privy to the conflicts felt by many teachers as they confronted their complicity with militarist instruction and consequently chose to leave teaching [Nozaki, 126]). Shigeko Kitani said, "I felt very liberalized from that [militarism,] you know. . . . [I had a] feeling of freedom, but at the same time I was very much surprised that, you know, the teachers turned 180 degrees around; they switched sides [seeing] America and England very viciously, but after the war they praised those countries with smiles on the face. Oh I couldn't believe it. I think they are ordered to praise America." Thus, for these interviewees, occupation, rather than producing docile bodies through the biopolitical project of education, generated subjects mistrustful of tutelage under occupation. While they felt constricted and suppressed under wartime fascism, they also resented the haughtiness of Americans who saw Japanese through the racial lens of Western colonial difference and erased memories of the atomic and incendiary aerial bombings of Japan. The pacifist politics of the Miwas—Kimitada's wanting Father Johnson to acknowledge Japan's wartime destitution and Emiko's wanting the American soldier to recognize the human cost of bombing—was based on remembrance. Both suggested a need to rewrite the popular historical record through an affective history that would mourn losses rather than through the teleological history of fascism being overcome by democracy and Japan moving toward development. Ogura, by contrast, was dubious even about the narrative of Japan's defeat. As his translator explained, "Afterward, when after he learned history, considering the history of America and Japan, he's not sure Japan loses the war."

Ogura's statement invites a rethinking of the interviewees' uneasy relationship to Japanese imperial nationalism. As noted earlier, Ogura was eager to share that the drawing of children cheering the emperor was a "banzai" salute, even though he attached no significance to it. In a sense, MacArthur's decision to let the Japanese keep the emperor as a symbol, despite his banning of several popular activities deemed martial, including samurai dramas, meant that affective continuities with a past of Japanese splendor, which was undoubtedly imperial, could be maintained even as Japan's militarist imperialism could be loathed. Although I did not pose the question of Japan's colonialism to the interviewees, it is interesting that in their condemnation of Japan's militarist nationalism, which had, in turn, wreaked violence and poverty on its own people, none of the interviewees mentioned or hinted about the violence that this colonialism had inflicted on other Asian nations, thus excluding what Viet Thanh Nguyen refers to as an alternative ethics of remembering (9). Their self-interpellation as victims of war or as pacifists overshadowed, or possibly disallowed, room for a historical reckoning with Japan's colonial past. The omission of the past was paradoxically enabled by occupation policies of benevolent reeducation that sought to strip remnants of ultranationalism and militarism but did not include education about Japanese colonialism, an exclusion congruent with the U.S. amnesia about its own colonial histories.

Although I have read the interviews symptomatically for their gaps and elisions and in the complex context of occupation, they suggest a plurality of memory formations that refuse to work teleologically toward resolutions. Michel Foucault's explanation of the genealogical approach that must "record the singularity of events outside of any monotonous finality" is useful in thinking about these memory constructions (*Language, Counter-Memory, Practice*, 139). Ogura's sudden declaration about feeling free at the end of occupation, for instance, is not the culmination of a progression of ideas or a clarifying vision that renders what preceded it simply false; it is a powerful affective memory that created him as an agential subject in the past. Activated in the present, alongside the historical memory of the Red purges that Shibusawa insistently brought up, it functioned to make his individual narration of wartime privations also a critique of occupation control. Similarly, Kimitada's recollections about occupation and occupation schooling included a distaste for the politics of leftist students, an admiration for MacArthur, and a disgust with brash soldiers. At the same time, his handout—which included information about Japanese militarism, GHQ's proscription of "totalitarian vocabularies," the episode with brothel-visiting soldiers, and the story about receiving Whitman chocolates—cast Kimitada as the urbane, sophisticated, knowledgeable historian well equipped to correct the historical memory of an uncomplicated, benign tutelage under occupation.

Foucault noted in an interview, "Since memory is actually a very important factor in struggle[,] . . . if one controls people's memory, one controls their dynamism. . . . It's vital to have possession of this memory, to control it, administer it, tell it what it must contain" (*Foucault Live*, 124). Part of occupation tutelage was a concerted effort to discipline popular memory, to propose what it should contain. My conversations with this group of Japanese suggested that their (socially constructed) memories escaped the ideological parameters of occupation tutelage. This does not mean that the oral narratives were simply counterhegemonic—actually, many subjects appreciated having a nonmilitarized education—but, rather, that the hegemony was not complete. While the rejection of militarism was indisputable, and the censorship of textbooks and *romaji* instruction paled in comparison with wartime devastation, occupation tutelage bred more skepticism and cynicism than control. Above all, the interviewees articulated the need for an affective history that questions the simple narrative of Americans reeducating and liberating an oppressed population.

Epilogue

The War on Terror and Education for Democracy

Shortly after the U.S. invasion of Iraq in 2003, George W. Bush devoted his weekly radio address to informing a skeptical nation that the occupation of Iraq was really one of building democracy through education. Instead of a curriculum devoted to indoctrinating the youth and teaching them hatred, U.S. efforts were designed to "build a stable and secure Iraq" through the rebuilding of schools, often with the personal intervention of American soldiers. "Our efforts," Bush said, "will help Iraq reclaim its proud heritage of learning, and bring it into the family of nations" ("Radio Address by George Bush"). The U.S. Agency for International Development (USAID) advertised in its request for proposals its efforts to "promote child-centered, inquiry-based, participatory teaching methods that lay a foundation for democratic practices and attitudes among children and educators and draw families into the life of the school communities" (quoted in Zehr). And finally, Andrea B. Rugh, an international education consultant with twenty-five years' experience living in "Arab" countries, opined that such methods would not work unless Iraqis were deeply involved in the process: "There's a sense in Arabic societies more of responsibility rather than rights. . . . They talk about responsibility—respect for elders and each other. It's very hard to have an egalitarian classroom when you have respect and authority" (quoted in Zehr).

These statements about education in Iraq following the military invasion eerily echo the ameliorative and subject-forming task of the tutelary project in the Philippines in the early twentieth century and in Japan more than half a century ago. Bush, sounding like the paternalist William McKinley at the turn of the twentieth century, used a familial trope to assure the United States that the occupation was necessary for Iraq's own good and to facilitate Iraq's emergence as a modern nation. However, as in the project of Japanese education for democracy, Iraqis had to be reeducated out of their hostility to the West. And as with the Japanese during occupation, educators such as Rugh relied on an Orientalist lens and lay colonial anthropology to characterize Iraq as an inherently undemocratic society. She suggested involving Iraqis in the process of child-centered Deweyan models of education to foster "democratic practices"; however, given the normalization of occupation within Rugh's program, and absent political critique, such practices simply encourage a mechanistic idea of dialogue without the epistemological curiosity needed to practice critical democracy (Freire and Macedo, 382).

Undoubtedly, the occupations of Japan and Iraq cannot be conflated. There are clear differences between the public demonstrations of authority by General Douglas MacArthur in his person and the offices of the Supreme Commander of Allied Powers and the attempt to exhibit democracy in Iraq by appointing a caretaker government months after the invasion. However, the endeavor to create an individualistic pedagogical subject critical of tradition and community, at once nationalist, democratic, and accepting of U.S. hegemony, continues, suggesting a continuity in technologies of U.S. empire. As different sites are effectively arrogated as U.S. militarized spaces, forms of schooling continue to function as complementary adjuncts to these spaces.

It is important to emphasize that racial difference has been central to these projects of education. As discussed earlier, there was a marked difference in approach regarding educational directives in Germany and Japan, even though the ostensible goal of dismantling the structures of fascism was similar in the two countries. Speaking comparatively about the Germans and Japanese during U.S. Senate hearings, Douglas MacArthur stated, "If the Anglo-Saxon was say 45 years of age in his development, in the sciences, the arts, divinity, culture, the Germans were quite as mature. The Japanese, however, in spite of their antiquity measured by time, were in a very tuitionary condition. Measured by the standards of modern civilization, they would be like a boy of 12 as compared with our development of 45 years" (Dower, *War without Mercy*, 303). Little wonder that educational advisers in Germany felt trepidation in recommending changes to a culture they felt was not simply at par with theirs but also a source of knowledge rather than "tuitionary."

Most other sites of U.S. colonialism and occupation, however, have been considered tuitionary. From the attempts to civilize Hawaiians through the teaching of English and the banning of the Hawaiian language to the Americanization of the "racially degenerate" Puerto Ricans through school plays, public parades, and English instruction (see Angulo, 30; Del Moral, 138–140); the promotion of technical education in Haiti; the attempts to reform the school system in Korea; and current educational efforts by the state and nongovernmental organizations (NGOs) in Afghanistan and Iraq, the role of the United States as tutor and bearer of democracy and the position of the nonwhite colonized/occupied as tuitionary have remained unquestioned. As Robert M. Spector wrote about the U.S. occupation of Haiti, it was not only economically and politically driven, but it also had a strong instructional component. The idea was "to tutor Haiti in Anglo-Saxon democracy. It was the Philippine experiment applied to the Caribbean" (viii). Hans Schmidt concurs, arguing that the United States "made a determined effort to indoctrinate Haitians with American concepts of political morality, pragmatism, and efficiency" (135).

Interestingly, even the brief period of the occupation of Korea by the U.S. Army Military Government in Korea (USAMGIK) from 1945 to 1948 witnessed a plethora of attempts to initiate educational reforms and mold the subjectivities of Koreans. Occupation officials held the abilities of Koreans in little regard. Archibald V. Arnold, the military governor, reported problems finding Koreans who could work with American integrity and efficiency and declared, as had officials in the Philippines decades earlier, that Koreans were unfit to run their country: "I have told them that it might be one year, ten years, or fifteen years" (quoted in Simons, 159). Similarly, the State-War-Navy Coordinating Committee suggested a trusteeship for Korea following occupation because Koreans were not fit "to exercise self-government" (Simons, 161). Americans propounded participatory learning, pragmatism, self-reliance, and individualism as paths to democratization. Public education also included inculcating Americanization and liberal capitalist democracy. Courses on English for Korean women, staffed by volunteers, were opened by the Women's Bureau, and booklets titled "Lessons for Democracy" were distributed en masse. A highly centralized system of education was instituted, often using officials who had served with the Japanese (Meade, 76), and nervous military officials sought to suppress student strikes by ordering the expulsion of students who refused to attend class even for a day (see Commander-in-Chief U.S. Army Forces, 71). Thus, strategies for educational reform were again very much a part of the occupation and carried out under the aegis of the military. Lessons in democracy (as self-expression), self-reliance (leading to material success), and individualism (propagated as the right to self-expression of abstract individuals apart from society and free of obligations to kinship networks) could function as bulwarks against communism. Simultaneously, these were technologies of subjectification into capitalist democracy, bolstered by a U.S. military presence.

In an age when outright colonialism of the sort practiced in the Philippines has virtually ended, but various forms of formal and informal U.S. occupation continue, the question of pacification through tutelage and subjectification is still relevant. For instance, the conjunction of sovereignty and governmentality was evident in the U.S. Army's Human Terrain System (HTS), started in 2006, which employed a diverse group of anthropologists, sociologists, and even American studies scholars to generate cultural knowledge that could be used to better control different areas, particularly Iraq and Afghanistan. As the website stated, "Sociocultural understanding and knowledge was believed to provide a unique method to help combat commanders consider the affects of military operations."[1] In turn, opening schools and universities under the aegis of education for democracy have been touted as a benefit of the invasions of both Afghanistan and Iraq, even as the schools function as sites of neocolonial subjectification.

Indeed, the rhetoric of pacification through education is endorsed by the Right and Left alike, with people on the Left including self-conscious critiques of imperialism in their arguments. The year 2007 saw the opening of the American University of Iraq, a private venture funded by Kurds and American neoconservatives, with ardent supporters of the Iraq War, including Fouad Ajami of Johns Hopkins University and Kanan Makiya of Brandeis University, on the board of directors. In a stinging critique of the American University of Iraq, Russ Baker and Kristina Borjesson criticized the operation of the university, but not its goals, which they saw as secular and lofty. The mission statement of the university reads that it is to "promote the development and prosperity of Iraq through the careful study of modern commerce, economics, business and public administration, and to lead the transformation of Iraq into a free and democratic society, through an understanding of the ideals of liberty and democracy." What Baker and Borjessen strongly critiqued was Provost Joshua Mitchell, a former Georgetown University professor of political theory, who functioned as "the classic colonial university official with the Bible in his pocket," but not the governing of occupation through the rhetoric of education for democracy. Neither the occupation itself nor education as the partner of occupation comes under their scrutiny.

Afghanistan, no less, has been cast as the object of colonial uplift, particularly through the abject figure of the burqa-clad woman awaiting freedom. This recycling of a familiar nineteenth-century colonial narrative of saving brown women has been harnessed by NGOs running educational programs. For instance, Paula Nirschel's Initiative to Educate Afghan Women, in which universities and colleges such as Bucknell, Mary Washington, Brenau, Hollins, and Mt. Holyoke participate, provides scholarships to Afghan women to study in the United States and requires them to return to Afghanistan to help with their homeland's reconstruction. We can think of this as a privatized version of the *pensionado* scheme. The initiative itself, described in terms of American benevolence, echoes Laura Bush's acclamation of the military invasion of Afghanistan as feminist rescue ("Radio Address by Mrs. Bush"). Nirschel was apparently "seized by the images of Afghan women shrouded in burqas: 'I had to get my hands on some of these women and help them get educated and bring their professionalism and their new feelings of self-worth back to their country'" (Teicher). Nowhere in Nirschel's initiative is there any mention of the U.S.-led bombing and occupation of Afghanistan or of local women's organizations such as the Revolutionary Association of Women of Afghanistan, which has been running schools for women since the 1970s and is resolutely opposed to occupation.

Today, education for democracy as a tactic of governmentality for the making of neoliberal subjects in areas of occupation, heavily reinforced by militarization, has proliferated in a variety of venues. For instance, Deborah Rodriguez, an adventurous hairdresser from Michigan, recounts in her salacious memoir *Kabul Beauty School* (2007) how she traveled to Kabul as part of an NGO, Care for All Foundation, helped open a beauty school in Kabul and started the NGO Beauty without Borders. Indeed, we can see the work of these beauticians as part of the biopolitical project of creating suitable neoliberal pedagogical subjects.[2] Liz Mermin's critical documentary *The Beauty Academy of Kabul* (2004) caricatures Rodriguez's mission of uplifting natives into modernity through the consumption of beauty products. Yet the thoroughly self-aware documentary refuses even to mention the U.S. invasion and occupation, confirming again the normalization of a military presence for benevolent tutelage.

Similarly, the use of education as a counterinsurgency strategy is evident in women's rights activism that tacitly assents to imperialism in the name of democracy and peace. The humanitarian Greg Mortensen is a good illustration of this: he claims he was inspired by children in remote areas of Pakistan using sticks to write their names in the dirt to build schools for them as part of the Central Asia Institute.[3] In *Three Cups of Tea* (2009), his memoir about helping to build schools in rural and war-ridden areas of Pakistan and Afghanistan, Mortensen never questions the agenda of the "war on terror," and in the acknowledgments, thanks "the peacemakers, and people serving in the military around the world, who also dedicate their lives to peace" (Mortensen and Relin, n.p.). This crude equation of military strength and peacemaking demonstrates once again the nexus of sovereignty and biopolitics central to U.S. colonialism and occupation. The book also makes clear the role of tutelage in projecting an image of American benevolence. As Fatima, a student at a remote school in Pakistan, says, "We love Americans. They are the most kind people for us" (Mortensen and Relin, 112). Mortensen, who became an informal adviser to the U.S. military in its counterinsurgency operations, was nominated by members of the U.S. Congress for the Nobel Peace Prize in 2009 (Bumiller).

Textbooks for children also remain important adjuncts to military operations. In the early 1980s, via a $51 million grant from USAID, the University of Nebraska, Omaha, produced textbooks for Afghan children designed to instigate resistance to Soviet occupation. The primers featured illustrations of guns, bullets, and soldiers. After 2002, George Bush affirmed the production of textbooks for Afghanistan with "respect for human dignity" instead of the earlier indoctrination (Stephens and Ottaway, A1). Therefore, the idea of education for democracy, under the aegis of the United States and against the backdrop of military presence, replaced the earlier mission of education for resistance. Similarly, when Creative Associates International won a no-bid contract for educational reform in Iraq soon after the invasion, it did so under the banner of "democracy promotion" (Saltman, 230). The production of appropriate textbooks was once again a central task of occupation.[4]

Of course, as this book has demonstrated, technologies of imperial pedagogical subjectification can never be totally successful. The attempt to colonize the signs and signifiers of linguistic and cultural identity in the Philippines and Japan through education was met in literary, filmic, and autobiographical discourses with various degrees of accommodation, redirection, appropriation, and resistance, often all at once. It is important, therefore, to briefly consider the extent to which educational reforms persisted in both of these sites and what their relative permanence or impermanence reveals about these technologies. The imposition of English in the Philippines and the proscription of the vernacular in U.S. colonial schooling was changed in 1939, during the commonwealth period, when Jorge Bocobo became the secretary of public instruction. The teaching of Pilipino (based on Tagalog and later renamed Filipino) began to be required of high school students in 1940. However, the 1987 constitution ratified both English and Filipino as official languages, with Filipino continuing as the national language. Although literature in Filipino and other vernaculars is thriving, with contemporary writers publishing in both English and Filipino and sometimes incorporating the two languages in the same text, the language of upward mobility continues to be English, and the perception of English as more suitable for academic subjects remains strong, despite research by educators suggesting that students learn best in their local languages (Bernardo, 22, 26). The use of English as the medium of instruction in premier institutions of higher learning, such as the University of the Philippines, Diliman, speaks to the hegemony of the language. At the same time, the emphasis on industrial education and the production of goods in schools has decreased dramatically, reflecting Filipinos' conception of themselves as a people capable of acquiring, and in need of, academic knowledge.

Yet despite anticolonial critiques, the historical project of American education continues to be assessed with a mixture of praise and trepidation. The hundred-year anniversary of the arrival of the Thomasites in the Philippines was marked in the country by a major centennial project that included conferences, lectures, film and dramatic presentations, exhibits, and book launches. Directed by Professor Judy Ick of the University of the Philippines, the project involved the U.S. Embassy, the American Studies Association of the Philippines, the Philippine-American Educational Foundation, and other Filipino educational institutions. The pamphlet for the Thomasite Centennial Project includes a thoroughly laudatory "white man's burden" history of the tutelary project, acclaiming the devotion and idealism of the Thomasites, "armed with books, pencils, paper and slates; and fired by high ideals and a genuine desire to help," and connects the Thomasite venture to contemporary programs, such as the Peace Corps and the Fulbright Student Program. The project also included a play written for the occasion by the award-winning playwright Tony Perez titled, "A Hundred Songs of Mary Helen Fee," based on Fee's memoir *A Woman's Impression of the Philippines.* Yet comments on the play by its director, Nonon Padilla, reveal the ambivalence in the collective historical memory of the Thomasites. Padilla commends Fee's memoir for its astute insights into the Filipino psyche and, almost echoing American Orientalist ideas about Filipinos, depicts Fee as a missionary whose "faith in Reason is tested by the world of emotions that Filipinos inhabited." At the same time, Padilla notes Fee's experience of Filipinos "suffering a newly imposed language imposed in schools" and her perseverance in her singular objective of sharing her knowledge and giving "her personal best."

The complex and fraught relations to the memory of U.S. colonial tutelage and the difficulties in negotiating the status of this memory today are evident in Padilla's comments about the apparent disagreements in the conceptualization of the play. While the original draft concluded with "the gloom of death and the histrionic practices of the locals mourning their dead," the team decided to end instead with Fee's comic story about Christmas in the Philippines, which includes misunderstandings but also shows Filipinos and Americans as Christians "in tune with the same wishes for unity, peace, and harmony."[5] But while diverse assessments about the tutelary project continue, the imprint on the educational system in the Philippines has been long-lasting. Ick says that a major part of the Philippine education system was patterned after America's and has called for recognizing the impact of American tutelage: "Whether it was good or bad, it doesn't matter. The point is it has become so much part of us" (Vergara, C6).

Although the period of Japanese occupation was short, the impact of educational reforms was palpable long after 1952. This was true partially because the beginning of occupation was also the end of years of prolonged war and of strict fealty to nationalism, which was enforced in schools. As discussed in Chapter 7 schooling during occupation in many ways could not be seen as anything but relief. Yet the specific changes ushered in during occupation have persisted to different degrees. The occupation's attempt to democratize the Japanese and decrease elitism had led to a major overhaul in the school structure. A 6-3-3 system of coeducational schools and a compulsory education of nine years replaced the earlier gender-segregated schools with only six years of compulsory schooling and a gymnasium-type structure. Despite post-occupation criticism of the dilution of excellence of middle schools, the system has been retained, with more than 95 percent of students receiving education until grade 12. As Toshio Nishi puts it, "The American-initiated mass educational reforms have revitalized the Japanese passion for learning and offered the people a broader horizon to explore" (xxxvi–xxxvii).

However, attempts to deculturate the Japanese through linguistic signifiers and social practices have met with limited success. Toward the end of occupation, the Civil Information and Education Section was itself recognizing the unfeasibility of replacing *kanji* with *romaji*. Although compulsory in schools, *romaji* has not become the medium of instruction or communication, and *kanji*, thought to be too difficult, time-consuming, and wasteful, continues to be a major part of the Japanese writing system, and the number of *kanji* characters taught in schools through secondary education has actually increased since 1946. Other attempts to change cultural practices to temper ultranationalism through authoritarian strictures likewise have had limited permanent impact. The course on morals (*shushin*), discontinued based on the recommendations of the U.S. Education Mission, had found its way back into the curriculum by 1959. The mission had held state Shintoism responsible for Japanese militaristic nationalism and had moved to abolish Shinto shrines in schools and to prohibit school visits to the shrines. MacArthur's personal and publicized belief in the democracy and social value of Christianity also furthered the strictures against Shintoism. Occupation authorities were successful in removing de jure state Shintoism and in secularizing Japanese education, but school visits to shrines—notably, the troubling official visits to the Yasukuni shrine—as well as the healthy continuity of Shintoism in Japanese life suggest the endurance of indigenous cultural practices. And to the dismay of many intellectuals, neonationalism and the search for an authentic and pure Japaneseness has been on the rise since the 1970s (Staaveren, 260). In schools, a democratic spirit was also propagated through the prohibition of the practice of paying obeisance to the emperor, who had renounced his divinity shortly after occupation. However, as scholars have noted, the continuation of imperial-era names and the principle of dynastic succession have enhanced the "political and symbolic authority of the emperor system" (Eiji, 520). It has no doubt contributed to the continuing amnesia about Japanese violence in Asia. The fact that reeducation as cultural colonization has had limited success in Japan while the political and economic goals of creating Japan as a capitalist ally, friendly nation, and strategic military partner have succeeded should offer a cautionary lesson about the ubiquitous appeal or universality of American cultural values—and, indeed, of Western modernity as a template for effecting change.

Given the continual use of tutelage as a form of subject making central to the maintenance of U.S. empire, analyses of different educational apparatuses in areas of occupation and control and the resistance to these apparatuses, particularly from those subject to it, remain integral to the task of critiquing imperialism today. Because the vast majority of U.S. imperial interventions since World War II have been in Asia, a transnational Asian American studies can be fundamental to the task of understanding these pedagogical forms of U.S. imperial governmentality.

Notes

INTRODUCTION

Epigraphs: Survey, 10–11; Snyder and Austin, 7.

1. Several critics have written about seeing Filipinos' needing American tutelage and schooling as a metaphor for colonial rule. Most significant is Julian Go (*American Empire and the Politics of Meaning*), who sees "tutelary colonialism" as a method of U.S. governance in the Philippines and Puerto Rico. He examines the "political education" of elites in both countries.

2. Go ("The Provinciality of American Empire") has addressed the fact that schooling was not implemented in Guam and Samoa, where it was deemed unfeasible.

3. I thank Leslie Bow for signaling this as a major argument.

4. The field of education has remained fairly impervious to questions of empire. The few studies of imperialism and education include Cameron McCarthy's *The Uses of Culture*, Willinsky's *Learning to Divide the World*, some essays in Thomas Ewing's collection *Revolution and Pedagogy*, and Roland Sintos Coloma's collection *Postcolonial Challenges in Education*. Coloma also lamented this lack of attention to empire in educational research in *Postcolonial Challenges in Education* (10). Recently there have been a few studies connecting U.S. colonialism and imperialism with education. Clif Stratton's *Education for Empire* is an excellent study of how textbooks in American schools naturalize paths for unequal citizenship, paralleling U.S. colonial policy. Tricia Gallagher-Geurtsen's *(Un)Knowing Diversity* is grounded in postcolonial methodologies and focuses on the colonized/minority students in the United States. Angulo summarizes education policies in countries occupied by the United States and outlines the conflicts between educators and administrators who wanted schools to serve humanitarian ends and produce enlightened citizens and those who wanted schools to serve the interests of capitalist imperialism.

5. I am grateful to Michael Hawkins for these comments on my work at the American Studies Association meeting in 2016.

6. Despite the fact that the Monroe Report of 1925 recommended a native language as an auxiliary medium, Pilipino was not allowed to be taught in public schools until 1940.

7. As Abe Ignacio and his colleagues point out, while *Puck* and *Judge* published cartoons that were generally supportive of colonization, the cartoons in *Life* were severely critical (Ignacio et al., 2, 24, 32).

8. Here I use the terms "racialization" and "racial project" as expounded by Michael Omi and Howard Winant (111, 125).

9. For methods of tribalizing Filipinos, see Kramer, 121–122.

10. Dower's *War without Mercy* is the most comprehensive analysis of ideas about the Japanese from the 1930s until occupation. Dower shows that although representations of the Japanese as apes did exist, Japan's victories led to perceptions of the Japanese as superhuman (187) and major academic studies and propaganda films stressed the cultural excess of the Japanese.

11. Many critics have commented that in the colonization of the Philippines, the United States employed tactics different from those of other colonial powers. Alfred McCoy argues that Filipino elites were required to play "an active role in the colonization of their own country." See "Images of a Changing Nation" in McCoy and Roces, 17.

12. The effect of U.S. policies was that this subject was also split along class lines. The U.S. restriction of the franchise to educated property owners created elite privilege. As Rafael suggests, this decree ensured access to legislative and civil service positions for elites ("Anticipating Nationhood," 69). I suggest that this access also created a desire among the subalterns for American education, a position best articulated by Bulosan.

13. See notes 1, 2, and 28.

14. *Annual Report of the General Superintendent of Education*, 30.

15. *New York Times*, March 2, 1949 quoted in Whiting, 39

16. *Official Journal of the Japanese Military Administration* 1942, 1:13, cited in Dalmacio, 82.

17. *Official Journal of the Japanese Military Administration of the Philippines*, 6:xix–xx, quoted in Goseingfiao, 231.

18. See "Address of the Director General of the Japanese Military Administration."

19. Although candidates were chosen through competitive exams and the process thus was putatively egalitarian, Kramer reminds us that the high school graduation requirement and the moral qualifications criteria generated upper-class candidates (205).

20. See Go, *American Empire and the Politics of Meaning*, 2–3, 27–28; Kramer, 201–203; Wesling, 12.

21. Espiritu calls for an intellectual history that "brings together a concern for the nation and transpacific relations and connects Asian experience on the American continent and in the Pacific world with critical histories of colonization, race, class, gender, ethnicity, and empire" (xvi). Sau Ling Cynthia Wong's landmark essay "Denationalization Reconsidered" similarly critiques arguments that see national and transnational perspectives as oppositions.

22. Some of these works include Glenn Anthony May's *Social Engineering in the Philippines*, Vicente L. Rafael's *White Love and Other Events in Filipino History* (2000), E. San Juan Jr.'s *After Postcolonialism*, Paul Kramer's *The Blood of Government*, Servando D. Halili Jr.'s *Iconography of the New Empire* (2006), Julian Go's *The American Colonial*

State in the Philippines, David Brody's *Visualizing American Empire*, and Jennifer M. McMahon's *Dead Stars*.

23. These works include Dower's *Embracing Defeat*, which places occupation policies within the history of U.S. imperialism; Koshiro's *Trans-Pacific Racisms and the U.S Occupation of Japan*, which analyzes shared racisms between Americans and Japanese; Takemae Eiji's *The Allied Occupation of Japan*, which argues for the lasting effect of SCAP's democratic reforms; and Michael S. Molasky's *The American Occupation of Japan and Okinawa* and Sharalyn Orbaugh's *Japanese Fiction of the Allied Occupation*, both of which examine representations of occupation in Japanese literature. Yoshikuni Igarashi's *Bodies of Memory* and Douglas N. Slaymaker's *The Body in Postwar Japanese Fiction* also include analysis of occupation literature.

24. See Fujiwara and Nagano's collection examining the United States in the Philippines and Japan as part of latecomer colonialism.

25. In *Empire and Education*, Coloma also deals with the pacification sought via American education and the raced and gendered hierarchies of the educational system. Other critics have compared colonial education policies with the education of minorities at home. While focusing mainly on southern literature, Peter Schmidt argues that the post-1898 colonies used Tuskegee as a model, creating a Jim Crow colonialism to uplift natives but delay their rights (6, 109–110).

26. See Nishi's *Unconditional Democracy*, Unger's *Literacy and Script Reform in Occupation Japan*, and Trainor's *Educational Reform in Occupied Japan*.

27. Wesling acknowledges this problem in her own study and includes a short section on Bulosan's *America Is in the Heart*.

28. Comparative studies of the Philippines and other sites of U.S. empire include Eric Love's *Race over Empire*; Go's *American Empire and the Politics of Meaning*; and Lanny Thompson's *Imperial Archipelago*. These studies of U.S. colonialism and imperialism have been synchronic. Post–World War II sites of U.S. imperialism therefore have not been seen in relation to the Philippines. Noah W. Sobe's collection *American Postconflict Educational Reform* and A. J. Angulo's *Empire and Education*, which deal with U.S. educational programs in areas of colonization and occupation, are more descriptive than analytical and do not engage with cultural works.

CHAPTER 1

1. William Howard Taft, letter written to be read at the meeting of supervisors of education (*Annual Reports of the War Department for the Fiscal Year Ended June 30, 1903*, 907).

2. Elliott approvingly quotes Madison Grant, who correlated skull shapes and intelligence to suggest that Filipinos could not change quickly (Elliott, Preface, n.p.).

3. In *American Pacificism*, Paul Lyons argues that ideas of oceanic people as carefree, happy islanders are different from ideas of Orientalism. Whereas Orientalism is based on knowledge, Pacificism is based on ignorance. I use the term "tropicalism" to describe the racial othering of Filipinos, because while they were often seen as happy islanders, the Philippines was subject to intense knowledge gathering.

4. *Report of the War Department*, 1901, pt. 4, 258, quoted in Forbes, 423.

5. As I discuss in Chapter 5, Okinawans were an exception and were tropicalized like Filipinos.

6. Letter from Major Gardiner, governor of Tayabas Province, in Atkinson, *Education in the Philippine Islands*, 1390.

7. The reality of American rule was that it empowered an *ilustrado* class by restricting franchise to property owners; putting ecclesiastic lands up for sale, which the mestizo elite quickly bought; and grooming these elites for political power so that cultural reproduction rather than change characterized the first decade of American rule (see B. Anderson, "Cacique Democracy in the Philippines," 11–12; Go, *American Empire and the Politics of Meaning*, 271; Kramer, 113.

8. Many Filipinos also viewed Filipino progress as dependent on learning English and "Anglo-Saxon" civilization (see Pardo de Tavera, 6).

9. Meg Wesling problematically combines Rawlins's and Barrows's remarks under one quotation and uses it as a basis to argue that Barrows thought literary education was of paramount significance (61).

10. *Proceedings of the Department of Superintendence*, 139, quoted in Fear-Segal, 103).

11. In the Senate hearings on the Philippines, while being interrogated about Filipinos providing labor for U.S. manufacturers, Barrows was, in fact, accused of favoring the interests of Filipinos over those of Americans (*Affairs*, 712).

CHAPTER 2

Epigraph: Osias, *The Story of a Long Career of Varied Tasks*, 90.

1. I am not dealing with educational reforms in Mindanao, which was treated differently from the rest of the Philippines.

2. These forms include foot dragging, false compliance, feigned ignorance, and slander. See J. Scott, *Weapons of the Weak*, xvi.

3. I disagree with critics who have dismissed differences between the Baldwin readers and those authored by Americans as early as 1904. Wesling points to the cosmetic nature of simply substituting "Jack" and "Mary" with "Juan" and "Maria." She also notes the inclusion of pieces designed to inculcate American exceptionalism and nationalism (91). Roger M. Thompson sees the same substitutions as evidence of cultural sensitivity and change (21–22).

4. Coloma argues that the readers are guides for a covert and hybrid nationalism, because they do not rely on only native sources ("Care of the Postcolonial Self," 306).

5. Osias writes, "Practical lessons in hygiene and sanitation are essential among barrio pupils.... 'One of the saddest things I saw,' said Booker T. Washington, 'was a young man ... sitting down in a one room cabin, with grease on his clothing, filth all around him, and weeds in the yard and garden, engaged in studying a French grammar'" (*Barrio Life and Barrio Education*, 13).

6. His interest in Philippine anthropology supposedly was sparked by a visit to the Philippine exhibit at the St. Louis World's Fair, where the controversial Igorot exhibit was justified on anthropological grounds. Beyer's work was thus a product of the machinery of colonial management even as it created an archive of cultural history for Filipinos.

7. See, e.g., the photograph captioned "Pupils in training department of Philippine Normal School participating in a patriotic drill" (*Twenty-First Annual*, 18).

8. Maria Teresa Trinidad Pineda Tinio examines essays, letters, and diaries written in Tagalog from 1900 to 1930 to demonstrate a nation-building effort in which Tagalog was central. She sees Osias's defense of English on the basis of the efficiency of a single language, in the famous Osias-Bocobo debates on language, as the rhetoric of a "good colonial" (Tinio, 193).

CHAPTER 3

1. Vicente Chu Reyes Jr. argues that, despite changes in the 1970s, the centralized system of education continued, and the Philippine Department of Education remains the biggest bureaucracy in the nation (10–11).
2. For a critique of the idea of mimicry as always subversive, see Moore-Gilbert, 134.
3. For blog comments, see http://signinandblogitout.blogspot.com/2010/09/hilda-cordero-visitation-of-gods.html.
4. Reynaldo Ileto, by contrast, has seen the earliest of peasant movements as coherent and rational (see *Pasyon and Revolution*).

CHAPTER 4

1. Elaine Kim sees Bulosan as a "goodwill ambassador" attempting to gain acceptance in America (57). Patricia Chu analyzes the feverish movement in America as testimony to Filipinos' inability to find a home in the country (19, 148–149). Michael Denning views Bulosan through Popular Front politics but sees *America* as only a migrant text (278–280). On gendering, see Lee, 6; on solidarity work, see Higadisha, 35–60.
2. When these stories were published, they were dished up as humorous, primitivist exotica. Harcourt, Brace billed them as belonging to a "universal and timeless comedy" with "a local touch." Bulosan reacted to such billings of his stories with outrage, writing, "I am not a laughing man. I am an angry man" ("I Am Not a Laughing Man," 121).
3. Arturo Roseburg notes the similarity of Father and Juan Tamad in "Philippine Humor" (17).
4. "The Wisdom of Uncle Santor" is in the collection *The Philippines Is in the Heart*.
5. Bulosan writes, "I . . . found that my brother Polon was one of the 25,000 volunteers in the Philippine National Guard. . . . Out of the eleven young men that volunteered in our town only three came back to live among us" ("The Laughter of My Father," 7).
6. I am referring to Foucault's notion of the docile body as one "that may be subjected, used, transformed and improved" and of discipline producing "subjected and practiced bodies" (*Discipline and Punish*, 136, 138).
7. Slotkin suggests that Bulosan uses this Igorot identified figure to demonstrate the racial hierarchies of imperialism within Filipino society itself.
8. Mr. Kinkaid, the president of Moral Progress for Filipinos, wrote, "How can a people who allow themselves to be known by the barbarous sport of cockfighting be allowed to govern themselves?" (quoted in Guggenheim, 139).
9. *Twenty-First Annual*, for instance, noted that in the 1919–1920 school year schoolchildren produced 1,312,307.28 pesos worth of industrial articles (34).
10. Cynthia Tolentino sees Bulosan creating the Filipino as "knowledge producer[,]

... defined by the capacity to gather, organize, generate, and disseminate knowledge that could compete with dominant and readily available representations of Filipinos" (383, 396). Although Tolentino's identification of Carlos as an oppositional knowledge producer is useful, the text repudiates the kind of knowledge producer she defines. In contrast to the colonial knowledge project of mapping, charting, and classifying, America proposes a constantly evolving counter-knowledge.

11. *America Is in the Heart* is not based totally on Bulosan's life. The Bulosans were relatively affluent, literate peasants, who owned two houses and supported their children's education. Bulosan came to the United States hoping to become a writer, and he never worked for extended periods in canneries or fields because of his poor health. He occasionally worked as a dishwasher but supported himself mainly via his writing (see Huang, 52–56).

12. See the cartoon "It's Up to Them," *Puck*, November 20, 1901, reprinted in Ignacio et al., 67.

13. For an analysis of the figure of the Asian American pet as an ambivalent space of resistance, see J. Kim, 142–143.

14. E. San Juan writes about Bulosan, "When AIH ends[,] . . . we do not pack up our bags and go back to the disenfranchised communities to enjoy the rewards of pax Americana. . . . [H]is utopianism, however much romanticized . . . proved resilient to compel him to re-engage with his new-found 'brothers' in the ILWU" (*Toward Filipino Self Determination*, 82).

15. See Chapter 2 for an analysis of this primer.

16. *The Volcano*, which has not received much critical attention, has generally been regarded as aesthetically weak (see Bernad, 308; Caspar, 82). L. M. Grow, however, views *The Volcano* as much more sophisticated than a propaganda novel and argues that Santos cannot create multidimensional characters "without undercutting his theme" (*The Novels of Bienvenido N. Santos*, 51).

17. Alfeo G. Nudas commends Santos for imbuing the novel with a telos, that of the Philippine nation's authenticity (245–258).

18. See the store's website at http://pbshistorypoleco.blogspot.com/2009/11/philippine-album-american-era.html (accessed August 22, 2013).

19. I am grateful to Allan Isaac for his comments about my paper on *Leche* at the American Studies Association meeting in 2013.

20. When I gave a talk on *Leche* in Manila in November 2016, the members of the audience said they could not afford to buy the paperback novel.

21. Robert Diaz, interview with R. Zamora Linmark, https://web.archive.org/web/20110522070521/http://www.coffeehousepress.org/blog-posts/spotlight-on-leche-by-r-zamora-linmark (accessed May 22, 2019).

CHAPTER 5

1. MacArthur, "Secret Memo to the Adjutant General," quoted in Hamilton, 471.

2. Clear about his Christianizing mission, MacArthur wrote, "I knew[,] however[,] that true religious freedom could never be achieved in Japan until a drastic revision was made in the ancient, backward, state-controlled subsidized faith known as Shintoism" (*Reminiscences*, 310).

3. Address of Japanese Minister of Education Yoshishige Abe at the first meeting of the U.S. Education Mission, March 8, 1946, in *Education in the New Japan*, 2:258, 260.

4. See Dower, *Embracing Defeat*, 272. Dower particularly mentions the firing of eleven thousand activist union members in 1949.

5. In the 1950s, Charles Marden saw contrasts between the characterizations of the Chinese, who were seen as "inferior, humble, ignorant," and the Japanese, who were seen as "aggressive, cunning, and conspiratorial[,] requiring more active dominant efforts to keep them in their place" (quoted in E. Kim, 123).

6. "Report of the United States Education Mission to Germany," September 20, 1946, 4, quoted in Shibata, 119.

7. For. Kallen, culture and democracy were mutually imbricated. Kallen insisted, "Cultural growth is founded upon Cultural Pluralism. Cultural Pluralism is possible only in a democratic society whose institutions encourage individuality in groups, in persons, in temperaments" (43).

8. Jean Toomer viewed behaviorists as providing the means by which the race problem could be solved (187).

9. For a discussion of different modernities, see Chakrabarty, 3–16, 141–147.

10. On the importance of Locke with respect to the U.S. Constitution as a document, see Gray, 3.

11. Morishima Michio's controversial *Why Has Japan Succeeded?* saw Wakon Yosai as problematic because the idea of Japan as "land of god" was central to the idea of Japanese spirit (23, 52). For a critique of the argument about Japan's separating a spiritual sphere from the West during the Meiji period, see Sakamoto, 113–128.

12. Okinawa was governed by the Far East Command of GHQ until 1950, when the U.S. Civil Administration of the Ryukyu (USCAR) was established. The Government of the Ryukyu Islands (GRI) was created in 1952.

13. Dean Acheson wrote to Truman in 1947, "Okinawa is of no economic value to Japan; . . . it was an economic liability. To us it is the western keystone of our military power vested in our air force island bases in the western Pacific" (Acheson, 357, quoted in Nishi, 352).

14. Analyzing three main strands of Okinawan studies from the 1920s to the 1980s, Masamichi S. Inoue suggests that Japanese scholars sought to assimilate Okinawa into Japan by seeing it as "the storehouse of ancient Japan" while ignoring conflicts. American anthropologists in the 1950s and 1960s focused on the non-Japanese aspects of Okinawa and the Okinawan oppression, thus implicitly justifying the U.S. policy of separating Japan and Okinawa. Finally, Okinawan scholars focused on a traditional Okinawa "untouched by power and history" (Inoue, 28–29).

15. This policy ended in 1961 when the Education Bureau of the Ryukyu published new guidelines for elementary schools (Uehara, 21)

16. Aiba et al., quoted in Nakamura, 86.

17. General Douglas MacArthur to Sally Butler, quoted in Koikari, 44.

18. Nakamura sees the Brides School texts as progressive compared with earlier missionary writings rooted in conversion, but she ignores the explicit proselytizing of "Christ Makes the Difference" in the Camp Kokura manual (Nakamura, 115).

19. The American Red Cross had run Brides Schools in Europe between 1943 and 1946. The main purpose of these schools was to deglamorize the United States for the women and to teach them about American geography and customs (Nakamura, 81–82).

Interestingly, the Red Cross did not run Brides Schools in the Philippines, although it did offer some orientations.

20. I thank Elena Tajima Creef for making these texts available to me.

CHAPTER 6

1. Douglas N. Slaymaker identifies "flesh writers" as the predominant group in postwar Japan, writing a literature of the flesh in rebellion against the idea of a spiritual national body or kotukai. He sees Kojima as part of the next generation who wrote about the crisis of male identity (Slaymaker, 2, 14).

2. For the erasure of Asian suffering in Japanese narratives, see Igarashi, 35–38.

3. Orbaugh also suggests that the teachers attempt "to make their status as respectable adults visible to the Americans who represent the current standard of 'adulthood' or 'teacherliness'" (135).

4. Tsuboi's novel covers mainly the wartime period.

5. In fact, teachers as purveyors of knowledge have little status in Kojima's stories. When Sano tells passengers he is a schoolteacher in "On the Train," a "wild laugh [rises] in the crowd and [rolls] from one person to the next like a roar of thunder" (quoted and translated in Orbaugh, 296).

6. For a reading of Gandhi's rejection of the manhood and dominance equation, see Nandy, 74.

7. Ann Sherif, by contrast, sees the story as dramatizing "the problem of retaining a cultural identity in the aftermath of defeat and the difficulties inherent in accommodating alien linguistic and conceptual systems" (107).

8. Molasky suggests that Shibamoto and Yamada represent "wartime militarists who, in postwar Japan, managed to disguise themselves as advocates of democracy" (34).

9. *Childhood Days* does feature the school, but the focus of the film is Shinji being bullied by his classmates at the countryside school.

10. See Harry Kreisler, "The Movie Experience: Conversation with Actress Sima Iwashita and Director Masahiro Shinoda," February 27, 1999, Institute of International Studies, University of California, Berkeley, http://globetrotter.berkeley.edu/conversations/Shinoda_Iwashita/shinoda_iwashita2.html (accessed May 8, 2016).

11. This directive was issued on September 20, but the implementation varied locally (see Nozaki, 124).

12. Anpo was the popular Japanese name for the Treaty of Mutual Cooperation, ratified in 1960, which allowed the United States to continue to use army bases in Japan.

13. Yet the novel problematically introduces Manchuria through Ken Otani (who is a "refugee" from the conquering army but forecloses any representation of the occupation of Manchuria). Japanese colonialism is thus both acknowledged and repressed.

14. See, e.g., King-Kok Cheung's analyses of "The Legend of Miss Sasagawara" and Obasan in *Articulate Silences* (54–73, 126–127); Elena Tajima Creef's reading of Mine Obuko in *Imaging Japanese America* (76–92); Morishima.

15. In his work on Holocaust remembrance, Michael Rothberg suggests that memory is not a zero-sum game in which attention to one historical event detracts from another. He shows how memory of the Holocaust has been productive for other groups. See also Jeffrey Santa Ana's analysis of Shaun Tan's creative use of historical memory (32–33).

16. Josephine Park sees this defiance as the boy's performance of an enemy role, which helps explain to him his bewildering incarceration (143–144). Marni Gauthier sees the novel as an emotional supplement to the 1981 Commission on Internment and a commentary on post-9/11 America (169–170).

17. The biblical story of Jesus healing a man's withered hand has resonated for many writers, including Thomas Hardy in "The Withered Arm" and H. G. Wells in "The Red Room."

CHAPTER 7

Epigraphs: Shigeko Kitani, interview with the author, Tokyo, November 2015; Rinjiro, 120–121.

1. I am thinking of symptomatic reading in the sense in which Louis Althusser describes Marx's reading of classical economists (see Althusser and Balibar, 28).

2. See the concept of affiliative postmemory in Hirsch; see also the idea of memory as something that involves work in Confino and Fritzsche, 5.

3. Luisa Passerini argues that all oral histories involve a self-consciousness, a "decision-making about the relationship between the self and history" (quoted in Gubrium and Holstein, 716).

EPILOGUE

1. The army discontinued the Human Terrain System in 2014 amidst widespread criticism by anthropologists. The website http://humanterrainsystem.army.mil/history.html (accessed August 1, 2012) has been taken down. However, army personnel continue to view HTS favorably and see sociocultural expertise as central to military operations (see Bradshaw and Esser).

2. For an analysis of the workings of neoliberal feminism in the novel and documentary, see Schueller.

3. Mortensen has been the object of a lot of controversy, accused of financial irregularities, overstating the number of schools built, and fabricating a story about being captured by the Taliban.

4. A blatant form of schooling Iraqis in Americanism was to rewrite history textbooks, expunging all references to Saddam and the Ba'ath Party ("A New History of Iraq").

5. All quotes are from the pamphlet "Thomasites 100 Years," n.p.

Works Cited

GOVERNMENT DOCUMENTS

"Address of the Director General of the Japanese Military Administration at the Opening Ceremonies of the Normal Institute," August 31, 1942. http://malacanang.gov.ph/5905-address-of-the-director-general-of-the-japanese-military-administration-at-the-opening-ceremonies-of-the-normal-institute-august-31-1942.

Affairs in the Philippine Islands: Hearings before the Committee on the Philippines of the United States Senate. 57th Cong., 1st sess., doc. no. 331, pt. 1. Washington, DC: U.S. Government Printing Office, 1902.

Annual Report of Major General Arthur MacArthur, U.S. Army, Commanding Division of the Philippines, Military Governor in the Philippine Islands, Manila: P.I., 1901.

Annual Report of the General Superintendent of Education, September 1904. Manila: Bureau of Printing, 1904.

Annual Reports of the Director of Education

    Eighth Annual Report of the Director of Education; July 1, 1907, to June 30, 1908. Manila: Bureau of Printing, 1908.

    Tenth Annual Report of the Director of Education for the Philippine Islands: July 1, 1909, to June 30, 1910, repr. ed. Manila: Bureau of Printing, (1910) 1957.

    Thirteenth Annual Report of the Director of Education: July 1, 1912, to June 30, 1913. Manila: Bureau of Printing, 1913.

    Fifteenth Annual Report of the Director of Education: January 1, 1914, to December 31, 1914. Manila: Bureau of Printing, 1915.

    Sixteenth Annual Report of the Director of Education; January 1, 1915, to December 31, 1915. Manila: Bureau of Printing, 1916.

    Twenty-First Annual Report of the Director of Education, January 1, 1920, to December 31, 1920. Manila: Bureau of Printing, 1921.

Twenty-Second Annual Report of the Director of Education: January 1, 1921, to December 31, 1921. Manila: Bureau of Printing, 1922.

Twenty-Fourth Annual Report of the Director of Education: January 1, 1923, to December 31, 1923. Manila: Bureau of Printing, 1924.

Twenty-Eighth Annual Report of the Director of Education, for the Calendar Year 1927. Manila: Bureau of Printing, 1928.

Annual Reports of the War Department for the Fiscal Year Ended June 30, 1903, Volume 7: Report of the Philippine Commission. Washington, DC: U.S. Government Printing Office, 1904.

Atkinson, Fred. *Education in the Philippine Islands*. Washington, DC: U.S. Government Printing Office, 1902.

———. "The Present Educational Movement in the Philippine Islands." In *Report of the Commissioner of Education for the Year 1900–1901*, vol. 2. Washington, DC: U.S. Government Printing Office, 1902.

Barrows, David P. "Memorandum on Public Instruction in Netherlands-India." *Ninth Annual Report of the Director of Education: July 1, 1908, to June 30, 1909*. Manila: Bureau of Printing, 1909.

Camp Kokura Brides School. American Red Cross, National Archives Records of the American Red Cross, 1947–1964. RG200, National Archives, College Park, MD, October 1956.

Commander-in-Chief, U.S. Army Forces, Pacific. *Summation of United States Army Military Government Activities in Korea*. No. 15, December 1946.

Cook, Katherine M. "Education of Certain Racial Groups in the United States and Its Territories." In *United States Department of Interior, Biennial Survey of Education, 1928–1930*, vol. 1. Washington, DC: U.S. Government Printing Office, 1932.

Education in the New Japan, vols. 1–2. Supreme Commander of Allied Powers, Civil Information and Education Section, Education Division. Tokyo, May 1948.

Far East Asia American Red Cross Brides School. National Archives Records of the American Red Cross, 1947–1964, RG200. National Archives, College Park, Maryland, 1959.

Garrison, Lloyd A., Superintendent of Education, Community Management Division, Granada Relocation Center, Amache, CO. *Final Report* (Education Section). Records of the War Relocation Authority (WRA), Record Group 210.2.1. National Archives and Records Administration, College Park, MD, 1945.

Guide to New Education in Japan, vol. 1. Ministry of Education. Tokyo, May 21, 1946.

MacArthur, Douglas. "Secret Memo to the Adjutant General." Cable 179 to AGWAR, Washington, DC, February 1, 1942, RG4 MMA.

MacArthur, Douglas, to Sally Butler, president, National Federation of Business and Professional Women's Clubs, May 5, 1948. Records of the U.S. Occupation of Japan, Record Group 5, box 12, folder "bus-buz."

Official Journal of the Japanese Military Administration of the Philippines. Department of Education, vol. 1, 1942.

———. Department of Education, vol. 6, 1942.

Primer of Democracy. English trans. Ministry of Education textbook, vol. 1, October 30, 1948.

———. English trans. Ministry of Education textbook, vol. 2, August 26, 1949.

"Radio Address by George Bush." October 18, 2003. https://georgewbush-whitehouse.archives.gov/news/releases/2003/10/20031018.html. Accessed August 1, 2016.

"Radio Address by Mrs. Bush." November 17, 2001. http://www.presidency.ucsb.edu/ws/?pid=24992. Accessed August 5, 2016.

"Report of the Philippine Commission." *Current History* 15, no. 5 (1922): 678–690.

Report of the United States Education Mission to Japan. Submitted to the Supreme Commander for the Allied Powers, Tokyo, March 30, 1946. Washington, DC: U.S. Government Printing Office, 1946.

Snyder, Harold E., and Margretta S. Austin, eds. *Educational Progress in Japan and the Ryukyus: A Report of a Conference of Major American Non-governmental Agencies Sponsored by the Commission on the Occupied Areas of the American Council on Education with the Cooperation of the Department of the Army*. Washington, DC: American Council on Education, 1950.

A Survey of the Educational System of the Philippine Islands by the Board of Educational Survey; Created under Acts 3162 and 3196 of the Philippine Legislature. Manila: Bureau of Printing, 1925.

LITERARY AND CRITICAL WORKS

Acheson, Dean. *Present at the Creation: My Years in the State Department*. New York: Norton, 1969.

Agamben, Giorgio. *Homo Sacer: Sovereign Power and Bare Life*, trans. Daniel Heller-Roazen. Stanford, CA: Stanford University Press, 1995.

Aiba, Kazuhiko, Jin Chen, Sachie Miyata, and Jun Nakasima, eds. *Manshu "tairiku no hanayome" ha doutsukuraretaka* [On How Manchuria's "Continental Brides" Were Constructed]. Tokyo: Akashi, 1996.

Akiyuki, Nosaka. "American Hijiki." In *Contemporary Japanese Literature: An Anthology of Fiction, Film and Other Writing since 1945*, trans. Jay Rubin, ed. Howard Hibbett, 436–468. New York: Knopf, 1977.

Albery, Nabuko. *Balloon Top*. New York: Pantheon, 1978.

Alidio, Kimberly A. "Between Civilizing Mission and Ethnic Assimilation: Racial Discourse, U.S. Colonial Education and Filipino Ethnicity, 1901–1946." Ph.D. diss., University of Michigan, Ann Arbor, 2001.

Althusser, Louis. "Ideology and Ideological State Apparatuses." In *Lenin and Philosophy, and Other Essays*, trans. Ben Brewster, 127–186. London: New Left, 1971.

Althusser, Louis, and Étienne Balibar. *Reading Capital*, trans. Ben Brewster. New York: Pantheon, 1971.

Anderson, Benedict. "Cacique Democracy in the Philippines: Origins and Dreams." *New Left Review* 169 (May/June 1988): 3–31.

———. *The Spectre of Comparisons: Nationalism, Southeast Asia and the World*. London: Verso, 1998

Anderson, Warwick. *Colonial Pathologies. American Tropical Medicine, Race, and Hygiene in the Philippines*. Durham, NC: Duke University Press, 2006.

Angulo, A. J. *Empire and Education: A History of Greed and Goodwill from the War of 1898 to the War on Terror*. New York: Palgrave, 2012.

Armstrong, Samuel Chapman. "The Indians." *American Missionary* 34, no. 12 (December 1880): 406–408.

Ashcroft, Bill. "Introduction: Spaces of Utopia." *Spaces of Utopia: An Electronic Journal*, 2d series, no. 1 (2012): 1–17. http://ler.letras.up.pt. Accessed June 30, 2017.

Atkinson, Fred. "Education in the Philippines." *The Outlook* 70 (April 5, 1902): 832–839.
Azuma, Eiichiro. *Between Two Empires: Race, History, and Transnationalism in Japanese America*. New York: Oxford University Press, 2005.
Bagley, William C. "The Report of the U.S. Educational [sic] Mission to Japan." *School and Society* 63 (June 1946): 388–389.
Baker, Russ, and Christina Borjesson. "The Empire Strikes Again: Sex, Oil, and Corruption at the American University of Iraq." *Salon*, February 16, 2011. http://www.salon.com/2011/02/16/american_university_iraq. Accessed August 4, 2016.
Baldwin, James. *School Reading by Grades: First Year*. New York: American Book, 1897.
Ballou, Robert O. *Shinto, the Unconquered Enemy: Japan's Doctrine of Racial Superiority and World Conquest*. New York: Viking, 1945.
Banton, Nila. *American Reading Instruction*. Newark, DE: International Reading Association, (1934) 2002.
Barthes, Roland. *Empire of Signs*. New York: Hill and Wang, 1983.
Bascara, Victor. *Model-Minority Imperialism*. Minneapolis: University of Minnesota Press, 2006.
———. "Up from Benevolent Assimilation: At Home with the Manongs of Bienvenido Santos." *MELUS* 29 I (Spring 2004): 61–78.
Beauchamp, Edward R., ed. *Education and Schooling in Japan since 1945*. New York: Routledge, 1998.
———. "Reforming Education in Postwar Japan: American Planning for a Democratic Japan, 1943–1946." *Journal of Curriculum and Supervision* 11 (Fall 1995): 67–86.
Beauchamp, Edward R., and James M. Vardaman, eds. *Japanese Education since 1945: A Documentary Study*. New York: M. E. Sharpe, 1994.
Becker, George F. "Are the Philippines Worth Having?" *Scribner's* 27 (June 1900): 739–752.
Bernad, Miguel A. "The Heroic Age in Philippine Literature." *Philippine Studies* 14 (1966): 299–308.
Bernardo, Allen B. I. "McKinley's Questionable Bequest: Over 100 Years of English in Philippine Education." *World Englishes* 23, no. 1 (2004): 17–32.
Best, Jonathan. *A Philippine Album: American Era Photographs, 1900–1930*. Makati City, Philippines: Bookmark, 1998.
Bhabha, Homi. *The Location of Culture*. New York: Routledge, 1994.
———. "The World and the Home." In *Dangerous Liaisons: Gender, Nation, and Postcolonial Perspectives*, ed. Anne McClintock, Aamir Mufti, and Ella Shohat, 445–455. Minneapolis: University of Minnesota Press, 1997.
Bourne, Randolph S. "Trans-National America." In *Theories of Ethnicity: A Classical Reader*, ed. Werner Sollors, 93–108. New York: New York University Press, 1996.
Bradshaw, Crystal, and Ronald J. Esser. "The Necessity of Socio-cultural Intelligence" *NCO Journal*, June 29, 2018. https://www.armyupress.army.mil/Journals/NCO Journal/Archives/2018/June/Socio-Cultural-Intelligence.
Bresnahan, Roger J. "Conversations with B. N. Santos." In *Reading Bienvenido N. Santos*, ed. Isagani R. Cruz, 98–127. Manila: De La Salle University Press, 1994.
Brody, David. *Visualizing American Empire: Orientalism and Imperialism in the Philippines*. Chicago: University of Chicago Press, 2010.
Buchanan, Andrew. "'Good Morning Pupil!' American Representations of Italianness and the Occupation of Italy, 1943–1945." *Journal of Contemporary History* 43, no. 2 (2008): 217–240.

Buencamino, Victor. *Memoirs of Victor Buencamino.* Manila: Jorge B. Vargas Filipiniana Foundation, 1977

Bulosan, Carlos. *America Is in the Heart.* Seattle: University of Washington Press, (1943) 1973.

———. "I Am Not a Laughing Man." *Amerasia Journal* 6, no. 1 (1979): 121–125.

———. *The Laughter of My Father.* New York: Bantam, (1944) 1946.

———. *The Philippines Is in the Heart: A Collection of Short Stories,* ed. E. San Juan Jr. Quezon City, Philippines: New Day, 1978.

Bumiller, Elisabeth. "Unlikely Tutor Giving Military Afghan Advice." *New York Times,* July 18, 2010. Academic OneFile. December 21, 2010.

Burton, Antoinette. *Dwelling in the Archive: Women Writing House, Home and History in Late Colonial India.* New York: Oxford University Press, 2003.

Caruth, Cathy. *Unclaimed Experience: Trauma, Narrative, and History.* Baltimore: Johns Hopkins University Press, 1996.

Caspar, Leonard. "Greater Shouting and Greater Silences: The Novels of Bienvenido N. Santos." *Solidarity* 3, no. 10 (1968): 82.

Chakrabarty, Dipesh. *Provincializing Europe: Postcolonial Thought and Historical Difference.* Princeton, NJ: Princeton University Press, 2000.

Chatterjee, Partha. *The Nation and Its Fragments: Colonial and Postcolonial Histories.* Princeton, NJ: Princeton University Press, 1993

Cheng, Anne Anlin. *The Melancholy of Race: Psychoanalysis, Assimilation, and Hidden Grief.* New York: Oxford University Press, 2001

Cheung, King-Kok. *Articulate Silences: Hisaye Yamamoto, Maxine Hong Kingston, and Joy Kogawa.* Ithaca, NY: Cornell University Press, 1993.

Chin, Frank, Jeffery Paul Chan, Lawson Fusao Inada, and Shawn Wong, eds. *Aiiieeeee! An Anthology of Asian-American Writers.* New York: Penguin, 1974.

Cho, Grace M. *Haunting the Korean Diaspora: Shame, Secrecy and the Forgotten War.* Minneapolis: University of Minnesota Press, 2008.

Chu, Patricia P. *Assimilating Asians: Gendered Strategies of Authorship in Asian America.* Durham, NC: Duke University Press, 2000.

Clymer, Kenton J. "Humanitarian Imperialism: David Prescott Barrows and the White Man's Burden in the Philippines." *Pacific Historical Review* 45, no. 4 (November 1976): 495–517.

Cohn, Bernard. *Colonialism and Its Forms of Knowledge: The British in India.* Princeton, NJ: Princeton University Press, 1996.

Coloma, Roland Sintos. "Care of the Postcolonial Self: Cultivating Nationalism in *The Philippine Readers.*" *Qualitative Research in Education* 2, no. 3 (October 2013): 302–327.

———. "Disidentifying Nationalism: Camilo Osias and Filipino Education in the Early Twentieth Century." In *Revolution and Pedagogy: Interdisciplinary and Transnational Perspectives on Educational Foundations,* ed. C. Thomas Ewing, 19–37. New York: Palgrave, 2005.

———. "Empire and Education: Filipino Schooling under United States Rule, 1900–1910." Ph.D. diss., Ohio State University, Columbus, 2004.

———, ed. *Postcolonial Challenges in Education.* New York: Peter Lang, 2009.

Confino, Alon, and Peter Fritzsche, eds. *The Work of Memory: New Directions Study of German Society and Culture.* Urbana: University of Illinois Press, 2002.

Constantino, Renato. "The Miseducation of the Filipino." *Weekly Graphic*, June 8, 1966, 1–27.

———. *The Second Invasion: Japan in the Philippines*. Quezon City, Philippines: Karrell, 1989.

Coontz, Stephanie. *The Way We Never Were: American Families and the Nostalgia Trap*. New York: Basic, 1993.

Cooper, Frederick. *Colonialism in Question: Theory, Knowledge, History*. Berkeley: University of California Press, 2005.

Cordero-Fernando, Gilda. *The Butcher, the Baker, the Candlestick Maker*. Manila: Benipayo, 1962.

Counts, George S. *Dare the School Build a New Social Order?* New York: John Day, 1932.

Craig, Austin. "The Kindergarten as an Americanizing Influence." *Philippine Teacher* 2, no. 8 (1906): 26–27.

Crawford, Miki Ward, Katie Kaori Hayashi, and Shizuko Suenaga. *Japanese War Brides in America: An Oral History*. Santa Barbara, CA: Praeger, 2010.

Creef, Elena Tajima. *Imaging Japanese America: The Visual Construction of Citizenship, Nation, and the Body*. New York: New York University Press, 2004.

Cruz, Denise. *Transpacific Femininities and the Making of the Modern Filipina*. Durham, NC: Duke University Press, 2012.

de Grazia, Victoria. *Irresistible Empire: America's Advance through Twentieth-Century Europe*. Cambridge, MA: Harvard University Press, 2005.

Delmendo, Sharon. *The Star-entangled Banner: One Hundred Years of America in the Philippines*. Quezon City: University of the Philippines Press, 2005.

Del Moral, Solsiree. "Negotiating Colonialism: 'Race,' Class and Education in Early-Twentieth-Century Puerto Rico." In *Colonial Crucible: Empire in the Making of the Modern American State*, ed. Alfred McCoy and Francisco A. Scarano, 135–145. Madison: University of Wisconsin Press, 2009.

Denning, Michael. *The Cultural Front: The Laboring of American Culture in the Twentieth Century*. London: Verso, 1997.

Derrida, Jacques. *Of Grammatology*, trans. Gayatri Chakravorty Spivak. Baltimore: Johns Hopkins University Press, 1974.

Dewey, John. *Characters and Events: Popular Essays in Social and Political Philosophy*. Ed. Joseph Ratner. New York: Holt, 1929.

———. *Democracy and Education: An Introduction to the Philosophy of Education*. New York: Macmillan, 1916.

———. *The School and Society*, rev. ed. Chicago: University of Chicago Press, (1900) 1915.

The Dial 41 (August 1906): 71.

Douglas, Mary. "Foreword: No Free Gifts." In *The Gift: The Form and Reason for Exchange in Archaic Societies*, by Marcel Mauss, trans. W. D. Halls, vii–xvii. New York: Norton, 1990.

———. *Purity and Danger: An Analysis of the Concepts of Pollution and Taboo*. New York: Routledge, 1978.

Dower, John. *Embracing Defeat: Japan in the Wake of World War II*. New York: W. W. Norton, 1999.

———. *War without Mercy: Race and Power in the Pacific*. New York: Pantheon, 1986.

Drinnon, Richard T. *Facing West: The Metaphysics of Indian-Hating and Empire-Building*. New York: New American Library, 1980.

Eiji, Takemae. *The Allied Occupation of Japan*, trans. Robert Ricketts and Sebastian Swann. New York: Continuum, 2002.
Elliott, Charles Burke. *The Philippines to the End of the Commission Government: A Study in Tropical Democracy*. Indianapolis: Bobbs-Merrill, 1917.
Elson, Ruth Miller. *Guardians of Tradition: American Schoolbooks of the Nineteenth Century*. Lincoln: University of Nebraska Press, 1964.
Emerson, Gertrude. "The Philippines Inside Out: The Special Mission, an Investigation and a New Harding Program." *Asia: The American Magazine on the Orient* 21 (November 1921): 903–911, 956, 958, 959.
Espiritu, Augusto Fauni. *Five Faces of Exile: The Nation and Filipino American Intellectuals*. Stanford, CA: Stanford University Press, 2005.
Eugenio, Damiana L. "Folklore in Philippine Schools," *Philippine Studies* 35, no. 2 (1987): 175–190.
Ewing, E. Thomas, ed. *Revolution and Pedagogy: Interdisciplinary and Transnational Perspectives on Educational Foundations*. London: Palgrave Macmillan, 2005.
Fabian, Johannes. *Time and the Other: How Anthropology Makes Its Object*. New York: Columbia University Press, 1983.
Fallace, Thomas D. *Race and the Origins of Progressive Education, 1880–1929*. New York: Teachers College Press, 2015.
Fanon, Frantz. *Black Skin, White Masks*, trans. Charles Lam Markmann. New York: Grove, 1967.
———. *The Wretched of the Earth*, trans. Constance Farrington. New York: Grove, (1963) 1968.
Fear-Segal, Jacqueline. *White Man's Club: Schools, Race, and the Struggle of Indian Acculturation*. Lincoln: University of Nebraska Press, 2007.
Fee, Mary Helen. *A Woman's Impression of the Philippines*. New York: Bibliobazar, (1910) 2006.
Fee, Mary Helen, Margaret A. Purcell, Parker Filmore, and John W. Ritchie. *The First Year Book*. New York: World Book, 1907.
Fermin, Jose D. 1904. *World's Fair: The Filipino Experience*. Quezon City: University of the Philippines Press, 2004.
Feuer, Lewis S. "John Dewey's Sojourn in Japan." *Teacher's College Record* 71, no. 1 (1969): 123–145.
Fonacier, Consuelo V., ed. *The Role and Mission of the University: Inaugural Addresses of the Presidents of the University of the Philippines*. Quezon City: University of the Philippines Press, 1971.
Forbes, W. Cameron. *The Philippine Islands*, vol. 1. Boston: Houghton Mifflin/Riverside, 1928.
Foucault, Michel. *Discipline and Punish: The Birth of the Prison*, trans. Alan Sheridan. New York: Random House, 1979.
———. *Foucault Live: Collected Interviews: 1961–1989*. New York: Semiotext(e), (1989) 1996.
———. "Governmentality." In *The Foucault Effect: Studies in Governmentality*, ed. Graham Burchell, Peter Miller, and Colin Gordon, 201–222. Chicago: University of Chicago Press, 1991.
———. *The History of Sexuality, Volume 1: An Introduction*, trans. Robert Hurley. New York: Random House, 1978.

———. *Language, Counter-Memory, Practice: Selected Essays and Interviews*, ed. Donald F. Bouchard. Ithaca, NY: Cornell University Press, 1977.
———. "Of Other Spaces." *Diacritics* 16, no. 1 (Spring 1986): 22–27.
Francisco, Adrianne Marie. "From Subjects to Citizens: American Colonial Education and Philippine Nation-Making, 1900–1934. Ph.D. diss., University of California, Berkeley, 2015.
Frederickson, George M. *The Comparative Imagination*. Berkeley: University of California Press, 2000.
Freer, William B. *The Philippine Experiences of an American Teacher: A Narrative of Work and Travel in the Philippine Islands*. New York: Scribner's, 1906.
Freire, Paulo. *Pedagogy of the Oppressed*, trans. Myra Bergman Ramos. New York: Continuum, (1970) 2005.
Freire, Paulo, and Donald Macedo. "A Dialogue: Culture, Language and Race." *Harvard Educational Review* 65, no. 3 (Fall 1995): 377–402.
Freud, Sigmund. *A General Introduction to Psychoanalysis*, trans. G. Stanley Hall. New York: Boni and Liveright, 1920.
———. "Mourning and Melancholia." In *The Standard Edition of the Complete Psychological Works of Sigmund Freud*, vol. 14, trans. James Strachey, 243–258. London: Hogarth, 1971.
Fujiwara, Kiichi, and Yoshiko Nagano, eds. *The Philippines and Japan under America's Shadow*. Singapore: National University of Singapore Press, 2011.
Gallagher-Geurtsen, Tricia. *(Un)Knowing Diversity: Researching Narratives of Neocolonial Classrooms through Youth's Testimonios*. New York: Peter Lang, 2012.
Garcia, J. Neil. "Reading Auras." In *Aura: The Gay Theme in Philippine Fiction in English*, ed. J. Neil C. Garcia, 9–38. Manila: Anvil, 2012.
Gauthier, Marni. *Amnesia and Redress in Contemporary American Fiction: Counterhistory*. New York: Palgrave, 2011.
Gayn, Mark. *Japan Diary*. New York: Tuttle, 1984.
Gibbs, David. *Advanced English Grammar and Composition*. New York: American Book, 1908.
———. *Elementary English Grammar and Composition*. New York: American Book, 1909.
———. *Lessons in English*. New York: American Book, 1905.
———. *Revised Insular Primer*. New York: American Book, 1906.
———. *Revised Insular Second Reader*. New York: American Book, 1914.
Gilroy, Paul. *Postcolonial Melancholia*. New York: Columbia University Press, 2006.
Go, Julian. *The American Colonial State in the Philippines*. Durham, NC: Duke University Press, 2003.
———, ed. *American Empire and the Politics of Meaning: Elite Political Culture in the Philippines and Puerto Rico during U.S. Colonialism*. Durham, NC: Duke University Press, 2008.
———. "The Provinciality of American Empire: 'Liberal Exceptionalism' and U.S. Colonial Rule, 1898–1912." *Comparative Studies in Society and History* 49, no. 1 (2007): 74–108.
Gold, Michael. *Jews without Money*. New York: Horace Liveright, 1930.
Gonzalez, N. V. M. *Kalutang: A Filipino in the World in Work on the Mountain*. Quezon City: University of the Philippines Press, 1995.
Gordon, Avery. *Ghostly Matters: Haunting and the Sociological Imagination*. Minneapolis: University of Minnesota Press, 1997.

Gosiengfiao, Victor. "The Japanese Occupation: The Cultural Campaign." *Philippine Studies* 14, no. 2 (1996): 228–242.

Gottlieb, Nanette. "Language and Politics: The Reversal of Postwar Script Reform Policy in Japan." *Journal of Asian Studies* 53, no. 4 (November 1994): 1175–1198.

Gray, John. *Liberalism*. Minneapolis: University of Minnesota Press, 1986.

Grewal, Inderpal. *Transnational America: Feminisms, Diasporas, Neoliberalisms*. Durham, NC: Duke University Press, 2003.

Grow, L. M. "The Architecture of the Interior: Angst and Nada in the Fiction of Edith Tiempo." *University of Windsor Review* 22, no. 2 (1989): 78–94.

———. "'The Laughter of My Father': A Survival Kit." *MELUS* 20, no. 2 (1995): 35–46.

———. *The Novels of Bienvenido N. Santos*. Quezon City, Philippines: Giraffe, 1999.

Gubrium, Jaber F., and James A. Holstein. *Handbook of Interview Research: Context and Method*. London: Sage, 2003.

Guggenheim, Scott. "Cock or Bull: Cockfighting, Social Structure, and Political Commentary in the Philippines." In *The Cockfight: A Casebook*, ed. Alan Dundes, 133–173. Madison: University of Wisconsin Press, 1994.

Guha, Ranajit. "On Some Aspects of the Historiography of Colonial India." In *Selected Subaltern Studies*, ed. Ranajit Guha and Gayatri Chakravorty Spivak, 37–44. New York: Oxford University Press, 1988.

Halili, Servando D., Jr., *Iconography of the New Empire: Race and Gender Images and the American Colonization of the Philippines*. Quezon City: University of the Philippines Press, 2006.

Hall, Stuart. "Cultural Identity and Diaspora." In *Colonial Discourse and Post-Colonial Theory*, ed. Patrick Williams and Laura Chrisman, 394–403. New York: Columbia University Press, 1994.

Hamilton, Nigel. *The Mantle of Command: FDR at War, 1941–1942*. New York: Houghton Mifflin, 2014.

Harris, Susan K. *God's Arbiters: Americans and the Philippines, 1898–1902*. New York: Oxford University Press, 2011.

Hayashi, Brian. *Democratizing the Enemy: The Japanese American Internment*. Princeton, NJ: Princeton University Press, 2008.

Higadisha, Cheryl. "Re-signed Subjects: Women, Work, and the World in the Fiction of Carlos Bulosan and Hisaye Yamamoto." *Studies in the Literary Imagination* 37, no. 1 (2004): 35–60.

Hirsch, Marianne. *The Generation of Postmemory: Writing and Visual Culture after the Holocaust*. New York: Columbia University Press, 2002.

Hochwalt, Frederick C. "United States Educational Mission to Japan." Report of the Proceedings of the Forty-Third Annual Meeting. *National Catholic Education Association Bulletin*, 1946, 378.

Houston, Jeanne Wakatsuki, and James D. Houston. *Farewell to Manzanar*. New York: Random House, 1973.

Hsu, Funie. "Colonial Articulations: English Instruction and the 'Benevolence' of U.S. Overseas Expansion in the Philippines, 1898–1916. Ph.D. diss., University of California, Berkeley, 2013.

Huang, Guiyou, ed. *Asian American Autobiographers: A Bio-bibliographical Critical Sourcebook*. Westport, CT: Greenwood, 2001.

Hunt, Michael. *Ideology and U.S. Foreign Policy*. New Haven, CT: Yale University Press, 1987.

Hunt, Thomas C., and Monalisa McCurry Mullins. *Moral Education in America's Schools: The Continuing Challenge.* Charlotte, NC: Information Age, 2005.

Ick, Judy Celine. "La Escuela del Diablo, Iskul ng Tao: Revisiting Colonial Public Education." In *Bearers of Benevolence: The Thomasites and Public Education in the Philippines*, ed. Mary Racelis and Judy Celine Ick, 261–272. Pasig City, Philippines: Anvil, 2001.

Igarashi, Yoshikuni. *Bodies of Memory: Narratives in Postwar Japanese Culture, 1945–1970.* Princeton, NJ: Princeton University Press, 2000.

Ignacio, Abe, Enrique de la Cruz, Jorge Emmanuel, and Helen Toribio, eds. *The Forbidden Book: The Philippine-American War in Political Cartoons.* San Francisco: T'Boli, 2004.

Ileto, R. C. *Pasyon and Revolution: Popular Movements in the Philippines, 1840–1910.* Quezon City, Philippines: Ateneo de Manila University Press, 1979.

———. "The 'Unfinished Revolution' in Philippine Political Discourse." *Southeast Asian Studies* 31, no. 1 (June 1993): 62–82.

Inoue, Masamichi S. *Okinawa and the U.S. Military: Identity Making in the Age of Globalization.* New York: Columbia University Press, 2007.

Iriye, Akira. "Continuities in U.S.-Japanese Relations," 1941–1949. In *The Origins of the Cold War in Asia*, ed. Yonosuke Nagai and Akira Iriye, 378–407. New York: Columbia University Press, 1977.

Irwin, Wallace. *Seed of the Sun.* New York: George H. Doran, 1921.

Ivy, Marilyn. *Discourses of the Vanishing: Modernity, Phantasm, Japan.* Chicago: University of Chicago Press, 1995.

Iwasbuchi, Koichi. *Recentering Globalization: Popular Culture and Japanese Transnationalism.* Durham, NC: Duke University Press, 2002.

Jaggar, Alison. "Love and Knowledge: Emotion in Feminist Epistemology." *Inquiry* 32 (1989): 151–176.

Jernegan, Prescott F. *The Philippine Citizen; A Text-Book of Civics, Describing the Nature of Government, The Philippine Government, and the Rights and Duties of Citizens of the Philippines.* Manila: Philippine Education, 1907.

Kalaw, Maximo M. *The Filipino Rebel: A Romance of American Occupation in the Philippines.* Manila: Filiniana Book Guild, (1929) 1964.

———. *Self-Government in the Philippines.* New York: Century, 1919.

Kallen, Horace M. *Culture and Democracy in the United States.* New York: Arno, (1924) 1970.

Kaplan, Amy, and Donald Pease, eds. *Cultures of United States Imperialism.* Durham, NC: Duke University Press, 1996.

Karasik, Daniel D. "Okinawa: A Problem in Administration and Reconstruction." *Journal of Asian Studies* 7 (May 1948): 254–267.

Keene, Donald, ed. *So Lovely a Country Will Never Perish: Wartime Diaries of Japanese Writers.* New York: Columbia University Press, 2010.

Kim, Elaine. *Asian American Literature: An Introduction to the Writings and Their Social Context.* Philadelphia: Temple University Press, 1982.

Kim, James. "Petting Asian America." *MELUS* 36, no. 1 (Spring 2011): 135–155.

Kim, Jodi. *Ends of Empire: Asian American Critique and the Cold War.* Minneapolis: University of Minnesota Press, 2010.

Kobayashi, Victor. *John Dewey in Japanese Educational Thought.* Ann Arbor: University of Michigan, School of Education, 1964.

Koble, Sean S. "Acting the Role of Gods: Shinoda Masahiro's Cinematic Confrontations with the Absolute Image." Master's thesis, University of Oregon, Eugene, 2014.
Koikari, Mire. "Exporting Democracy? American Women, 'Feminist Reforms,' and the Politics of Imperialism in the U.S. Occupation of Japan, 1945–1952." *Frontiers* 23, no. 1 (2002): 23–45.
Kojima, Nobuo. "The American School" (1954). In *Contemporary Japanese Literature: An Anthology of Fiction, Film, and Other Writings since 1945*, ed. Howard Hibbett, 120–144. New York: Knopf, 1977.
Koshiro, Yukiko. *Trans-Pacific Racisms and the U.S Occupation of Japan*. New York: Columbia University Press, 1999.
Kramer, Paul. *The Blood of Government: Race, Empire, the United States and the Philippines*. Chapel Hill: University of North Carolina Press, 2006.
Kristeva, Julia. *Powers of Horror: An Essay on Abjection*, trans. Leon S. Roudiez. New York: Columbia University Press, 1982.
Lanzona, Vina A. "The Philippines—Engendering Counterinsurgency: The Battle to Win the Hearts and Minds of Women during the Huk Rebellion in the Philippines." In *Hearts and Minds: A People's History of Counterinsurgency*, ed. Hannah Gurman, 50–77. New York: New Press, 2013.
Lee, Rachel. *The Americas of Asian American Literature: Gendered Fictions of Nation and Transnation*. Princeton, NJ: Princeton University Press, 1999.
Leong, Nancy. "Racial Capitalism." *Harvard Law Review* 126 (June 2013): 2153–2226.
Lewis, William D., Albert Lindsay Rowland, Elizabeth J. Marshall, and Manuel L. Carreon. *Rizal Readers, Fifth Reader*. Philadelphia: John C. Winston, 1917.
——. *Rizal Readers, Seventh Reader*. Philadelphia: John C. Winston, 1917.
Lim, Eng-Beng. *Brown Boys and Rice Queens: Spellbinding Performance in the Asias*. New York: New York University Press, 2013.
Lim, Shirley Geok-lin, John Gamber, Stephen Hong Sohn, and Gina Valentino, eds. *Transnational Asian American Literature: Sites and Transits*. Philadelphia: Temple University Press, 2006.
Linmark, R. Zamora. *Leche*. Minneapolis: Coffee House, 2011.
Locke, John. *Second Treatise of Government*, ed. C. B. MacPherson. Indianapolis: Hackett, (1962) 1980.
Lomawaima, K. Tsianina. "Estelle Reel, Superintendent of Indian Schools, 1898–1910: Politics, Curriculum, and Land." *Journal of American Indian Education* 35, no. 3 (May 1996): 5–31.
Love, Eric. *Race over Empire*. Chapel Hill: University of North Carolina Press, 2004.
Lowe, Lisa. *Intimacies of Four Continents*. Durham, NC: Duke University Press, 2015
Lucken, Michael. *Imitation and Creativity in Japanese Arts: From Kishida Ryusei to Miyazaki Hayao*. New York: Columbia University Press, 2016.
Lye, Colleen. *America's Asia: Racial Form and American Literature, 1893–1945*. Princeton, NJ: Princeton University Press, 2005.
Lyons, Paul. *American Pacificism: Oceania in the US Imagination*. New York: Routledge, 2006.
MacArthur, Douglas. *Reminiscences: General of the Army*. New York: McGraw-Hill, 1964.
Macherey, Pierre. *A Theory of Literary Production*, trans. Geoffrey Wall. New York: Routledge, 2006.

Maki, John M. *A Yankee in Hokkaido: The Life of William Smith Clark*. New York: Lexington, 2002.
Makin, John H. "Japan's Investment in America: Is It a Threat?" *Challenge* 31, no. 6 (November–December 1988): 8–16.
Margold, Jane A. "Egalitarian Ideals and Exclusionary Practices: U.S. Pedagogy in the Colonial Philippines." *Journal of Historical Sociology* 8, no. 4 (1995): 375–394.
Marshall, T. H. "Citizenship and Social Class." In *Citizenship and Social Class and Other Essays*. Cambridge: Cambridge University Press, 1950, 1–85.
Martin, Dalmacio. "Education and Propaganda in the Philippines during the Japanese Occupation." Master's thesis, Stanford University, Stanford, CA, March 1953.
Martin, Isabel Pefianco. "American Education and Philippine Literature." *Philippine Studies* 49, no. 1 (2001): 113–122.
———. "Pedagogy: Teaching Practices of American Colonial Educators in the Philippines." *Kritika Kultura* 1 (2002): 90–100.
May, Elaine Tyler. *Homeward Bound: American Families in the Cold War Era*. New York Basic, 1988.
May, Glenn Anthony. *Social Engineering in the Philippines: The Aims, Execution and Impact of American Colonial Policy, 1900–1913*. Westport, CT: Greenwood, 1980.
McCarthy, Cameron. *The Uses of Culture: Education and the Limits of Ethnic Affiliation*. New York: Routledge, 1997.
McClintock, Anne. *Imperial Leather: Race, Gender and Sexuality in the Colonial Context*. New York: Routledge, 1995.
McCoy, Alfred, and Alfredo Roces. *Philippine Cartoons: Political Caricature of the American Era 1900–1941*. Quezon City, Philippines: Vera-Reyes, 1985.
McCoy, Alfred, and Francisco A. Scarano, eds. *Colonial Crucible: Empire in the Making of the Modern American State*. Madison: University of Wisconsin Press, 2009.
McDonald, Keiko. *Reading a Japanese Film: Cinema in Context*. Honolulu: University of Hawai'i Press, 2006.
McGuffey, William Holmes. *Fourth Eclectic Reader*, rev. ed. New York: John Wiley and Sons, 1920.
———. *Fifth Eclectic Reader*, rev. ed. New York: American Book, 1879.
McMahon, Jennifer M. *Dead Stars: American and Philippine Literary Perspectives on the American Colonization of the Philippines*. Quezon City: University of the Philippines Press, 2011.
Mead, Arthur S. "The Ryukyu Islands." In *Educational Progress in Japan and the Ryukyus: A Report of a Conference of Major American Non-governmental Agencies*, ed. Harold E. Snyder and Margretta S. Austin, 19–21. Washington, DC: American Council on Education, 1950.
Meade, E. Grant. *American Military Government in Korea*. New York: Columbia University Press, 1951.
Mears, Helen. *Mirror for Americans: Japan*. Boston: Houghton Mifflin, 1948.
Melville, Herman. *Typee*. New York: Airmont, (1844) 1965.
Michio, Morishima. *Why Has Japan Succeeded? Western Technology and the Japanese Ethos*. New York: Cambridge University Press, 1984.
Mignolo, Walter. "Delinking: The Rhetoric of Modernity, the Logic of Coloniality, and the Grammar of De-coloniality." *Cultural Studies* 21, no. 2 (2007): 449–514.
———. *Local Histories/Global Designs*. Princeton, NJ: Princeton University Press, 2000.

Miller, Stuart Creighton. *Benevolent Assimilation: The American Conquest of the Philippines, 1899–1903.* New Haven, CT: Yale University Press, 1982.
Milligan, Jeffrey Ayala. *Islamic Identity, Postcoloniality, and Educational Policy: Schooling and Ethno-Religious Conflict in the Southern Philippines.* New York: Palgrave, 2005.
Minear, Richard H. "The Wartime Studies of Japanese National Character." *Japan Interpreter* 13 (Summer 1980): 36–59.
Molasky, Michael S. *The American Occupation of Japan and Okinawa: Literature and Memory.* New York: Routledge, 1999.
Moore-Gilbert, Bart. *Postcolonial Theory: Contexts, Practices, Politics.* New York: Verso, 1977.
Morishima, Emily Hiramatsu. "Remembering the Internment in Post–World War II Japanese American Fiction." Ph.D. diss., University of California, Los Angeles, 2010.
Mortensen, Greg, and David Oliver Relin. *Three Cups of Tea: One Man's Mission to Promote Peace . . . One School at a Time.* New York: Penguin, 2009.
Nakagawa, Kerry Yo. *Japanese American Baseball in California: A History.* Charleston, SC: History Press, 2014.
Nakamura, Masako. "Families Precede Nation and Race? Migration and Integration of Japanese War Brides after World War II." Ph.D. diss., University of Minnesota, Minneapolis, 2010.
Nandy, Ashish. *At the Edge of Psychology: Essays in Politics and Culture.* New York: Oxford University Press, 1980.
Nealon, Jeffrey. *Post-Postmodernism: Or, the Cultural Logic of Just-in-Time Capitalism.* Stanford, CA: Stanford University Press, 2012.
"A New History of Iraq." *The Guardian*, November 24, 2003. https://www.theguardian.com/education/2003/nov/25/schools.schoolsworldwide. Accessed November 12, 2018.
Newsom, Sidney C., and Levona Payne Newsom. *Third Reader.* Boston: Ginn, 1904.
Nguyen, Viet Thanh. *Nothing Ever Dies: Vietnam and the Memory of War.* Cambridge, MA: Harvard University Press, 2016.
Nishi, Toshio. *Unconditional Democracy: Education and Politics in Occupied Japan 1945–1952.* Stanford, CA: Hoover Institution Press, 1982.
Nozaki, Yoshiko. "Educational Reform and History Textbooks in Occupied Japan." In *Democracy in Occupied Japan: The U.S. Occupation and Japanese Politics and Society,* ed. Mark E. Caprio and Yoneyuki Sugita, 120–146. New York: Routledge, 2007.
Nudas, Alfeo G. "B. N. Santos's *The Volcano*: A Telic Contemplation." In *Reading Bienvenido N. Santos,* ed. Isagani R. Cruz and David Jonathan Bayot, 245–258. Manila: De La Salle University Press, 1994.
Okamura, Ryo. *Jigoku ue no hanami kance.* Tokyo: Kobunsha, 2003.
Omi, Michael, and Howard Winant. *Racial Formation in the United States.* 2d ed. New York: Routledge, 1994.
Orbaugh, Sharalyn. *Japanese Fiction of the Allied Occupation: Vision, Embodiment, Identity.* Boston: Leiden, 2007.
Oshima, Masanori. "What a Japanese Expects of the Philippines." *Philippine Review,* November 1943.
Osias, Camilo. "The Aspiration of the Filipinos." *Western Courier* 5, no. 20 (May 28, 1908): 162–166.
———. *Barrio Life and Barrio Education.* New York: World Book, 1921.

———. *The Filipino Way of Life: The Pluralized Philosophy*. Boston: Ginn, 1940.
———. *The Philippine Readers, Book One*. Boston: Ginn, 1927.
———. *The Philippine Readers, Book Two*. Boston: Ginn, (1924) 1932.
———. *The Philippine Readers, Book Three*. Boston: Ginn, 1922.
———. *The Philippine Readers, Book Five*, rev. ed. Boston: Ginn, 1932.
———. *The Philippine Readers, Book Six*, rev. ed. Boston: Ginn, 1929.
———. *The Philippine Readers, Book Seven*, rev. ed. Boston: Ginn, (1924) 1932.
———. *The Story of a Long Career of Varied Tasks*. Quezon City, Philippines: Manlapaz, 1971.
Otsuka, Julie. *When the Emperor Was Divine*. New York: Knopf, 2002.
Palmer, Frederick. "White Man and Brown Man in the Philippines." *Scribner's* 27 (1900): 76–86.
Palumbo-Liu, David. *Asian/America: Historical Crossings of a Racial Frontier*. Stanford, CA: Stanford University Press, 1999.
Pardo de Tavera, Trinidad H. "The Heritage of Ignorance." In *Thinking for Ourselves: A Representative Collection of Filipino Essays*, ed. Vicente Hilario and Eliseo Quirino, 1–17. Manila: Oriental Commercial, 1928.
Park, Josephine. "Alien Enemies in Julie Otsuka's *When the Emperor Was Divine*." *Modern Fiction Studies* 59, no. 1 (2013): 135–155.
Peterson, William. "Success Story Japanese-American Style." *New York Times*, January 9, 1966, 20, 33–39.
Phelps, David. "The Closed World: The Films of Shinoda Masahiro—Surface Play and Subterfuge in the Movies of a Modern Classicist." *Senses of Cinema* 61 (December 2011). http://sensesofcinema.com/2011/feature-articles/the-closed-world-the-films-of-shinoda-masahiro-surface-play-and-subterfuge-in-the-movies-of-a-modern-classicist. Accessed November 19, 2018.
Philippine Education 8, no. 4 (July 1911).
Portelli, Alessandro. "Oral History as Genre." In *Narrative and Genre: Contexts and Types of Communication*, ed. Mary Chamberlain and Paul Thompson, 23–47. New York: Routledge, 1998.
Porter, Gene Stratton. *Her Father's Daughter*. New York: Doubleday, 1921.
Prakash, Gyan. "Civil Society, Community, and the Nation in Colonial India." *Etnografica* 6, no. 1 (2002): 27–39.
Pratt, Mary Louise. *Imperial Eyes: Travel Writing and Transculturation*. New York: Routledge, 1992.
Pyle, Kenneth B. *The Making of Modern Japan*. Lexington, MA: D. C. Heath, 1978.
Quezon, Manuel L. "America's Pledge to the Philippines." *Asia: The American Magazine on the Orient* 21 (November 1921): 912, 960.
Quijano, Anibal. "Coloniality and Modernity/Rationality." *Cultural Studies* 21, nos. 2–3 (March/May 2007): 168–178.
Rabson, Steve. "Introduction." In *Okinawa: Two Postwar Novellas*. Berkeley: University of California, Institute of East Asian Studies, 1989.
Rafael, Vicente L. "Anticipating Nationhood: Collaboration and Rumor in the Japanese Occupation of Manila." *Diaspora* 1, no. 1 (1991): 67–82.
———. *Motherless Tongues: The Insurgency of Language amid Wars of Translation*. Durham, NC: Duke University Press, 2016.
———. *White Love and Other Events in Filipino History*. Durham, NC: Duke University Press, 2000.

Reimold, Orlando Scheirer. *First Primary Language Book*, rev. ed. New York: World Book, 1914.
———. *Industrial Studies and Exercises*. New York: World Book, 1911.
———. *Second Primary Language Book*, rev. ed. New York: World Book, 1914.
Retamar, Roberto Fernández. *Caliban and Other Essays*, trans. Edward Baker. Minneapolis: University of Minnesota Press, 1989.
Reyes, Vicente Chu, Jr. *Mapping the Terrains of Educational Reform: Global Trends and Local Responses in the Philippines*. New York: Routledge, 2016.
Rinjiro, Sodei. *Dear General MacArthur: Letters from the Japanese during the American Occupation*, ed. John Junkerman, trans. Shizue Matsuda. New York: Rowman and Littlefield, 2001.
Rodriguez, Deborah. *Kabul Beauty School: An American Woman Goes behind the Veil*. New York: Random House, 2007.
Rogers, Lawrence. *Long Belts and Thin Men: The Postwar Stories of Kojima Nobuo*. Fukuoka, Japan: Kurodahan, 2016.
Rosaldo, Renato. "Imperialist Nostalgia." *Representations* 26 (Spring 1989): 107–122.
Roseburg, Arturo G. "Philippine Humor." *Far Eastern Faculty Journal* 4 (1958): 5–19.
Rothberg, Michael. *Multidirectional Memory: Remembering the Holocaust in the Age of Decolonization*. Stanford, CA: Stanford University Press, 2009.
Ruscetta, Louis John. "Education for Philippine Pacification: How the U.S. Used Education as Part of Its Counterinsurgency Strategy in the Philippines from 1898 to 1909." Master's thesis, U.S. Army Command and General Staff College, Fort Leavenworth, KS, 2012.
Said, Edward. *Orientalism*. New York: Vintage, 1979.
Sakai, Naoki. "Transpacific Complicity and Comparatist Strategy: Failure in Decolonization and the Rise of Japanese Nationalism." In *Globalizing American Studies*, ed. Brian T. Edwards and Dilip P. Gaonkar, 240–268. Chicago: University of Chicago Press, 2010.
Sakamoto, Rumi. "Japan, Hybridity, and the Creation of Colonialist Discourse." *Theory, Culture, Society* 13, no. 3 (1996): 113–128.
Saltman, Kenneth J. "Corporate Education and 'Democracy Promotion' Overseas: The Case of Creative Associates International in Iraq, 2003–4." In *American Post-Conflict Educational Reform*, ed. Noah W. Sobe, 229–250. New York: Palgrave, 2005.
San Juan, E. *After Postcolonialism: Remapping Philippines–United States Confrontations*. Lanham, MD: Rowman and Littlefield, 2000.
———. "Introduction." In *On Becoming Filipino: Selected Writings of Carlos Bulosan*, 1–46. Philadelphia: Temple University Press, 1995.
———. *The Philippine Temptation: Dialectics of Philippines-U.S. Literary Relations*. Philadelphia: Temple University Press, 1996.
———. *Toward Filipino Self Determination: Beyond Transnational Globalization*. Albany: State University of New York Press, 2010.
Santa Ana, Jeffrey. *Racial Feelings: Asian America in a Capitalist Culture of Emotion*. Philadelphia: Temple University Press, 2015.
Santos, Bienvenido N. "The Excursionists" (1960). In *Brother, My Brother*, 159–171. Makati City, Philippines: Bookmark, 1991.
———. "The Filipino Writer in English as Storyteller and Translator." In *Reading Bienvenido N. Santos*, ed. Isagana R. Cruz and David Jonathan Bayot, 35–44. Manila: De La Salle University Press, 1999.

———. *Memory's Fictions: A Personal History*. Quezon City, Philippines: New Day, 1993.
———. *The Volcano*. Quezon City, Philippines: New Day, (1965) 1986.
Schlund-Vials, Cathy J. *War, Genocide, and Justice: Cambodian Memory Work*. Minneapolis: University of Minnesota Press, 2012.
Schmidt, Hans. *The United States Occupation of Haiti: 1915–1934*. New Brunswick, NJ: Rutgers University Press, 1995.
Schmidt, Peter. *Sitting in Darkness: New South Fiction, Education, and the Rise of Jim Crow Colonialism, 1865–1920*. Jackson: University of Mississippi Press, 2011.
Schmitt, James Erwon. "From the Frontlines to Silent Spring: DDT and America's War on Insects, 1941–1962." *Concept* 39 (2016): 1–29.
Schudson, Michael. "Dynamics of Distortion in Collective Memory." In *Memory Distortion: How Minds, Brains and Societies Reconstruct the Past*, ed. Daniel L. Schacter, 346–367. Cambridge, MA: Harvard University Press, 1995.
Schueller, Malini Johar. "Cross-Cultural Identification, Neoliberal Feminism, and Afghan Women." *Genders* 53 (Spring 2011). https://www.colorado.edu/gendersarchive1998-2013/2011/04/01/cross-cultural-identification-neoliberal-feminism-and-afghan-women.
Scott, David. "Colonial Governmentality." *Social Text* 43 (Fall 1995): 191–220.
Scott, James C. *Domination and the Arts of Resistance: Hidden Transcripts*. New Haven, CT: Yale University Press, 1992.
———. *Weapons of the Weak: Everyday Forms of Peasant Resistance*. New Haven, CT: Yale University Press, 1985.
"Seeds for Democracy." *Rome [Georgia] News Tribune*, March 27, 1953.
Sherif, Ann. *Mirror: The Fiction and Essays of Kodaya Aija*. Honolulu: University of Hawai'i Press, 1999.
Shibata, Masaka. *Japan and Germany under U.S. Occupation: A Comparative Analysis of Post-war Educational Reform*. New York: Lexington, 2005.
Simons, Geoff. *Korea: The Search for Sovereignty*. New York: St. Martin's, 1995.
Simpson, Caroline Chung. *An Absent Presence: Japanese Americans in Postwar American Culture*. Durham, NC: Duke University Press, 2001.
———. "'Out of an Obscure Place': Japanese War Brides and Cultural Pluralism in the 1950s." *Differences* 10, no. 3 (1998): 47–76.
Slaymaker, Douglas N. *The Body in Postwar Japanese Fiction*. New York: Routledge, 2004.
Slotkin, Joel. "Igorots and Indians: Racial Hierarchies and Conceptions of the Savage in Carlos Bulosan's Fiction of the Philippines." *American Literature* 72, no. 4 (December 2000): 843–866.
Sobe, Noah W., ed. *American Post-conflict Educational Reform*. New York: Palgrave, 2005.
Soliven, Benito. "The Revival of Ancient Philippine Culture." *Teacher's College Journal* 1 (October 1939): 19, 24.
Sone, Monica. *Nisei Daughter*. Seattle: University of Washington Press, 1953.
Spector, Robert M. W. *Cameron Forbes and the Hoover Commissions to Haiti (1930)*. Lanham, MD: University Press of America, 1985.
Spicer, Edward H. "Anthropologists and the War Relocation Authority." In *The Uses of Anthropology*, ed. William Goldschmidt, 217–237. Washington, DC: American Anthropological Association, 1979.
Spivak, Gayatri Chakravorty. "Can the Subaltern Speak?" In *Colonial Discourse and*

Post-colonial Theory: A Reader, ed. Patrick Williams and Laura Chrisman, 66–111. New York: Columbia University Press, 1994.

Staaveren, Jacob Van. *An American in Japan 1945–1948: A Civilian View of Occupation.* Seattle: University of Washington Press, 1994.

Starn, Orin. "Engineering Internment: Anthropologists and the War Relocation Authority." *American Ethnologist* 13, no. 4 (1986): 700–720.

Starr, Frederick. "A Review of Philippine School Books." *Philippine Republic* 3, no. 10 (1926): 12–13.

Steinberg, David Joel. *Philippine Collaboration in World War II.* Ann Arbor: University of Michigan Press, 1967.

Stephens, Joe, and David B. Ottaway. "From U.S., the ABC's of Jihad: Violent Soviet-Era Textbooks Complicate Afghan Education Efforts." *Washington Post*, March 23, 2002, A1.

Stoler, Ann Laura. *Race and the Education of Desire: Foucault's History of Sexuality and the Colonial Order of Things.* Durham, NC: Duke University Press, 1995.

Stratton, Clif. *Education for Empire: American Schools, Race, and the Paths of Good Citizenship.* Berkeley: University of California Press, 2016.

Sturtevant, David R. *Popular Uprisings in the Philippines: 1840–1940.* Ithaca, NY: Cornell University Press, 1976.

Teicher, Stacy A. "From Kabul to a U.S. Campus." *Christian Science Monitor*, vol. 22 (October 2002). http://www.csmonitor.com/2002/1022/p13s01-lehl.html. Accessed November 19, 2018.

Thakur, Yoko H. "History Textbook Reform in Allied Occupied Japan, 1945–52." In *Education and Schooling in Japan since 1945*, ed. Edward R. Beauchamp, 21–38. New York: Routledge, 1998.

Theobold, H. C. *The Filipino Teacher's Manual.* New York: World Book, 1907.

Thiong'o, Ngugi wa. *Decolonising the Mind: The Politics of Language in African Literature.* Portsmouth, NH: Heinemann, 1981.

"Thomasites 100 Years: 1901: A Century of Education for All." American Historical Collection, F 325.18, Ateneo University, Manila, n.d., n.p.

Thompson, Lanny. *Imperial Archipelago: Representation and Rule in the Insular Territories under U.S. Dominion after 1898.* Honolulu: University of Hawai'i Press, 2010.

Thompson, Roger M. *Filipino English and Taglish: Language Switching from Multiple Perspectives.* Philadelphia: John Benjamines, 2003.

Thomson, James C., Jr., Peter W. Stanley, and John Curtis Perry. *Sentimental Imperialists: The American Experience in East Asia.* New York: Harper, 1981.

Tiempo, Edith. "The Dam." In *Aura: The Gay Theme in Philippine Fiction in English*, ed. J. Neil Garcia, 81–89. Manila: Anvil, 2012.

———. "The Dimensions of Fear." In *Aura: The Gay Theme in Philippine Fiction in English*, ed. J. Neil Garcia, 90–97. Manila: Anvil, 2012.

Tinio, Maria Teresa Trinidad Pineda. "The Triumph of Tagalog and the Dominance of the Discourse on English: Language Politics in the Philippines during the American Colonial Period." Ph.D. diss., National University of Singapore, 2009.

Tolentino, Cynthia. "In the 'Training Center of the Skillful Servants of Mankind': Carlos Bulosan's Professional Filipinos in an Age of Benevolent Supremacy." *American Literature* 80, no. 2 (June 2008): 381–406.

Toomer, Jean. "Race Problems and Modern Society." In *Theories of Ethnicity*, ed. Werner Sollors, 168–190. New York: New York University Press, 1996.

Townsend, Henry S. *Primary Geography*. New York: American Book, 1917.

Trainor, Joseph C. *Educational Reform in Occupied Japan: Trainor's Memoir*. Tokyo: Meisei University Press, 1983.

Tsuboi, Sakae. *Twenty-Four Eyes*, trans. Akira Miura. Tokyo: Tuttle, (1952) 1983.

Uehara, Kozue. "Why Do We Teach and Learn English? Discourses of English Teaching and Learning during the U.S. Occupation of Okinawa, 1945–1972." *Komaba Journal of English Education* 3 (2012): 3–24.

Unger, J. Marshall. *Literacy and Script Reform in Occupation Japan*. New York: Oxford University Press, 1996.

Ventura, Sylvia Mendez. *A Literary Journey with Gilda Cordero-Fernando*. Quezon City: University of the Philippines Press, 2005.

Vergara, Alex Y. "A Is for Apple, B Is for Boy . . . T Is for Thomasites." *Philippine Daily Inquirer*, June 3, 2001.

Viswanathan, Gauri. *Masks of Conquest: Literary Study and British Rule in India*. New York: Columbia University Press, 1989.

Wallerstein, Immanuel. *The Capitalist World-Economy*. Cambridge: Cambridge University Press, 1979.

Webster, Noah. *A Grammatical Institute of the English Language: Comprising, an Easy, Concise, and Systematic Method of Education, Designed for the Use of English Schools in America*. Hartford, CT: Hudson and Godwin, 1783.

Wesling, Meg. *Empire's Proxy: American Literature and U.S. Imperialism in the Philippines*. New York: New York University Press, 2011.

Whiting, Allen. *China Crosses the Yalu: The Decision to Enter the Korean War*. Stanford, CA: Stanford University Press, 1968.

Williams, Raymond. *Marxism and Literature*. New York: Oxford University Press, 1977.

Willinsky, John. *Learning to Divide the World: Education at Empire's End*. Minneapolis: University of Minnesota Press, 1998.

Wolff, David, Bruce W. Menning, David Schimmelpenninck, and John W. Steinberg, eds. *The Russo-Japanese War in Global Perspective: World War Zero*, vol. 2. Boston: Leiden, 2007.

Wong, Sau Ling Cynthia. "Denationalization Reconsidered: Asian American Cultural Criticism at a Theoretical Crossroads." *Amerasia Journal* 21, nos. 1–2 (1995): 1–28.

Worcester, Dean C. *The Philippines Past and Present*, vol. 2. Norwood, MA: Macmillan, 1914.

Wyatt-Brown, Bertram. *A Warring Nation: Honor, Race, and Humiliation in America and Abroad*. Charlottesville: University of Virginia Press, 2014.

Yoshimizu, Ayaka. "Hello, War Brides: Heteroglossia, Counter-memory, and the Autobiographical Work of Japanese War Brides." *Meridians* 10, no. 1 (2009): 111–136.

Zehr, Mary Ann. "U.S. to Remake School System in Postwar Iraq." *Education Week* 22, no. 31 (April 16, 2003). https://www.edweek.org/ew/articles/2003/04/16/31iraq.h22.html. Accessed November 19, 2018.

Zelizer, Barbie. "Reading the Past against the Grain: The Shape of Memory Studies." *Critical Studies in Mass Communication* 12, no. 2 (June 1995): 214–238.

Index

Abe, Yoshishige, 158, 164, 201–202
Abjection, 119, 133–134, 140, 252
Achebe, Chinua, 21
Acheson, Dean, 265n13
Afghanistan, education for, 3, 16, 251–254
African Americans, 133, 160, 194, 195; and education, 18, 40, 51–52, 58, 63, 80, 117; and Filipinos, 9–10, 34, 39. *See also* Industrial education
Agamben, Giorgio, 208
Aguinaldo, Emilio, 10, 35, 46, 80
Ajami, Fouad, 252
Akiyuki, Nosaka, 205
Albery, Nobuko, 4, 19, 28, 203; *Balloon Top*, 217–219
Althusser, Louis, 22, 58, 140, 267n1 (chap. 7)
Americanization, 28, 168, 250–251; Filipino nationalism as, 49; of Filipinos, 49–62, 112, 114, 142; of Japanese, 3, 166, 177, 203, 216, 223–224. *See also* Flags
American literature: as alienating, 97, 137; as civilizing, 30
Amorsolo, Fernando, 77, 79, 80
Anderson, Benedict, 15
Anderson, Warwick, 56
Angulo, A. J., 259n4, 261n28
Armstrong, Samuel Chapman, 51
Arnold, Archibald V., 251
Ashcroft, Bill, 152

Asian American studies, 5, 30, 111; and transnationalism, 257
Atkinson, Fred, 6, 25, 34, 38, 39, 40, 41, 43, 49, 51, 52
Azuma, Eiichiro, 30, 222

Bacho, Peter, 22
Bagley, William, 18
Bailey, C. J., 49
Baker, Russ, 252
Bakla, 26, 94
Baldwin Readers, 63–65, 68
Ballantine, Joseph, 166
Ballou, Robert, 162
Barrows, David, 14, 17, 25, 34, 38, 40, 41, 42, 44–45, 46–49, 51–53, 64–65, 164, 262n9, 262n11
Barthes, Roland, 176
Bascara, Victor, 30, 128
Beauchamp, Edward R., 157
Benjamin, Harold, 167
Best, Jonathan, 148
Beveridge, Albert, 17, 47
Bewley, Luther B., 50, 51, 54
Beyer, H. Otley, 78, 262n6 (chap. 2)
Bhabha, Homi, 4, 26, 75, 91, 165, 190, 210
Biopower, 13
Bonifacio, Andrés, 77, 79, 82, 83, 84–85, 107, 152

Index

Borjesson, Kristina, 252
Bourne, Randolph S., 168
Bowles, Gordon, 167
Bresnahan, Roger J., 129
Brides Schools in occupation Japan, 19, 189–199. *See also* Racial capital
Brink, G. N., 37
Buck, H. H., 51
Buencamino, Victor, 74
Bulosan, Carlos, 4, 19, 24, 26–27, 49, 91, 107, 108, 109; *America Is in the Heart*, 118–127; "The Education of My Father," 111, 115–118; *The Laughter of My Father*, 110–112; "My Mother's Boarders," 111, 112–115
Bush, George W., 249, 250, 254

Caciquismo, 42, 46, 57, 119
Capitalist democracy, education in, 6, 11, 28, 159, 183, 186, 195, 203, 214, 223, 227, 251
Capra, Frank, 162
Carlisle Indian Industrial School, 39, 51
Carmack, Edward, 47, 49
Censorship in occupation Japan, 29, 158, 165, 171, 184, 202, 223, 233, 247
Césaire, Aimé, 152
Chakrabarty, Dipesh, 11, 85–86
Chatterjee, Partha, 13, 75, 181, 182
Cheng, Anne Anlin, 128, 139
Cheung, King-Kok, 137
Child-centered models of learning, 18, 249–250; in Japan, 8, 20, 167; in Philippines, 43
Chin, Frank, 30
Christianizing mission, 218; of Douglas MacArthur, 158, 256, 264n2
Chu, Patricia, 263n1 (chap. 4)
Civilizing mission, 6, 158; in Philippines, 45, 98, 103. *See also* Barrows, David
Clark, William S., 17, 171
Clymer, Kenton J., 48
Cohn, Bernard, 5–6
Cold War allies: Japan, 160, 170, 178, 189–203, 217–218, 234; Philippines, 102–103
Collaborative dissent, 5, 26, 63, 74. *See also* Osias, Camilo
Collective memory, 29, 142–147, 183, 230, 234–235, 239. *See also* Memory
Coloma, Roland Sintos, 31, 39, 73, 74, 259n4, 261n25, 262n4
Colonial Japan, 15, 183, 203, 229, 257
Colonial paternalism, 2, 4, 134, 170, 218
Community and kinship, 4, 11, 12, 54, 60; alienation from, 91–93; as resistance, 27, 97, 103–108, 113–125, 203, 214–219, 221–227
Constantino, Renato, 7, 21–22, 36, 80, 83, 90, 97

Cooper, Frederick, 4
Coppola, Francis Ford, 148
Cordero-Fernando, Gilda, 4, 19, 26, 58, 91–92; "A Harvest of Humble Folk," 102–108; "The Visitation of the Gods," 101–102
Counts, George S., 167
Craig, Austin, 49
Crone, Frank I., 51, 53
Curricular reform, 3, 8, 18, 22, 33–35, 42–55, 104, 156–186

Decivilizing Japanese, 164
Decolonial thinking, 4, 109–154
De Grazia, Victoria, 157, 158
Demasculinization, 205–217. *See also* Masculinity
Denning, Michael, 263n1 (chap. 4)
Derrida, Jacques, 149
Dewey, George, 6
Dewey, John, 18, 20, 43, 159, 160, 169, 170, 175, 179, 250
Diaz, Junot, 149
Douglas, Mary, 130, 150
Dower, John, 14, 30, 40, 158, 162, 214, 225, 250, 260n10
Drinnon, Richard, 30
DuBois, Fred, 17

Educational reform, 3, 8, 18, 22, 33–35; in Japan, 156–186; in Philippines, 42–60, 104
Education for democracy, 29, 157, 167, 174, 224, 233, 249–258
Eiji, Takemae, 30, 207, 223, 257
Elliott, Charles Burke, 34, 36, 42, 261n2
Elson, Ruth Miller, 63
Emerson, Gertrude, 78
Emerson, Ralph Waldo, 11, 34
Emperor worship: continuity of, 218, 219, 225; as defiance, 225–226; strictures against, 10, 157–158, 162, 166, 184, 223
English, imposition of in Philippines, 3, 5, 6–7, 17, 36, 37, 45–51, 52, 59, 62, 67, 75, 86, 90, 96, 116–117, 120–121, 127, 131, 133, 139, 145, 172
Epistemology of folk, 91, 110–127, 144
Espiritu, Augusto, 30, 128, 133, 260n21
Eugenio, Damaiana L., 78
Ewing, Thomas, 259n4

Fabian, Johannes, 12
Fallace, Thomas, 18
Fanon, Frantz, 11, 122, 124, 131, 134, 204
Fansler, Harriot Ely, 78

Fee, Mary Helen, 36, 44, 62, 64, 65–67, 70, 77, 79, 80; *The First Year Book,* 65–67; *A Woman's Impression of the Philippines,* 36, 64, 66, 255
Feuer, Lewis L., 169
The First Philippine Reader, 142, 145
Flags, 49–51; as Americanization, 59, 68–70; and nationalism, 80–83
Forbes, W. Cameron, 7, 35
Foucault, Michel, 12, 13, 18, 22, 104, 246, 247, 263n6
Frederickson, George M., 15
Freer, William B., 40, 41, 50, 51, 59, 96
Freire, Paulo, 22
Freud, Sigmund, 128, 132, 139, 205, 226, 232

Gallagher-Geurtsen, Tricia, 259n4
Garcia, J. Neil, 93
Garrison, Lloyd A., 223–224
Gayn, Mark, 207
German racialization, 12, 158, 161–163, 250
Gibbs, David, 52, 62, 64, 65, 67, 68, 70, 77, 79, 80, 86, 145; *Lessons in English,* 68, 70–71; representations of Moros, 71–72
Gildersleeve, Virginia C., 167
Givens, Willard E., 167
Glissant, Édouard, 152
Globalization and neocolonialism, 27, 143
Go, Julian, 24, 30, 259n1, 260n22, 261n28
Gold, Michael, 113
Gonzalez, N. V. M., 89, 90
Gordon, Avery, 99
Gosiengfiao, Victor, 20
Gottlieb, Nanette, 173
Governmentality, 12–14, 16, 28, 55, 56, 252
Grow, L. M., 99, 112, 264n16
Guide to New Education in Japan, 28, 180–184, 213–214

Hagedorn, Jessica, 22
Haiti, U.S. educational reforms in, 3, 16, 29, 251
Halbwachs, Maurice, 29
Hale, Edward Everett, 68, 83, 84
Halili, Servando, 9, 260n22
Hall, Robert King, 176
Hall, Stuart, 77
Hampton, 3, 39, 51, 52
Harris, Susan K., 85
Hawai'i, 3, 15, 16, 18, 51, 109, 146, 150, 250
Hayashi, Brian, 155
Hayashi, Fumiko, 23
Hegemony, 3–5, 12, 26–27, 60, 62–63, 74, 80, 86, 125, 158, 161, 180, 189, 230, 232, 243, 247, 250, 255

Hirohito (emperor), 7, 20, 210, 211, 219, 222, 225
Homoeroticism, 94–98, 208
Houston, James D., 23, 28, 220; *Farewell to Manzanar,* 220–222
Houston, Jeanne Wakatsuki, 4, 23, 28, 220; *Farewell to Manzanar,* 220–222
Huk Rebellion, 102–105
Human Terrain System, 252, 267n1 (epi.)
Hutchins, William J., 196

Ick, Judy, 89–90, 255–256
Igarashi, Yoshikuni, 216, 261n23
Ignacio, Abe, 260n7
Igorots, 149; depictions of, 71, 116, 138, 139, 148. *See also* Primitivism
Ilustrado, 42, 43, 90, 138, 262n7 (chap. 1)
Imitators, 11; Filipinos as, 25, 35, 44, 101, 175; Japanese as, 161, 165, 172, 182, 208
Individualism, 6, 11, 14, 19, 25, 28, 34, 35, 46, 54, 85, 86, 103, 105, 122, 126, 142, 153, 159, 166, 168, 170, 173, 177, 179, 186, 187, 203, 214, 219, 223, 227, 238, 251
Industrial education, 10; in Philippines, 10, 17, 33–34, 39, 51–55, 57–60, 64–65, 115, 117–118, 126, 255
Inoue, Masamichi S., 265n14
Intersectional memory, 4, 28, 203, 220. *See also* Memory
Iraq, 3, 16, 249–252; textbooks for, 267n4
Irwin, Wallace, 160
Iwakashi, Peter Junichi, 243

Japanese colonization of Philippines, 19–21
Japanese internment, 23, 164, 194; links with occupation, 23, 28, 203, 219–228
Jefferson, Thomas, 46, 52, 65, 76, 164
Jenks, Maud Huntley, 148
Jernegan, Prescott, 50

Kalaw, Maximo, 107, 114
Kallen, Horace M., 168, 265n7
Kandel, Isaac L., 167, 171
Kanji: elimination of, 8, 27, 169, 173–177; race and, 176
Kaplan, Amy, 30
Karasik, Daniel D., 188
Katipunan, 69, 73, 85
Kawaguchi, Sachie, 232, 233, 234
Keene, Donald, 225
Kennan, George, 12
Kenyatta, Jomo, 74
Kikuji, Nakamura, 223
Kim, Elaine, 263n1 (chap. 4), 265n5
Kim, Jodi, 30

Kipling, Rudyard, 8, 41
Kitani, Osamu, 235–237, 238, 241, 244–245
Kitani, Shigeko, 229, 235, 237, 244–245
Kobayashi, Victor, 159
Koikari, Mire, 191
Korea, U.S. educational reforms in, 251
Koshiro, Yukiko, 21, 160, 178, 186, 261n23
Kramer, Paul, 24, 30, 46, 69, 260n19, 260n22
Kristeva, Julia, 134
Kuniyoshi, Obara, 170

Lanzona, Vina A., 105
Laurel, Jose P., 21
Leong, Nancy, 193
Linmark, R. Zamora, 4, 19, 26, 27, 91, 109, 110; and antitourism, 148; *Leche*, 141–153
Locke, John, 54, 55, 179, 195
London, Jack, 17
Longfellow, Henry Wadsworth, 7, 131, 139
Love, Eric, 261n28
Lowe, Lisa, 30
Lutz, W. E., 37
Lyons, Paul, 34, 188, 261n3

Mabini, Apolinario, 11, 77, 79, 82–83, 84
MacArthur, Arthur, 7, 35
MacArthur, Douglas, 1, 9, 28–29, 35, 155, 167, 171, 211–212, 215, 217, 226–227, 230, 233–234, 242, 244–247, 256, 264n2; and censorship, 158, 178; Christianizing Japanese, 158, 256, 264; and Japanese constitution, 207; and masculinity, 225; and Philippines, 8, 155, 163; views of Japanese, 18, 182, 191, 250
Macherey, Pierre, 232
Makiya, Kanan, 252
Malays, 10, 46, 71, 86, 99
Marden, Charles, 265n5
Marshall, T. H., 195
Martin, Isabel Pefianco, 48
Masculinity: colonial, 7, 28, 96, 202, 205–208, 211, 240; native, 113, 117; nonhegemonic, 208, 213, 226
May, Glenn Anthony, 30, 43, 51, 260n22
McCarthy, Cameron, 259n4
McClintock, Anne, 50
McCoy, Alfred, 30, 260n11
McDonald, Keiko, 211
McGuffey Readers, 63–65, 68
McKinley, William, 2, 3, 33, 75, 250
McMahon, Jennifer, 34, 261n22
Mead, Arthur E., 188
Mears, Helen, 165

Meiji modernity, 202, 240, 241
Melancholia, 4, 27, 110, 128, 129, 134; cultural, 210. *See also* Santos, Bienvenido
Melville, Herman, 40, 208
Memorization: as Filipino trait, 44; as Japanese trait, 172, 174, 175, 176
Memory: collective, 29, 142, 144, 146, 147, 183, 230, 234–235, 239; individual, 147, 229–248; intersectional, 220
Mermin, Liz, 253
Michener, James, 192
Michio, Morishima, 265n11
Mignolo, Walter, 27, 123, 141
Militarism of Japanese, 12, 17, 29, 158, 164–166, 169, 201–202, 204, 221, 226, 236, 237, 241, 243, 245, 246, 247
Miller, Stuart Creighton, 33
Milligan, Jeffrey Ayala, 30
"The Miseducation of the Filipino," 22, 90
Mitchell, Joshua, 252
Miwa, Emiko, 238, 243–245
Miwa, Kimitada, 238, 239–245
Model minority, Japanese brides as, 191, 192, 194, 195, 196, 198, 199
Modernity, 12, 17, 27, 41, 45, 47, 56, 85, 86, 91, 97–105, 110, 113, 114, 116, 118, 122, 158, 168, 171, 173, 177, 205, 253, 257; of Japan, 161, 164, 176, 179, 181–182, 202, 240–241; the Other of, 123
Molasky, Michael, 30, 188, 208, 261n23
Monroe Report (*A Survey of the Educational System of the Philippine Islands*), 1, 25, 35, 36, 41, 54, 55, 65, 122, 260n6
Moros, representation of, 71–72, 86. *See also* Gibbs, David; Racialization
Mortensen, Greg, 253–254, 267n3 (epi.)
Mourning, 28, 128, 211, 214, 216
Mulvanity, E. D., 194
Muñoz, José Esteban, 73–74

Nakamura, Masako, 192, 265n18
Nationalism, 4, 16, 22, 64, 68; anticolonial, 25, 181–182; in Japan, 28, 29, 162, 164–166, 173, 177, 181–182, 186–188, 213–219, 226, 227, 230, 235–246; in Philippines, 35, 50, 62, 73–87, 131, 135
Native Americans, 63, 155; and education, 39, 40, 117; and Filipinos, 72, 117
Nealon, Jeffrey, 143–144
Negritos, 10, 71, 72, 75, 76, 86, 100, 139
Neocolonialism, 27, 90, 92, 106, 128, 129, 140, 143–144
Newsom, Levona Payne, 72, 73, 79

Newsom, Sidney, 72, 73, 79
Ngugi wa Thiong'o, 21, 206
Nguyen, Viet Thanh, 246
Nirschel, Paula, 252, 253
Nishi, Toshio, 176, 177, 181, 183, 184, 256
Nkrumah, Kwame, 74
Nobuo, Kojima, 4, 19, 28, 202; "The American School," 203–209
Nozaki, Yoshiko, 212
Nudas, Alfeo G., 264n17
Nugent, D. R., 1, 7

Ōe, Kenzaburō, 23
Ogura, Norio, 232–236, 244, 245, 246, 247
Okamura, Ryo, 210
Okinawa, 1–3, 186–189, 203, 239–240, 261n5
Omi, Michael, 190, 260n8
Ong, Han, 22
Orbaugh, Sharalyn, 201, 207, 261n23, 266n3, 263n5
Orientalism, 12, 25, 27, 34; and Filipinos, 38–44; and Japanese, 158–169, 180–182, 261n3
Oshima, Masanori, 20
Osias, Camilo, 19, 22, 25, 39, 60, 61, 111, 116, 127, 262n5, 263n8 (chap. 2); and collaborative dissent, 26; and nationalism, 26, 63, 73–86; and racial categories of Filipinos, 75–76, 86
Otsuka, Julie, 4, 23, 28, 203, 220; *When the Emperor Was Divine*, 222–227

Pacifism, Japanese, 28, 189, 208, 229, 230, 239, 243, 246
Padilla, Nonon, 255
Panlasigui, Isidoro, 78
Park, Josephine, 267n16
Passerini, Luisa, 267n3 (chap. 7)
Pax Americana, 28, 157, 201, 217–218, 229
Pease, Donald, 30
Pedagogical subjects, 2–5, 11, 14, 18, 22, 24, 26–29, 34; Filipinos, 25, 26, 48, 50, 54, 58–60, 90–92, 98–111, 116–153; Japanese, 156–160, 175–179, 191, 196–199, 204, 226, 233, 243, 250, 253, 254
Pensionado program, 23, 39, 73, 74, 86, 109, 127, 138, 253
Perez, Tony, 255
Peterson, William, 195
Philippine-American War, 6, 13, 17, 30, 115, 118, 142, 147, 153
Phillips, William A., 42
Pilipino, 48, 229, 254, 260n6

Popular culture representations of Japanese, 160–164
Portelli, Alessandro, 231
Potsdam Declaration, 165, 183, 189
Prakash, Gyan, 13
Pratt, Mary Louise, 97, 140
Pratt, Richard, 3
Primer of Democracy, 27, 159, 177–180, 224, 225
Primers: in Philippines, 25, 52, 64–87, 126, 142, 145; in United States, 63
Primitivism, 116, 138, 140, 162
Progressivist education, 8, 14, 18, 29, 43, 44, 79, 159, 167, 168, 169, 170, 175
Puerto Rico, 3, 15, 16, 18, 39, 259n1
Pyle, Kenneth, 176

Quezon, Manuel, 14, 78, 85, 114, 131
Quijano, Anibal, 11, 123, 147

Racial capital, 124; Japanese brides as, 28, 160, 191, 193–194, 197, 199
Racialization: of Filipinos, 5, 6, 8, 10, 11, 33–60, 72, 122; of Germans, 12, 158, 161–163, 175, 250; of Japanese, 5, 6, 8, 10, 11, 16, 155–186, 189–199. *See also* Racial capital
Racial management, 8, 22
Rafael, Vicente, 30, 90, 95, 260n12, 260n22
Rawlins, Joseph, 47, 48, 49, 262n9
Reeducation of Japanese, 10, 11, 12, 157–159, 164, 171, 183–185, 220, 223; critique of, 209–220, 224–226, 230–257
Reimold, Orlando Scheirer, 62, 64, 65, 70, 72, 73, 77, 79, 126
Report of the United States Education Mission to Japan, 8, 18, 27, 159, 167–177
Retamar, Roberto Fernández, 42
Reverse Course, 11, 16, 158, 190; changing racialization of Japanese, 158, 160, 178, 179
Reyes, Vicente Chu, Jr., 263n1 (chap. 3)
Rinjiro, Sodei, 229
Rizal, José, 15, 20, 50, 56, 72, 76, 77, 79, 80, 82, 83, 84, 122, 144
Rizal Readers, 64, 76, 77, 80
Robinson Crusoe, 7, 11, 72, 73, 126
Rodriguez, Deborah, 253
Rodwell, W. W., 36
Romaji, 5, 8, 27, 31, 172–177, 205, 206, 223, 231, 233, 247, 256
Roosevelt, Theodore, 16
Roseburg, Arturo, 263n3 (chap. 4)
Rote learning, 60, 175, 184–186

Rothberg, Michael, 266n15
Rugh, Andrea B., 249

Said, Edward, 41, 42, 159, 166
Sakai, Naoki, 187
Sandiko, Teodoro, 41
San Juan, E., 30, 111, 117, 122, 260n22, 264n14
Santos, Bienvenido, 4, 19, 23, 26, 27, 49, 91, 108, 109, 110, 127–128, 264n16; "The Excursionists," 136–141; *The Volcano*, 129–136
Santos, Tomas, 135
Scarano, Francisco A., 30
Schooling. *See* Governmentality
School system and Americanization. *See* Americanization
Schudson, Michael, 29, 230
Scott, David, 14
Scott, James C., 22, 25–26, 63, 70, 125, 232
Script reform in Japan, 31, 172–176. *See also* Kanji; Romaji
Sherif, Ann, 266n7
Shibata, Masaka, 162–163
Shibusawa, Sakae, 232, 233, 234, 247
Shinoda, Masahiro, 4, 19, 28, 129, 203; *MacArthur's Children*, 209–217
Shinohara, Kidehiko, 197
Shintoism, 10, 162, 164, 165, 177, 179, 256, 264n2; prohibition of shrines, 8, 158, 184
Sibayan, Bonifacio, 83
Simpson, Caroline Chung, 192
Slaymaker, Douglas N., 261n23, 266n1
Slotkin, Joel, 115, 263n7
Sobe, Noah W., 261n28
Soliven, Benito, 21
Sone, Monica, 222
Spanish colonialism, 7, 15, 20, 44, 77, 102, 107, 129, 143, 178; hierarchical, 25, 35, 42, 43, 50, 57, 65, 153; inadequate schooling in, 7, 42
Spector, Robert M., 251
Spivak, Gayatri Chakravorty, 59, 117–118
Staaveren, Jacob Van, 28, 160, 167, 175, 196, 209; *An American in Japan, 1945–1948*, 184–186
Starr, Frederick, 62, 86
Stoddard, Alexander J., 167
Stoddard, George D., 167
Stratton, Clif, 259n4
Stratton-Porter, Gene, 161, 164
Subaltern spaces, 110–112
A Survey of the Educational System of the Philippine Islands (Monroe Report), 1, 25, 35, 36, 41, 54, 55, 65, 122, 260n6

Tada'ichi, Hirakawa, 207
Taft, William Howard, 33, 38, 45, 46, 51, 133, 261n1
Tagalog, 19, 37, 45–46, 73, 83, 84, 86, 89, 146, 152, 172, 254; as inferior, 47, 48
Taylor, John, 162
Teahouse of the August Moon, 1–3
Textbooks: in colonial Philippines, 19, 25, 26, 65–87; in occupation Japan, 177–184. *See also* Americanization; Osias, Camilo
Theobold, H. C., 25; *The Filipino Teacher's Manual*, 55–59
Thomasites, 6, 26, 36, 89, 95, 229, 255
Thompson, Lanny, 261n28
Thompson, Roger, 83, 262n3
Tiempo, Edith, 4, 19, 26, 49, 91–92; "The Dam," 94–98; "The Dimensions of Fear," 98–101
Tinio, Maria Teresa Trinidad Pineda, 263n8 (chap. 2)
Tolentino, Cynthia, 263n10
Toomer, Jean, 168, 265n8
Trainor, Joseph J., 156, 157, 174, 187
Tropicalism, 12, 34, 40, 42, 57, 188, 261n3
Tsuboi, Sakae, 207, 266n4
Tsuchiya, Shizuko, 238
Tubneb, E. G., 38
Tuitionary condition: of Filipinos, 8–9, 33, 34, 38, 42, 48, 61, 78, 86, 95; Germany not seen as tuitionary, 12; of Japanese, 18, 250
Turner, E. G., 44
Tuskegee, 3, 39, 51, 52, 117, 261n25
Tydings-McDuffie Act of 1934, 15–16

Ultranationalism: of Germans, 162; of Japanese, 6, 164, 173, 182, 183, 201, 221, 230, 246, 256. *See also* Nationalism
Unger, J. Marshall, 173

Vardaman, James M., 157,
Ventura, Sylvia Mendez, 101
Vergara, Alex Y., 256
Viswanathan, Gauri, 5

Wanamaker, Pearl A., 167
War on terror, 249–258
Washington, Booker T., 34, 39, 51, 58, 65, 74, 104, 262n5
Webster, Noah, 68
Wesling, Meg, 24, 121–122, 261n27, 262n9 (chap. 1), 262n3 (chap. 2)
White, Frank, 25, 33–34, 36–37, 40, 51, 53
Whittier, John Greenleaf, 131
Willinsky, John, 3, 12, 150, 259n4

Winant, Howard, 190, 260n8
Woods-Forbes report, 40, 83, 86, 112
Woodson, Carter, 21
Worcester, Dean, 14–15
World's Fair, St. Louis, 116, 138, 262n6 (chap. 2)

Yasuoka, Shōtaro, 23
Yoshimizu, Ayaka, 192
Yoshio, Nagano, 170

Zelizer, Barbie, 29, 231

MALINI JOHAR SCHUELLER is a Professor of English at the University of Florida. She is the author of *Locating Race: Global Sites of Post-colonial Citizenship*, *U.S. Orientalisms: Race, Nation, and Gender in Literature, 1790–1890*, and *The Politics of Voice: Liberalism and Social Criticism from Franklin to Kingston*. She is also the director of the award-winning documentary *In His Own Home*.

Also in the series *Asian American History and Culture*:

Shelley Sang-Hee Lee, *Claiming the Oriental Gateway: Prewar Seattle and Japanese America*
Isabelle Thuy Pelaud, *This Is All I Choose to Tell: History and Hybridity in Vietnamese American Literature*
Christian Collet and Pei-te Lien, eds., *The Transnational Politics of Asian Americans*
Min Zhou, *Contemporary Chinese America: Immigration, Ethnicity, and Community Transformation*
Kathleen S. Yep, *Outside the Paint: When Basketball Ruled at the Chinese Playground*
Benito M. Vergara Jr., *Pinoy Capital: The Filipino Nation in Daly City*
Jonathan Y. Okamura, *Ethnicity and Inequality in Hawai'i*
Sucheng Chan and Madeline Y. Hsu, eds., *Chinese Americans and the Politics of Race and Culture*
K. Scott Wong, *Americans First: Chinese Americans and the Second World War*
Lisa Yun, *The Coolie Speaks: Chinese Indentured Laborers and African Slaves in Cuba*
Estella Habal, *San Francisco's International Hotel: Mobilizing the Filipino American Community in the Anti-eviction Movement*
Thomas P. Kim, *The Racial Logic of Politics: Asian Americans and Party Competition*
Sucheng Chan, ed., *The Vietnamese American 1.5 Generation: Stories of War, Revolution, Flight, and New Beginnings*
Antonio T. Tiongson Jr., Edgardo V. Gutierrez, and Ricardo V. Gutierrez, eds., *Positively No Filipinos Allowed: Building Communities and Discourse*
Sucheng Chan, ed., *Chinese American Transnationalism: The Flow of People, Resources, and Ideas between China and America during the Exclusion Era*
Rajini Srikanth, *The World Next Door: South Asian American Literature and the Idea of America*
Keith Lawrence and Floyd Cheung, eds., *Recovered Legacies: Authority and Identity in Early Asian American Literature*
Linda Trinh Võ, *Mobilizing an Asian American Community*
Franklin S. Odo, *No Sword to Bury: Japanese Americans in Hawai'i during World War II*
Josephine Lee, Imogene L. Lim, and Yuko Matsukawa, eds., *Re/collecting Early Asian America: Essays in Cultural History*
Linda Trinh Võ and Rick Bonus, eds., *Contemporary Asian American Communities: Intersections and Divergences*
Sunaina Marr Maira, *Desis in the House: Indian American Youth Culture in New York City*
Teresa Williams-León and Cynthia Nakashima, eds., *The Sum of Our Parts: Mixed-Heritage Asian Americans*
Tung Pok Chin with Winifred C. Chin, *Paper Son: One Man's Story*
Amy Ling, ed., *Yellow Light: The Flowering of Asian American Arts*
Rick Bonus, *Locating Filipino Americans: Ethnicity and the Cultural Politics of Space*
Darrell Y. Hamamoto and Sandra Liu, eds., *Countervisions: Asian American Film Criticism*
Martin F. Manalansan IV, ed., *Cultural Compass: Ethnographic Explorations of Asian America*

Ko-lin Chin, *Smuggled Chinese: Clandestine Immigration to the United States*
Evelyn Hu-DeHart, ed., *Across the Pacific: Asian Americans and Globalization*
Soo-Young Chin, *Doing What Had to Be Done: The Life Narrative of Dora Yum Kim*
Robert G. Lee, *Orientals: Asian Americans in Popular Culture*
David L. Eng and Alice Y. Hom, eds., *Q & A: Queer in Asian America*
K. Scott Wong and Sucheng Chan, eds., *Claiming America: Constructing Chinese American Identities during the Exclusion Era*
Lavina Dhingra Shankar and Rajini Srikanth, eds., *A Part, Yet Apart: South Asians in Asian America*
Jere Takahashi, *Nisei/Sansei: Shifting Japanese American Identities and Politics*
Velina Hasu Houston, ed., *But Still, Like Air, I'll Rise: New Asian American Plays*
Josephine Lee, *Performing Asian America: Race and Ethnicity on the Contemporary Stage*
Deepika Bahri and Mary Vasudeva, eds., *Between the Lines: South Asians and Postcoloniality*
E. San Juan Jr., *The Philippine Temptation: Dialectics of Philippines-U.S. Literary Relations*
Carlos Bulosan and E. San Juan Jr., eds., *The Cry and the Dedication*
Carlos Bulosan and E. San Juan Jr., eds., *On Becoming Filipino: Selected Writings of Carlos Bulosan*
Vicente L. Rafael, ed., *Discrepant Histories: Translocal Essays on Filipino Cultures*
Yen Le Espiritu, *Filipino American Lives*
Paul Ong, Edna Bonacich, and Lucie Cheng, eds., *The New Asian Immigration in Los Angeles and Global Restructuring*
Chris Friday, *Organizing Asian American Labor: The Pacific Coast Canned-Salmon Industry, 1870–1942*
Sucheng Chan, ed., *Hmong Means Free: Life in Laos and America*
Timothy P. Fong, *The First Suburban Chinatown: The Remaking of Monterey Park, California*
William Wei, *The Asian American Movement*
Yen Le Espiritu, *Asian American Panethnicity*
Velina Hasu Houston, ed., *The Politics of Life*
Renqiu Yu, *To Save China, To Save Ourselves: The Chinese Hand Laundry Alliance of New York*
Shirley Geok-lin Lim and Amy Ling, eds., *Reading the Literatures of Asian America*
Karen Isaksen Leonard, *Making Ethnic Choices: California's Punjabi Mexican Americans*
Gary Y. Okihiro, *Cane Fires: The Anti-Japanese Movement in Hawaii, 1865–1945*
Sucheng Chan, *Entry Denied: Exclusion and the Chinese Community in America, 1882–1943*

www.ingramcontent.com/pod-product-compliance
Lightning Source LLC
Chambersburg PA
CBHW061252230426
43665CB00026B/2911